Grounding Cognition

One of the key questions in cognitive psychology is how people represent knowledge about concepts such as football or love. Recently, some researchers have proposed that concepts are represented in human memory by the sensorimotor systems that underlie interaction with the outside world. These theories represent a recent development in cognitive science to view cognition no longer in terms of abstract information processing, but in terms of perception and action. In other words, cognition is grounded in embodied experiences. Studies show that sensory perception and motor actions support human understanding of words and object concepts. Moreover, even understanding of abstract and emotion concepts can be shown to rely on more concrete, embodied experiences. Finally, language itself can be shown to be grounded in sensorimotor processes. This book brings together theoretical arguments and empirical evidence from several key researchers in this field to support this framework.

Diane Pecher is assistant professor at the Erasmus University Rotterdam (The Netherlands). She received a Ph.D. from the University of Amsterdam in 1999. Her dissertation *Dynamics of Semantic Memory* was supervised by Jeroen G. W. Raaijmakers. Her research is funded by a grant from the Netherlands Organization of Scientific Research (NWO).

Rolf A. Zwaan is Professor of Psychology at Florida State University. He received his Ph.D. from Utrecht University, The Netherlands, in 1992 and is the author of more than 60 scientific publications. His journal publications include articles in *Psychological Science*, *Cognition*, and *Psychological Bulletin*. His research is funded by grants from the National Institutes of Health.

Grounding Cognition

The Role of Perception and Action in Memory, Language, and Thinking

Edited by

DIANE PECHER
Erasmus University Rotterdam

ROLF A. ZWAAN
Florida State University

CAMBRIDGE
UNIVERSITY PRESS

PUBLISHED BY THE PRESS SYNDICATE OF THE UNIVERSITY OF CAMBRIDGE
The Pitt Building, Trumpington Street, Cambridge, United Kingdom

CAMBRIDGE UNIVERSITY PRESS
The Edinburgh Building, Cambridge CB2 2RU, UK
40 West 20th Street, New York, NY 10011-4211, USA
477 Williamstown Road, Port Melbourne, VIC 3207, Australia
Ruiz de Alarcón 13, 28014 Madrid, Spain
Dock House, The Waterfront, Cape Town 8001, South Africa

http://www.cambridge.org

First published 2005

Printed in the United States of America

Typeface Palatino 10/12 pt.   *System* LATEX 2$_\varepsilon$ [TB]

A catalog record for this book is available from the British Library.

Library of Congress Cataloging in Publication Data
Grounding cognition : the role of perception and action in memory,
language, and thinking / edited by Diane Pecher and Rolf A. Zwaan.
   p. cm.
ISBN 0-521-83464-3 (hardback)
   1. Cognitive science.   2. Mind and body.   I. Pecher, Diane.
II. Zwaan, Rolf A.   III. Title.
BF311.G768   2005
153.2 – dc22   2004016031

ISBN 0 521 83464 3 hardback

Contents

List of Contributors

Lawrence W. Barsalou, Emory University, Atlanta, Georgia, USA

Raymond Becker, University of Wisconsin, Madison, Wisconsin, USA

Anna M. Borghi, University of Bologna, Bologna, Italy

Laura A. Carlson, University of Notre Dame, Notre Dame, Indiana, USA

Ying Feng, Indiana University, Bloomington, Indiana, USA

Raymond W. Gibbs, Jr., University of California, Santa Cruz, California, USA

Arthur M. Glenberg, University of Wisconsin, Madison, Wisconsin, USA

Robert L. Goldstone, Indiana University, Bloomington, Indiana, USA

Monica Gonzalez-Marquez, Cornell University, Ithaca, New York, USA

David Havas, University of Wisconsin, Madison, Wisconsin, USA

Ryan Kenny, University of Notre Dame, Notre Dame, Indiana, USA

Ronald W. Langacker, University of California, San Diego, California, USA

Brian MacWhinney, Carnegie Mellon University, Pittsburgh, Pennsylvania, USA

Carol J. Madden, Florida State University, Tallahassee, Florida, USA

Diane Pecher, Erasmus University Rotterdam, Rotterdam, The Netherlands

Jesse J. Prinz, University of North Carolina, Chapel Hill, North Carolina, USA

Daniel C. Richardson, Stanford University, Stanford, California, USA

Mike Rinck, Technical University of Dresden, Dresden, Germany

Brian J. Rogosky, Indiana University, Bloomington, Indiana, USA

Michael J. Spivey, Cornell University, Ithaca, New York, USA

Katja Wiemer-Hastings, Northern Illinois University, DeKalb, Illinois, USA

Rolf A. Zwaan, Florida State University, Tallahassee, Florida, USA

Introduction to *Grounding Cognition*

The Role of Perception and Action in Memory, Language, and Thinking

Diane Pecher and Rolf A. Zwaan

Fifty years of research in cognitive science have demonstrated that the study of cognition is essential for a scientific understanding of human behavior. A growing number of researchers in the field are proposing that mental processes such as remembering, thinking, and understanding language are based on the physical interactions that people have with their environment. Rather than viewing the body as a support system for a mind that needs to be fueled and transported, they view the mind as a support system that facilitates the functioning of the body. By shifting the basis for mental behavior toward the body, these researchers assume that mental processes are supported by the same processes that are used for physical interactions, that is, for perception and action. Cognitive structures develop from perception and action.

To fully understand why this idea is so exciting, we need to look at the history of cognitive science. One of the major ideas propelling the cognitive revolution was the computer metaphor, in which cognitive processes are likened to software computations (Turing, 1950). Just like software can run on different hardware systems, so can cognitive processes run independently from the hardware in which they happened to be implemented, the human brain and body. Furthermore, just as computer programs, the human mind was thought to manipulate abstract symbols in a rule-based manner. These symbols were abstract because they were not derived from interactions with the environment by way of sensory organs and effectors.

Traditional cognitive theories assume that the meaning of a concept consists of the links between the abstract symbol for that concept and the abstract symbols for other concepts or for semantic features. However, this view has fundamental problems, as has been demonstrated in an increasing number of contributions to the literature (e.g., Barsalou, 1999; Glenberg, 1997; Pulvermüller, 1999). Two of these problems are the transduction problem (Barsalou, 1999) and the grounding problem (Harnad, 1990). The transduction problem is the problem of how perceptual experiences are translated into the arbitrary symbols that are used to represent concepts. In traditional artificial intelligence (AI) research, this problem was solved by way of divine intervention on the part of the programmer. Brooks (1987) provides this example. The following two complex propositions are true of a chair [CAN[SIT-ON, PERSON, CHAIR]], [CAN[STAND-ON, PERSON, CHAIR]], but it would be a gross oversimplification to state that these propositions provide an exhaustive description of chairs. For example, some chairs have back support, others do not, some chairs have wooden frames, others have metal frames, some chairs can be folded, and others cannot. In order for AI programs to work, programmers abstract concrete entities, actions, and events to atomic concepts such as PERSON, CHAIR, and SIT. These are the concepts the computer works with. It can therefore be argued that traditional AI programs do not display intelligence, because they do not address the transduction problem in a theoretically meaningful way (Brooks, 1987; Pfeifer & Scheier, 1999).

The grounding problem is the problem of how the symbols are mapped back onto the real world. Many models of conceptual memory assume that the meaning of a symbol is captured in its relations to other symbols (e.g., semantic network models). However, without any reference to the outside world such symbols are essentially meaningless. Therefore, it seems more fruitful to consider cognition to be grounded in the human body and its interaction with the environment, and thus in perception and action. Rather than being merely input and output devices, perception and action are considered central to higher cognition. Some recent experiments have shown that perceptual and motor representations play a role in higher cognitive processes such as understanding language and retrieving information from memory (Glenberg & Kaschak, 2002; Pecher, Zeelenberg, & Barsalou, 2003; Solomon & Barsalou, 2001; Spivey, Tyler, Richardson, & Young, 2000; Stanfield & Zwaan, 2001; Zwaan, Stanfield, & Yaxley, 2002). Many of these and other experiments are described in the contributions to this volume.

As yet, there is no unified embodied theory of cognition. In an insightful review of the literature, Wilson (2002) identified six rather diverse claims about embodied cognition: (1) cognition is situated; (2) cognition is time-pressured; (3) we off-load cognitive work onto the environment; (4) the environment is part of the cognitive system; (5) cognition is for action; (6) offline cognition is body based. She argues that the sixth claim is the best documented and the most powerful of these claims. According to this claim, sensorimotor functions that evolved for action and perception have been co-opted for use during offline cognition. Offline cognition occurs when sensorimotor functions are decoupled from the immediate environment and subserve what we might call "displaced thought processes," i.e., thoughts about situations and events in other times and places. Most of the research presented in this volume can be viewed as addressing this sixth claim about embodied cognition (except for Borghi's chapter, which also addresses the fifth claim). The eleven chapters that follow are clustered around five topics: (1) The interaction between cognition and spatial and action processes, (2) understanding emotional and abstract concepts, (3) the grounding of grammar in embodied experiences, (4) examining the role of sensorimotor processes and representation in language comprehension, and (5) mental representations.

It is crucial for the embodied framework to demonstrate that cognition is grounded in bodily interactions with the environment. The way people represent and understand the world around them is directly linked to perception and action. Thus, it needs to be shown that sensorimotor patterns are activated when concepts are accessed. In her chapter, Anna Borghi investigates the idea that concepts are for action. During interaction with the environment, people need to be able to quickly perform actions on objects. In an extensive review of the available evidence, Borghi shows that motor information is activated automatically by direct visual input but also by the activation of concepts via words and by goals. This evidence provides strong support for the idea that concepts should be thought of as a set of sensorimotor patterns that allow the organism to interact with the physical world, rather than as a collection of abstract symbols.

Laura Carlson and Ryan Kenny review results from a series of experiments that show how the perception of space and the understanding of spatial terms is grounded in physical action. These experiments investigated how terms such as "above" or "below" are understood in the context of space around a specific object. The results showed that the way people usually interact with these objects affects how the space around these objects is perceived. The results also showed that prior exposure to a specific interaction with the object biased the perception of space around the object towards that function.

As is shown in a number of studies and the first two chapters, there is evidence that perception and action play a crucial role in the representations of objects. Critics of the embodied view have argued that it might be a problem to extend this finding to abstract concepts such as "truth" or "political power," which do not refer directly to concrete objects people interact with physically. The representation of abstract concepts in terms of sensorimotor processes poses a challenge to the embodied view. There have been two proposals for mechanisms by which people represent abstract concepts. The first proposal comes from cognitive linguistics and states that abstract concepts are understood via metaphors. For example, "time" might be understood by metaphorical mapping on "movement in space." Evidence for such metaphorical mapping comes from expressions such as "time flies." The second proposal argues that both concrete and abstract concepts are representations of situations, and that the difference between them is merely one of focus.

In his chapter, Ray Gibbs discusses how people's bodily actions are used to support the use of language and abstract thought. His first claim is that language developed from perception and action. By metaphorical extension, words that originally referred to concrete objects and actions acquired new and more abstract meanings. His second point is that understanding of abstract concepts is grounded in patterns of bodily experiences called image schemas (Lakoff, 1987). These image schemas are sensorimotor structures that organize experiences. He discusses results from psychological experiments that support this notion.

Jesse Prinz presents an analysis of how moral concepts ("good" and "bad") are understood. Whether something is good or bad cannot be perceived directly, which leads to the question of how moral judgments can be grounded in perception. Prinz argues that moral concepts are grounded in emotions such as anger and disgust. He further argues that emotions are perceptions of one's own bodily state. This way, moral concepts are grounded in perception.

Art Glenberg, David Havas, Raymond Becker, and Mike Rinck argue that part of understanding language about emotions is to put the body in the corresponding state. They present two experiments in which they use the Strack, Martin, and Stepper (1988) procedure to manipulate mood. In this procedure participants hold a pen in their mouth. If they hold the pen with their teeth, their mouth is forced into a smile. If they hold the pen with their lips a partial frown is forced. They show that judgments of emotional sentences are facilitated if the mood of the sentence is congruent with the mood induced by the pen manipulation.

A different solution to the problem of abstract concepts is provided by Larry Barsalou and Katja Wiemer-Hastings. In their chapter, they suggest that accessing the situation in which a concept occurs is an important factor in understanding and representing both concrete and abstract concepts. Concrete and abstract concepts might differ in the focus of attention. Concrete concepts depend mainly on objects in the situation whereas abstract concepts depend mainly on events and introspections. Another difference is that the representations of abstract concepts are more complex than those for concrete concepts. Barsalou and Wiemer-Hastings discuss an exploratory study, which provides initial evidence for this view.

An area that at first sight does not seem to provide fertile ground for an embodied approach is language. After all, language is typically thought of as consisting of systematically organized strings of auditory and visual symbols, which are arbitrarily related to their referents and meaning. On this view, language processing by definition is the manipulation of abstract, amodal, and arbitrary symbols. However, careful analyses by cognitive linguists such as Langacker (1987, 1991), Lakoff (1987), Talmy (2002a, 2002b), Givón (1992), and Goldberg (1995) have begun to uncover the sensorimotor foundations of grammar. Continuing this line of research,

Ron Langacker in his chapter shows how simple perceptual processes such as visual scanning are essential to the meaning of sentences such as "A scar extends from his ankle to his knee," or "A scar extends from his knee to his ankle," and also underlie the meaning of more abstract sentences such as "The rainy season starts in December and runs through March."

Along similar lines, Brian MacWhinney views grammar as a set of cues for perspective taking. He argues that perspective taking is based upon our interactions with the world, but can be expanded to situations that are distant in time or space. He then goes on to show that the perspective theory provides a coherent account for a variety of linguistic phenomena, such as deixis, syntactic ambiguity, and pronominal reference.

Rolf Zwaan and Carol Madden discuss a set of empirical data collected in their lab, pointing to the conclusion that visual representations are routinely activated when people understand words and sentences. They present a theory of sentence comprehension according to which meaning is construed by activating and integrating sensorimotor representations in mental simulations of the described situation.

Michael Spivey, Daniel Richardson, and Monica Gonzalez-Marquez likewise argue that language and sensorimotor processes can smoothly interface. They review a series of experiments from their lab that provide strong support for this general thesis and for more specific predictions derived from theories of meaning in cognitive linguistics, for example predictions regarding the role of image schemata in language comprehension.

Finally, Rob Goldstone, Ying Feng, and Brian Rogosky describe ABSUR-DIST, a computational model, which translates between two conceptual systems, for example between two people trying to talk about the same concepts. They show that both internal relations between concepts and external grounding contribute to alignments between systems. They argue that internally and externally based sources of meaning are mutually reinforcing.

The collection of ideas in this book and the empirical support obtained for them present an exciting new approach to the study of cognition. The number of researchers who are investigating the role of the body in cognition is growing, and we hope that this book will contribute to that development.

ACKNOWLEDGMENTS

We would like to thank the following individuals who have provided excellent "inside" and "outside" reviews of the chapters in this volume: Larry Barsalou, Anna Borghi, Gordon Bower, Laura Carlson, Andy Clark, Seana Coulson, Kenny Coventry, Delphine Dahan, Stefan Frank, Ray Gibbs, Art

Glenberg, Sam Glucksberg, Mike Kaschak, Fred Keijzer, Ron Langacker, Carol Madden, Mike Masson, Teenie Matlock, Ted Sanders, Micheal Spivey, Brian MacWhinney, Margaret Wilson, and René Zeelenberg. We would also like to thank Kiki Zanoli for her help with preparing the index.

Part of this chapter was written while Rolf Zwaan was a Fellow at the Hanse Institute for Advanced Study in Delmenhorst, Germany. Rolf Zwaan's research is also supported by grant MH-63972 from the National Institutes of Health.

References

Barsalou, L. W. (1999). Perceptual symbol systems. *Behavioral & Brain Sciences 22*, 577–660.

Brooks, R. A. (1987). Intelligence without representation. *Artificial Intelligence 47*, 139–159.

Glenberg, A. M. (1997). What memory is for. *Behavioral and Brain Sciences 20*, 1–55.

Glenberg, A. M., & Kaschak, M. P. (2002). Grounding language in action. *Psychonomic Bulletin & Review 9*, 558–565.

Givón, T. (1992). The grammar of referential coherence as mental processing instructions. *Linguistics 30*, 5–55.

Goldberg, A. (1995). *Constructions: A Construction Grammar Approach to Argument Structure*. Chicago: University of Chicago Press.

Harnad, S. (1990). The symbol grounding problem. *Physica D 42*, 335–346.

Lakoff, G. (1987). *Women, Fire, and Dangerous Things: What Categories reveal about the Mind*. Chicago: University of Chicago Press.

Langacker, R. L. (1987). *Foundations of Cognitive Grammar, Vol. 1, Theoretical Prerequisites*. Stanford, CA: Stanford University Press.

Langacker, R. L. (1991). *Foundations of Cognitive Grammar, Vol. 2, Descriptive Application*. Stanford, CA: Stanford University Press.

Pecher, D., Zeelenberg, R., & Barsalou, L. W. (2003). Verifying conceptual properties in different modalities produces switching costs. *Psychological Science 14*, 119–124.

Pfeifer, R., & Scheier, C. (1999). *Understanding Intelligence*. Cambridge, MA: Cambridge University Press.

Pulvermüller, F. (1999). Words in the brain's language. *Behavioral & Brain Sciences 22*, 253–336.

Solomon, K. O., & Barsalou, L. W. (2001). Representing properties locally. *Cognitive Psychology 43*, 129–169.

Spivey, M., Tyler, M., Richardson, D., & Young, E. (2000). Eye movements during comprehension of spoken scene descriptions. *Proceedings of the 22nd Annual Conference of the Cognitive Science Society* (pp. 487–492). Mahwah, NJ: Erlbaum.

Stanfield, R. A., & Zwaan, R. A. (2001). The effect of implied orientation derived from verbal context on picture recognition. *Psychological Science 12*, 153–156.

Strack, F., Martin, L. L., & Stepper, S. (1988). Inhibiting and facilitating condition of facial expressions: A non-obtrusive test of the facial feedback hypothesis. *Journal of Personality & Social Psychology 54*, 768–777.

Talmy, L. (2000a). *Toward a Cognitive Semantics, Vol. I: Concept Structuring Systems*, Cambridge, MA: MIT Press.

Talmy, L. (2000b). *Toward a Cognitive Semantics, Vol. II: Typology and Process in Concept Structuring*. Cambridge, MA: MIT Press.

Turing, A. (1950). Computing machinery and intelligence. *Mind 59*, 433–460.

Wilson, M. (2002). Six views of embodied cognition. *Psychonomic Bulletin & Review 9*, 625–636.

Zwaan, R. A., Stanfield, R. A., & Yaxley, R. H. (2002). Language comprehenders mentally represent the shapes of objects. *Psychological Science 13*, 168–171.

2

Object Concepts and Action

Anna M. Borghi

Successful interaction with objects in the environment is the precondition for our survival and for the success of our attempts to improve life by using artifacts and technologies to transform our environment. Our ability to interact appropriately with objects depends on the capacity, fundamental for human beings, for categorizing objects and storing information about them, thus forming concepts, and on the capacity to associate concepts with names. Concepts serve as a kind of "mental glue" that "ties our past experiences to our present interactions with the world" (Murphy, 2002). These concepts are the cognitive and mental aspects of categories (Barsalou, Simmons, Barbey, & Wilson, 2003).

The generally accepted view sees concepts as being made of propositional symbols related arbitrarily to their referents. This implies that there exists a process by which sensorimotor experience is translated into amodal symbols. By proposing that concepts are, rather, grounded in sensorimotor activity, many authors have shown the limitations of this view (Barsalou, 1999; Harnad, 1990; Thelen & Smith, 1994). According to Barsalou (1999), concepts are perceptual symbols – i.e., recordings of the neural activation that arises during perception – arranged as distributed systems or "simulators." Once we have a simulator it is possible to activate simulations, which consist in the reenactment of a part of the content of the simulator.

This view presupposes a close relationship among perception, action, and cognition. Many recent theories argue against the existence of a separation between perception and action, instead favoring rather a view that incorporates motor aspects in perception (Berthoz, 1997). In theories that posit perception and action as separate spheres (Sternberg, 1969; Pylyshyn, 1999), it is not possible to envision action systems as having effects on perception, because the assumption is that the perceptual process takes place in the same way, independent from the kind of response involved – manual, by saccade, etc. (Ward, 2002). The primary limitation of this view is that it is not adaptive. It is difficult to imagine the evolution of the human perceptual system as something other than an ongoing process of finding appropriate responses to the environment. Perception cannot be simply the recording of sensorial messages. It must be influenced and filtered by action.

A growing body of research emphasizes the interconnections between the "low-level" or sensorimotor processes and the "high-level" or cognitive processes. It has been proposed that cognition is embodied, i.e., that it depends on the experiences that result from possessing a body with given physical characteristics and a particular sensorimotor system. This view of cognition is clearly in opposition to the classical cognitivist view according to which the mind is a device for manipulating arbitrary symbols.

The aim of this chapter is to provide indications that may serve as tools for evaluating the claims that concepts are grounded in sensorimotor experiences and that "knowledge is for acting" (Wilson, 2002). I will argue that object concepts support direct interaction with objects and that when concepts refer to objects through words, they activate action information.

This idea is compatible with two possibilities. Concepts can be conceived of directly as patterns of potential action (Glenberg, 1997) or as being made of "perceptual symbols" from which it is possible to quickly extract data that serve to inform action (Barsalou, 1999). If concepts directly evoke actions, they allow us to respond quickly to environmental stimuli. However, particular situations and goals may make it necessary to interact with objects in different ways, in which case we have to read concepts as clues to interaction and not simply as blueprints that tell us how to act (Duncker, 1945).

I will argue that both claims are true. Concepts automatically activate motor information for simple interaction with their referents, particularly with manipulable objects. However, when it comes to performing complex goal-oriented actions with complex objects, we may access more general perceptual and situational information and utilize it more flexibly.

OBJECT CONCEPTS AND INTERACTION WITH OBJECTS

Imagine you are using a computer. The concept "computer" supports the current interaction with the current computer. For example, before pressing each key on the keyboard, you access motor images that tell you where the different keys are.

In this perspective, the function of a concept consists of activating online simulations that support interaction with objects. Such simulations may also occur when there is no specific task requirement. Furthermore, this online use of concepts doesn't necessarily imply the mediation of awareness. One could be unaware of the position of the keys on the keyboard. Access to previous experience, however, allows us to understand that the keys have to be pressed instead of pinched. The unconscious mediation of conceptual knowledge makes it possible for us to extract information from the object so that we are able to interact with it successfully. The actions suggested by a particular object are known as affordances (Gibson, 1979). In this section, I will first discuss the ways in which concepts help us combine affordances with previous experience of objects. I will then discuss evidence demonstrating that concepts support action.

Affordances and Interaction with Objects

The affordance an individual derives from an object is neither objective nor subjective. "It is equally a fact of the environment and a fact of behavior" (Gibson, 1979, p. 129). Depending on the constraints of one's body, on the perceptual characteristics of the object in question, and on the situation at hand, we derive different affordances from objects. Perception is filtered and influenced by action, so affordances are interactive. An object blocking our way might afford the action of stopping, but not if the object is very low in relationship to our body.

Also, affordances are variable. As we use an object, its affordances may change. Before we use tools, we conceive of them as separate objects, with their own affordances. As we use them they can change from being mere objects, and may become extensions of our body (Hirose, 2001). There is evidence that peripersonal space is dynamic and can be extended and contracted through the use of a tool (Farne & Ladavas, 2000).

One might ask why we need conceptual knowledge if affordances support us in interacting successfully with objects. This question is crucial. When do concepts come into play? According to Gibson, and in the ecological tradition, affordances are based on intrinsic perceptual properties of objects. These properties are registered directly by the perceptual system without the mediation of object recognition or semantic knowledge. "You do not have to classify and label things in order to perceive what they afford" (Gibson, 1979, p. 134). In this view, the environment is thought to contain all the information the motor system needs to interact with objects, surfaces, substances, and other living entities. The behavioral possibilities afforded by objects are entirely specified by the pattern of stimulation that the object produces in the perceiver.

There are, however, some problems with this theory. Consider the different affordances derived from a rock blocking our way, and those derived from a bicycle. In the case of the rock, we quickly derive the affordance of stopping or of removing the obstacle. In the case of the bicycle, the handle may afford the action of grasping it, the seat of sitting upon it, etc. Thus, we may need to access conceptual information in order to know to which affordances to react.

In fact, the ability to use an object appropriately implies a capacity for combining the affordances it provides with our previous experience of that object and/or with any preexisting knowledge of its function. To ride a bike, we need to access previous experience with bikes. This experience need not be direct. Infants of four months, for example, acquire information regarding the affordances of an object by observing others rather than through direct experience (Mareschal & Johnson, 2003).

Furthermore, our goals in approaching an object can have an effect on our actions in relation to that object. The action of grasping the receiver of a telephone might come to us automatically, but using a telephone to call someone is the result of a mediation of goals, which differ from those involved in cleaning a telephone.

There are cases in which an object's shape might afford a certain response, but appropriate usage may require a different response. Klatzky, McCloskey, Doherty, and Pellegrino (1987) showed that for most objects the appropriate hand posture may be predicted on the basis of the object's structure, but for some objects structure and function diverge: a knife elicits a pinch response but functions with a clench posture. This suggests that in order to interact appropriately with certain kinds of objects, we have to combine the affordances they directly elicit with knowledge of the object and its function.

Two Routes to Action? An influential view regarding the relationships between action and conceptual knowledge claims that there are two different routes to action: a direct visual route, mediated by the dorsal system, and another route that implies access to semantics and is mediated by the ventral system. This view is supported by behavioral data (Rumiati & Humphreys, 1998). Further evidence concerns double dissociation found in patients with optic aphasia who fail to name visually presented objects but whose ability to gesture with them is preserved, and in apraxics, who are able to name and recognize objects but not to act appropriately with them.

However, recent data suggest that a direct nonsemantic route to action might exist, but that it is very limited and that there are deep interactions among perception, action, and knowledge. Experiments with action-decision and size-decision tasks conducted using Positron Emission Tomography (PET) indicated that words and pictures do not activate different neural areas (Phillips, Humphreys, Noppeney, & Price, 2002). Rather, pictures activate the same areas but to a lesser degree, probably due to the role played by affordances in facilitating motor responses. The only specific areas activated for pictures concerned novel objects, where it is necessary to spend some time in structural processing, as there is no previous usage or action information to access. Buxbaum, Sirigu, Schwartz, and Klatzky (2003) found that apraxics are able to associate an appropriate hand posture to novel objects but not to real objects. Thus, affordances in the classic, Gibsonian sense might be activated only by novel objects.

When we have previous experience with objects, it comes into play and influences interaction with them.

A less restrictive possibility is that manipulatory gestures in response to an object's affordances can be performed without accessing conceptual knowledge, but that it is impossible to perform gestures appropriate to the object's use as mediated by goals. Along these lines, Buxbaum et al. (2003) suggest that prehensile postures such as pinch and clench might be mediated simply by the dorsal system, thus not requiring access to knowledge regarding an object, while exploratory hand postures such as palm and poke, linked as they are with object identity, are always mediated by the ventral system. However, prehensile postures should also be related to object identity. Even a simple action such as grasping a familiar object by its handle requires a motor representation of how to grasp, and an object relative representation of where to grasp based on the object identity. Preshaping, manipulation, and tactile exploration of objects are mediated by knowledge. For example, even without visual feedback from the hand, the size of the grip aperture correlates with the object's size. However, knowledge is not sufficient: visual stimuli potentiate object affordances. Prehensile movement directed at objects within the peripheral visual field are inaccurate and improper (Jeannerod, 1994).

With a dual task paradigm, Creem and Proffitt (2001) showed that the ability to grasp common objects such as a hammer or a toothbrush appropriately, by, for example, reaching for a handle even if it is not oriented toward us, decreased with a semantic interference task, but not with a spatial interference task. This suggests that combining conceptual knowledge with affordances derived from objects is a necessary component of grasping them in an appropriate manner (Buxbaum, Schwartz, & Carew, 1997).

This mediation of conceptual knowledge is unconscious. Actions are driven by implicit knowledge of object attributes. The response is automatic. However, the implicit and explicit modes of processing are not isolated (Jeannerod, 1997). Klatzky et al. (1987) presented evidence that people have explicit knowledge of how to manipulate objects. People are able to reliably report which class of hand shape (clench, pinch, poke, palm) would be used to manipulate a certain object, which objects can be manipulated given a certain hand shape, and in which functional context (hold–pick up; feel–touch; use) a given hand shape had to be used.

Overall, the data are compatible with a second view, according to which there is an integrated distributed system for semantics, vision, and action rather than separate modules (Allport, 1985). Different information is activated depending on the goal being pursued. According to this view, semantic and sensorimotor information interact by allowing appropriate object use in such a manner that "the contribution from the functional/associational domain is actually enhanced by the involvement of sensorimotor elements recruited directly from perception" (Buxbaum et al., 1997, p. 248).

This does not mean that visual input and memory input have the same effect on action. For example, Wing, Turton, and Fraser (1986) have shown that grasping directed at memorized objects involves larger grip aperture than grasping directed at visual objects. In interaction with the memory input the visual input is necessary to adjust the grip appropriately. Neither sensorimotor nor semantic information is necessary and sufficient for performing appropriate actions. The visual input potentiates the affordances associated with the object – e.g., the handles, or the kind of grasp (Tucker & Ellis, 1998, 2001). This notion is compatible with the idea that we may have forms of representations or world models, but that they are partial and action-based and must be integrated with information on the current environment and needs (Clark, 1997).

Neural Basis: "What" and "How" Systems

The fact that we can do different things with objects is the basis for Jeannerod's (1994, 1997) proposal that we have both a pragmatic and a semantic representation of objects. Pragmatic representation, which is largely automatic, involves a rapid visuomotor transformation of the object, which is simply considered as a goal for acting. When our action is based on a pragmatic representation, we program and adjust object-oriented actions online in response to object properties. Semantic representation implies the integration of the features of an object into a meaningful identity, and it is generally conscious. The actions it generates are based on the memorized characteristics of objects. On the basis of this distinction, an object's attributes can be classified with regard to different aspects of object-oriented behavior. Size, shape, and texture are probably relevant to both forms of representation, color just to the semantic, weight just to the pragmatic.

Notice that these two forms of object representation are not separate; they may be integrated and influence each other. Anatomically, this is possible given the many connections linking the dorsal ventral systems.

In fact, this distinction between pragmatic and semantic representation is compatible – but does not overlap – with Milner and Goodale's (1995) hypothesis that we have two differently specialized visual processing systems. The dorsal system, originally conceived of as a spatial system used for coding the location of an object ("where" system), is now seen as a "how" system, dedicated to the computation of the movements of the effectors required to bring objects into proximity. It has been demonstrated in experiments conducted on monkeys that a large population of neurons in the dorsal stream is involved in the coding of hand grasping movements. The teams of Rizzolatti and Sakata have highlighted the role played by neurons in area F5 of the monkey, an area that forms the rostral part of the ventral premotor cortex, and in the intraparietal sulcus (area AIP). Canonical F5 neurons discharge both when the monkey sees the object and when it performs a goal-directed action such as manipulating, holding, tearing, or grasping a graspable 3D object. Some of these neurons are selective for different types of grip: precision grip, finger prehension, whole-hand prehension (Rizzolatti & Luppino, 2001). Overall, the dorsal system can be conceived of as an integrated perception-action system specialized in forming visuomotor representation of objects based on their physical characteristics and in transforming visual information into information regarding the graspability of objects in terms of affordances. This happens when information about goals is not specified and when correctness of action is guaranteed even when there is no functional information about objects.

Unlike the dorsal system, which operates in real time, the ventral system is specialized in computing and storing information about objects over long time intervals. As we have seen, in most cases conceptual information has to be combined with visual information for a person to interact correctly with objects, for example, to access what kind of grip is appropriate for manipulating them. In these cases, the dorsal system may receive input from the ventral system. This leads to a reconsideration of the idea that semantic knowledge is represented only in the ventral stream. Instead, it seems plausible that object knowledge is represented in various areas and that the premotor cortex plays a major role. Dorsal and ventral premotor activation might be part of a frontotemporal circuit connecting object meaning with motor responses.

A Possible Mechanism: Motor Imagery. More and more authors share the view that visual object representation includes motor information. A plausible mechanism for allowing this is the automatic activation of motor imagery. Motor imagery is a special kind of mental imagery involving the self. It corresponds to a subliminal activation of the motor system. Recently it has been shown that this system is involved not only in producing movements, but also in imagining actions, learning by observation, understanding the behavior of other people and recognizing tools (Decety, 1996; Jeannerod & Frak, 1999). In monkeys, neurons in area F5 discharge even when acting with the object is not required by the task (Fadiga, Fogassi, Gallese, & Rizzolatti, 2000). Similarly, in humans tools or graspable objects activate the premotor cortex even when no response is required. The mechanism of simulation guarantees that the system is flexible enough to shift to other action simulations if the situation requires it.

Behavioral Evidence

From Vision to Action. Recently much behavioral evidence has been provided in support of the idea that visual representation of objects includes the partial activation of the motor patterns associated with their affordances. For example, a glass is represented by making accessible the information that it can be reached and grasped in order to drink from it. Ellis and Tucker (2000) formulated the name "microaffordances" to refer to this phenomenon. Microaffordances are elicited automatically, independent of the goal of the actor. Accordingly, microaffordances typically do not pertain to complex actions, which are probably mediated by the actor's goal, such as drinking. Rather, they facilitate simple and specific kinds of interaction with objects. These simple interactions with objects also imply the activation of conceptual knowledge. In fact, microaffordances are more specific than Gibsonian affordances. They do not elicit grasping, but a specific component of grasping, which is suitable to a particular object.

Ellis and Tucker demonstrated this by presenting participants with real objects of different size located behind a screen (Ellis & Tucker, 2000; Tucker & Ellis, 2001). Participants had to categorize the objects as natural or artifact, or to respond to a high or low auditory stimulus, using either a power grip or a precision grip. A compatibility effect between the kind of grasp and a task-irrelevant dimension, the object's size, was found. The effect was also generated when the object was located outside the reaching space, which suggests that seeing the object activates the simulation of a specific component of grasping. A similar compatibility effect was found between the direction of the wrist rotation and the kind of grasp required by the object. For example, objects such as bottles facilitated responses with a clockwise wrist rotation, while objects such as toothbrushes facilitated a counterclockwise wrist rotation.

Microaffordances are not only elicited as a response to the size of an object. Tucker and Ellis (1998) conducted an experiment in which they presented participants with photographs of objects with handles, such as cups. The cups were presented upright or upside down, with the handle extending to the left or to the right of the object. Participants had to indicate whether the object was upright or reversed by pressing a left or a right key. Results showed a clear effect of the compatibility between the position of the handle and the orientation of the key, indicating that seeing an object can potentiate a certain response. In a further study, Phillips and Ward (2002) presented participants with a visual objects prime such as a frying pan with a handle. Its handle could be on the left, on the right, or in the middle, and it could be placed nearer to or further from the participant. The prime was followed after a varying stimulus onset asynchrony (SOA) by an imperative target requiring a left or right hand or footpress. The researchers found that there was a correspondence effect between handle orientation and the key the participant pressed regardless of the modality (e.g., hands uncrossed, hands crossed, foot response). This correspondence effect increased with SOA. The absence of an effect of depth could mean that participants accessed conceptual information, as they mentally reached for the handle even if it was not oriented toward them. Their interpretation of the results favors the idea that the affordances of an object do not potentiate a specific response code for the hand or limb more suited to respond, but rather activate a more abstract spatial code, which may potentiate a wide variety of responses to the afforded side of space.

More interestingly, these data suggest that participants form a simulation of their interaction with the objects, being sensitive to the relationship among the (irrelevant) object property, the handle location, the current position of their limbs in space, and the force of the effectors. The sensitivity to the current position of the limbs explains why in the crossed hand condition the hand closer to the handle is more activated. As the frying pan visually presented on the screen was empty, it might have been simpler and more economical for participants to grasp it with the hand closer to the handle. If the pan were presented with something (possibly heavy) inside, it could have been more useful to activate the ipsilateral hand. Of course, these studies test the immediate motor response to visual affordances. They do not investigate planning of a sequence of actions. If this were the case, then probably the most activated hand would be the ipsilateral hand, as it is easier to use when performing a series of actions. This sensitivity to the strength of their effectors explains why Tucker and Ellis (1998) did not find the compatibility effect when the effectors to provide the answer were two different fingers of the same hand and why Phillips and Ward (2002) found it with foot response. Unlike the foot, fingers are too close to each other to imply a different orientation of our bodily axis toward an object located in front of us. Furthermore, fingers might be too weak to move a cup, whereas feet are surely strong enough to remove a pan by pushing its handle. Thus, visual stimuli evoke a simulation of the interaction with the object in which object properties are not activated per se (e.g., handle location), but in interaction with the body properties (e.g., effectors location and force), and the current situation (e.g., empty frying pan).

From Action to Perception. The visual presentation of an object is not the only factor to potentiate the affordances associated with it. The intention to perform an action modulates visual processing by favoring perceptual features that are action-related.

Bekkering and Neggers (2002) found that the first eye movement was more accurate in selecting a target-object situated, with a given orientation, among distractors, when the object had to be grasped afterward than when it had to be pointed to. Given that orientation is relevant for grasping but not for pointing, the results suggest that action planning influences visual processing.

Various experiments demonstrate the effects of motor-visual priming. Preparation to grasp an object facilitates the detection and discrimination of visual shapes congruent with it. Craighero, Fadiga, Rizzolatti, and Umilta (1999) trained participants to prepare a grasping movement toward a bar oriented clockwise or counterclockwise. They then had to grasp it as quickly as possible after presentation of a picture representing a bar oriented either clockwise or counterclockwise or a circle. Grasping response times were quicker when the orientation of the visually presented bar and that of the bar to grasp matched. The congruency effect was still present when the participants used effectors other than the hands or made a response not affected by a postural relation with the grasping movement (i.e., blinking with both eyelids). It disappeared when the visual properties of the presented target did not match with those for which the grasping movement was prepared, as a pencil with the same orientation of the bar, which could not be grasped in the same way as the bar. Thus the effect was not due to orientation effects per se, but to the matching of the motor affordances of the visual object with those of the real object.

Motor preparation also evokes a representation of the prepared action in visual terms. Vogt, Taylor, and Hopkins (2003) demonstrated this with a simple response procedure. Participants, given the instruction "clockwise" or "counterclockwise" and a prime, were asked to grasp a bar in the indicated orientation. By manipulating the perspective of the hand presented as a prime, which could either match the end posture of the observer's own hand ("Own perspective") or the end posture of the hand of another person ("Other perspective"), they found a congruency effect for the "Own perspective" when a neutral hand stimulus was given as a preview and for the "Other perspective" when the prime stimuli was preceded by a fixation dot. The results suggest that there are two different priming effects: a visuomotor priming effect, driven by a visual stimulus (the hand) that automatically evokes a motor response, and a motor-visual priming, planning driven, which enhances the visual processing of body parts in the Own perspective. Both mechanisms are relevant from an evolutionary standpoint. We need to react quickly to unexpected appearance of hands of conspecifics, just as we automatically react to visual objects, and we also need to select perceptual stimuli relevant for acting.

Borghi, Di Ferdinando, and Parisi (2002) ran Artificial Life simulations that explain how the action intention influences categorization. They simulated an organism living in a bidimensional environment containing four different objects. The organism had a visual system with which he/she saw one object at a time and a movable two-segment arm. He/she was aware of the arm's position at any given time thanks to proprioceptive input from the arm's segments. The organism's behavior was controlled by an artificial neural network. In the simulation, the organism had to group the stimuli by pressing the same button, in two categories that, depending on the task or action intention (which was encoded in a set of additional input units), could be formed by perceptually very similar, moderately similar, or different objects. Categories formed by perceptually dissimilar objects are goal-derived categories, i.e., categories based on common goals rather than on perceptual similarity between their members (Barsalou, 1991). Task information overrode perceptual information. The internal representations of the neural networks reflected the current task and not the perceptual similarity between the objects. However, the networks tended to form action-based categories more easily (e.g., in fewer generations) when perceptually similar objects had to be responded to by pressing the same button than when perceptual similarity and action to perform were not congruent. At hidden layers nearer the sensory input, where task information still had not arrived, internal representations reflected perceptual information.

Visual processing is not only influenced by action intention. We also implicitly code action relations of the causal kind between objects, and this influences visual selection (Riddoch, Humphreys, Edwards, Baker, & Willson, 2003). Patients with extinction, i.e., patients who, in the presence of two stimuli, report seeing only one of them, identified pairs of objects that were action-related in a correct and an incorrect way (e.g., corkscrew going into the cork at the top or at the bottom of a wine bottle). Patients were more likely to select two items in a trial if they were in the correct position for action, and if they were linked by an action relation (e.g., hammer and nail) rather than an associative relation (e.g., pencil associated with the most frequently associated word, pen).

Interactive Properties and Categorization. Iachini and Borghi (2004) used a sorting task to test the importance of interactive properties for categorization. The material consisted of boxes varying in shape (square vs. triangular), size (small vs. large), and kind of handle (liftable vs. not liftable). The boxes were built to make it possible to lift them without using the handle, but participants had to extend the hand in an unnatural position. Also, size was manipulated, but not in such a way as to deeply influence interaction with objects. Depending on the condition, during the learning phase participants had to observe the boxes (only vision); to touch and lift the boxes without seeing them (only motor); to observe, touch, and lift the boxes (vision and motor); and to observe the experimenter touching and lifting the boxes (mirror). Then participants had to sort the boxes into two groups.

If sorting tasks were predicted by perceptual salience, shape should be the preferred dimension for sorting, followed by size. If the objects activate a simulation of the possible actions to perform with them, whether they were easy to lift should acquire relevance. This hypothesis was confirmed. Across conditions, sorting was predicted by both shape and liftability, which differed significantly from size. The relevance of shape can be explained by the fact that shape automatically activates motor information.

From Vision to Function? The findings reported thus far indicate that there is an interaction between action-relevant object properties, such as shape and part location, size and orientation, and the kind of action to perform. Viewing an object automatically activates action related properties, and motor preparation influences the perceptual processing of an object.

However, the studies reported do not address the issue of whether the visual perception of an object automatically invokes motor representation of the object's function. To test for this, Bub, Masson, and Bukach (2003) asked participants to learn to associate a color to one of four hand postures (pinch, poke, open grasp, close grasp) to mimic in relation to an object. Photos of objects were presented, which could be congruent or not with the hand posture (e.g., a needle is congruent with a pinch posture). Participants had to respond with a given posture to the color of the picture. There was no congruency effect between the hand posture and the object. The congruency effect appeared only when it was required to direct attention to the object identity.

The results indicate that images of objects do not automatically evoke their function. This happened only when information about function and form evoked the same motor response. This suggests that manipulation and functional information might differ and that only the first is automatically elicited by visual stimuli.

Buxbaum, Veramonti, and Schwartz (2000) report cases of apraxic patients with impaired manipulation knowledge but intact function knowledge. These cases double dissociate from a case of an agnosic described by Sirigu, Duhamel, and Poncet (1991) who was able to determine how to manipulate certain objects, but was not able to define their function or the context in which they would be utilized.

Gerlach, Law, and Paulson (2002) used PET on participants who had to decide whether an object was natural or man-made in a picture categorization task. The left premotor cortex, concerned with motor function, was more activated during categorization of manipulable objects, such as vegetables, fruit, and clothing, than during categorization of animals and nonmanipulable artifacts. The effect of manipulability was independent of the function and the category of the object.

Kellenbach, Brett, and Patterson (2003) asked participants to judge actions and functions associated with manipulable and nonmanipulable artifacts (e.g., a hammer or a traffic light). PET showed that the response of the left ventral premotor cortex and the left middle temporal gyrus was stronger in the case of manipulable objects, whereas no regions of the cortex were more activated by function relative to action judgments about artifacts. These results indicate that the brain responds preferentially to how we interact with objects, rather than to what they are used for, and confirm that action and function information do not overlap.

Summary

The neural and behavioral data presented in this section are consistent with the idea that interaction with objects occurs in different ways. In the case of novel objects affordances directly guide actions. In the case of known objects, there are two possible outcomes. When we perform simple actions, visual input and object knowledge support us as we extract affordances automatically ("knowing how"). In this case concepts can be seen as patterns of potential action that support us in extracting affordances (Glenberg, 1997). When we perform complex actions, visual input and object knowledge are integrated with functional knowledge of objects, goals, and sensitivity to context. This integration makes it possible to extract the affordances relevant for current goals and for an appropriate object use ("knowing what for"). In this case, concepts should rather be thought of as residuals of perceptual experience, from which it is possible to extract action information that is relevant for the current situation quickly (Barsalou, 1999). Both visions of concepts are true depending on the situation.

OBJECT CONCEPTS, ACTION, AND LANGUAGE

Evidence reviewed in the first section suggests that visual stimuli activate motor-action information and that motor preparation enhances visual processing. The second section of the chapter focuses on object concepts expressed through words, i.e., concept-nouns. The hypothesis tested is that concept-nouns also activate action and motor information (Barsalou, 2003).

Affordances and Concept-Nouns

If object information is stored in terms of affordances, it is plausible that words that refer to objects activate the same affordances as the objects themselves. However, the same object could actually possess many affordances. In the case of a car, the steering wheel could afford driving, while the seat could afford sitting. Thus, it is plausible that not all affordances are activated during a simulation, only affordances elicited by canonical actions as well as affordances relevant for the current goals (Zwaan, Stanfield, & Yaxley, 2002; Carlson & Kenny, Chapter 3, this volume).

Borghi (2004) verified whether objects are represented as patterns of potential actions by focusing on their parts. In a first experiment, three groups of participants were required to perform an imagery decision task. They had to decide if they could imagine using or acting with, building, or seeing certain objects. For a subset of critical concept-nouns – all complex artifacts such as bicycle, mixer, piano – they were also required to produce the names of component parts. In the building and seeing situations, participants produced more part names. It appeared that when they sim- ulated action using one of the objects, they selectively focused on certain parts. The produced parts were submitted to a group of raters who judged the importance of each part for using or acting with, building and seeing each object. The average rating of each part for each perspective (action- use, building, and vision) was then multiplied by the frequency of the produced parts for each participant and by the position in which the part was produced. Results showed that parts produced more frequently and earlier across situations were those rated as relevant for acting with the object. However, depending on the kind of simulated interaction with ob- jects (building vs. vision), different parts became salient for concepts. In a second experiment, participants were simply required to produce the parts of the critical concept-nouns without performing the imagery deci- sion task. Also in this neutral condition the parts relevant for actions were rated as most important and produced earlier. This suggests that object concepts are action-based. In addition, the number of parts produced in the neutral situation paralleled that of parts produced in the action situa- tion and was lower than the number of parts produced in the building and vision situations. Much as occurred in the action situation, participants in the neutral situation focused selectively on a certain number of parts. Interestingly, these parts were those relevant for acting with objects. The results indicate that affordances relevant for canonical actions with objects are activated, but that the activation of affordances is modulated by the simulated situation.

In language comprehension, sentence structure guides the selection of affordances. In various papers, Glenberg and collaborators have shown that sentences combine and are understood if the combination, or mesh, of affordances works. For example, if we can mentally envision that the combination of affordances can accomplish a goal described by a sentence, we understand the sentence and judge that it makes sense. Glenberg and Robertson (2000) found that sentences such as "After wading barefoot in the lake, Erik used his shirt to dry his feet" were judged more sensible than sentences like "After wading barefoot in the lake, Erik used his glasses to dry his feet." This indicates that affordances derived from objects in the world, not words, constrain the way in which ideas can be meshed and combined.

Borghi (2004) asked participants to read sentences describing actions (e.g., "The woman shared the orange"). The sentences were followed by the name of a part of the object mentioned in the sentence or by the name of a part of something else. Participants had to press one key if the name referred to a part of the object mentioned in the sentence, another key if it did not. Parts of the objects were either parts from which it was easy to extract affordances or not. For example, the action of sharing the slices of an orange can be more easily simulated than the action of sharing its pulp, due to the perceptual properties of the parts "slices" and "pulp." Parts from which it was easy to derive affordances for the goal expressed by the sentence were processed earlier than other parts.

Altmann and Kamide (1999) obtained similar results in an experiment with eye-tracking. Participants had to inspect a semirealistic scene while listening to sentences such as "The boy will eat the cake." Once they heard the verb, they oriented their eyes to the only object in the display that could be eaten and was therefore compatible with the simulated action (see also Chambers, Tanenhaus, Eberhard, Filip, & Carlson, 2002).

Klatzky, Pellegrino, McCloskey, and Doherty (1989) demonstrated that participants form an action simulation in which they verify the compatibility between the specific posture to use and the action to perform on the object. Iconic and verbal primes corresponding to hand shapes speeded the sensibility judgment of sentences compatible with them. For example, the hand shape for "pinch" speeded the sensibility judgment for "aim a dart."

Concepts Elicit Actions: Indirect Evidence

Evidence shows that concept-nouns elicit perceptual, situational, functional and causal information, which might be relevant for situated actions.

Shape. There is much evidence of the importance for object concept-nouns of intrinsic properties, i.e., properties likely to remain relatively constant in a variety of situations, such as shape and size (Jeannerod, 1994). These properties are both perceptual and motor, and they orient actions.

Different studies have shown the importance of shape and parts for object concept-nouns (Tversky & Hemenway, 1984). Evidence on the "shape bias" shows that from the age of two, children extend names to objects similar in shape (Smith & Samuelson, 1997). During sentence comprehension, adults mentally represent the object shape. For example, the sentence "The ranger saw the eagle in the sky" led to a faster recognition of a picture of a bird with outstretched wings than of a bird with folded wings (Zwaan et al., 2002).

We are also sensitive to the iconic order in which parts of objects are presented. Semantic relatedness judgments regarding pairs of words that respect the iconic order ("attic" presented above "basement") were quicker than judgments regarding pairs of words that did not respect it ("basement" presented above "attic") (Zwaan & Yaxley, 2003).

Size. Even if not so salient as shape, size is also important for concept-nouns, probably due to its relevance for action, as preliminary data by Setti (personal communication) indicate. Participants were provided semantic association judgments for pairs of words referring to objects of the same or of different sizes. When prime and target were the same size, responses were quicker and more accurate than when size differed. In a further study the target followed sentences with either a manipulation or a neutral verb (e.g., The boy grasped vs. saw the grapefruit). Participants had to evaluate whether the second word was from the same category as the word in the sentence. Responses were quicker when object size corresponded, even though the neutral and the manipulation sentences did not differ. However, in an explicit task, participants consistently answered that size was more important for performing actions referred to by manipulative than by neutral verbs.

Attention. The implicit intention to perform a particular action could lead to a selective focus on different perceptual properties. Wu and Barsalou (2001) asked participants to produce the features of objects such as a watermelon and a half watermelon. With both imagery and neutral instructions, with "watermelon" participants produced primarily external properties such as skin and green. With "half watermelon" they produced mostly internal properties such as red and seeds. The results may depend on the different actions typically associated with a watermelon and a half watermelon.

Eye-tracking studies show that participants listening to stories describing objects orient their eyes in the direction of the imagined object. For example, they orient their eyes upward while listening to someone talk about skyscrapers, downward while listening to someone talk about canyons (Spivey & Geng, 2001; see Spivey, Richardson, & Gonzales-Marquez, Chapter 11, this volume).

Perspective. If concepts are made of perceptual symbols, they should have perspectives, as percepts have perspectives. Perspectives pertain to interaction and vary depending on the relation between our body and the object (see Zwaan & Madden, Chapter 10, this volume). Given this potential variation in perspective, it would be adaptive to first access the perspectives relevant for more frequent actions, before eventually shifting to other perspectives if the situation requires.

Borghi and Barsalou (2002) asked participants to imagine a scenario, e.g., being inside or outside a prison, and to answer whether in that situation they could expect to find a certain object. For a subset of concept-nouns, participants had to produce object characteristics. Seven raters evaluated to what extent the properties produced across the scenarios would be experienced from different perspectives (e.g., "inside," "outside"). The ratings were then multiplied for the production frequency. The procedure was repeated in five experiments accessing different perspectives: inside-outside, near-far, top-bottom, toward-away, and visual-motor-auditory. Evidence of the existence of both entrenched and situational perspectives arose. Entrenched perspectives provide default ways of constructing simulations, such as perceiving objects from the outside, from the front, up close, and visually. They are clearly action-based: Typically we act with objects located in front of us, and close to us, and we experience them through vision and touch. Default perspectives sometimes reinstate themselves, perhaps because of their informativeness, even when situational perspectives are appropriate. So, even when asked to adopt a situational perspective imagining being far from an object, participants adopted an entrenched perspective zooming in on it: 'pizza' always elicited more frequently near properties (e.g., olive oil) than far properties (e.g., round). Typically, however, situational perspectives override default perspectives, inducing perspectives relevant in the current situation, such as perceiving objects from the inside, from above, at a distance, or auditorally. So participants produced more frequently inside than outside properties (e.g., claustrophobic versus guard-tower) when imagining being inside a prison.

Borghi, Glenberg, and Kaschak (in press) examined whether or not the knowledge of object spatial organization in parts is accessed in a different way depending on the perspective relevant for the actions to perform. After reading a sentence describing an object from an inside perspective ("You are driving a car") or an outside perspective ("You are fueling a car"), participants had to verify whether a word appearing after the sentence named a part of the object ("steering wheel" or "trunk") by pressing two different keys. There was clearly a perspective effect in that participants verified respective parts (inside or outside) with greater speed when the sentence they read was related directly to the perspective. Another experiment demonstrated that relative distance to objects within a perspective also affects response. For example, given the inside perspective of sitting in an airplane, participants were quicker to verify the part name "tray table" than "cockpit." This suggests that object parts are differentially accessed depending on the perspective and that perspective is related to the action to perform.

Motion. For interacting with different kinds of objects and entities, it is important to know how they typically move. Setti and Borghi (2003) asked two groups of participants to write how objects referred to by concept-nouns of different ontological kind move or are moved. The ontological categories included natural kinds (animals and plants), artifacts (complex artifacts and means of transport), nominal kinds, and "ambiguous" kinds or concepts, which could be considered natural as well as artifact, such as milk. From the analyses of the nouns and verbs produced it emerged that there are three parameters for organizing information about the motion of an object. The most important parameter is the ability to produce a displacement, which distinguishes animals and nominal kinds – which are able to change their position – from plants, which can grow, but cannot produce a displacement. The second parameter is speed, which distinguishes means of transport, which move quickly, from plants, which move slowly. The third parameter is self-induced movement, which distinguishes nominal kinds from other concepts (Mandler, 1992). All these parameters are grounded in action. While interacting with objects and entities we use information on their displacement and speed. Knowing whether movement is self-induced is also relevant for interactions as that between hunter and prey in chase.

Context. Interacting successfully with objects implies knowing not only their perceptual and motion properties, but also where to find them. Much evidence indicates that concept-nouns activate thematic relations, i.e., relations referring to situations in which their referents typically occur. Traditionally it has been assumed that thematic organization is relevant only for pre-school conceptual knowledge and that it is substituted at a later point in development by taxonomic, hierarchical organization. Recent studies highlight the relevance of thematic relations in adults (Lin & Murphy, 2001). Borghi and Caramelli (2001, 2003) found that thematic relations were produced more frequently than taxonomic ones in children aged 5, 8, and 10, and in adults. Most interestingly, among thematic relations action relations were the most often produced among 5-year-olds. Older children and adults tended rather to produce spatial relations. Objects were linked first to a specific action and at a later point thought of as embedded in contexts where typical actions are performed.

Borghi, Caramelli, and Setti (2004) asked participants to produce locations associated with basic- and superordinate-level concept-nouns (e.g., steak, food). With both neutral and imagery instructions, participants produced more object-locations (e.g., "plate") with basic-level concept-nouns, where one or a few category members can be found, whereas with superordinate-level concept-nouns they produced more setting-locations (e.g., kitchen), where more category members can coexist. The same results were found in a location-verification task. Again, the results may by explained by the action intention: as basic-level concepts generally refer to single instances, it is more productive while acting with them to focus on a specific location. The case is different for superordinate-level concepts, which refer to multiple instances.

Situatedness. The reported evidence suggests that concepts retain information on typical contexts of objects. However, sensitivity to the current context is also a clear advantage for acting. Barsalou (1987) has shown in many experiments that concepts activate different information depending on the participant, on the moment of the day, and on the context, on the point of view adopted. On the developmental side, Smith (Smith & Samuelson, 1997) has stressed the importance of variability in word extension tasks.

Function. Evidence showing the centrality of function for categorization, especially of artifacts, is in line with the adaptive view of categorization presented here. The affordance view of function suggests in fact that the capacity to infer an object's function depends on experience and prior knowledge of how to use an object. In antithesis to this view, the intentional view of function underlines the role played by the intention of the designer of the artifacts. However, Chaigneau and Barsalou (in press) show that when participants are given adequate information on both the actual use of the object and the setting in which it would be used, as well as its design history, the use of an object dominates over design history in the judgments expressed by participants.

Causality. The importance of causal relations for categorization is widely recognized (Keil, 1989; Sloman, Love, & Ahn, 1998). However, it is not always recognized that causality is deeply grounded in action. One of the reasons why thematic relations are more accessible than taxonomic relations may stem from the fact that, unlike taxonomic relations, they are linked by causal relations. In particular, action and function relations presuppose causal relations – between agents and actions, between agents and the effects and products of actions, etc.

Preliminary data by Borghi, obtained with a typicality rating task performed on part names of weapons and of other artifacts, suggest that we are sensitive to the causal relations between object parts and that this sensitivity is grounded in action. The parts to rate were divided into three categories. Causal parts are those with which we typically come into contact, such as a car's steering wheel. Effect parts are those whose movement is dependent on another agent (think of the relationship between the wheels of a car and the steering wheel). Structural parts are parts that are not related to typical actions, such as the roof of a car. Both cause and effect parts, which are action-related, were judged more salient than structural parts, while the importance of effect parts was higher for weapons, lower for other artifacts.

Concepts Elicit Actions: Direct Evidence

The reported evidence supports the view that concepts are residuates of perceptual experiences. The information accessed most easily is that relevant for typical actions, but depending on the situation we may access information useful for less typical actions. Thus action experiences are reflected in concepts, but the evidence available thus far does not lead to the conclusion that motor information is automatically activated.

Neuroimaging studies and behavioral studies support the hypothesis that some kinds of motor information are directly elicited by concept-nouns. It has been demonstrated, for example, that action is a powerful cue for recalling information on objects. Magniè, Ferreira, Giuliano, and

Poncet (1999) report the case of an agnosic patient who recognized only objects with which he could recall associated actions – tools, kitchen utensils, clothes, body parts – but not animals and musical instruments (he didn't play any instrument).

Neuroimaging. Neuroimaging studies show that object knowledge is organized as a distributed system. In this system object attributes are stored near the same modality-specific areas that are active as objects are being experienced (Martin, Ungerleider, & Haxby, 2001; Pulvermüller, 1999). This goes against the claim, defended by widely accepted theories regarding concept organization and representation in the brain, that conceptual information is functionally and physically independent of modality-specific input and output representations and that the appropriate level of analysis for studying conceptual organization is that of whole categories, not of features (Mahon & Caramazza, in press). PET indicated that naming of tools, compared to naming of animals (importantly, animals were large four-legged animals, such as elephants), differentially activated the left middle temporal gyrus, an area very close to the area assumed to store information about object movement, which is also activated by action-generation tasks, and the left premotor cortex, generally activated when participants imagine themselves grasping objects with their dominant hand (Martin, Wiggs, Ungerleider, & Haxby, 1996). This suggests that action and manipulation information is automatically activated by viewing objects and pictures, and that the same areas are involved when forming motor imagery and when activating information on tools. Using fMRI, Simmons, Pecher, Hamann, Zeelenberg, and Barsalou (2003) show that brain activation during a verification task of modal properties (Pecher, Zeelenberg, & Barsalou, 2003) reflects the processed properties but is also distributed in different areas. In particular, in trials with motor properties, many areas are active, particularly visual areas. This evidence supports a close relationship between visual and motor properties.

Behavioral. Behavioral studies support the hypothesis that motor information is directly activated in the processing of concept-nouns. Borghi et al. (in press) demonstrated with a part-verification task that concept-nouns of object parts directly activate the motor system. Sentences such as "There is a horse in front of you" were followed by parts chosen so that actions directed toward them (on the real object) required a movement upward (the head of the horse) or downward (the hoof of the horse). Responding by pressing a button in a direction compatible with the part location (e.g., responding upward to verify that a horse has a head) was faster than responding in a direction incompatible with the part location.

Preliminary evidence by Borghi and Nicoletti indicates that processing artifacts activates the kind of grip appropriate to use them. Participants categorized words and pictures in natural and artifacts by pressing different buttons. Categorization times were slower for artifacts that are typically used with a precision and a power grip (e.g., harp), than for artifacts used with two power grips (e.g., rake).

What happens with concept-nouns that refer to objects with which we typically interact in different ways? Action intentions expressed linguistically may modulate the activation of the motor system. Glenberg and Kaschak (2002) asked participants to provide sensibility judgments by pressing a button either moving the hand towards the body or away from the body. They found a compatibility effect between the action to perform and the sentence to process: for example, the sentence "Close the drawer" was responded to more quickly while moving the hand away from the body, and the sentence "Open the drawer" while moving the hand toward the body.

Preliminary evidence by Borghi indicates that the movement performed influences judgments on size. Participants judged the size of objects requiring a precision grip (e.g., pencil) and a power grip (e.g., eggplants) in four conditions, when asked to move their hands in order to simulate a precision grip movement or a power grip movement and when asked to use pliers of two different sizes to mimic the same movements. Size ratings produced in the precision grip condition were lower than those produced in the power grip condition.

Summary

Overall, neuroimaging and behavioral evidence is consistent with the idea that concept-nouns activate motor responses automatically. This has been demonstrated thus far only for simple manipulatory actions such as grasping and reaching the object's parts, directly afforded by characteristics such as shape and size, and not for complex actions involving access to functional knowledge. Barsalou and Borghi (2004) found that when asked what is typically included in complex actions such as eating, participants produced mostly microactions, such as chewing. Microaffordances probably operate at this microlevel.

The difference between manipulation and function information has interesting implications. It helps explain that the fact that children extend names on the basis of shape rather than of function is not due to their scarce sensitivity to action information (Landau, Smith, & Jones, 1998). In fact, shape certainly incorporates motor information, even if not functional information.

TRUE ONLY FOR MANIPULABLE OBJECTS?

We have seen that concepts support interaction with objects, mostly through the use of motor imagery. Motor imagery may facilitate simple interaction with objects – responding to their organization in parts, holding them, grasping them. This is especially true for manipulable objects, independent of their ontological kind. Manipulable natural kinds, such as flowers, evoke behavioral effects similar to those evoked by manipulable artifacts. Motor imagery may also be activated for microinteractions with nonmanipulable objects. Consider buildings, for example. We do not typically manipulate them, but we may manipulate their parts.

The difference between artifacts and natural kinds might arise when we consider goal-driven actions. Simple artifacts, at least, such as cups, are designed so that information relevant for microinteractions is congruent with functional information. Probably responses to natural kinds are more frequently mediated by goals than response to artifacts, as we typically act with natural kinds in different ways and have to extract different affordances depending on our goals – we typically drink from glasses, while we can feed, caress, and perform surgery on cats. This could explain why natural kinds activate the visual areas of the cortex more than tools. Accessing more perceptual properties may guarantee more action flexibility (Parisi, personal communication, 2001).

Thus, on the basis of the evidence, it can be concluded that manipulable object concepts, and in some cases object concepts overall, directly activate motor information concerning microinteractions with their referents, i.e., interactions not mediated by goals. This is true both when we interact directly with objects and when we process concept-nouns. Evidence that concepts automatically activate motor information related to their functional characteristics is less compelling.

Things become more complicated if we consider concepts that do not refer to objects, such as abstract concepts like freedom and truth (see Barsalou & Wiemer-Hastings, Chapter 7, this volume). The acquisition of these concepts may be grounded in interactions we have with the world and their possession can be useful for acting in the world, but they probably do not elicit motor images. However, they might elicit situations through mental imagery. Preliminary evidence by Borghi, Caramelli, and Setti (2004) (unpublished manuscript) indicates that more than 80% of the relations produced with abstract concepts such as risk are situations. Furthermore, a growing body of evidence shows that abstract concepts can also refer indirectly to bodily experiences. Boroditsky and Ramscar (2002) showed that abstract concepts such as time are understood through the experience-based domain of space.

CONCLUSION

This chapter shows that object concepts play an important adaptive role. In the presence of objects and when objects are referred to by words they activate action simulations to facilitate interaction with objects. Concepts directly evoke simple motor responses and can therefore be seen as patterns of potential action (Glenberg, 1997). However, to guarantee the flexibility necessary for interactions mediated by goals, concepts should rather be conceived of as made of "perceptual symbols," from which to extract information relevant for the hic-and-nunc (Barsalou, 1999). These two visions of concepts are complementary and share the assumption that concepts are grounded in sensorimotor activity.

In the presence of objects, concepts help to combine affordances with previous experiences. This occurs primarily at an unconscious level. In some cases we might simply react to novel objects, in which case affordances are a direct invitation to act. In other cases, we may need to know how to manipulate objects in order to interact with them successfully. Evidence shows that visual information potentiates microaffordances, i.e. affordances associated with object manipulation, which automatically evoke motor responses. In other cases we might need to know how to use objects, i.e., to know what kind of affordances to extract, given the current situation and goals.

What happens with concepts expressed by words? They keep track of our interaction with objects. First of all, they keep track of the experience of object manipulation. They activate microaffordances such as those elicited by shape and size, and these microaffordances automatically evoke motor responses. Second, concept-nouns keep track of information relevant for more complex interactions with objects by activating perceptual, contextual, functional, and causal information. This allows us to activate the affordances relevant for the current situation and goals, thus facilitating situated action. Evidence seems to indicate that at this "higher" level the motor system is not automatically activated, but that its activation is mediated by access to general perceptual and situational information.

ACKNOWLEDGMENTS

Thanks to Andrea di Ferdinando, Tina Iachini, Diane Pecher, Rolf Zwaan, and two anonymous reviewers for useful comments on an earlier draft and to Ann Gagliardi for help with English.

References

Allport, D. A. (1985). Distributed memory, modular subsystems, and dysphasia. In S. K. Newman, R. Epstein (Eds.), *Current Perspectives in Dysphasia* (pp. 32–60). Edinburgh: Churchill Livingstone.

Altmann, G. T. M., & Kamide, Y. (1999). Incremental interpretation at verbs: Restricting the domain of subsequent reference. *Cognition 73*, 247–264.

Barsalou, L. W. (1987). The instability of graded structure, implications for the nature of concepts. In U. Neisser (Ed.), *Concepts and Conceptual Development:*

Ecological and Intellectual Factors in Categorization (pp. 101–140). Cambridge, UK: Cambridge University Press.

Barsalou L. W. (1991). Deriving categories to achieve goals. In G. H. Bower (Ed.), *The Psychology of Learning and Motivation: Advances in Research and Theory* (vol. 27, pp. 1–64). San Diego, CA: Academic Press.

Barsalou, L. W. (1999). Perceptual symbol systems. *Behavioral & Brain Sciences 22*, 577–609.

Barsalou, L. W. (2003). Situated Simulation in the Human Conceptual System. *Language and Cognitive Processes*, 18, 513–562.

Barsalou, L. W., & Borghi, A. M. (2004). The MEW theory of knowledge: Evidence from concepts for settings, events, and situations.

Barsalou, L. W., Simmons, W. K., Barbey, A. K. & Wilson, C. D. (2003). Grounding conceptual knowledge in modality-specific systems. *Trends in Cognitive Science 7*, 84–91.

Bekkering, H., & Neggers, S. W. (2002). Visual search is modulated by action intentions. *Psychological Science 13*, 370–374.

Berthoz, A. (1997). *Le sens du movement*. Paris: Odile Jacob.

Borghi, A. M. (2004). Objects, concepts, and action: Extracting affordances from objects' parts. *Acta Psychologica 115*, 1, 69–96.

Borghi, A. M., & Barsalou, L. W. (2002). Perspectives in the conceptualization of categories.

Borghi, A. M., & Caramelli, N. (2001). Taxonomic relations and cognitive economy in conceptual organization. In J. D. Moore & K. Stenning (Eds.), *Proceedings of the 23rd Meeting of the Cognitive Science Society* (pp. 98–103). London: Erlbaum.

Borghi, A. M., & Caramelli, N. (2003). Situation bounded conceptual organization in children: From action to spatial relations. *Cognitive Development 18*, 1, 49–60.

Borghi, A. M., Caramelli, N., & Setti, A. (2004). Conceptual information on objects' location.

Borghi, A. M., Di Ferdinando, A., & Parisi, D. (2002). The role of perception and action in object categorization. In J. A. Bullinaria & W. Lowe (Eds.), *Connectionist Models of Cognition and Perception* (pp. 40–50). Singapore: World Scientific.

Borghi, A. M., Glenberg, A. M., & Kaschak, M. P. (in press). Putting words in perspective. *Memory & Cognition*.

Boroditsky, L., & Ramscar, M. (2002). The roles of body and mind in abstract thought. *Psychological Science 13*, 185–189.

Bub, D. N., Masson, M. E. J., & Bukach, C. M. (2003). Gesturing and naming: The use of functional knowledge in object identification. *Psychological Science 14*, 467–472.

Buxbaum, L. J., Schwartz, M. F., & Carew, T. G. (1997). The role of semantic memory in object use. *Cognitive Neuropsychology 14*, 219–254.

Buxbaum, L. J., Sirigu, A., Schwartz, M. F., & Klatzky, R. (2003). Cognitive representations of hand posture in ideomotor apraxia. *Neuropsychologia 41*, 1091–1113.

Buxbaum, L. J., Veramonti, T., & Schwartz, M. F. (2000). Function and manipulation tool knowledge in apraxia: Knowing "what for" but not "how." *Neurocase 6*, 83–97.

Chaigneau, S. E., & Barsalou, L. W. (in press). The role of function in categories. *Theoria et Historia Scientiarum*.

Chambers, C. G., Tanenhaus, M. K., Eberhard, K. M., Filip, H., & Carlson, G. N. (2002). Circumscribing referential domains during real-time language comprehension. *Journal of Memory and Language 47*, 30–49.

Clark, A. (1997). *Being There*. Cambridge, MA: MIT.

Craighero, L., Fadiga, L., Rizzolatti, G., & Umilta, C. (1999). Action for perception: A motor-visual attentional effect. *Journal of Experimental Psychology: Human Perception and Performance 25*, 1673–1692.

Creem, S. H., & Proffitt, D. R. (2001). Grasping objects by their handles: A necessary interaction between perception and action. *Journal of Experimental Psychology: Human Perception and Performance 27*, 1, 218–228.

Decety, J. (1996). The neurophysiological basis of motor imagery. *Behavioural Brain Research 77*, 45–52.

Duncker, K. (1945). On problem solving. *Psychological Monographs 58*, 5, 270.

Ellis, R., & Tucker, M. (2000). Micro-affordance: The potentiation of components of action by seen objects. *British Journal of Psychology 91*, 451–471.

Fadiga, L., Fogassi, L., Gallese, V. & Rizzolatti, G. (2000). Visuomotor neurons: Ambiguity of the discharge or "motor" perception? *International Journal of Psychophysiology 35*, 165–177.

Farne, A., & Ladavas, E. (2000). Dynamic size-change of hand peripersonal space following tool use. *Neuroreport 11*, 1–5.

Gerlach, C., Law, I., & Paulson, O. B. (2002). When action turns into words. Activation of motor-based knowledge during categorization of manipulable objects. *Journal of Cognitive Neuroscience 14*, 1230–1239.

Gibson, J. J. (1979). *The Ecological Approach to Visual Perception*. Boston: Houghton Mifflin.

Glenberg A. M. (1997). What memory is for. *Behavioral & Brain Sciences 20*, 1–55.

Glenberg, A. M., & Kaschak, M. P. (2002). Grounding language in action. *Psychonomic Bulletin & Review 9*, 558–565.

Glenberg, A. M., & Robertson, D. A. (2000). Symbol grounding and meaning: a comparison of high dimensional and embodied theories of meaning. *Journal of Memory and Language 43*, 379–401.

Harnad, S. (1990). The symbol grounding problem. *Physica D 42*, 335–346.

Hirose, N. (2001). An ecological approach to embodiment and cognition. *Cognitive Systems Research 3*, 289–299.

Iachini, T., & Borghi, A. M. (2004). Conceptualization and sensorimotor interaction with objects.

Jeannerod, M. (1994). Object oriented action: Insights into the reach grasp movement. In K. M. B. Bennet & U. Castiello (Eds.), *Insights into the Reach to Grasp Movement* (pp. 3–15). Amsterdam: Elsevier.

Jeannerod, M. (1997). *The cognitive neuroscience of action*. Cambridge, MA: Blackwell.

Jeannerod, M., & Frak, V. (1999). Mental imaging of motor activity in humans. *Current Opinion in Neurobiology 9*, 735–739.

Keil, F. (1989). *Concepts, Kinds, and Cognitive Development*. Cambridge, MA: MIT.

Kellenbach, M. L., Brett, M., & Patterson, K. (2003). The importance of manipulability and action in tool representation. *Journal of Cognitive Neuroscience 15*, 30–46.

Klatzky, R. L., McCloskey, B. P., Doherty, S. & Pellegrino, J. W. (1987). Knowledge about hand shaping and knowledge about objects. *Journal of Motor Behavior 19*, 187–213.

Klatzky, R. L., Pellegrino, J. W., McCloskey, B. P. & Doherty, S. (1989). Can you squeeze a tomato? The role of motor representations in semantic sensibility judgments. *Journal of Memory and Language 28*, 56–77.

Landau, B., Smith, L., & Jones, S. (1998). Object shape, object function, and object name. *Journal of Memory and Language 38*, 1–27.

Lin, E. L., & Murphy, G. L. (2001). Thematic relations in adults' concepts. *Journal of Experimental Psychology: General 130*, 1, 3–28.

Magniè, M. N., Ferreira, C. T., Giuliano, B., & Poncet, M. (1999). Category specificity in object agnosia: Preservation of sensorimotor experiences related to object. *Neuropsychologia 37*, 67–74.

Mahon, B. Z., & Caramazza, A. (in press). The organization of conceptual knowledge in the brain: Living kinds and artifacts. In E. Margolis & S. Laurence (Eds.), *Creations of the mind: Essays on artifacts and their representation.* Oxford: Oxford University Press.

Mandler, J. M. (1992). How to build a baby, II: Conceptual primitives. *Psychological Review 99*, 587–604.

Mareschal, D., & Johnson, M. H. (2003). The "what" and "where" of object representations in infancy. *Cognition 88*, 259–276.

Martin, A., Ungerleider, L. G. & Haxby, J. V. (2001). Category Specificity and the brain: The sensory-motor model of semantic representations of objects. In M. S. Gazzaniga M. S. (Ed.), *The Cognitive Neurosciences*, 2nd edition. Cambridge, MA: MIT.

Martin, A., Wiggs, C. L, Ungerleider, L. G., & Haxby, G. V. (1996). Neural correlates of category specific knowledge. *Nature 379*, 649–652.

Milner, A. D., & Goodale, M. A. (1995). *The Visual Brain in Action.* Oxford: Oxford University Press.

Murphy, G. L. (2002). *The Big Book of Concepts.* Cambridge, MA: MIT.

Pecher, D., Zeelenberg, R., & Barsalou, L. W. (2003). Verifying conceptual properties in different modalities produces switching costs. *Psychological Science 14*, 119–124.

Phillips, J. A., Humphreys, G. W., Noppeney, U., & Price, K. J. (2002). The neural substrates of action retrieval: An examination of semantic and visual routes to action. *Visual Cognition 9*, 662–684.

Phillips, J. C., & Ward, R. (2002). *S-R* correspondence effects of irrelevant visual affordance: Time course and specificity of response activation. *Visual cognition 9*, 540–558.

Pulvermüller, F. (1999). Words in the brain's language. *Behavioral and Brain Sciences*, 22, 253–336.

Pylyshyn, Z. (1999). Is vision continuous with cognition? The case for cognitive impenetrability of visual perception. *Behavioral and Brain Sciences 22*, 341–423.

Riddoch, J. M., Humphreys, G. W., Edwards, S., Baker, T., & Willson, K. (2003). Seeing the action: Neuropsychological evidence for action-based effects on object selection. *Nature Neuroscience 6*, 82–89.

Rizzolatti, G., & Luppino, G. (2001). The cortical motor system. *Neuron 31*, 889–901.

Rumiati, R. I., & Humphreys, G. W. (1998). Recognition by action: Dissociating visual and semantic routes to action in normal observer. *Journal of Experimental Psychology: Human Perception and Performance 24*, 631–647.

Setti, A., & Borghi, A. M. (2003). Information about motion in concepts of different ontological kinds. In F. Schmalhofer, R. M. Young, & F. Katz (Eds.), *Proceedings of the First Meeting of the European Society of Cognitive Science*, Osnabrück 2003 (p. 438). London: Erlbaum.

Simmons, W. K., Pecher, D., Hamann, S. B., Zeelenberg, R. & Barsalou, L. W. (2003). fMRI evidence for modality-specific processing of conceptual knowledge on six modalities. *Meeting of the Society for Cognitive Neuroscience*, New York.

Sirigu, A., Duhamel, J. R., & Poncet, M. (1991). The role of sensorimotor experience in object recognition. A case of multimodal agnosia. *Brain 114*, 2555–2573.

Sloman, S. A., Love, B. C., & Ahn, W. (1998). Feature centrality and conceptual coherence. *Cognitive Science 22*, 189–228.

Smith, L. B., & Samuelson, L. L. (1997). Perceiving and Remembering: Category Stability, Variability, and Development. In K. Lamberts & D. Shanks (Eds.), *Knowledge, Concepts, and Categories* (pp. 161–195). Hove, UK: Psychology Press.

Spivey, M. J., & Geng, J. J. (2001). Oculomotor mechanisms activated by imagery and memory: Eye movements to absent objects. *Psychological Research 65*, 235–241.

Sternberg, S. (1969). The discovery of processing stages: Extensions of Doder's method. In W. G. Koster (Ed.), *Attention and Performance II*. Amsterdam: North-Holland Publishing Company.

Thelen, E., & Smith, L. B. (1994). *A Dynamic Systems Approach to the Development of Cognition and Action*. Cambridge, MA: MIT.

Tucker, M., & Ellis, R. (1998). On the relations between seen objects and components of potential actions. *Journal of Experimental Psychology: Human Perception and Performance 24 3*, 830–846.

Tucker, M., & Ellis, R. (2001). The potentiation of grasp types during visual object categorization. *Visual Cognition 8*, 769–800.

Tversky, B., & Hemenway, K. (1984). Objects, parts, and categories. *Journal of Experimental Psychology: General 113*, 169–193.

Vogt, S., Taylor, P., & Hopkins, B. (2003). Visuomotor priming by pictures of hand pictures: Perspective matters. *Neuropsychologia 41*, 941–951.

Ward, R. (2002). Independence and integration of perception and action: An introduction. *Visual Cognition 9*, 385–391.

Wilson, M. (2002). Six views of embodied cognition. *Psychonomic Bulletin & Review 9*, 625–636.

Wing, A. M., Turton, A., & Fraser, C. (1986). Grasp size and accuracy of approach in reaching. *Journal of Motor Behaviour 18*, 245–260.

Wu, L. L. & Barsalou, L. W. (2001). Grounding concepts in perceptual simulation: I: Evidence from property generation.

Zwaan, R., Stanfield, R. A., & Yaxley, R. H. (2002). Do language comprehenders routinely represent the shapes of objects? *Psychological Science 13*, 168–171.

Zwaan, R. A., & Yaxley, R. H. (2003). Spatial iconicity affects semantic-relatedness judgments. *Psychonomic Bulletin and Review*, 10, 954–958.

3

Constraints on Spatial Language Comprehension

Function and Geometry

Laura A. Carlson and Ryan Kenny

Consider the following scenario. You arrive at work early one morning and head for the office coffeepot. A colleague of yours is already there pouring herself a cup of coffee. Upon seeing you, she says "Place your cup below the pot." You interpret her statement as an indication that she will pour you a cup of coffee, and you put your cup in the appropriate location. Of interest in the current chapter are the processes and representations that underlie your apprehension of her utterance and your subsequent action. At a minimum, apprehension involves matching the relevant objects in the environment with the referents in the utterance (i.e., linking the cup in your hand with "your cup," the coffee pot in her hand with "the pot"). For utterances of this type, these objects have different roles. One object is referred to as the located object, and it is the object whose location is being specified. It is also considered the focal object that is profiled in the utterance (Langacker, 1987; see also Zwaan & Madden, Chapter 10, this volume). The other object is referred to as the reference object. Due to its size, shape or salience within the discourse, the reference object is assumed to offer a viable reference point from which to define the location of the located object (Landau & Jackendoff, 1993; Langacker, 1993; Talmy, 1983). However, with respect to the goal of the utterance, this object is backgrounded relative to the located object (Langacker, 1987).

Apprehension also involves mapping the spatial term "below" to an appropriate region of space surrounding the coffeepot (Langacker, 1993, 2002; Logan & Sadler, 1996; Miller & Johnson-Laird, 1976). This region has been referred to as a preposition's search domain (Langacker, 1993; Miller & Johnson-Laird, 1976). However, defining the search domain is not straight-forward, as it can be constrained by numerous influences including perceptual, geometric, social and functional factors (Miller & Johnson-Laird 1976). The problem is illustrated in Figure 3.1, in which several possible placements of the cup are illustrated. The degree to which these placements represent the "below" spatial relation varies in interesting ways. First

1a 1b
1c 1d

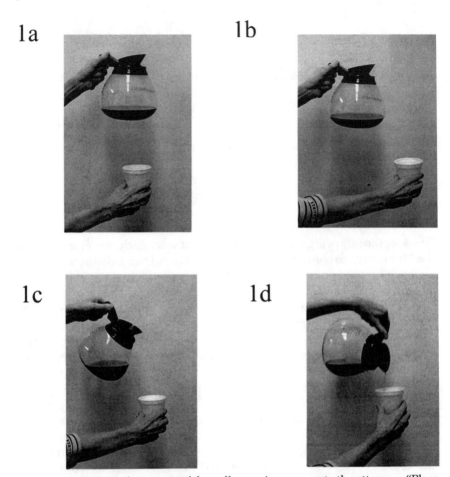

FIGURE 3.1. Various placements of the coffee cup in response to the utterance "Place the cup below the pot." Panel a illustrates a placement directly below the pot, in the so-called good region for "below" (Logan and Sadler, 1996). Panel b illustrates a placement off to the side, in the so-called acceptable region for "below" (Logan and Sadler, 1996). Based on a geometric definition of "below," a is a more acceptable placement than b. Panels c and d illustrate the same type of placement as in b, but the change in the orientation of the pot makes these more acceptable. Based on a functional definition of "below," c and d are more acceptable than b and possibly a.

compare panel 1a that represents a placement in which the cup is directly below the center of the pot and panel 1b that represents a placement in which the cup is below but off to the side. Typically, ratings of the acceptability of the spatial term "below" as a description of these types of placements favor the placement in 1a over 1b (Carlson-Radvansky & Logan, 1997; Hayward & Tarr, 1995; Logan & Sadler, 1996). One interpretation of this effect is that the "best" placement of the located object is defined on the basis of the geometric properties of the reference object, most usually its center of mass for projective relations such as "below" or "above" (Gapp, 1995; Regier, 1996; Schirra, 1993).

However, now consider the placements in panels 1c and 1d. The spatial term "below" is more acceptable as a description of the spatial relation between the objects for these placements relative to the placement in 1b, despite being in the same geometric spatial relation. One interpretation of this effect is that the change in orientation of the reference object highlights the potential functional interaction between the objects. This functional interaction then biases the interpretation of the spatial term. Indeed, this functional interaction may be so strongly inferred, that some may prefer panel 1b to panel 1a. More generally, this example is consistent with a growing body of work demonstrating both geometric and functional influences on the interpretation of spatial language (Carlson-Radvansky, Covey & Lattanzi, 1999; Carlson-Radvansky & Radvansky, 1996; Carlson-Radvansky & Tang, 2000; Coventry, 1998, 1999; Coventry, Carmichael, & Garrod, 1994; Coventry, Prat-Sala, & Richards, 2001; Garrod, Ferrier, & Campbell, 1999; Vandeloise, 1988; 1991; for an excellent review, see Coventry & Garrod, 2004).

Nevertheless, the manner in which geometric and functional factors jointly constrain the interpretation of spatial language, and how their relative strengths are determined and combined is unknown. We focus on this point in this chapter. Specifically, we begin by overviewing the theoretical importance of geometric and functional factors, and illustrate the joint combination of these factors within a given data set (Carlson-Radvansky, Covey, & Lattanzi, 1999). Next, we offer an explanation of these effects that focuses on the ideas of activation and construal within the immersed experiencer framework of Zwaan (2004; see also Coventry & Garrod, 2004). This allows us in turn to make particular predictions about the factors that should constrain these effects, as reflected in the relative strength of the geometric and functional influences. We offer preliminary evidence in support of these predictions. Finally, we conclude by underscoring the importance of examining the interpretation of a spatial term not as an abstract definition but rather as a reflection of a simulated event that combines the current utterance with the goals, situational context, and knowledge of the interlocuters (Clark, 1997; Coventry & Garrod, 2004; Zwaan, 2004; Zwaan & Madden, Chapter 10, this volume).

GEOMETRIC AND FUNCTIONAL INFLUENCES ON INTERPRETING SPATIAL TERMS

Geometric Influence

Defining spatial relations with respect to geometric properties of the objects is beneficial because it offers a definition that can be generalized across particular objects. This is important, because spatial terms such as "below" and "near" form a closed class in English (Landau & Jackendoff, 1993), with a limited number of terms available that have to be used to specify the spatial relations among a virtually unlimited number of open class nouns. Yet, despite the many different combinations of objects that can be used, there is an obvious sense in which in many contexts the spatial term conveys the same meaning, as in "The cloud is below the moon," "The bird is below the window," and "The cup is below the coffeepot" (for extended discussion, see Coventry & Garrod, 2004). One might even argue for a metaphorical extension (Lakoff, 1987) that covers more abstract objects in this relation, as in "The chairperson of the department is below the President of the University." For one example of a complete cataloging of all the various uses of a given term, see Brugman's (1988) analysis of "over"; see Coventry and Garrod (2004) for further discussion. A geometric account strives to achieve this commonality in part by minimizing the role of the particular objects being related, and focusing only on the information that remains constant across varied uses of this term. One way to accomplish this would be to schematize the objects (Herskovits, 1986, 1998; Landau & Jackendoff, 1993; Talmy, 1983), representing them in a relatively abstract form that preserves only the information required for computing the spatial relation. For example, the located object could be represented as an idealized point, and the reference object could be represented as an abstract axial-based shape, preserving the axes that indicate the internal structure of the object and define its sides, information that is necessary for some spatial terms (e.g., across). Determination of the geometric properties of this shape (e.g., midpoint, center-of-mass) could thus be calculated in a similar manner across all possible objects.

One Example of a Formal Geometric Approach. The geometric approach has been widely adopted, both theoretically (Bennett, 1975; Hayward & Tarr, 1995; Logan & Sadler, 1996; Talmy, 1983) and computationally (e.g., Gapp, 1995; Regier, 1996; Regier & Carlson, 2001; Schirra, 1993) as a means of defining the space surrounding the reference object. For example, within Regier and Carlson's (2001) attention vector-sum model (AVS), an attentional beam is anchored at a point within the reference object, radiating out to encompass the located object. This is illustrated in Figure 3.2, panel a, with the rectangle as the reference object, and the filled circle as the located object. Attentional strength is maximal at the focus of the beam, and drops off with distance, consistent with other characterizations of an attentional drop-off (Downing & Pinker, 1985; LaBerge & Brown, 1989). As a result, some parts of the reference object receive more attention than other parts. In addition to the attentional beam, the direction of the located object with respect to the reference object is represented as a population of vectors that project from each point along the reference object to the located object, as

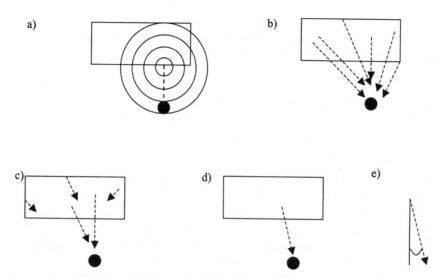

FIGURE 3.2. Illustration of the attention vector sum model as applied to "below." Panel a shows the attentional beam focused on a point on the reference object. Panel b shows vectors rooted at each point within the reference object, pointing to the located object. Panel c shows that each vector is weighted by the amount of attention allocated to its point on the reference object. Panel d shows that the overall direction is a sum of the weighted vectors from Panel c. Panel e shows that this overall direction is then evaluated relative to a reference orientation, in this case vertical for "below," with degree of deviation from the reference orientation mapping onto the acceptability of using "below" to describe the relationship between the located and reference objects (adapted from Figure 5 in Regier and Carlson (2001). Grounding spatial language in perception: An empirical and computational investigation. *Journal of Experimental Psychology: General 130, 273–298*).

illustrated in Figure 3.2, panel b. The representation of direction as a sum over a population of vectors has been observed in diverse neural subsystems (e.g., Georgopoulos, Schwartz, & Kettner, 1986; Wilson & Kim, 1994), suggesting that it may be a widely used means of encoding direction. The attentional beam and the vector sum are combined by weighting each vector as a function of the amount of attention being allocated to its point on the reference object, shown in Figure 3.2, panel c. The resulting weighted vectors are then summed to create an overall direction (Figure 3.2, panel d) and its alignment with respect to a reference direction (such as vertical for "below"), is measured (Figure 3.2, panel e). In general, perfect alignment with the reference direction corresponds to the best use of a spatial term (e.g., Figure 3.1, panel a). Acceptability drops off in a linear fashion with increasing deviations from the reference axis (e.g., Figure 3.1, panel b) to a certain cut-off, below which the term is not considered acceptable, regardless of the vector sum.

The AVS model was developed and tested across a wide range of geometric shapes, including rectangles, triangles and L-shaped figures. It outperforms other geometrically based competitor models, quantitatively providing strong fits to empirical data, and qualitatively exhibiting critical effects in its output. The success of this type of model (see also Gapp, 1995; Schirra, 1993) is an endorsement of the viability of a geometric approach, at least with respect to these stimuli and task demands.

Functional Influence

A large literature has emerged that demonstrates that when geometric information is held constant across two possible arrangements of objects, the arrangement that preserves the functional or dynamic/kinematic interaction between the two objects is preferred, indicating that geometric information alone is not sufficient for defining spatial terms (Vandeloise, 1991; for review, see Coventry & Garrod, 2004). Indeed, Coventry & Garrod (2004) distinguish between two types of extrageometric influences: conceptual information relating to knowledge of object function and object association, and dynamic/kinematic information relating to the interaction of the objects, including ideas of support, containment and locational control.

One Example of a Functional Influence. One example of functional information constraining the interpretation of spatial language comes from Carlson-Radvansky, Covey, and Lattanzi (1999). They presented participants with thirty-two pairs of pictures of real world objects, containing a reference object and a located object. Participants were asked to place the located object above or below the reference object. Two criteria were used for selecting the reference objects: First, each object had to have a functionally important part that could be offset from the center of the object when viewing the object from the side (see Figure 3.3 for examples). Second, the functional part had to be interacted with from "above" or "below" (e.g., one squeezes toothpaste onto the bristles of a toothbrush from "above"). For each reference object, two located objects that were matched in size and shape were selected. One was related to the functionally important part of the reference object (e.g., a tube of toothpaste for a toothbrush as the reference object), and the other was not functionally related, although its size and shape allowed it to be used in conjunction with the reference object in a similar, albeit not always successful, manner (e.g., a tube of oil paint). A given participant performed the placement task with each reference object and one located object; one half of a given subject's trials used functionally related located objects and one half used functionally unrelated located objects. Across participants, each type of located object was used with each reference object.

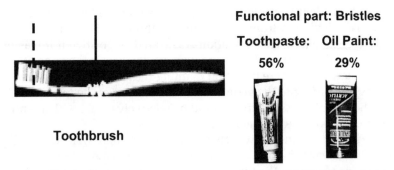

Functional part: Bristles

Toothpaste:	Oil Paint:
56%	29%

Toothbrush

Functional part: Spout

Mug:	Yogurt cup:
66%	23%

Tea Kettle

Functional part: Slot

Coin:	Ring:
67%	60%

Piggy Bank

FIGURE 3.3. Three sample objects from Carlson-Radvansky, Covey, and Lattanzi (1999). Reference objects are on the left, and the located objects (functional and nonfunctional) are on the right. On each of the reference objects, the solid line runs through the center-of-mass of the object; the dashed line runs through the object's functional part. Placements were measured as deviations from the center-of-mass line, with these deviations coded as positive if they were in the direction of the functional part. The numbers correspond to percentages of the distance for the average placements for each type of located object.

The dependent variable was the placement of the located object, measured as a deviation from a line running through the center of mass of the reference object. This deviation was coded as positive if it was in the direction of the functional part, and negative if it was in the opposite direction. If placements were based on defining the spatial terms "above" and "below" according to the geometric center of mass of the reference object, then the size of the deviations would be relatively small, with a randomly determined positive or negative sign.

The important finding was that for all objects there was an overall positive bias toward the functional part. Note that across the set of objects, the distance between the functional part and the center of mass of the object varied considerably, making it difficult to interpret the magnitude of this bias when expressed in millimeter measurements. To take this variation into account, we expressed the functional bias as a percentage of the distance of the deviation from the center-of-mass of the object, relative to the distance between the center-of-mass of the object and the center of the functional part. Within this scheme, 0% would indicate a placement above or below the center of mass, and 100% would indicate a placement directly over or under the functional part.

Figure 3.3 illustrates functional and nonfunctional located objects and lists their percentage deviations for three sample reference objects. For example, for the toothbrush, the functionally related object (toothpaste) was placed 56% of the distance away from the center of mass line toward the functional part. On average across objects, functionally related located objects were placed 72% of the distance toward the functional part. It is important to note that there was no labeling or explicit mention to the participants of the functional part of the reference object; rather, the instructions were simply to place one object above or below the other object. As such, participants could have placed the located object above or below any part of the reference object. Nevertheless, the identity of the located object and its typical function with respect to the reference object were apparently recognized by participants, and this served to bias their placements toward the relevant functional part.

On average, functionally unrelated located objects were placed at 45% of the distance between the center of mass and the functional part, exhibiting a smaller but nonetheless significant functional bias. This finding indicates that people also considered a functional interaction between these two objects. This may not be surprising, given that the nonfunctional located objects were selected to allow the same type of interaction as the functional located objects. However, these interactions were not common and would often be unsuccessful. For example, for a lamp as a reference object, the functional located object was a light bulb and the nonfunctional located object was an avocado. One could screw both the lightbulb and the avocado into the light socket, but only the former action would produce light.

For an indepth analysis of the functional bias across objects and types of interaction see Carlson and Covell (in press).

Combining Geometric and Functional Influences

While the Carlson-Radvansky et al. (1999) data strongly indicate a role for the functional interaction among the objects, it is not the case that functional information was the only source of influence on these placements. While deviations were positive, the size of the deviations was less than 100%, indicating an incomplete bias. The fact that the deviations all fell between the center of mass of the reference object and the functional part indicates that both geometric and functional factors influenced how these terms were defined (Carlson-Radvansky et al., 1999). Similarly, Coventry, Prat-Sala, and Richards (2001) observed varying influences of functional and geometric factors as a function of the orientations of the object, the portrayed success of their interaction, and the particular spatial term that was being used. For example, they found that the terms "over" and "under" were more strongly influenced by functional effects whereas "above" and "below" were more strongly influenced by geometric factors.

Given evidence in favor of both sets of factors, the interesting question becomes determining how these are combined during the apprehension of a spatial term. The general consensus (Carlson, 2000; Carlson-Radvansky et al., 1999; see also Coventry et al., 2001; Coventry & Garrod, 2004) is that there is a weighted combination of these two types of factors, with the relative emphasis on geometric versus functional factors varying across the types of objects and their depicted interaction, the spatial term being used, and the context. Of course, such an account then requires one to specify exactly how the weights are set as a function of these factors, an issue we address in the remaining sections of this chapter.

One Example of a Formal Combination of Geometry and Function. An implementation that successfully combines geometric and functional factors is provided in a modification to AVS (Regier, Carlson, & Corrigan, in press). Specifically, a functional parameter is included in the model that corresponds to the functional importance of a given point on the reference object. The total amount of attention that is paid to a particular point on the reference object depends upon both a distance parameter (as in the original AVS) and this functional parameter. This is inspired in part by work by Lin and Murphy (1997) that demonstrates greater attention to functionally important parts of objects. The functional parameter can be set to values ranging from 0 to 1. A value of 0 indicates that the corresponding point on the reference object is not functionally important. In this case, attentional allocation to the point would depend solely on distance. For

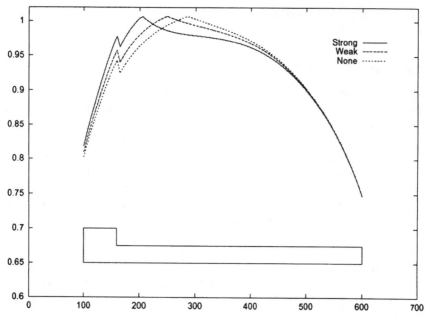

FIGURE 3.4. Simulation data for the toothbrush as the reference object using AVS with the functional parameter set for a strong bias (.8 = solid line), a weak bias (.3 = dashed line) or no bias (0 = dotted line) (from Regier, Carlson, & Corrigan, in press).

objects with functional parts, the functional parameter would be set to a positive value between 0 and 1, selectively biasing the allocation of attention to points within the functional part. We successfully fit the data from Carlson-Radvansky et al. (1999) by running AVS with three settings for the functional parameter: 0, corresponding to no functional bias; .3 corresponding to a weak functional bias, intended to represent the functionally unrelated located object; and .8 corresponding to a strong functional bias, intended to represent the functionally related located object. The simulation data are shown in Figure 3.4. The model outputs a value between 0 and 1 that corresponds to an acceptability rating, with 1 indicating the best use of above. Note that when attentional allocation to the bristles was strong (solid line; $F = .8$), the peak is about 73% of the distance toward the functional part. When the attentional allocation was weak (dashed line; $F = .3$), the peak was at 46% of the distance. These correspond very closely to the empirical data obtained by Carlson-Radvansky et al. (1999), where the overall bias was 72% and 45% toward the functional part, respectively. The AVS model thus offers a means of combining the geometric and functional influences on the parsing of space around the reference object.

UNDERSTANDING THE FUNCTIONAL INFLUENCE

A Possible Theoretical Account

Zwaan (2004; Zwaan & Madden, Chapter 10, this volume) presents an immersed experiencer framework for language comprehension in which language is a cue to the comprehender to construct an experiential simulation with perceptual and action components of the derived situation (for similar ideas, see Coventry & Garrod, 2004). Within this perspective, interpretation of a word activates experiences with its referents, with activations across words combining during a process of construal that constrains interpretation. Construal can operate both forward and backward, with words constraining meanings of preceding and following words, consistent with the idea that online interpretation of an utterance is incremental (Chambers, Tanenhaus, Eberhard, Filip, & Carlson, 2001). For example, Zwaan (2004) argues that in interpreting the phrase "red squirrel" red may activate many diverse shades associated with that label; however, only a subset of these shades will be appropriate for squirrel; these relevant shades will correspond to the articulated construal of "red squirrel." More generally, the process of construal involves the following components: time, a spatial region, perspective, a focal entity, a possible background entity, the relation of the focal entity to the background entity, and features of the entities such as size or color.

With respect to spatial language, of central interest are the focal and background entity and their relation, specified within a perspective at an inferred time and place. The same activation and construal processes should operate amid these components. For example, Langacker (1993, 2002) has argued that the search domain of a given spatial term profiles a particular portion of the reference object, an idea referred to as an active zone that is highlighted within the current attentional frame or articulated within the simulated model (Zwaan, 2004). Since the located object is the focal entity in the utterance, it is likely that its relationship with the reference object would help to define the active zone, given the goal of the comprehender to construct a situation consistent with the description that makes use of activated knowledge about the objects including how they interact. For example, for the utterance "Place the toothpaste tube above the toothbrush," it is likely that stored representations of previous encounters of these objects and their interaction would get activated (Coventry & Garrod, in press; Zwaan & Madden, Chapter 10, this volume). Because these involved using the toothpaste in conjunction with a particular part of the toothbrush, this would bias the active zone to be defined with respect to part of the object (the bristles) rather than the whole object. In addition, stored representations of the "above" relation would also be activated across diverse sets of located and reference objects; this would constitute activation of the geometric component. Crucially, there would be an intersection among these sets in which there was a convergence between function and geometry, given that toothpaste tubes are usually "above" toothbrushes in their typical interaction. Therefore, the definition of "above" as applied to this utterance would be constrained by both geometry and function. In contrast, in the case of the tube of oil paint, any previous encounters of the interaction of these objects would be activated, although this is presumed to be few, in addition to the activation of representations of the "above" relation. It is also possible that an imagined interaction would also be constructed in which the objects were functionally interacting, consistent with an attempt to define a situation model that provided a meaning for the association between the two objects (Coventry & Garrod, 2004). In general, however, the convergence for function and geometry would be smaller, and one would expect a smaller or absent functional effect. This would be the case for spatial descriptions that relate objects that are not functionally related objects, as in "The stapler is to the left of the telephone," or "The keys fell behind the toaster."

Predictions Derived from This Account

If this type of account is correct, then factors that impact the simulated interaction between the located object and the reference object should significantly alter the respective strengths of the functional and geometric influences. We will focus on three aspects of this issue. First, many objects have many functional parts, and different objects typically interact with these parts. If the located object as the focal entity defines the active zone on the reference object (Langacker, 1993, 2002), then the functional bias should shift across parts of an object when different located objects are used. In our experiments, we test this by using reference objects with multiple parts that offer different affordances (Borghi, Chapter 2, this volume), and manipulating the identity of the located object.

Second, the functional bias observed by Carlson-Radvansky et al. (1999) relied on the use of a spatial term (i.e., "above" and "below") that also corresponded to the direction of interaction between the objects. Based on the account presented above, the association between the objects should not be sufficient for exhibiting a strong functional effect. Rather, the objects must be placed in a spatial relationship that enables them to fulfill their function, consistent with a simulated interaction between them. Thus, a functional bias should only be observed for terms that allow the objects to be placed in a manner that is consistent with their interaction. In our experiments, we test this by comparing placements of located objects relative to reference objects that interact with each other from the side, and collect data for the terms "above," "below," and "near." The vertical terms constrain placement of the located object to the upper or lower sides of the reference object, locations that are inconsistent with the direction of interaction. In contrast, "near" enables placements with respect to any side, thereby enabling placements that could fulfill the interaction.

Third, as reviewed by Borghi (Chapter 2, this volume) there is a distinction between the kinds of knowledge about an object that becomes activated during identification, with some evidence in favor of automatic activation of action information. However, Bub, Masson, and Bukach (2003) demonstrate that information about the function of the object is not automatically activated during identification. Thus, this type of information is more strategically available (Borghi, Chapter 2, this volume). When the objects are unrelated, there is no possibility of simulating an interactive relation, and therefore a geometrically defined relation should take precedence. In our experiments we test this by using a neutral located object (a bean bag) that doesn't interact with the reference object at all. This object will not highlight a particular functional part; rather, definitions of spatial terms in these cases should be geometrically based. As a strong test of this idea, we also include a manipulation of context in which we highlight a particular part of the reference object, and then evaluate whether the neutral located object will make use of this part. If the functional effect is due to the construction of a situation model that simulates an interaction, then even this biasing context should be ineffective for defining the spatial relation with respect to the salient part. That is, although that part was made salient previously, it is no longer relevant within the context of the placement task, and therefore should not bias placements.

INITIAL EMPIRICAL EVIDENCE

The Contribution of the Identity of the Located Object

Many objects have many parts. For example, for the objects in Figure 3.3, the toothbrush has bristles and a grip, the tea kettle has a lid, a basin, a handle, and a spout; the piggy bank has the bank, features of the pig, and the slot. How then is one part selected as functionally important? The idea under investigation is that the located object as the focal entity picks out the part of the reference object with which it typically interacts. For example, a tube of toothpaste would pick out the bristles of the toothbrush, however, a hand would pick out the handle. If the located object helps determine the functional importance of the parts of the reference object, then the locus of the functional bias should change as the identity of the located object changes.

To test this idea, Carlson and Kenny (2004) selected 15 reference objects with multiple parts, with the constraint that two of the parts were on the ends of the object, maximally distant from each other, and equidistant from the center point when viewed from the side. The direction of interaction with the functional parts was unconstrained across objects, but most typically was from the side. For each reference object, three located objects were selected: one that interacted with each part of the reference object, and a neutral beanbag object. Because the beanbag does not bias any particular functional part, this type of neutral object thus enabled us to assess the relative salience of the parts of the reference object independently of the located object. Note that such salience could be due to factors other than functional importance, such as perceptual prominence. Three sample objects are shown in Figure 3.5, including a curling iron as a reference object and a wig and a power strip as the located objects; headphones as a reference object and a model head or cd player as the located objects; and a trumpet as a reference object and a mute and a mouthpiece as the located objects. For convenience, we will refer to the leftmost part as F1 and the rightmost part as F2. However, it should be noted that mirror-reversed versions of the objects were used across participants, such that for some participants F1 appeared on the left and F2 appeared on the right, and for others F1 appeared on the right and F2 appeared on the left. Each participant was presented with each reference object in conjunction with one of the located objects, and was asked to place the located object above or below the reference object. Across participants, each reference object was paired with each located object and each spatial term; the reported preliminary data are based on 4 participants receiving each combination.

Of critical interest were the placements around the reference object as a function of the identity of the located object. It was expected that the beanbag as a neutral object would be placed geometrically above or below the center of the reference object, the best geometric placement for these terms (Regier & Carlson, 2001). However, if one of the parts of the reference object was more salient than the other, then the beanbag might be placed relative to that part. More interesting, with respect to the functionally related located objects, three outcomes were possible. First, it is possible that the functional effect observed by Carlson-Radvansky et al. (1999) would not generalize to this set of objects with multiple parts, and that participants would be guided by geometric factors, placing the located objects above or below the center of the reference object. Second, all placements could be made with respect to a single part, indicating a particular salience that was independent of function. Third, placement of the located objects could be biased toward their appropriate functional parts, resulting in clusters of placements around F1 and F2. This would suggest that the identity of the located object plays a primary role in determining the functional importance of the parts of the reference object, and this has a corresponding impact on the manner in which the objects are spatially related. This possibility is consistent with the idea that the located object

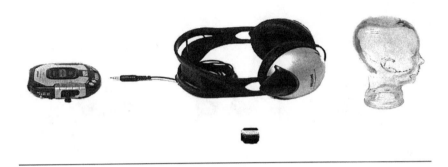

FIGURE 3.5. Sample objects from Carlson and Kenny (2004). In each panel, the central object is the reference object, the object directly below the reference object is the beanbag, and the remaining two objects are the functionally related located objects, positioned next to the functional part with which they typically interact. At the top, the reference object is a curling iron, and the located objects are a wig and a power strip. In the middle, the reference object is a pair of headphones, and the located objects are a CD player and a head. At the bottom, the reference object is a trumpet, and the located objects are a mute and a mouthpiece.

as the focal entity defines the active zone of reference object by virtue of their simulated interaction.

Above and below placements for the sample reference objects from Figure 3.5 are presented in Figure 3.6, as a function of the type of located object. Outlines of the located object indicate the orientation and positioning of each placement. The left column illustrates placements of the located object that interacted with the functional part designated as F1 (leftmost

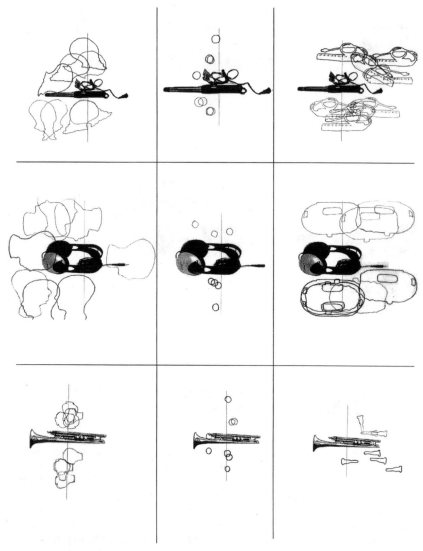

FIGURE 3.6. Placements of the located objects above and below the three sample objects (curling iron in top row, headphones in middle row, and trumpet in bottom row). The first column illustrates placements of the located object associated with the functional part of the object designated as F1 ("a wig" with "the curling iron tip"; "a head" with the "headphones"; "a mute" with "the trumpet"). The second column illustrates placements of the beanbag. The third column illustrates placements of the located object associated with the functional part of the object designated as F2 ("a powerstrip" for "the plug of the curling iron"; "a cassette player" for "the jack of the headphones"; "a mouthpiece" for "the mouth of the trumpet").

part in the figure); the center column illustrates placements of the beanbag, and the right most column presents placements of the located object that interacted with the functional part designated as F2 (rightmost part in the figure). The thin black line running through the reference object indicates its midpoint, and is by definition equidistant from each of the functional parts.

Given this organization, one can immediately observe a number of effects across these sample objects. First, the beanbags in the center column tend to cluster above and below the midpoint of the reference object, indicated by their small and randomly distributed deviations from the midpoint line. Second, there are placements that are geometrically based. For example, all placements of the mute above and below the trumpet (bottom panel, left column) are clustered around the midpoint line. Third, there are placements that are biased toward a functionally appropriate part. For example, all but one of the mouthpiece placements above and below the trumpet (bottom panel, right column) are biased toward the side of the trumpet with the mouth. Similarly, for the headphones, several of the head placements (middle panel, left column) are clustered around the part that covers one's ears, with one placement even changing the orientation of the head to better enable the functional interaction. This is an interesting case, because it switches reference frames, defining "above" with respect to the intrinsic sides of the headphones rather than with respect to the picture environment or the orientation of the viewer (see Carlson, 1999, for a review of how a given reference frame is selected when multiple frames are possible). In contrast, placements of the compact disc player are clustered around the jack end of the headphones. Fourth, for the most part the bias is intermediate, rather than at a geometric placement or at a functional placement. For example, for the curling iron, placements of the wig are biased toward the tip end but are not completely over or under the tip, whereas placements of the power strip are biased toward the plug end but not completely over or under the plug.

These data are preliminary in that we only have a few observations per object per condition; nevertheless, the plots are suggestive of certain trends. To further evaluate these trends, we quantified these effects by measuring across all objects the deviations from the midpoint of the located object from the midpoint line, with placements toward F1 (on the left) arbitrarily assigned a negative value, and placements toward F2 (on the right) arbitrarily assigned a positive value. Note that across objects, the distance from the midpoint to either functional part varied, making it difficult to interpret deviations expressed in millimeters. Accordingly, following Carlson-Radvansky et al. (1999), we converted the deviations into percentages of the distance from the midpoint toward the functional part. As such, 0% would indicate a placement over the midpoint of the object; −100% would indicate a placement over the leftmost functional part; and +100% would indicate a placement over the rightmost functional part.

For the located object associated with F1, mean deviations were −16%; for the located object associated with F2, mean deviations were +11%, and for the beanbag, mean deviations were −3%. There was a significant difference between the deviations for F1 and F2, indicating that the identity of the located object had an influence on the way in which participants spatially related the objects, biasing them to place functionally related objects in a direction toward the appropriate functional part. Note, however, that the relative size of this bias is somewhat small, indicating a predominant influence of geometric factors that resulted in placements that generally clustered around the midpoint of the reference object.

Note that the size of the located object varies across the different objects, and for some objects, the located objects are very large. This caused us to worry that estimating the placement of the located object by its midpoint might not be accurately characterizing the type of placement. Accordingly, we examined each reference object, and classified the placements of the two functional located objects into three categories: (1) geometric (clustered around the midpoint): 62% fell into this category; (2) toward the appropriate functional part: 28% fell into this category; or (3) toward the inappropriate functional part: 10% fell into this category. For the beanbag, the placements were classified as geometric: 72% falling into this category; or toward a functional part: 28% falling into this category. While the majority of the placements were clearly geometric, (consistent with the deviation analyses above), there was evidence in favor of a small but significant functional bias, with the percentages of placements falling into the functional parts categories significantly above 0. This bias was observed for both the functionally related located objects and the beanbag, despite the finding that the size of the deviation for the beanbag was very small in the preceding analysis.

In summary, although preliminary, these data indicate the presence of both geometric and functional influences on participants' determination of how to spatially relate the two objects. There were two sources of the functional bias. First, certain parts of the reference object were considered salient, as indicated by the presence of a small bias with the neutral located object. Second, as expected, the identity of the located object contributed to the functional bias. For example, the presence of a functional bias was more apparent for functionally related located objects than for the neutral located object. In addition, when the functional bias was observed, it reflected placements relative to the appropriate functional part, not simply random deviations from the center of the object. These biases indicate that the functional interaction of the objects has a small but significant impact on the way in which participants parse space into regions around the reference object. Nevertheless, it is clear that the predominant factor in these placements was geometric.

The Direction of Interaction

It is important to note that the size of this functional bias is much smaller (<20%) than the influence obtained by Carlson-Radvansky et al. (1999) (72% for functionally related objects; 45% for functionally unrelated objects). One possible reason for this difference is the nature of the interaction between the objects. Recall that in the Carlson-Radvansky et al. (1999) study, the reference objects were selected with the constraint that the located object interacted with it from above or below. Thus, placing the located object above or below the reference object resulted in a placement that served to facilitate the interaction between the objects (e.g., toothpaste "above" the bristles of the toothbrush). In contrast, in the present set of stimuli, the located object typically interacted with the relevant part of the reference object from the side. For example, the mute and mouthpiece are applied to their respective parts on the trumpet by moving in from the left or right direction; the head must be tilted and move from the left to fit within the headphones; and the curling iron clasps the hair from the sides. This horizontal direction of interaction is typical for the set of items that we used. Thus, an association between the objects is not sufficient for obtaining a strong functional bias. Rather, the placement of the objects with respect to the spatial term must enable a fulfillment of the simulated interaction. We assessed this idea by conducting the placement task with the spatial term "near." We selected "near" because Prasada and Ferenz (2001) used a rating task to show that "near" is influenced by the functional interaction among the objects. Similarly, "near" is related semantically to "approach," and Morrow and Clark (1988) observed effects of object characteristics on judgements of distance associated with the term "approach." This makes it likely that the term "near" will be susceptible to the functional bias in our placement task. Second, and most importantly, the definition of "near" is not restricted to a particular part of the object. Indeed, Logan and Sadler (1996) had participants place an "X" near an "O," and found that the placements were scattered close to but all around the O, consistent with a geometric definition based on distance from the edges of the reference object, without further specification of a particular edge. Thus "near" offers an important contrast to the terms "above" and "below" that restrict placements to a particular side of the object. As discussed previously, this type of restriction may alter the degree of functional influence, particularly if the direction of interaction between the located objects and the reference object is not from "above" and "below."

The "near" condition was embedded in the "above" and "below" trials in the preceding experiments, with all participants receiving all terms, and each term paired with each type of located object across participants. The predictions for "near" were similar to those for "above" and "below," although a stronger functional bias was anticipated, given that the spatial term no longer restricted placements to a particular side that may or may not have coincided with the direction of interaction between the objects. More specifically, with "near" it was expected that participants would be able to place the located object at any side, and could therefore position their placements so as to facilitate the interaction between the objects, should they wish to do so.

Figure 3.7 shows the near placements around the three sample reference objects from Figure 3.5, broken down by type of located object. The differences between Figures 3.6 and 3.7 are readily apparent. First, placements of the neutral object in the center columns are generally clustered around the two functional parts rather than around the midpoint of the object. Second, placements are functionally biased toward the appropriate functional part, with occasional exceptions. Third, the gradation in the functional placements that was observed for above and below that seemed to reflect a combination of functional and geometric factors is much less evident for near. Rather, the functional placements tend to illustrate a complete bias. Note also that placements of the located objects were generally consistent with the direction of interaction between the objects, enabling fulfillment of their interaction.

We quantified these effects, following the procedures used for the "above" and "below" data. Specifically, for the located object functionally related to F_1 (the leftmost part in Figure 3.7), the mean percentage deviation of the placements was −56%; for the located object related to F_2 (the rightmost part), the mean percentage deviation was +36%; and the mean percent deviation for the beanbag was −30%, indicating a bias toward the leftmost functional part. These deviations were all greater than 0, with a significant difference between the deviation associated with F_1 and the deviation associated with F_2. In addition, all of these deviations were significantly greater than the size of the deviations observed in the "above" and "below" data. These data indicate a substantial functional influence due to the identity of the located object, with placements biased toward the appropriate functional part, and an influence due to the functional parts of the reference object, as indicated by the bias to place the neutral object near F_1. Thus, as in the "above" and "below" data, in addition to the contribution of the identity of the located object, there was also an effect due to the salience of a particular part of the reference object. Whether this part was highlighted by virtue of its functional importance, perceptual prominence or some other dimension is unclear.

As with the "above" and "below" data, we also classified the placements as geometric, with 18% of placements occurring in this category; functional, with 60% of the placements occurring in this category, and consistent with the opposite function, with 22% falling into this category. For the beanbag placements, 72% were in the functional category and 28% were geometric.

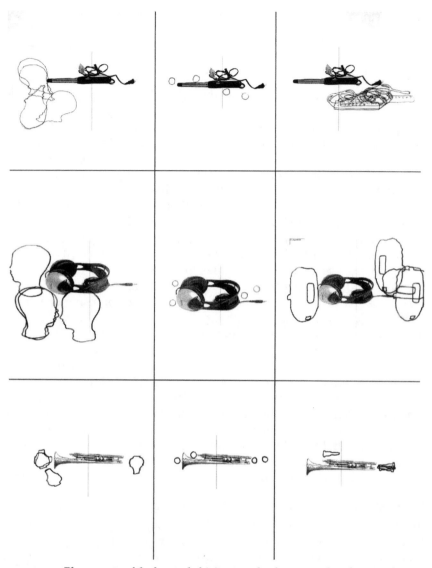

FIGURE 3.7. Placements of the located objects near the three sample reference objects. See Figure Caption 3.6 for description of the layout.

These classifications for the functionally related objects are largely a reversal of the pattern of data observed for "above" and "below," and indicates that "near" placements are more susceptible to functional influences than geometric influences. We attribute this to the fact that "near" placements were not restricted to any particular edge of the reference object, and thus could be placed so as to facilitate the interaction between the objects, consistent with a simulation of the interaction between the objects.

The Contribution of Context

The last factor that we examined had to do with the context in which the placement task occurred. Thus far, participants were provided with cutout photographs of real objects, and asked to perform a simple task that involved spatially relating the objects. On the basis of the functional bias, we have been inferring that participants were evaluating how the objects interacted, with this interaction making a particular part more salient, resulting in a bias toward that part. If this is the case, then one should not observe the effect with a located object that does not participate in this interaction, such as the beanbag. This was observed. Moreover, this effect should remain absent, even when providing a context in which the part of the reference object participates in a functional interaction, if the placement task involves an object that cannot fulfill this interaction. Carlson and Kenny (2004) tested this idea in the following manner. Prior to the placement task, participants were shown a video of a person using one of the located objects in conjunction with the reference object, thereby highlighting a particular function and by extension a particular part of the object. For a given reference object, some participants viewed an interaction with F_1, and others viewed an interaction with F_2. We also included a neutral video condition in which the reference object appeared in isolation, in order to assess any default preferences for particular parts of the object. Stills from one of the video clips are shown in Figure 3.8, with the bottle opener as the reference object, and a wine bottle (associated with F_1) and a beer bottle (associated with F_2) as the located objects. Participants then performed the placement task using a neutral object (e.g. bean bag) that did not bias any particular part as the located object, using the terms "above," "below," and "near."

Placement data for three sample objects are shown in Figure 3.9, with the squares above and below the reference object representing "above" and "below" placements, respectively, and the circles representing "near" placements. The left column represents placements following videos that emphasized the functional part designated as F_1 (on the left of the object). The middle column represents placements following videos with the reference object in isolation. The right column represents placements following videos that emphasized the functional part designated as F_2 (on the right of the object). Two effects are apparent: First, "above" and "below" placements are predominantly geometric, clustering around the midpoint of the reference object, regardless of the video context (compare across columns). Second, "near" placements are more distributed, with some reflecting geometric placements that are and some reflecting functional placements that are located next to one of the functional parts. Note, however, that even for

Emphasize F1

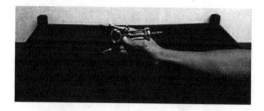

Reference object by itself

Emphasize F2

FIGURE 3.8. Sample video clips illustrating interactions between the located objects and the reference object. In the top panel, the located object ("wine bottle," shown to the right) interacts with "the corkscrew part of the bottle-opener"; in the bottom panel, the located object ("beer bottle") interacts with "the opener part of the bottle-opener." In the middle panel, the reference object is shown by itself.

these "near" placements, these functional placements do not seem to be constrained to the part that was emphasized in the video. For example, for the curling iron, for F1 context, one object was placed near F1 and another was placed near F2; for F2 placements, one object was placed near F1. Other examples of this are the scattered placements for F1 with the headphones, and F2 for the trumpet.

F1   F2

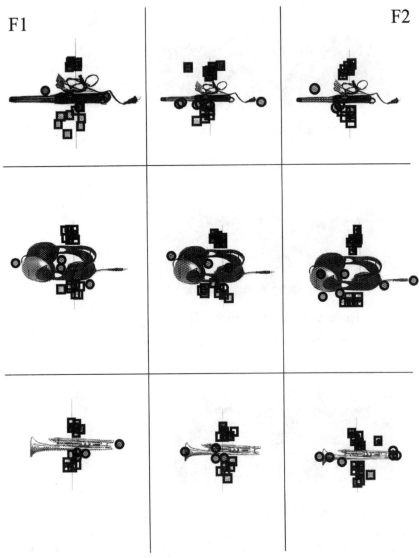

FIGURE 3.9. Placements of the neutral located object (beanbag) above and below (designated by squares) and near (designated by circles) the three sample reference objects. The first column shows placements when functional part F1 on the reference object (on the left in the figure) was emphasized in the preceding video. The middle column shows placements when the reference object was presented by itself in the preceding video. The last column shows placements when the functional part F2 on the reference object (on the right) was emphasized in the preceding video.

TABLE 3.1. *Percentages of Distance toward Emphasized Functional Part as a Function of Spatial Term and Video Condition. A Negative Deviation Indicates a Bias toward F1. A Positive Deviation Indicates a Bias toward F2*

Video	Above/Below	Near
Neutral	−2	−11
Emphasized F1	−3	−22
Emphasized F2	−3	+8

We quantified these data by coding the placements as deviations from the midpoint of the reference object toward a functional part, with deviations toward F1 coded arbitrarily as negative, and toward F2 coded arbitrarily as positive. The two columns in Table 3.1 present deviations reported as percentages of the distance between the midpoint and the functional part, as a function of video condition and spatial term. Negative values indicate a bias toward F1, and positive values indicate a bias toward F2. The deviations for "above" and "below" were not significantly different from 0, indicating geometrically based placements around the midpoint of the object. In contrast, the placements for "near" in the F2 context differed significantly from placements in the F1 context and in the neutral context, indicating that the video served to highlight the F2 function and bias placements accordingly. Placements in the F1 and neutral context did not differ, both exhibiting a bias toward F1, indicating that it is a salient part of the reference object. Note, however, that the size of these deviations is quite small. In sum, these data show that emphasizing a part of the reference object prior to the placement task minimally alters where participants place an unrelated object in response to a spatial description.

Summary of Empirical Findings

Across these various data sets several findings emerge that characterize how function and geometric information constrain the comprehension of spatial language. First, the identity of the located object is important. Stronger functional biases were observed with a located object that was functionally related to the reference object, with the bias in the direction that was consistent with the appropriate functional part. Second, the parts of a reference object seem to differ in importance, with some default preferences for certain parts over others, as observed in the "near" data with a neutral reference object. Third, the strength of the functional influence varies across spatial term, with "near" exhibiting stronger effects than "above" or "below." One reason for this is that for the objects that we used, "near" enabled placements that were consistent with a simulated interaction between the objects, whereas "above" and "below" did not. We favor this explanation because it provides a possible account of why there may be term differences, rather than simply describing such differences. Fourth, prior exposure to the reference object in the context of a particular interaction caused only a slight bias toward the emphasized functional part in a placement task with a neutral object. This was only for the term "near," and was smaller than that observed without a video but using functionally related located objects. The next step is to test whether previous exposure to the interaction with the object would magnify the functional bias, assessed by showing the videos followed by a placement task using the functionally related objects rather than the neutral object used here. A larger bias may be expected because the depicted interaction on the video is consistent with the presumed simulated interaction. Fifth, in addition to varying degrees of functional bias, all studies had placements that were based on geometric factors, with most of the "above" and "below" placements around the midpoint of the reference object.

CONCLUSION

This chapter began by motivating the use of both geometric and functional influences on the interpretation of spatial language, arguing for the importance and impact of each type of factor. One particular functional effect (Carlson-Radvansky et al., 1999) was taken as an example of a combination of geometric and functional influences. A theoretical account of the functional bias was offered that was based on the general idea that language comprehension is best understood with respect to an embodied theory of meaning rather than a set of amodal propositional representations (e.g., Barsalou, 1999; Coventry & Garrod, in press; Gibbs, 2003; Glenberg, 1997; Glenberg & Kaschak, 2002; Pecher, Zeelenberg, & Barsalou, 2003; Zwaan, Stanfield, & Yaxley, 2002). Specifically, interpretation of a spatial description was examined in the context of the immersed experiencer framework (Zwaan, 2004), and several predictions were derived that focused on the idea that the located object as the focal entity defined an active zone on the reference object (Langacker, 1993, 2002) around which the search domain of the spatial term was defined. When the focal entity did not functionally interact with the reference object, the search domain was defined by the geometric properties of the spatial term. This is consistent with idea that a function of an object is not automatically activated during identification (Bub et al., 2003), but rather requires the strategic construction of a viable situation model that is based on perceptual simulations of the objects and their relation (Barsalou, 1999) and that is consistent with the affordances of the objects and the actions that can operate upon them (Glenberg, 1997).

Thus, along these lines, we infer that when asked to place one object above another object, participants are actively considering how these objects interact, calling up their conceptual knowledge and past experiences with these objects, with this information dictating how the spatial term is understood. An important feature of this account is that it emphasizes the interpretation of language not in isolation but as an act (Clark, 1997) of activation and construal (Zwaan, 2004) that takes into account goals, context and previous knowledge, thereby linking the processing of language to other more general cognitive processes such as memory, perception, attention and action (see especially, Spivey, Richardson & Gonzalez-Marquez, Chapter 11, this volume; Zwaan & Madden, Chapter 10, this volume).

ACKNOWLEDGMENTS

These experiments were conducted as part of the second author's senior honors thesis. We are grateful to the Undergraduate Research Opportunity Program sponsored by the Institute for Scholarship in the Liberal Arts, College of Arts and Letters, University of Notre Dame for supporting this work. Many thanks to Claudia Gonzalez and Rina Tamayo for help in coding the data. Address correspondence to: Laura Carlson, Department of Psychology, 118-D Haggar Hall, University of Notre Dame, Notre Dame, IN 46556; email: Lcarlson@nd.edu; phone: 574-631-6511.

References

Barsalou, L. W. (1999). Perceptual symbol systems. *Behavioral and Brain Sciences 22*, 577–660.

Bennett, D. C. (1975). *Spatial and Temporal Uses of English Prepositions: An Essay in Stratificational Semantics*. London: Longman.

Brugman, C. (1988). *The Story of "Over": Polysemy, Semantics and the Structure of the Lexicon*. Garland Press.

Bub, D. N., Masson, M. E. J., & Bukach, C. M. (2003). Gesturing and naming: The use of functional knowledge in object identification. *Psychological Science 14*, 467–472.

Carlson, L. A. (1999). Selecting a reference frame. *Spatial Cognition and Computation 1*, 365–379.

Carlson, L. A. (2000). Object use and object location: The effect of function on spatial relations. In E. van der Zee & U. Nikanne (Eds.), *Cognitive Interfaces: Constraints on Linking Cognitive Information* (pp. 94–115). Oxford: Oxford University Press.

Carlson, L. A., & Covell, E. R. (in press). Defining functional features for spatial language. In L. A. Carlson & E. van der Zee (Eds.), *Representing functional features for language and space: Insights from perception, categorization and development*. Oxford: Oxford University Press.

Carlson, L. A., & Kenny, R. (2004). Constraints on spatial language by form and function. Unpublished manuscript.

Carlson-Radvansky, L. A., Covey, E. S., & Lattanzi, K. L. (1999). "What" effects on "where": Functional influences on spatial relations. *Psychological Science 10*, 516–521.

Carlson-Radvansky, L. A., & Logan, G. D. (1997). The influence of reference frame selection on spatial template construction. *Journal of Memory and Language 37*, 411–437.

Carlson-Radvansky, L. A., & Radvansky, G. A. (1996). The influence of functional relations on spatial term selection. *Psychological Science 7*, 56–60.

Carlson-Radvansky, L. A., & Tang, Z. (2000). Functional influences on orienting a reference frame. *Memory & Cognition 28*, 812–820.

Chambers, C. G., Tanenhaus, M. K., Eberhard, K. M., Filip, H., & Carlson, G. (2001). Circumscribing referential domains in real-time language comprehension. *Journal of Memory and Language 47*, 30–49.

Clark, H. H. (1997). *Using Language.* Cambridge: Cambridge University Press.

Coventry, K. R. (1998). Spatial prepositions, functional relations and lexical specification. In P. Olivier and K. Gapp (Eds.), *The Representation and Processing of Spatial Expressions* (pp. 247–262). Hillsdale, NJ: Lawrence Erlbaum Associates.

Coventry, K. R. (1999). Function, geometry, and spatial prepositions: Three experiments. *Spatial Cognition and Computation 2*, 145–154.

Coventry, K. R., & Garrod, S. C. (2004). *Saying, Seeing and Acting: The Psychological Semantics of Spatial Prepositions.* Hove, UK: Psychology Press, Taylor & Francis.

Coventry, K. R., Carmichael, R., & Garrod, S. C. (1994). Spatial prepositions, object-specific function and task requirements. *Journal of Semantics 11*, 289–309.

Coventry, K. Prat-Sala, M., & Richards, L. (2001). The interplay between geometry and function in the comprehension of "over," "under," "above," and "below." *Journal of Memory and Language 44*, 376–398.

Downing, C., & Pinker, S. (1985). The spatial structure of visual attention. In M. Posner and O. Marin (Eds.), *Attention and Performance XI* (pp. 171–187). Hillsdale, NJ: Lawrence Erlbaum.

Gapp, K.-P. (1995). Angle, distance, shape, and their relationship to projective relations. In J. D. Moore & J. F. Lehman (Eds.), *Proceedings of the 17th Annual Conference of the Cognitive Science Society* (pp. 112–117), Mahwah, NJ: Cognitive Science Society.

Garrod, S. C., Ferrier, G., & Campbell, S. (1999). In and on: Investigating the functional geometry of spatial prepositions. *Cognition 72*, 167–189.

Georgopoulos, A. P., Schwartz, A. B., & Kettner, R. E. (1986). Neuronal population coding of movement direction. *Science 223*, 1416–1419.

Gibbs, R. W. (2003). Embodied experience and linguistic meaning. *Brain and Language 84*, 1–15.

Glenberg, A. M. (1997). What is memory for? *Behavioral and Brain Sciences 20*, 1–55.

Glenberg, A. M., & Kaschak, M. P. (2002). Grounding language in action. *Psychonomic Bulletin & Review 9*, 558–565.

Hayward, W. G., & Tarr, M. J. (1995). Spatial language and spatial representation. *Cognition 55*, 39–84.

Herskovits, A. (1986). *Language and Spatial Cognition: An Interdisciplinary Study of the Prepositions of English.* Cambridge: Cambridge University Press.

Herskovits, A. (1998). Schematization. In P. Olivier & K.-P. Gapp (Eds.), *Represen-tation and Processing of Spatial Expressions* (pp. 149–162). Mahwah, NJ: Lawrence Erlbaum Associates.

LaBerge, D., & Brown, V. (1989). Theory of attentional operations in shape identi-fication. *Psychological Review 96*, 101–124.

Lakoff, G. (1987). *Women, Fire and, Dangerous Things: What Categories Reveal About the Mind*. Chicago: University of Chicago Press.

Landau, B., & Jackendoff, R. (1993). "What" and "where" in spatial language & spatial cognition. *Behavioral & Brain Sciences 16*, 217–265.

Langacker, R. W. (1987). *Foundations of cognitive grammar*. (Vol. 1). Stanford, CA: Stanford University Press.

Langacker, R. W. (1993). Grammatical traces of some "invisible" semantic con-structs. *Language Sciences 15*, 323–355.

Langacker, R. W. (2002). A study in unified diversity: English and Mixtec locatives. In N. J. Enfield (Ed.), *Ethnosyntax: Explorations in Grammar and Culture* (pp. 138–161). Oxford: Oxford University Press.

Lin, E. L., & Murphy, G. L. (1997). Effects of background knowledge on object categorization and part detection. *Journal of Experimental Psychology: Human Per-ception & Performance 23*, 1153–1169.

Logan, G. D., & Sadler, D. D. (1996). A computational analysis of the apprehension of spatial relations. In P. Bloom, M. A. Peterson, L. Nadel & M. Garrett (Eds.), *Language and Space* (pp. 493–529). Cambridge, MA: MIT Press.

Miller, G. A., & Johnson-Laird, P. N. (1976). *Language and perception*. Cambridge, MA: Harvard University Press.

Morrow, D. G., & Clark, H. H. (1988). Interpreting words in spatial descriptions. *Language and Cognitive Processes 3*, 275–291.

Pecher, D., Zeelenberg, R., & Barsalou, L. W. (2003). Verifying properties from different modalities for concepts produces switching costs. *Psychological Science 14*, 119–124.

Praseda, S., & Ferenz, K. (2001). Is the catch near the television? Functional infor-mation and talking about distances. Unpublished manuscript.

Regier, T. (1996). *The human semantic potential: Spatial language and constrained con-nectionism*. Cambridge, MA: MIT Press.

Regier, T., & Carlson, L. A. (2001). Grounding spatial language in perception: An Empirical and Computational Investigation. *Journal of Experimental Psychology: General 130*, 273–298.

Regier, T., Carlson, L. A., & Corrigan, B. (in press). Attention in spatial language: Bridging geometry and function. To appear in L. A. Carlson & E. van der Zee (Eds.), *Representing functional features for language and space: In-sights from perception, categorization and development*. Oxford: Oxford University Press.

Schirra, J. (1993). A Contribution to Reference Semantics of Spatial Prepositions: The Visualization Problem and its Solution in VITRA. In C. Zelinsky-Wibbelt (Ed.), *The semantics of prepositions: From mental processing to natural language processing* (pp. 471–515). Berlin: Mouton de Gruyter.

Talmy, L. (1983). How language structures space. In H. L. Pick & L. P. Acredolo (Eds.), *Spatial Orientation: Theory, research and application* (pp. 225–282). New York: Plenum Press.

Vandeloise, C. (1988). Length, width, and potential passing. In B. Rudzka-Ostyn (Ed.), *Topics in Cognitive Linguistics* (pp. 403–427). Amsterdam: John Benjamins.

Vandeloise, C. (1991). *Spatial Prepositions: A Case Study from French*. Chicago: University of Chicago Press.

Wilson, H. R., & Kim, J. (1994). Perceived motion in the vector sum direction. *Vision Research 34*, 1835–1842.

Zwaan, R. A. (2004). The immersed experiencer: Toward an embodied theory of language comprehension. To appear in B. H. Ross (Ed.), *The Psychology of Learning and Motivation*. Vol. 44 (pp. 35–62). New York: Academic Press.

Zwaan, R. A., Stanfield, R. A., & Yaxley, R. H. (2002). Language comprehenders mentally represent the shapes of objects. *Psychological Science 13*, 168–172.

4

Embodiment in Metaphorical Imagination

Raymond W. Gibbs, Jr.

How would you describe the way you think about your life? When asked this question, many people immediately embrace some convenient metaphor to characterize their self-conception. Consider two narratives from individuals in their late 40s who had re-entered college to finally obtain their degrees. The first, Sara, talked of her life as being a journey. She said that completing school was critical "because it's important to where I want to end up." It represents "this little highway to, um, a new life, I guess. Each one of the steps I take down this road was well thought out. You take your journey and end up back where you started and you see it in a new way, and you see it for the first time, and I really believe that's what I did" (Horton, 2002, p. 283).

A different person, Porter, described his life as a kind of play within a play. He said, "I think that when you do that, when you create a play within a play, and you say, well, if my life was already, which it seems to be, a staged production, up and running, ready to go, there were no surprises ... it was a set production.... It was me. I was the character in the play that had become the protagonist. I am in my own show right now, absolutely. I get to be the star in my show" (Horton, 2002, p. 284).

Taking journeys and participating in plays are embodied activities that serve as crucial foundations for how Sara and Porter imaginatively think of their lives at that moment. The impulse toward metaphor is centered around thinking of some abstract idea or event in terms of some familiar bodily experience (e.g., being in a play, taking journeys). But people also desribe their lives in terms of events that they have not directly experienced. Consider the following narrative from a married man, Sam, where he discusses his wife's infertility and its effect on their lives (Becker, 1997, pp. 66–7):

It (infertility) became a black hole for both of us. I was so happy when I was getting married, and life for me, was consistently getting better. And she was continuously depressed. Everything was meaningless because she couldn't have a baby. And so it was a tremendous black hole, it was a real bummer. I mean, in the broadest, deepest sense of the term. It was very upsetting to me because it was like no matter what . . . it seemed like every time . . . I was, like, taking off and feeling good, and she was dragging me down. . . . It was just like everything was going down the black hole. . . . The notion of the black hole is that it's this magnet – this negative magnet in space through which all matter is irretrievably drawn – that was the image that I had of it. It was just sucking everything down out of our lives. Down this negative hole. It was bad.

Sam describes the black hole (i.e., the infertility) as a terrible constricting force that prevents him and his wife from experiencing the pleasures and responsibilities of parenthood. This black hole sucks significant, much desired elements out of their relationship, and as a metaphor, reflects a dismal image of their deteriorating marriage, one that both partners seem to have little control over. Although Sam has never fallen into a black hole, the metaphor seems apt precisely because we can simulate what that event must be like, given some of the embodied actions we have experienced in our lives, such as feeling forcefully drawn to something or someone, or falling and feeling out of control.

My main argument in this chapter is that significant aspects of people's imaginative abilities arise from, and continue to be structured by, pervasive patterns of embodied activity. Imagination may refer to the scenes we construct as we read a novel, recall images of past life experiences, or experience strong emotions rising into consciousness. But human imagination is also an unconscious process that uses metaphor to map aspects of long-term memory onto immediate experience. Much of the work in support of this claim comes from the systematic analysis of linguistic statements. Some cognitive scientists argue that how people talk about their lives is not the best place to find evidence on how they truly think. After all, words often fail to describe the external world, and it is likely the case that language is inadequate to capture much about the detailed richness of inner mental experience. My claim, however, is that the language people use to describe their experiences reveals a deep-seated, cognitive imperative to make sense of the world in terms of our bodies (and in terms of embodied metaphor). I suggest that the linguistic evidence demands explanation within a more general psychological account of human conceptual systems and human imagination.

HYPOTHESES ON EMBODIED METAPHORICAL IMAGINATION

Cognition is what happens when the body interacts with the physical/cultural world. Minds are not internal to the human body, but exist as webs encompassing brains, bodies, and world. In a similar way, "embodiment" refers to the dynamical interactions between the brain, the body, and the physical/cultural environment. My specific use of the term "embodiment" is intended to capture important aspects of people's phenomenological experiences of their bodies in action. People need not be conscious of these sensations (e.g., proprioception), yet there are important regularities in bodily experiences that are tacitly incorporated into higher-level cognition. This possibility does not deny the fundamental importance of bodily processes such as neural activity, which is, of course, a prime focus of research in cognitive science. My aim here, however, is to emphasize the relevance of recurring patterns of bodily action and sensations in grounding people's creation and use of symbols.

A key part of understanding how embodiment provides the grounding for perception, cognition, and language is to study how people imaginatively use aspects of their phenomenal experience to structure abstract concepts. This study naturally leads to the topic of metaphor given its role in mapping concrete aspects of subjective bodily experiences onto abstract knowledge domains. Embodiment shapes metaphorical thought and language at different levels with each level reflecting a different time-scale, ranging from slow-moving linguistic evolution, to fast-moving aspects of immediate, online language production and comprehension.

Consider the following hypotheses. Each specifies a different level of the interaction of embodiment and linguistic meaning.

1. Embodiment plays a role in the development and changes in the meanings of words and expressions over time.
2. Embodiment motivates the linguistic meanings that have currency within linguistic communities, or may have some role in an idealized speakers/hearers' understanding of language.
3. Embodiment motivates speakers' use and understanding of why various words and expressions mean what they do.
4. Embodiment functions automatically and interactively in people's online use and understanding of linguistic meaning.

These hypotheses reflect a hierarchy of possibilities about the interaction of embodied experience with different aspects of language use and understanding. Because they relate to different time-scales in which linguistic meaning occurs, each hypothesis requires appropriate methods of empirical study, with certain disciplines better able to provide evidence in support of these different possibilities. The research described below comes from both cognitive linguistics (Hypotheses 1 and 2) and experimental psycholinguistics (Hypotheses 3 and 4). For space reasons, I focus more on the latter two hypotheses, and only give selected examples of research pertaining to Hypotheses 1 and 2.

HYPOTHESIS 1: EMBODIMENT AND THE EVOLUTION
OF LANGUAGE

There is much interest in cognitive science on the role that evolving brain processes play in the evolution of language. But people's recurring phenomenological experiences in the world also serve as the grounding for the development of language referring to abstract concepts. A specific demonstration of how embodiment shaped language evolution is seen in historical studies of metaphor. Sweetser (1990) has shown in detail how many polysemous words in Indo-European languages acquired their nonphysical meanings via metaphorical extensions from earlier acquired, concrete, embodied meanings. To take just one example, the metaphorical mappings between the idea of visually seeing things to intellectually understanding things defines a pathway for semantic change. The presence of conceptual metaphors like UNDERSTANDING IS SEEING explains not only how words change their meanings historically (i.e., why the physical sense of "see" gets regularly extended via metaphor at a later point to have a nonphysical meaning), but also motivates for contemporary speakers just why it is that polysemous words have the specific meanings they do (e.g., why it just makes sense to us to talk about understanding ideas using expressions like "I clearly see the point you're making in this essay"). With few exceptions, words in Indo-European languages meaning "see" regularly acquire the meaning "know" at widely scattered times and places. It appears, then, that the development of the abstract idea of "knowing," and words referring to this concept, is based on some arbitrary convention, but is grounded in recurring patterns of embodied activity. A great deal of cognitive linguistic research on language change and the historical development of language is consistent with this important claim (Blank & Koch, 1999; Winters, 1992).

HYPOTHESIS 2: EMBODIMENT MOTIVATES CONTEMPORARY
LINGUISTIC MEANING

Image Schemas

Why do people talk in the ways they do about abstract ideas and events? Cognitive linguists have long argued that many of our concepts, including abstract ones, are grounded in, and structured by, various patterns of our perceptual interactions, bodily actions, and manipulation of objects (Johnson, 1987; Lakoff, 1987; Lakoff & Johnson, 1999; Talmy, 1988). Specific patterns of force dynamics underlie our embodied understanding of abstract concepts (Talmy, 1988). Forces are viewed as physical, embodied entities (an agonist) acting in competition against other forces (an antagonist), with each entity having varying strengths and tendencies. We understand these entities primarily from our own bodily experiences such as pushing and being pushed, moving objects, and feeling the forces acting within our bodies as we move about the environment. These patterns are experiential gestalts, called "image schemas" that emerge throughout sensorimotor activity as we manipulate objects, orient ourselves spatially and temporally, and direct our perceptual focus for various purposes.

Image schemas can be defined generally as dynamic analog representations of spatial relations and movements in space. Even though image schemas are derived from perceptual and motor processes, they are not themselves sensorimotor processes. Instead, image schemas are "primary means by which we construct or constitute order and are not mere passive receptacles into which experience is poured" (Johnson, 1987, p. 30). In this way, image schemas are different from the notion of schemata traditionally used in cognitive science that are abstract conceptual and propositional event structures. By contrast, image schemas are imaginative, nonpropositional structures that organize experience at the level of bodily perception and movement. Image schemas exist across all perceptual modalities, and one necessary for there to be any sensorimotor coordination in our experience. As such, image schemas are at once visual, auditory, kinesthetic, and tactile. Finally, image schemas cover a wide range of experiential structures that are pervasive in experience, have internal structure, and can be metaphorically elaborated to enhance understanding of more abstract conceptual domains. Most generally, image schemes are those recurring bodily experiences that help solve different adaptive problems for people as they live in complex physical environments.

Consider a few examples of image schemas. The BALANCE schema is something that is learned "with our bodies and not by grasping a set of rules" (Johnson, 1987, p. 74). Balancing is such a pervasive part of our bodily experience that we are seldom aware of its presence in everyday life. We come to know the meaning of balance through the closely related experiences of bodily equilibrium or loss of equilibrium. Each of us has experienced occasions when we have trouble standing, have too much acid in our stomachs, when our hands get cold, our heads feel too hot, our bladders feel distended, our sinuses become swollen, and our mouths feel dry. In these and numerous other ways we learn the meanings of lack of balance or equilibrium. We respond to imbalance and disequilibrium by warming our hands, drinking, draining our bladders, and so forth until we feel balanced once again. Our BALANCE image schema emerges, then, through our experiences of bodily equilibrium/disequilibrium and maintaining our bodily systems and functions in states of equilibrium.

Our BALANCE image schema is metaphorically elaborated in a large number of abstract domains of experience (e.g., psychological states, legal relationships, and formal systems) (Johnson, 1987). For of bodily and visual equilibrium, there seems to be one basic scheme consisting of a point or axis

around which forces and weights must be distributed so that they counter-
act or balance one another. Our experience of bodily balance and the perception of balance is connected to our understanding of balanced personal-
ities, balanced views, balanced systems, balanced equilibrium, the balance
of power, the balance of justice, and so on. In each of these examples, the
mental or the abstract concept of balance is understood and experienced in
terms of our physical understanding of balance. Image schemas have internal logic or structure that determine the roles these schemas can play
in structuring various concepts and patterns of reasoning. It is not unusual that a large number of unrelated concepts (for the systematic, psychological, moral, legal, and mathematical domains) all just happen to
make use of the same word "balance" and related terms. We use the same
word for all these domains because they are structurally related by the
same sort of underlying image schemas, and are metaphorically elaborated
from them.

Consider the embodied roots of another salient image schema,
STRAIGHT (Cienki, 1998). The term "straight" is employed in many physical and abstract ways. For instance:

"The straight edge of the table."
"Stand up straight."
"I can't think straight."
"It rained for three days straight."
"Tell it to me straight."
"Let me get this straight."
"He's not straight, but gay."
"I couldn't keep a straight face."

Why do we use "straight" in these rather different ways? The concept of
straight has an important role in our sensory experience. Research shows
that collinearity of points or elements in a visual pattern has an important
role in visual perception (Foster, 1982). For example, classic Gestalt studies on empirical grouping, visual detection in moving fields, visual acuity
in movement, visual texture discrimination, and visual discrimination of
briefly presented dot figures all show that perception of straightness is a
fundamental property of how we see and make sense of visual events.
Straight lines are more quickly and easily seen then curved lines. Horizontal and vertical straight lines, especially, are more easily perceived than
are oblique straight lines (Attneave & Olson, 1967). These findings partly
explain why people can talk of things being straight both as gestalt forms
(e.g., "The straight edge of the table"), and as a kind of orientation, such
as vertical (e.g., "The picture on the wall is not straight") (Zubin & Choi,
1984).

Finally, the SOURCE-PATH-GOAL schema first develops as we learn
to focus our eyes and track forms as they move throughout our visual

field. From such experiences, a recurring pattern becomes manifest in tracking a trajector from point A to another point B. Later on, as we move our bodies in the real world, ranging from experiences of reaching for objects to moving our entire bodies from one location to another, more varied SOURCE-PATH-GOAL experiences become salient. Although SOURCE-PATH-GOAL experiences may vary considerably (e.g., many objects, shapes, types of paths traveled), the emergent image-schematic structure of SOURCE-PATH-GOAL can be metaphorically projected onto more abstract domains of understanding and reasoning (Johnson, 1987). This metaphorical mapping preserves the structural characteristics or the cognitive topology of the source domain (Lakoff, 1990). Thus, the SOURCE-PATH-GOAL schema gives rise to conceptual metaphors such as PURPOSES ARE DESTINATIONS, which preserve the main structural characteristics of the source domain (i.e., SOURCE-PATH-GOAL). Not surprisingly, the SOURCE-PATH-GOAL schema serves as the source domain for the pervasive conceptual metaphor LIFE IS A JOURNEY (see Sara's narrative above).

I now present detailed examples of how image schemas, and the conceptual metaphors they give rise to, underlie several kinds of abstract ideas and concepts. This work is based on systematic analyses of linguistic expressions referring to different conceptual domains. Most generally, the evidence discussed here supports the idea that people use their understanding of different embodied activities to imaginatively structure more abstract ideas and events.

Linguistic Action

Linguistic action refers to a wide range of different kinds of speech events. One analysis of 175 body-part metaphors in a large corpus showed that body parts and bodily functions are essential source domains for characterizing people's description of talk (Goossens, Pauwels, Rudzka-Ostyn, Simon-Vanderberger, & Varpays, 1995). There are several ways through which people's understanding of human embodiment is metaphorically projected to structure linguistic action.

The first way involves body parts that play a role in speaking, which are put to a different use (e.g., eating and breathing). For instance, phrases such as "feed" and "force/ram/thrust" something down someone's throat" depicts specific interactions between two people in which the speaker transmits something to a listener, and the listener obtains the information by eating it.

A second group characterizes speaking as eating (or part of the process of eating), such as "chew the fat," or "chew the rag" (i.e., "to chat or complain"). Given that both fat and a rag can be chewed a long time, with little nutritional value coming from these activities, these idiom phrases express the idea of talking about something a long time with little new information to be gained from the experience.

The phrase "eat one's words" (i.e., to admit that one has said something in error) illustrates a different metaphor through linguistic action. By referring to the directionality of eating (i.e., ingesting), compared with the directionality of speaking (i.e., exteriorizing), these idioms express the idea that the speaker's words were somehow destroyed by making them go back to the place where they arose. This hypothetical action renders the speaker's utterance mute as it no longer has the originally intended effect upon the audience.

On the other hand, the term "regurgitate" (i.e., to report what one has already heard or learned) depicts the same direction of action as does speech and expresses the idea that the speaker has once ingested some idea, but not quite digested it completely (like people with food or liquid) so that it can indeed be thrown up and out of the body.

The experience of breathing underlies many metaphorical phrases for linguistic action, in part because breathing is very much a part of speaking (e.g., "He breathed words of love into her ear"). The phrase "waste one's breath" characterizes the air one breathes as a valuable resource, one that is essential to proper bodily functioning, which should not be expended needlessly. To "cough up" something is to remove a substance (e.g. blood, phlegm) that causes bodily, and often breathing, discomfort. When a speaker "chokes back" something, he or she attempts to prevent something from escaping the body, thus expressing the idea of someone exerting great control over what he or she has started to say.

The metaphor "spit out" reflects the idea that the speaker has something of value in the body which through effort he or she is able to gather up (spit or phlegm) and say (expectorate).

Various expressions for linguistic action center around the movement of the visible speech organs. "Keeping one's mouth shut," "Open one's lips," and "closed lipped" describes positions of the mouth and lips to stand for either the presence or absence of speech. Saying something "tongue in cheek" or "to lie through one's teeth" also express different types of linguistic actions (e.g., in gesture, lie) in which contours of the face and mouth metaphorically structure our understanding of what a speaker is communicating.

The bodily posture and experience of listeners captures something about how linguistic actions are understood. When someone "turns a deaf ear" or when something "goes in one ear and out the other," it's clear that the listener is not dedicating the right body part of successful communication.

Our sensory apparatus plays important roles in various aspects of our metaphorical conceptualization of speaking. For instance, the metaphor "sniff" (i.e., to say something in a complaining manner) rests on the embodied experience that the act of perceiving something with our noses is often accompanied by a special noise (i.e., sniffing). The sniffing noise represents that a person has perceived something of value that is transferred to the idea that a listener has understood something of substance. Sniffing noises are often made when something objectionable is smelled, and this gets mapped into the domain of linguistic communication to express the idea that the listener has just comprehended an unpleasant idea.

Violent physical action provides a rich source domain for characterizing many kinds of linguistic actions. The sport of boxing, in particular, provides the embodied actions underlying many linguistic concepts like "pulling one's punches," "spar," or "beating someone to the punch." For "pulling one's punch," speakers soften the impact of what they say for listeners. When speakers "spar" with listeners, the interaction is less serious, more playful, than is a full-fledged fight. And when speakers "beat someone to the punch," they make a point or argument before their listeners do.

Several metaphors for linguistic action focus on restricted movement. "Tongue tied," "hold your tongue," and "bite your tongue" all refer to the silent consequences of being unable to speak, mostly through self-control. Somewhat related are phrases where some object is clumsily handled, such as "fumble," or when one's actions are awkward, as in "heavy-handed" or "left-handed compliment." When a speaker successfully exchanges information to another, often in cases when a speaker offers a reward to someone else in exchange for something, he or she "hands it to someone."

The embodied experience of walking motivates various speech actions with different parts of walking movements being tied to specific ways of speaking. When someone "backtracks" while speaking, he or she reverses directions on the path they started out on to correct what has already been stated. A different error arises when someone "puts his foot in his mouth," indicating, via the metaphor of a serious mishandling of the body when walking, that a grave mistake has been made in saying what was just said.

The metaphorical structuring of linguistic action via significant patterns of embodied experience is, of course, tied to image schemas. For instance, the image schema BALANCE (i.e., a symmetrical arrangement of forces around a point or axis) motivates various phrases referring to a person's attempt to restore equilibrium of the body (and mind). When people say "get something off my chest," they describe a forceful action to remove an impediment that causes imbalance. Speakers who get something off their chests remove oppressive forces by merely talking to an appropriate person, often the person most responsible for placing the burden or impediment on the speaker. "Getting something off one's chest," just like "blowing off steam" and "coughing something up" restore a sense of balance or well-being to an individual.

The image schema CONTAINMENT underlies many metaphorical concepts related to our understanding of linguistic action. For instance, our mouths, like our bodies, are experienced as containers, such that when the container is open, then linguistic action is possible, and when closed, there is only silence. To be "closed-lipped" reflects the silent, closed container, and when one "bites one's lip," the closing of the mouth and lips is done quickly with great force. When someone "lies through their teeth," the container is perceived as a hiding place where true information resides, but the container is somewhat defective and we can see through the speaker's shameless attempt to lie about something when the truth can partly be seen. Some metaphors talk of entering the mouth container, as when "one puts words in someone's mouth" or "force/ram/thrust something down someone's throat," with the more forceful the entering into the container reflecting greater intensity on the speaker's linguistic action.

These selected examples clearly illustrate how image schemas connect the domains of embodied action with the domain of linguistic action. Generally, this examination of metaphor and linguistic action reveals how people use their intuitive phenomenological sense of their bodies to make sense of, and structure, more abstract conceptual domains.

Political Ideas

Embodied schemas and metaphors are pervasive in talk about politics and political ideas. One analysis of the debates in the United States in 1990 over the Gulf War showed that several image schemas enabled people to reason about international politics (Beer, 2001). Balance is central term in international relations. "Balance of power" expresses the shared wisdom of foreign policy. The terms "balance" and its cognates occur in the debate a total of 107 times. In the case of "balance," we come to understand more clearly an entire complex of related application. Rep. Peter Fazio (D-Oregon) uses "balance" to lay out the national pieces of the Gulf region and attempts to structure the forces of that region on a very complex board: "If we think about what is the long-term effect here, we have embraced Iraq to counter Iran. Now we are embracing Syria to counter Iraq. After we decapitated Iraq in this war, if that is what happens, what then is next in the region? How do we instill a new government in Iraq? How do we balance the forces in the region? Will we have to occupy Iraq? Will we have to defend Iraq against Syria or Turkey or Iran in the near future in order to gain so-called or restore so-called balance in the region?" (CR, H-132).

Blockage includes many cognates such as "block, blockage, blockaded, blockading, blockages, blocked, blocking," and "blocks." Related words are "embargo, force, intervention, penetration," and "sanctions." "Blockage" itself appears relatively infrequently, but "blockade" is used 69 times. In the case of the Gulf War, blockage is the form of an economic embargo was the major alternative strategic option. "Embargo" and its cognates appear 260 times. Opposite terms, such as "unblockage" or its distant cognates "liberation" and "free" appear 167 times. "Penetration" is the opposite of blockage in another dimension. When liberation relieves or dissolves the blockage, penetration pierces it. "Penetration" was used infrequently, but the notion of "intervene" was used 374 times. "Intervention," like "blockage" is a standard means of foreign policy and is densely connected in the theory and practice of international relations.

Center-periphery has wide play in international political economy. "Center" emerges as the key term in this dyad, appearing 37 times compared with "periphery's" three. "Center" evokes a very clear circular spatial grid. Indeed, as Sen. Steven Symms (R-Idaho) used "center," he conjured up an image of a spider – Saddam Hussein – sitting at the center of a web of domestic power" "The Iraqi dictator sits at the center of a web of state, party, military, and secret police organizations" (*CR*, S-380). When the web spreads outward beyond the national boundaries of Iraq, it entangles an ever-growing number of participants including the international world of terrorism. However, as in a real web, control always remains at the center. Indeed, as Sen. Orrin Hatch (R-Utah) suggested: "We all know that the world's most vicious terrorists have taken up residence in Baghdad.... Terrorists are on the move, and weapons and equipment are being put into place. Iraq stands at the center of three actions, providing the crucial support – false passports, sophisticated equipment, vast sums of money – that only a state sponsor of terror has available" (*CR*, S-385).

"Periphery" is an opposite of "center" and its textual uses illustrates another important dimension of bodily orientation. For example, Sen. Paul Sarbanes (D-Maryland) distinguishes between vital (or central) and peripheral components of the national interest: "Of course, we have interests in the Gulf. But it is essential to distinguish between peripheral interests and vital interests. Vital interests exist when our national security is truly a risk. Vital interests are those you kill and die for" (*CR*, S-154). In same way, peripheral elements of the human body – such as skin or even limbs – may be sacrificed in order to maintain the "center" of the body – the life essence, or "soul."

"Compulsion" is used as a frame to distinguish between free and slave societies, the free American Self and the enslaved Other. One of the marks distinguishing the oppressive regime of Saddam Hussein is the use of compulsory labor. The theme of compulsion also enters the democratic debate in Congress. Sen. Joseph Lieberman (D-Connecticut) made it clear that he did not wish to create an unseemly compulsion of the president to go to war. Rather, he wanted Congress to share the collective responsibility for the actions that must be taken: "I make my choice today to support the President of the United States, to give him not a compulsion to go to war, but an authorization to commit our troops to battle should he determine it necessary to protect our national security" (*CR*, S-376).

"Container" obviously translates into "containment," one of the major orienting terms of postwar international relations. As Sen. Kerry (D-Massachusetts) pointed out: "We sustained our fight against the Soviets for 40 years after Stalin took over Eastern Europe. We contained Stalinism, and in time, an isolated and decaying Soviet Union has been going through a process of caving in" (*CR*, S-249). The proposed strategy of containment took on a more economic flavor. As Sen. Sarbanes spoke of the Iraqi case, the assumption of those who supported a sanctions policy was, that over time, "the bite of these economic sanctions were felt and the punitive containment – the embargo, the blockage, the use of force to make the sanctions effective through the blockade – as that bite (became) stronger and stronger with the passage of time, it would over time lead to his departure from Kuwait" (*CR*, S-151). Finally, the *New York Times* talked of the wider political and military containment when mentioning what happens if economic containment was not effective: "the conflict would then become regionally destabilizing, on a scale that is difficult precisely to define but that could become also impossible to contain" (*CR*, S-155).

This discussion demonstrates how many key political concepts can be traced back to bodily referents. Balance is connected to the balance of power, physical blockage to blockade, center-periphery to core and marginal interests, compulsion to the use of force and coercion, contact to diplomatic discourse and military friction, and container to containment.

Illness

People routinely use a wide range of metaphorical expressions as they talk about their subjective experiences of illness. A common observation is that metaphor provides the imaginative tools for communication about senseless suffering, yet also offers a plan for personal transformation in coping with illness (Siegelmann, 1990). Metaphor appears to have both representational and determinative functions for individuals by not only representing past experience, but also serving as filters to rejuvenate how people view their past experiences and project their futures. Patients focus their attention on certain metaphorical ways of viewing their illnesses that are useful to their specific experiences and backgrounds (Low, 1996).

One recent project examined in detail the embodied metaphors six women employed in their narratives about their experiences with cancer (Gibbs & Franks, 2002). Six women in recovery from different forms of cancer were interviewed and asked to talk about their learning that they had cancer, their treatment and subsequent recovery. These interviews lasted from 20 to 35 minutes. Overall, the women produced 796 individual linguistic metaphors (an average of 132 metaphors per person). These diverse linguistic metaphors were structured by just 22 conceptual metaphors, such as CANCER IS AN OBSTACLE ON LIFE'S JOURNEY and EMOTIONAL EFFECT IS PHYSICAL IMPACT. Seventy-seven percent of the women's metaphorical language reflected embodied metaphors in the sense that the source domains (e.g., obstacles on life's journey) involved some aspect of recurring sensorimotor experience. For example, the women employed language like "to get through," "to get over" something, and talked of "to move into a new space." One woman commented that "having cancer was like walking off the face of the earth." A different woman described her cancer experience in the following manner: "When people say that the world is round it is a lie. It's flat and I know what the edge looks like." Another woman noted that "cancer is something that pulls you back to the core of life itself," and another said that "cancer forced me to begin stripping away a lot of things that don't matter." Finally, one woman talked of her experiences in particularly poetic terms when she personified cancer as a dancer partner: "I felt like my spirit was able to sing again and that I had taken off the cloak of disease – that I had been carrying this cloak of disease for about six months and that in dancing I had taken it off and my spirit was singing again." Note the skin-like quality of the emotional experience mentioned here as the woman soon learned to take off "the cloak of disease."

Embodied metaphor clearly plays a major role in women's imaginative understanding of their cancer experiences. Most notably, these instances show the primacy of the body in movement through "affective space" (Cataldi, 1996) in people's descriptions of their self-concepts, their illnesses, and their emotions. A separate analysis revealed, in fact, that 82% of the language these women used to talk about themselves involved embodied movement as a tactile (against the skin) experience.

Theories

Theories are abstract entities referring to folk and scientific explanations of human and natural events. But people actually speak of theories in rather concrete ways. For instance, speakers will say "Your data can't support the theory," "Your theory is weak," "Your theory needs to be buttressed," or "Your theory needs a better foundation," These statements reflect a particular entailment of the common conceptual metaphor THEORIES ARE BUILDINGS. People also talk about theories being woven together or unraveling, which reflect the idea that THEORIES ARE FABRIC. At first glance, these imaginative constructions do not seem to be especially embodied, even if part of our knowledge of buildings and fabric comes from our embodied interactions with them. Moreover, there are clearly some aspects of buildings and fabric that are not mapped onto our understanding of theories. For example, one never hears a speaker talk of a theory lacking windows, needing a new air-conditioning unit, or being a pretty pink wool.

The cognitive linguistic research on image schemas and conceptual metaphor has provided significant evidence on the embodied grounding of imaginative abstract thought. But consideration of the THEORIES

ARE BUILDINGS and THEORIES ARE FABRIC conceptual metaphors raises several problems for standard conceptual metaphor theory. First, conceptual metaphors appear to differ in the way they are experientially grounded (Grady, 1997, 1999). For instance, consider the well-known conceptual metaphor MORE IS UP (e.g., "Inflation is up this year"). It is easy to correlate having more of some objects or substance (i.e., quantity) with seeing the level of those objects or substance rise (i.e., verticality). But many conceptual metaphors do not suggest such straightforward experiential correlations, such as THEORIES ARE BUILDINGS or THEORIES ARE FABRICS. Moreover, the fact that some aspects of buildings and fabric are not mapped onto the domain of theories shows that there are gaps in metaphorical mapping processes.

An interesting solution to these problems suggests that conceptual metaphors are not the most basic level at which metaphorical mappings exist in human thought and experience. Grady (1997) argued that the strong correlation in everyday embodied experience leads to the creation of or "primary" metaphors. Some of the most prominent primary metaphors are:

INTIMACY IS CLOSENESS (e.g., "We have a close relationship.")
DIFFICULTIES ARE BURDENS (e.g., "She's weighed down by responsibilities.")
AFFECTION IS WARMTH (e.g., "They greeted me warmly.")
IMPORTANT IS BIG (e.g., "Tomorrow is a big day.")
MORE IS UP (e.g., "Prices are high.")
SIMILARITY IS CLOSENESS (e.g., "Those colors aren't the same, but they're close.")
ORGANIZATION IS PHYSICAL STRUCTURE (e.g., "How do theories fit together?")
HELP IS SUPPORT (e.g., "Support your local charities.")
TIME IS MOTION (e.g., "Time flies.")
STATES ARE LOCATIONS (e.g., "I'm close to being in a depression.")
CHANGE IS MOTION (e.g., "My health has gone from bad to worse.")
PURPOSES ARE DESTINATIONS (e.g., "He'll be successful, but isn't there yet.")
CAUSES ARE PHYSICAL FORCES (e.g., "They push the bill through Congress.")
KNOWING IS SEEING (e.g., "I see what you mean.")
UNDERSTANDING IS GRASPING (e.g., I've never been able to grasp complex math.")

These metaphorical correlations arise out of our embodied functioning in the world. In each case, the source domain of the metaphor comes from the body's sensorimotor system. A primary is a metaphorical mapping for which there is an independent and direct experiential basis and independent linguistic evidence. A "compound" or "complex" metaphor, on the other hand, is a self-consistent metaphorical complex composed of more than one primitive. Complex metaphors are created by blending primary metaphors and thereby fitting together small metaphorical pieces into larger metaphorical wholes.

For instance, consider the following three primitive metaphors: PERSISTING IS REMAINING ERECT, STRUCTURE IS PHYSICAL STRUCTURE, and INTERRELATED IS INTERWOVEN. These three primitives can be combined in different ways to give rise to compound metaphors that have traditionally been seen as conceptual metaphors. But the combination of these primitives allows for metaphorical concepts without gaps. Thus, combining PERSISTING IS REMAINING ERECT with STRUCTURE IS PHYSICAL STRUCTURE provides for a compound THEORIES ARE BUILDINGS, which nicely motivates the metaphorical inferences that theories need support and can collapse, etc., without any mappings such as that theories need windows. In a similar way, the combination of STRUCTURE IS PHYSICAL STRUCTURE AND INTERRELATED IS INTERWOVEN gives rise to a different metaphorical compound for theories, namely, THEORIES ARE FABRICS. This compound metaphor gives rise to the reasonable inferences that theories can unravel or may be woven together, without generating entailments such as that theories are colorful in the way that some fabrics have colors.

This view of the embodied basis for metaphorical thought and language solves the "poverty of mapping" problem often noted for conceptual metaphor, and other theories of metaphor (Grady, 1997). There is no need to posit specific mechanisms that override parts of source-to-target domain mappings in primary metaphors because of the positive correlation in embodied experience between the source and target domains (Grady, 1997).

All of the above only bears on the embodied motivation for ordinary talk as a system of language. None of this linguistic evidence directly addresses the possibility that people actually use their bodies to help create many of the abstract concepts described in embodied metaphorical terms. But the cognitive linguistic evidence is highly suggestive of this possibility. At the very least, psycholinguists must explain why people talk in the systematic ways they do in terms of embodied metaphor. The linguistic evidence cannot be dismissed just because it comes from nonexperimental research.

HYPOTHESIS 3: EMBODIMENT IN INTERPRETING METAPHORICAL LANGUAGE

The cognitive linguistic evidence described thus far suggests that embodied experience has a significant role in grounding various aspects of thought and language. This work highlights the idea that there are important linkages between recurring patterns of embodied activities, abstract concepts, and the imaginative language used to describe these abstract concepts. But do people really work in this way? This section describes experimental studies showing that embodied metaphor provides at least part of the tacit knowledge people have as to why many words and phrases have the particular meanings they do and that embodied metaphor plays some role in people's conscious interpretation of language. A key element of much of this work is that people's embodied experiences are specifically examined apart from language and are then used to make empirical predictions about individuals' use and understanding of linguistic meaning. I explore this in the context of experimental studies on word meaning, idiomatic expressions, and metaphorical talk of desire.

Word Meaning

Words are traditionally defined in terms of semantic features that are usually abstract and thought to reflect different conceptual relations. Yet scholars now argue that some aspects of word meanings arise from, and are mentally represented in terms of, embodied experience. Consider the word "stand" in the following sentences:

> "Please stand at attention."
> "He wouldn't stand for such treatment."
> "The clock stands on the mantle."
> "The law still stands."
> "He stands six-foot five."
> "The part stands for the whole."
> "She had a one-night stand with a stranger."

These sentences represent just a few of the many senses of "stand" that are common in everyday speech and writing. Some of these senses refer to the physical act of standing (e.g., "Please stand at attention," "The clock stands on the mantle," "He stands six-foot five"), others have nonphysical, perhaps figurative, interpretations (e.g., "We stood accused of the crime," "The part stands for the hole," "He wouldn't stand for such treatment"). What are the principles that relate the different physical and nonphysical senses of "stand" in the examples noted above?

Gibbs, Beitel, Harrington, and Sanders (1994) demonstrated that the different senses of the polysemous word "stand" are motivated by different image schemas that arise from our bodily experience of standing. A group of participants were first guided through a brief set of bodily exercises to get them to consciously think about their own physical experience of standing. For instance, participants were asked to stand up, to move around, bend over, to crunch, and to stretch out on their tip-toes.

After this brief standing exercise, participants then read brief descriptions of 12 different image schemas that might possibly have some relationship to the experience of physical standing (e.g., VERTICALITY, BALANCE, RESISTANCE, ENABLEMENT, CENTER-PERIPHERY, LINKAGE). Finally, the participants rated the degree of relatedness of each image schema to their own embodied experience of standing. The results of this first study showed that five image schemas are primary to people's bodily experiences of standing (i.e., BALANCE, VERTICALITY, CENTER-PERIPHERY, RESISTANCE, and LINKAGE).

A second experiment asked people to sort 35 different senses of "stand" into five groups based on their similarity of meaning. An analysis of these groups revealed that participants did not categorize physical senses of "stand" separately from the nonphysical or figurative senses. For example, the physical idea of standing in "to stand at attention" was often grouped with the metaphorical senses of "stand" in "let the issue stand" and "to stand the test of time."

The third experiment in this series examined the relationship between the five image schemas for the physical experience of standing and the various senses of "stand" studied in Experiment 2. Once again, participants were first asked to stand up and focus on different aspects of their bodily experience of standing. As they did this, the participants were presented with verbal descriptions of the five image schemas BALANCE, VERTICALITY, CENTER-PERIPHERY, RESISTANCE, and LINKAGE. Afterwards, the participants were given a list of 32 senses of "stand" and asked to rate the degree of relatedness between each sense and the five image schemas. These ratings allowed us to construct an image schema profile for each of the 32 uses of "stand." For example, "it stands to reason" and "as the matter now stands" both have the same image schema profile (in their rank-order of importance) of LINKAGE–BALANCE–CENTER/ PERIPHERY–RESISTANCE–VERTICALITY. The expressions "don't stand for such treatment" and "to stand against great odds" are both characterized by the image schema profile RESISTANCE–CENTER/PERIPHERY– LINKAGE–BALANCE–VERTICALITY.

The primary goal of this study, though, was to assess whether the senses of "stand," seen as being similar in meaning in the second experiment, were reliably predictable from the image schema profiles obtained in this study. Statistical analyses showed that knowing the image schema profiles for different senses of "stand" allowed us to predict 79% of all the groupings of "stand" in Experiment 2. These data provide strong support for the hypothesis that people's understandings of the meanings of "stand" are partly motivated by image schemas that arise from their bodily experiences of standing. A fourth study showed that participants' sortings of "stand" in different groups can not be explained simply in terms of their understanding of the contexts in which these words appeared. Thus, people did not sort phrases, such as "don't stand for such treatment" and "to stand against great odds," because these phrases refer to the same types of situations. Instead, it appears that people's similarity judgments are best attributed to their tacit understanding of how different patterns of image schemas motivate different uses of the polysemous word "stand."

These studies demonstrate that people make sense of different uses of "stand" because of their tacit understanding of several image schemas that arise partly from the ordinary bodily experience of standing. These image schemas not only produce the grounding for many physical senses of "stand" (e.g., "he stands six-foot five," "stand in the way," and "stand at attention"), but also underlie people's understanding of complex, metaphorical uses (e.g., "the part stands for the whole," "as the matter now stands," and "the engine can't stand the constant wear"). People perceive different senses of "stand" as similar in meaning partly on the basis of the underlying image schema profile for each use of the word in context (see Beitel, Gibbs & Sanders, 2000). Thus, people tacitly recognize some connection between these schematic bodily experiences and different aspects of linguistic meaning, including meanings that are highly abstract and/or metaphorical.

Idiomatic and Conventional Expressions

There is a extensive literature demonstrating that conceptual metaphors may play a role in people's understanding of individual phrases and larger textual units (see Gibbs, 1994, 1999). Consistent with the claims of cognitive linguists, there is also evidence that people tacitly recognize the embodied nature of many conceptual metaphors. One set of psycholinguistic studies examined how people's intuitions of the bodily experience of containment, and several other image schemas, which serve as the source domains for several important conceptual metaphors, underlie speakers' use and understanding of idioms (e.g., "blow your stack," "spill the beans"). These studies were designed to show that the specific entailments of idioms reflect the source to target domain mappings of their underlying conceptual metaphors (Gibbs, 1992). Most importantly, these metaphorical mappings preserve the cognitive topology of these embodied, image-schematic source domains (e.g., heated fluids in the bodily container onto anger).

Participants in a first study were questioned about their understanding of events corresponding to particular bodily experiences that were viewed as motivating specific source domains for conceptual metaphors (e.g., the experience of one's body as a container filled with fluid). For instance, participants were asked to imagine the embodied experience of a sealed container filled with fluid, and then they were asked something about causation (e.g., "What would cause the container to explode?"), intentionality (e.g., "Does the container explode on purpose or does it explode through no volition of its own?"), and manner (e.g., "Does the explosion of the container occur in a gentle or a violent manner?").

Overall, the participants were remarkably consistent in their responses to the various questions. To give one example, people responded that the cause of a sealed container exploding its contents is the internal pressure caused by the increase in the heat of the fluid inside the container. They also reported that this explosion is unintentional because containers and fluid have no intentional agency, and that the explosion occurs in a violent manner. These brief responses provide a rough, nonlinguistic profile of people's understanding of a particular source domain concept (i.e., heated fluid in the bodily container). These profiles are rough approximations of what cognitive linguistics and others refer to as the "image-schematic structures" of the source domains (Gibbs & Colston, 1995; Lakoff, 1990).

These different image schematic profiles about certain abstract concepts allowed me to predict something about people's understanding of idioms. My idea was that people's intuitions about various source domains map onto their conceptualizations of different target domains in very predictable ways. For instance, people's understanding of anger should partly be structured by their folk concept for heated fluid on the bodily container as described above. Several studies showed this to be true (Gibbs, 1992). Not surprisingly, when people understand anger idioms, such as "blow your stack," "flip your lid," or "hit the ceiling," they inferred that the cause of anger is internal pressure, that the expression of anger is unintentional, and is done is an abrupt violent manner. People do not draw these same inferences about causation, intentionality, and manner when comprehending literal paraphrases of idioms, such as "get very angry."

More interesting, though, is that people's intuitions about various source domains map onto their conceptualizations of different target domains in very predictable ways. For instance, several later experiments showed that people find idioms to be more appropriate and easier to understand when they are seen in discourse contexts that are consistent with the various entailments of these phrases. Thus, people find it easy to process the idiomatic phrase "blow your stack," when this was read in a context that accurately described the cause of the person's anger as being due to internal pressure, where the expression of anger was unintentional and violent (all entailments that are consistent with the entailments of the source to target domain mappings of heated fluid in a container onto anger). However, readers took significantly longer to *read* "blow your stack" when any of these entailments were contradicted by the preceding story context.

These psycholinguistic findings provide additional evidence that people's metaphorical concepts underlie their understanding of what idioms mean in written texts. Moreover, they provide significant experimental evidence that people's intuitions about their embodied experiences can predict something about their use and understanding of idioms, expressions that are partly motivated by bodily based conceptual metaphors.

A very recent research project on embodiment and metaphorical meaning looked at people's interpretations of metaphorical expressions about human desires (Gibbs, Lima, & Francuzo, 2004). This work also independently examined people's embodied experiences and used this information to make predictions about people's understandings of linguistic meaning. The metaphorical mapping of hunger onto desire is frequently found in talk of various kinds of desires, including lust and the desires for both concrete objects and abstract ideas/events. Thus, American English speakers often talk of abstract desires in terms of hunger.

"He hungers for recognition."
"He hungers for adventure."
"He had a hunger for power."
"He hungers for revenge."

Asserting this metaphorical relationship is not just a conventional or arbitrary way of speaking about desire, because there appears to be rich, systematic correspondences between feeling hunger and feeling different aspects of desire. Gibbs et al. (2004) investigated whether university students in two cultures, the United States and Brazil, metaphorically understand different desires in terms of their embodied experiences of hunger. If hunger and desire are highly correlated, and if people metaphorically make sense of their desires partly in terms of hunger, then these more prominent parts of their hunger experiences should be invariantly mapped onto their different concepts for desire. Thus, people should subsequently view certain ways of talking about desires in terms of specific hunger experiences more acceptable than less prominent aspects of feeling hunger.

A first study presented American and Brazilian college students with three types of symptoms that may possibly result from a person being hungry (these were translated into Brazilian Portuguese for the Brazilian participants). "Local" symptoms referred to specific parts of the body, "general" symptoms referred to whole body experiences, and "behavioral" symptoms referred to various behaviors that may result as a consequence of a person being hungry. Each of these three symptoms included items that we presumed may be closely related to the experience of being hungry, items possibly being related, and items not at all related to hunger. An analysis of these ratings showed that both English and Portuguese speakers gave similar ratings to the different items. For example, the two groups of participants agreed that strong effects of hunger on the human body include the stomach grumbles, thought of food makes one's mouth water, one has a stomachache, and one has a headache (local symptoms); one feels discomfort, becomes weak, becomes dizzy, gets annoyed, and has an appetite (general symptoms); and the person feels out of balance, becomes emotionally fragile, and becomes very anxious (behavior symptoms).

The two groups of participants also agreed on those items that were not related to their hunger experiences. Examples of these items include: the knees swell, the feet hurt, the hands itch, and the fingers snap (local symptoms); one wants to run, doesn't wish to see anyone, becomes talkative, and gets a fever (general symptoms), and one behaves normally, and one can work well (behavior symptoms). Overall, these findings indicate significant regularities in people's embodied experiences of hunger, at least as suggested by speakers from these two different cultures.

A second study examined whether people's folk knowledge about hunger is correlated with their understandings of difference experiences of desire. English and Portuguese speakers were asked to give their intuitions about two types of questions. The first set of questions focused on how people's bodies felt when experiencing three types of desire: love, lust, and the desire for things other than human beings, such as fame, adventure, money, etc. (the "other" category). Participants were asked to read each question and then rate the relevance of various bodily experiences (e.g., becomes dizzy, weak, annoyed, talkative) when that person was in love, lust, or experiencing some other desire.

The second set of questions focused on people's intuitions about the acceptability of different ways of linguistically expressing desire. Similar to the body questions, half of the items were constructed from strongly (or highly) rated bodily experiences for hunger as shown in the first study, with the other half came from weakly (or lowly) rated hunger items. These linguistic questions were posed for three types of desire (i.e., love, lust, and other) as was the case for the body questions. The participants' task was simply to read each statement (e.g., "My whole body aches for you," "I have a strong headache for knowledge," "My hands are itching for you," "My knees ache for information about my ancestry") and rate whether it was an acceptable way of talking in their respective language.

An analysis of the mean ratings showed that the findings for both the Body and Linguistic questions are generally consistent across English and Portuguese for the three types of symptoms for the three types of desire (love, lust, other). For instance, in regard to students' ratings of the acceptability of different linguistic expressions, both the American and Brazilian students viewed "I have a great appetite for money" and "I have a stomach pain for my old way of life" as being reasonable, acceptable ways of talking about different desires. But they also rated expressions such as "I became talkative for adventure" and "My knees swell for information about my ancestry" as being unacceptable ways of talking about desire.

Overall, then, the findings showed how knowing something about people's embodied experiences of hunger allows scholars to empirically predict which aspects of desire will, and will not, be thought of, and talked about, in terms of our complex embodied understandings of hunger. This evidence is generally consistent across two different languages and cultural communities. People use their knowledge of their bodily experiences/actions as the primary source of metaphorical meaning and understanding.

None of the studies described above indicate that people are using their "in-the-moment" felt sense of their bodies when thinking about and understanding the language referring to abstract concepts. The work discussed here only suggests that parts of our abstract concepts are linked to embodied, metaphorical experiences, which motivates people's interpretation of different metaphorical words and phrases.

HYPOTHESIS 4: EMBODIMENT AND IMMEDIATE
LANGUAGE PROCESSING

The final hypothesis states that embodiment plays a role in the immediate processing of metaphorical statements. I describe here two very different sets of studies in support of this claim. The first series of experiments demonstrated that people compute or access embodied metaphors during their immediate understanding of idioms like "blew his stack" (Gibbs, Bogdonvich, Sykes, & Barr, 1997). In these studies, participants read stories ending with idioms and then quickly gave lexical decision responses to visually presented letter-strings that reflected either something about the conceptual metaphors underlying these idioms (e.g., "heat" for ANGER IS HEATED FLUID IN A CONTAINER having just read "John blew his stack") or letter-strings that were unrelated to these conceptual metaphors (e.g., "lead").

There were two important findings from this study. First, people were faster to make these lexical decision responses to the related metaphor targets (i.e., "heat") having just read idioms than they were to either literal paraphrases of idioms (e.g., "John got very angry") or control phrases (e.g., phrases still appropriate to the context such as "John saw many dents"). Second, people were faster in recognizing related metaphorical targets than unrelated ones having read idioms, but not literal paraphrases or control phrases. This pattern of results suggests that people are immediately computing or accessing at least something related to the conceptual metaphor ANGER IS HEATED FLUID IN A CONTAINER when they read idioms. In another experiment, participants were faster to make lexical decision responses to metaphor targets (e.g., "heat") having read an idiom motivated by a similar conceptual metaphor (e.g., "John blew his stack") than an idiom with roughly the same figurative meaning but motivated by a different conceptual metaphor (e.g., "John bit her head off," which is motivated by the conceptual metaphor ANGER IS ANIMAL BEHAVIOR). Again, it appears that people compute or access the relevant conceptual metaphor, including embodied source domains, for an idiom during some aspect of their processing of these phrases.

It is important to be careful in interpreting the results of psycholinguistic studies like those just described. Thus, the Gibbs et al. (1997) data should only be understood as showing that people quickly see a tight association between their understanding of certain idioms and particular conceptual metaphors. These results do not necessarily imply that people actually compute or access conceptual metaphors when they are actively processing the meanings of idioms in real time. Nor do these data tell us whether people must compute or access an idiom's underlying conceptual metaphor in order to interpret what that idiom figuratively means.

Furthermore, the Gibbs et al. (1997) findings do not tell us whether people actively construct metaphoric representations (i.e., the conceptual metaphor) when understanding idioms or are people merely accessing in an associative manner preexisting conceptual metaphors when processing certain idioms. When people read an idiomatic expression like "John blew his stack," they may very well quickly access the conceptual metaphor ANGER IS HEATED FLUID IN A CONTAINER given that this metaphor is so closely tied to the idiom, even if the metaphor is not needed to actually understand what the idiom means in discourse. People may not actually compute a source-(HEATED FLUID IN A CONTAINER)-to-target (ANGER) domain mapping, and draw all the complex set of inferences associated with the conceptual metaphor, during ordinary understanding of conventional language.

Finally, the fact that conceptual metaphors may be active during some part of idiom understanding does not mean that people are activating embodied image schemas. Thus, in understanding "John blew his stack," readers do not necessarily activate or re-experience specific image schemas such as CONTAINMENT as part of their interpreting the figurative meaning of the idiom. My personal view is that online language processing is best characterized as a simulation process in which people create embodied scenarios, much as if one were in a flight simulator, appropriate to the discourse situation. Under this view, experiences of containment may indeed shape online production and comprehension of expressions like "John blew his stack." Although the data from Gibbs et al. (1997) are consistent with this idea, these results do not directly confirm it to the exclusion of other theoretical possibilities.

The last line of research I wish to discuss investigated the possible influence of bodily action on people's speeded processing of simple metaphoric phrases, as "stamp out a feeling," "push an issue," "sniff out the truth" and "cough up a secret," each of which denote physical actions upon abstract items. Wilson and Gibbs (2004) hypothesized that if abstract concepts are indeed understood as items that can be acted upon by the body, then performing a related action should facilitate sensibility judgments for a figurative phrase that mentions this action. For example, if participants first move their leg as if to kick something, and then read "kick around the idea," they should verify that this phrase is meaningful faster than when they first performed an unrelated body action.

Participants first learned to perform various specific bodily actions (e.g., throw, stamp, push, swallow, cough, grasp) given different nonlinguistic cues. Following this, participants were individually seated in front of a computer screen. The experiment consisted of a series of trials where an icon flashed on the screen, prompting the participant to perform the appropriate bodily action. After doing this, a string of words appeared on the screen and participants had to judge as quickly as possible whether the word string was "sensible."

Analysis of the speeded sensibility judgments showed that participants responded more quickly to the metaphorical phrases that matched the preceding action (e.g., the motor action kick was followed by "kick around the idea"), than to the phrases that did not match the earlier movement (e.g., the motor action chew was followed by "kick around the idea"). People were also faster in responding to the metaphor phrases having performed a relevant body moment than when they did not move at all. In short, performing an action facilitates understanding of a figurative phrase containing that action word, just as it does for literal phrases. A second study showed that same pattern of bodily priming effects when participants were asked to imagine performing the actions before they made their speeded responses to word strings. This result reveals that real movement is not required to facilitate metaphor comprehension, only that people mentally simulate such action.

Most generally, people do not understand the nonliteral meanings of these figurative phrases as a matter of convention. Instead, people actually understand "toss out a plan," for instance, in terms of physically tossing something (i.e., plan is viewed as a physical object). In this way, processing metaphoric meaning is not just a cognitive act but involves some imaginative understanding of the body's role in structuring abstract concepts.

CONCLUSION

My main claim in this chapter is that embodied activity is an essential part of the grounding for thought and language. There is significant evidence from both cognitive linguistics and psycholinguistics to support all four major hypotheses on how embodiment serves to create and maintain certain forms of abstract thought and the language people use to describe these metaphorical concepts. Of course, the four hypotheses discussed here are not the only ways that embodied actions influence imaginative thought and language. But distinguishing between these different time-scales is critical to studying the various roles that embodiment plays in grounding human cognition.

The data discussed here offer an important challenge to cognitive science accounts that ignore people's phenomenological bodily experience in theories of higher-order cognition and linguistic meaning. Simply put, people's recurring bodily actions serve as the fundamental grounding for how and why people think and talk in the specific ways that they do. This claim does not imply that there are no language-specific and cultural-specific constraints on thought and language. Yet the extensive literature by cognitive linguistics and psycholinguistics, only some of which is described in this chapter, points to major links between bodily experiences, abstract thought, and metaphorical language. Not all psychologists agree with these conclusion, especially in regard to whether conceptual, embodied metaphors are accessed during ordinary verbal metaphor comprehension (Glucksberg, 2001; Keysar, Shen, Glucksberg, & Horton, 2000). Psychologists sometimes defend their neglect of embodied, conventional metaphors by arguing that some cognitive linguistic analyses are contrary to their own intuitions. Thus, psychologists voice skepticism about the intuitive, introspectionist methods of cognitive linguistics, but then justify their neglect of conventional metaphors because of their own intuitions! It would be far better, in my view, for psychologists and others, to study explicitly embodied metaphors for abstract concepts, according to accepted empirical methods, make decisions about cognitive linguistic claims based on these studies, and to not simply dismiss this work out of hand.

My work directly establishes the importance of full-scale tactile-kinesthetic activity, and not just purely visual/perceptual processes, in theories of symbol grounding. An important aspect of this research is my attempt to systematically explore, even if crudely, people's intuitions about their bodies and actual human movement, in motivating aspects of human imagination. Thus, I employ cognitive linguistic analyses to generate possible bodily correlates for higher-order thought, but then investigate people's subjective bodily experiences independent of language to form empirical predictions about people's understandings of different forms of language. I urge others to adopt this research strategy when conducting experimental studies on the embodied grounding of thought and language.

The work described in this chapter does not distinguish between the possibility that sensorimotor activity is actively recruited in metaphor comprehension and the idea that functionally-independent conceptual representations are activated when metaphors referring to abstract concepts are understood. Even if these conceptual representations for abstract concepts are independent of immediate bodily action, they still may be partly formed via sensorimotor processes and retain something about their embodied origins. Under this latter possibility, people's bodily experiences of handling physical objects may be used in creating, and maintaining elaborate conceptual representations for many abstract concepts. But these "embodied" concepts need not be continually tied, and immediately influenced, by ongoing body activity. Future empirical research must clarify which of these different possibilities best describe various aspects of linguistic understanding.

Most generally, the present findings are consistent with the idea that many aspects of linguistic processing are tied to what the body is doing at any one moment. People may, for instance, be creating embodied simulations of speakers' messages that involve moment-by-moment "what must it be like" processes that make use of ongoing tactile-kinesthetic experiences. These simulations processes operate even when people encounter language that is abstract, or refers to actions that are physically impossible to perform. This interpretation of the evidence describe in this chapter is also congruent with a body of emerging evidence in cognitive science showing intimate connections between perceptual/sensorimotor experience and language understanding (Barsalou, 1999; Glenberg & Roberston, 2000; Glenberg & Kaschak, 2002; Richardson, Spivey, Barsalou, & McRae, 2003; Zwaan, Stanfield, & Yaxley, 2002). One possibility to consider is that embodied metaphors may not be explicitly represented as enduring structures in long-term memory, as often assumed by many cognitive linguists. They may, however, be created on-the-fly as imaginative simulations given very specific constraints within the particular brain, body, world interactions that hold at any moment in time. Under this view, people conceptualize specific situations, including those in which language is involved, by simulating themselves as full-bodied participants in these events. Image schemas and embodied metaphors may regularly arise from these imaginative simulation processes, and need not be static entities in long-term memory waiting to get accessed or activated.

References

Atneave, F., & Olson, R. (1967). Discriminability of stimuli varying in physical and retinal orientation. *Journal of Experimental Psychology 74*, 149–157.

Barsalou, L. W. (1999). Perceptual Symbol Systems. *Behavioral and Brain Sciences 22*, 577–609.

Becker, A. (1997). *Disrupted lives*. Berkeley: University of California Press.

Beer, F. (2001). *The Meanings of War and Peace*. College Station: Texas A&M Press.

Beitel, D., Gibbs, R., & Sanders, P. (2000). Psycholinguistic perspectives on polysemy. In H. Cuykens & B. Zawada (Eds.), *Polysemy in cognitive linguistics* (pp. 213–239). Amsterdam: Benjamins.

Blank, A., & Koch, P. (Eds.) (1999). *Historical Semantics and Cognition*. Berlin: Mouton.

Cataldi, S. (1996). *Emotion, depth, and flesh*. Albany: SUNY Press.

Cienki, A. (1998). STRAIGHT: An image schema and its metaphorical extensions. *Cognitive Linguistics 9*, 107–149.

Foster, D. H., & Gravano, S. (1982). Overshoot of curvature in visual apparent motion. *Perception Psychophysics 31*, 411–420.

Gibbs, R. (1992). What do idioms really mean? *Journal of Memory and Language 31*, 485–506.

Gibbs, R. (1994). *The Poetics of Mind: Figurative Thought, Language, and Understanding*. New York: Cambridge University Press.

Gibbs, R. (1999). Taking metaphor out of our heads and putting it into the cultural world. In R. Gibbs & G. Steen (Eds.), *Metaphor in Cognitive Linguistics* (pp. 145–166). Amsterdam: Benjamins.

Gibbs, R., Beitel, D., Harrington, M., & Sanders, P. (1994). Taking a stand on the meanings of "stand": Bodily experience as motivation for polysemy. *Journal of Semantics 11*, 231–251.

Gibbs, R., Bogdonovich J., Sykes, J., & Barr, D. (1997). Metaphor in idiom comprehension. *Journal of Memory and Language 37*, 141–154.

Gibbs, R., & Colston, H. (1995). The cognitive psychological reality of image schemas and their transformations. *Cognitive Linguistics 6*, 347–378.

Gibbs, R., & Franks, H. (2002). Embodied metaphor in women's narratives about their experiences with cancer. *Health Communication 14*, 139–166.

Gibbs, R., Lima, P., & Francuzo, E. (2004). Metaphor is grounded in embodied experience. *Journal of Pragmatics 36*, 1189–1210.

Glenberg, A. M., & Kashak, M. P. (2002). Grounding language in action. *Psychonomic Bulletin and Review 9*, 558–565.

Glenberg, A. M., & Roberston, D. A. (2000). Symbol grounding and meaning: A comparison of high-dimensional and embodied theories of meaning. *Journal of Memory and Language 43*, 379–401.

Glucksberg, S. (2001). *Understanding Figurative Language: From Metaphor to Idioms*. New York: Oxford University Press.

Goosens, L., Pauwels, B., Rudzka-Ostyn, M., Simon-Vanderberger, J., & Varpays, J. (1995). *By Word of Mouth: Metaphor, Metonymy, and Linguistic Action in a Cognitive Perspective*. Amsterdam: Benjamins.

Grady, J. (1997). THEORIES ARE BUILDINGS revisited. *Cognitive Linguistics 8*, 267–290.

Grady, J. (1999). A typology for conceptual metaphor: Correlation vs. resemblance. In R. Gibbs & G. Steen (Eds.) *Metaphor in cognitive linguistics* (pp. 79–100). Amsterdam: Benjamins.

Horton, S. (2002). Conceptualizing transition: The role of metaphor in describing the experience of change at midlife. *Journal of Adult Development 9*, 277–290.

Johnson, M. (1987). *The Body in Mind* (p. 30). Chicago: University of Chicago Press.

Keysar, B., Shen, Y., Glucksberg, S., & Horton, W. (2000). Conventional language: How metaphorical is it? *Journal of Memory & Language 43*, 576–593.

Lakoff, G. (1987). *Women, Fire, and Dangerous Things: What Categories Reveal About the Mind*. Chicago: Chicago University Press.

Lakoff, G. (1990) The invariance hypothesis: Is abstract reason based on image schemas? *Cognitive Linguistics 1*, 39–74.

Lakoff, G., & Johnson, M. (1999). *Philosophy in the Flesh*. New York: Basic Books.

Low, S. (1996). Embodied metaphors: Nerves as lived experiences. In T. Csordas (Ed.), *Embodiment and Experience* (pp. 139–162). New York: Cambridge University Press.

Richardson, D., Spivey, M., Barsalou, L., & McRae, K. (2003). Spatial representations activated during real-time comprehension of verbs. *Cognitive Sciences, 27,* 767–780.

Siegelmann, E. (1990). *Metaphor and Meaning in Psychotherapy.* New York: Norton.

Sweetser, E. (1990). *From Etymology to Pragmatics: The Mind-Body Metaphor in Semantic Structure and Semantic Change.* Cambridge: Cambridge University Press.

Talmy, L. (1988). Force dynamics in language and cognition. *Cognitive Science 12,* 49–100.

Wilson, N., & Gibbs, R. (2004). Body movement primes metaphor comprehension Manuscript submitted for publication.

Winters, M. (1992). Diachronicity within synchrony: The challenge of cognitive grammar. In M. Putz (Ed.), *Thirty Years of Linguistic Evolution* (pp. 503–512). Amsterdam: Benjamins.

Zubin, D., & Choi, S. (1984). Orientation and gestalt: Conceptual organizing principles in the lexicalization of space. In D. Testen, V. Mishra, & J. Drogo (Eds.), *Papers from the Parasession on Lexical Semantics* (pp. 333–345). Chicago: Chicago Linguistic Society.

Zwaan, R. A., Stanfield, R. K., & Yaxley, R. H. (2002). Language comprehenders mentally represent the shapes of objects. *Psychological Science 13,* 168–171.

5

Passionate Thoughts

The Emotional Embodiment of Moral Concepts

Jesse J. Prinz

In the 18th century, David Hume said that every idea is built up from copies of prior impressions. In modern terminology: all concepts are built up from stored records of perceptual states. This empiricist credo is enjoying a resurgence these days. Researchers in numerous fields are seriously investigating the hypothesis that thought has a perceptual basis. They are questioning the rationalist assumptions that have dominated cognitive science since its inception in the 1950s. Empiricism is still a fringe movement, however. It is often dismissed as gratuitously radical and utterly indefensible. That attitude has become something of a dogma, but it derives from two serious worries. One of them has to do with innate ideas. Empiricists have tended to be antinativists, and the current orthodoxy in cognitive science is to postulate a considerable amount of innate knowledge. I think the orthodoxy is mistaken, but I will have little to say about that here. The second major reason for rejecting empiricism has to do with abstract ideas. We often think about things that are far removed from sensory experience. There is no way to paint a mental picture of truth, justice, democracy, or necessity. If empiricism is to have any hope of success, it must be able to explain how we come to think about things at this level of abstraction.

I think the objection from abstract ideas must be dismantled piecemeal. There are different kinds of abstract ideas, and these must be accommodated in different ways. Several chapters in this volume address this issue (see especially Chapter 7 by Barsalou & Wiemer-Hastings, Gibbs, and Chapter 11 by Spivey, Richardson, & Gonzalez-Marquez). Barsalou and Wiemer-Hastings emphasize situational meaning. They say that, for both abstract and concrete concepts people simulate situations where those concepts apply. In the case of abstract concepts, however, people are likely to focus on events and introspectable psychological states, in their simulations, rather than objects or entities. Gibbs and Spivey et al. emphasize the role of spatial metaphors in understanding abstract concepts.

In this chapter, I contribute to these efforts by focusing on a single class of abstract ideas: moral concepts. *Justice, obligation, right,* and *wrong* are examples. Good and evil have no taste, smell, or visage. Consequently, it is hard to understand how our concepts of these things could be stored copies of percepts. I will defend an answer to this challenge. Unlike other authors in this volume, I will not emphasize situational meaning or metaphor, though both are surely relevant to a complete theory of moral concepts. We do simulate moral scenarios when we engage in moral deliberation, and we do speak metaphorically of evil forces, the balance of justice, and the path to righteousness. I will not develop these points here. The proposal that I want to explore is much older; it is a version of the answer that Hume himself proposed in accounting for moral concepts.

A number of factors make morality an especially important domain for researchers interested in how cognition gets grounded. First, moral cognition has direct links to action, and action plays a central role in contemporary revivals of empiricism. Second, moral cognition is intimately linked to emotion, and emotion is linked to the body. Thus, moral cognition offers a case study in cognitive embodiment. Third, moral cognition is highly sophisticated and likely to be uniquely human, so it offers a nice counterpoint to research on more rudimentary capacities. Finally, moral cognition is informed by culture. It offers insights into social aspects of the human mind. I will touch on each of these themes.

Before discussing moral cognition, I present an overview of the kind of empiricism that I favor. I offer a more detailed treatment elsewhere (Prinz 2002), and my position builds on the work of Barsalou (1999). This is an extension of those efforts.

CONCEPT EMPIRICISM

Empiricism Defined

The term "empiricism" has been used in a number of different ways. It sometimes refers to an epistemological doctrine, according to which all knowledge must be justified by appeal to experience. It sometimes refers to a semantic doctrine, according to which the meaning of a word can be specified in terms of observable confirmation conditions. It sometimes refers to a learning theory, according to which simple principles of perceptual similarity, association, and conditioning drive the acquisition of mature cognitive capacities. I do not wish to defend any of these hypotheses. The empiricist theory that I favor has to do with the nature of conceptual representations, the information they encode, and their primary functions.

This brand of empiricism is best approached by asking what concepts are for. Rationalist philosophers often presume that concepts are primarily for thinking or reflecting, implying that these activities can occur without any interaction with the physical world (see Fodor, 2004). The Cartesian conception of the mind as a pure reflecting ego is a philosophers' fiction. Such a mind would never have evolved. Concepts must allow us to do something. But what do they allow us to do? Psychologists sometimes imply that concepts are tools for sorting things or categorizing. The majority of empirical work on concepts investigates categorization. Categorization is a peculiar task, from an ecological perspective. We very rarely categorize things for categorization's sake. Instead, we categorize things because we want to bring past knowledge to bear on the present, and we want to learn new things about the entities that we encounter in the world. Psychologists certainly recognize this, and they emphasize the role of concepts in learning and induction (e.g., Murphy & Medin, 1985). But the lesson might be pushed a little farther. Millikan puts the point by saying that concepts are for reidentification ("there's another one of those") rather than categorization. I have used the term "detection" to capture a similar idea (Prinz, 2002). Millikan also speaks of "tracking" categories. This latter term is especially useful, because it conveys the idea that categories may vary from context to context. We track categories across their transformations. If we shift from categorization to tracking, we will immediately recognize that conceptual representations must be variable and context-sensitive. Work reviewed in Barsalou (1987) has borne this out.

The idea of tracking is an improvement over "categorization," because tracking is more flexible and useful in the real world. But the idea of tracking is still too passive. It implies that concepts are primarily in the business of knowledge enrichment. In actuality, concepts are tools for negotiating successful interactions with categories. They allow us to react appropriately to category instances and to plan future interactions. These activities require that we learn about categories, but also that we be able to apply that knowledge. A passive tracker would not survive very long. Instead, concepts must serve what I will call "active tracking." They must encode information about categories that helps us respond to them behaviorally. In Gibson's (1979) terms, concepts must encode information about what actions categories afford.

If concepts are tools for active tracking, then they must be grounded. We must know when to apply them, and we must know what courses of action are available to us when they apply. That information must be available to our senses or to the systems that coordinate our behavioral responses. Prevailing theories of concepts assume that this information is encoded in an amodal format. A moment's reflection suggests that this assumption is bizarre. If concepts are applied to perceived entities and used to guide actions, there is no reason to translate the sensory or motor codes into an amodal format.

Here we encounter the core tenet of empiricism. Locke, Hume, and other classical empiricists of Britain, claimed that the mental representations used in thought are modality specific. They are couched in the codes used by sensory input systems, not in an amodal code. Thought has no common currency. This old-fashioned idea is supported by the points that we have just been considering. If concepts are essentially tracking tools, then we should expect them to be couched in sensory codes.

The idea of active tracking adds two dimensions that are not emphasized in the classical empiricist picture: context sensitivity and action-oriented feature encoding. Let me remark on these in turn. Locke and Hume give the impression that concepts are stable. They remain constant over time and context. But this is hard to reconcile with active tracking. To track an object, concept must be pliable. A conceptual representation of a bird must encode what the bird looks like while standing, and while in flight. This can be done, in part, by noting invariants, but invariants, such as the triangular shape of a beak, abstract away from details that are useful for prediction. The fact that birds can both stand and fly may be useful information for the would-be bird hunter. There is good reason to retain information that allows us to represent a range of variation.

One might think that tracking objects requires the introduction of amodal symbols. We need some way of retaining constancy as our images are transformed during an episode of dynamic tracking. As a bird image transforms from standing to soaring, we need a way of marking the fact that the same bird is being represented. Amodal representations seem to fit the bill (so to speak). If we tag our dynamic bird images with amodal labels, we can keep track of the fact that those images correspond to a single object. This would spell trouble for the empiricist. But there is no need for the empiricist to go this route. To identify two different representations with the same object, one doesn't need a third representation to remain constant across them. That merely multiples representations, and it raises the question: how does an amodal label get appended to sensory images? The constancy problem has a much simpler solution. The most one would need is a way of indexing representations to a common mental file – a distributed storage site in long-term memory. This might require the computational equivalent of memory addresses, but addresses need not be regarded as symbols. They are not representations of anything, and they are not the vehicles of thought. They are just ways of linking representations to each other. Context sensitivity does not require the introduction of amodal representations. The dynamic character of perceptual representations is consistent with the spirit of classical empiricism.

Turn now to the second way in which the present proposal seems to depart from classical empiricist approaches. I said that concepts contain both perceptual representations and motor representations. Locke and Hume emphasized inputs, not outputs. But allowing for motor representations in conceptualization preserves the spirit of the classical view. First of all, Locke and Hume do use the term "sensation" to include experiences of the acting body. Locke invokes the felt body in explaining how we acquire concepts of *solidity* and *power*. The experience of motor command may be mediated by input systems, such as kinesthesia, proprioception, and haptic touch. These senses allow one to bring the motoric into the purview of the senses. Second, the division between input systems and outputs systems may be blurrier than Locke and Hume had realized. Consider Milner and Goodale's (1995) account of the dorsal visual action system. On one reading of their data, the visual system can sense the affordances of an object. Vision can be action-guiding. If Locke and Hume had a complete theory of perception at their disposal, they would have appreciated this fact and incorporated it into their theory. Third, the main thrust of empiricism is the denial of an amodal code. Motor representations are not amodal. To include these representations among our conceptual building blocks is no concession to rationalism. Classical empiricists neglected the active body, and that was a serious oversight, but one can bring the body back in without abandoning the basic ideas that were driving Locke and Hume. Embodied empiricism is a natural outgrowth of classical empiricism.

The embodied empiricist theory that I want to defend can be broken down into three core hypotheses:

1. Concepts serve as tools for tracking categories.
2. The concept for a given category will be implemented by different representations on different occasions.
3. Those representations are stored records (or combinations of stored records) of perceptual states and/or motor commands.

The first hypothesis is defended by Millikan (2000) and Prinz (2002). The other two, which follow naturally from the first, have been defended by Barsalou (1987, 1999) and Prinz (2002). All three have roots in the classical British empiricists of Great Britain. The third hypothesis is what makes the theory recognizably empiricist. It echoes the Humean credo that ideas all derive from impressions.

Empirical Support for Empiricism

In the preceding section, I offered a theoretical argument for empiricism. If we consider what concepts are for, it is natural to suppose that they are built up from stored perceptual-motor states. But theoretical arguments require confirmation in the lab. Is there any empirical support for Hypothesis 3? Every chapter in this volume testifies to an affirmative answer. I will mention a few important finding here.

On the face of it, empiricism may seem incompatible with evidence from neuroscience. There are polymodal association areas of the brain that are thought to contain amodal symbols. These areas receive inputs from multiple sensory modalities, and they are especially prevalent in frontal cortex, which is associated with higher cognition. Do such findings refute concept empiricism? I don't think so. While these areas play a role in higher cognition, they do not function alone. Damasio (1989) has argued that polymodal association areas are "convergence zones" that serve to reactivate modality specific areas during cognitive tasks (see also Warrington & McCarthy 1983; Simmons & Barsalou, 2003). They store records about what sensory states were concurrently active during prior encounters with objects and events. Cognitive tasks require the reactivation of those sensory records. This is consistent with empiricism.

Barsalou and his colleagues have amassed a body of evidence that is consistent with convergence zone theory (see Simmons & Barsalou, 2003, for a review). Some of that evidence comes from neuroimaging. Simmons et al. (2003) conducted an fMRI study in which subjects were asked to confirm whether members of a category can have certain properties (e.g., "can leaves be rustling?"). Outside of the scanner, the categories and properties were rated for the extent to which they are experienced in each of five sense modality and the extent to which they are associated with motor response. For example, experiences of leaves might be rated as highly visual, somewhat auditory, and largely nonolfactory. These ratings were then correlated with brain activity in sensory specific areas. The category and property sensory ratings had an 0.7 correlation with activity in sensory areas, and explained almost 50% of the variance. These results show that property verification tasks cause spontaneous activation in modality-specific brain areas, and those activations can be predicted by the perceptual profile of the category. Other researchers have obtained similar results (see Martin & Chao, 2001). Chao, Haxby, and Martin (1999) found that the same modality-specific areas of the brain are active when subjects recognize pictures of a category and when they read the name. Chao and Martin (2000) found brain activation in areas associated with motor response when subjects viewed pictures of tools.

Barsalou and colleagues have also found behavioral evidence in support of empiricism. For example, Pecher et al. (2003) gave subjects a property verification task, in which they need to confirm whether or not a named feature is true of a named category. Subjects would answer "yes" to LEAVES-rustling and "no" to CARNATION-black. All of the features were colors, sounds, or other observable qualities. Pecher et al. wanted to know if these features were represented using an amodal code or a modality specific code. They reasoned that if subjects were reactivating sensory states to perform the task, there should be a temporal cost to shifting from a feature in one modality to a feature in another. This is just what they found. In performing conceptual tasks, subjects apparently reengaged perceptual representations. Category names also seem to engage motor responses. For example, Spivey et al. (2000) found that subjects tended to look up when they heard stories about tall buildings, and they tended to look down when they heard about canyons.

I think that the evidence for perceptual/motor grounding is very strong. Rather than utilizing purely amodal representations, we seem to call up perceptual features and action commands when we perform conceptual tasks. This suggests that concepts are collections of perceptual and behavioral features that are reactivated "off-line" in thought. But one might think these findings are limited to concrete concepts, i.e., concepts of objects and relations that we can readily observe. There has been comparatively little investigation of empiricist accounts of abstract concepts. Abstract concepts pose a significant challenge. If conceptual tasks reactivate perceptual states, then perceptual states must be reactivated when we use abstract concepts. That sounds bizarre. By definition, abstract concepts do not designate observable things. What perceptual features could possibly be involved?

MORAL CONCEPTS

Emotions in Moral Cognition

Abstract concepts are too varied to consider collectively in one paper. My strategy here will be to consider one class of abstract concept within an empiricist framework. These are the moral concepts. More specifically, I want to consider the fundamental concepts of (morally) *good* and *bad*.

When we say that something is morally bad, we do not seem to be commenting on its appearance. We are not suggesting that it looks or tastes a particular way. There is an obvious retort to this. Moral truths reside not in the world, but in us. They are evaluations, not observations. This is, in a certain sense, exactly right, but it only highlights the problem. How can empiricism accommodate judgments that are not observationally grounded? The answer is that moral judgments are observationally grounded. They are grounded in observations of ourselves. To judge that something is morally bad is to recognize an aversive response to it. Morally relevant events cause emotional responses in us. We recognize that some event is morally significant by emotionally reacting to it in a particular way or by recognizing that it is similar to events that have stirred our emotions on other occasions. Emotions, I will suggest, are perceptions of our bodily states. To recognize the moral value of an event is, thus, to perceive the perturbation that it causes.

Minus the bit about the body, this is essentially what Hume (1739) proposed. He said that to judge that something is morally bad is to experience disapprobation, and to judge something good is to experience approbation. The resources of contemporary psychology provide an opportunity to build on Hume's suggestion. First, we know a lot more about emotions now, and second, we have tools for testing whether Hume's proposal is descriptively accurate.

The terms "approbation" and "disapprobation" are really just place-holders. It is unlikely that they name particular discrete emotions. There is no distinctive feeling of moral disapproval or approval. Recent evidence suggests that moral emotions may vary as a function of the forms of conduct that elicit them. This is most evident in the case of negative moral judgments. When we judge that an act is morally bad, the emotional experience depends on the nature of the act.

A striking demonstration of this owes to Rozin et al. (1999), who extended the work of Shweder et al. (1997). Shweder et al. had argued that moral rules fall into three different categories. Some involve autonomy. These are rules that pertain to individuals and their rights. Prohibitions against harming or stealing are autonomy prohibitions, because they are affronts to the rights of individuals. Other moral rules involve community. These pertain to the social order, including issues of ranking within a social hierarchy. Disrespect for the elderly, for social superiors, and for public property are all crimes against community. Finally, there are moral rules pertaining to what Shweder et al. call "divinity." These rules, which are less prevalent in secular societies, involve the divine order. Crimes of religious impurity are the paradigm cases of divinity rule violations. In secular societies, there are residual rules of divinity. Many of these concern sexual propriety. To engage in bestiality, for example, makes one impure. We tend to think of some acts as "unnatural." In general, I think rules of divinity can be thought of as rules that protect the natural order. Unnatural acts may not harm individuals or community resource; they are an affront to nature itself.

Rozin et al. used this taxonomy to determine whether violates of different kinds of rules elicits different emotions. They presented subjects with descriptions of a variety of different kinds of morally questionable conduct and asked them to report how they would feel towards the perpetrators. The pattern of responses was robust. Subjects were angered by those who violated autonomy rules, contemptuous towards those who committed crimes against community, and disgusted by those who committed divinity transgressions (such as people who performed deviant sexual acts). They conclude that there is a mapping from transgression-types to emotional responses. They call this the CAD Hypothesis, for Community/Contempt, Autonomy/Anger, and Divinity/Disgust.

Rozin et al.'s finding might be extended in a variety of ways. They show that emotions vary as a function of transgression-types. It is also quite clear that emotions vary as a function of who commits the transgression. In their study, the perpetrators are strangers. What happens when the perpetrator is the self? I think there are likely to be systematic interactions between transgression- and transgressor-type. If you violate an autonomy rule, you may feel guilty. If you violate a rule of community, you may be more likely to feel ashamed. When you violate a divinity rule, you may feel a combination of shame and self-directed disgust. There may also be affects of victim identity in the case of autonomy and community norms. If a stranger is the victim of a transgression, reactions may be less intense than if the self or a loved one is a victim. I would guess, however, that these differences are more quantitative that qualitative. It seems to be a distinctive feature of morality that we respond emotionally in cases in which we are not involved. This is the third-party nature of moral response. I am angry if one stranger harms another, even if I am unaffected.

The preceding observations can be summarized by saying that moral disapproval takes on various forms. It is context sensitive. The same may be true for moral approbation. We may feel gratitude or admiration when a stranger does something good, and we might feel pride or self-righteousness when we do good ourselves. Disapprobation and approbation refer to ranges of emotions. In a word, they are "sentiments." Sentiments can be defined as dispositions to experience different emotions in different contexts (Prinz, 2004). For example, the sentiment of liking ice cream may involve feeling happiness when ice cream is obtained, sadness when it is unavailable, and craving when it comes to mind. Disapprobation and approbation are sentiments that can be defined as dispositions to experience various different emotions as a function of context.

The Rozin et al. study goes some way toward supporting this theory. It shows that people naturally and systematically associate emotions with moral transgressions. Further evidence for the role of emotions in moral conceptualization can be found elsewhere. Haidt et al. (unpublished manuscript) asked subjects to indicate whether they found certain forms of conduct morally objectionable. For example, they asked subjects to imagine a situation in which a brother and sister engage in consensual incest using effective birth control. When subjects report that this is wrong, they ask them to justify that evaluation. It turns out that people have difficulty providing reasons, and when reasons are provided they can easily be short circuited. When subjects reply that incest can lead to birth defects, the experimenters remind them that birth control was used. Eventually subjects give up on reasons and declare that incest is "just wrong," or wrong because it is disgusting. Emotions seem to drive their judgments. I suspect that much the same results would be obtained if subjects were asked about murder rather than incest. If asked why murder is wrong, it would be hard to provide an answer. If pushed, one might contrive to say that murder is wrong because it violates the victim's rights, but it would be hard for most people to articulate why it is wrong to violate rights, much less explain what rights are or where they come from. Some people might say that murder is wrong because one wouldn't want to be killed oneself, but this answer only explains why it's prudent to illegalize murder. Moreover, those who appeal to their own well-being when they justify prohibitions against murder are implicitly appealing to their emotions. We all think, "If someone tried to kill *me*, I would be outraged." Trained philosophers may be able to provide reasons for moral claims, but untrained moral reasoning seems to be emotionally grounded.

Further evidence for this conclusion comes from the literature on moral development (see Eisenberg, 2000, for review). The most effective means of training children to be moral are parental love withdrawal, power assertion, and the induction of sympathy through drawing attention to the consequences of action (Hoffman, 2000). All of these methods affect a child's emotional state. Love withdrawal is especially effective. It induces sadness in children by convincing them that they may lose the affection and support of their caregivers. Elsewhere I have argued that this becomes the foundation for guilt (Prinz, 2003). Guilt is a species of sadness directed at one's own transgressions. Eventually the sadness induced by love withdrawal is transferred to the action, and we become sad about what we have done, rather than being sad about the consequences. This transfer can be driven in part by mechanisms as simple as classical conditioning. Other moral emotions may be learned by emulating adults and by having experiences as the victim of moral transgressions. If a child is physically harmed by another child, anger is a natural result. Moral disgust can be transmitted by parental displays of disgust, bolstered perhaps by fear induction. Moral disgust is most likely to be inducible in the context of actions that involve the body, because it derives from nonmoral disgust, which is evolved to protect against contamination of the body (Rozin et al., 1993).

The claim that emotions are central to moral development and moral judgment is consistent with findings from neuropsychology. There is evidence that early injuries in areas of the brain associated with the top-down regulation of emotional response (ventromedial prefrontal cortex) lead to antisocial behavior (Anderson et al., 1999). There is also at least one documented case of antisocial behavior resulting from a ventromedial injury in adulthood (Blair & Cipolotto, 2000). These findings suggest that emotional impairments compromise moral cognition. Neuroimaging studies with healthy subjects are consistent with these results (see Greene & Haidt, 2002, for a review). Greene et al. (2001), for example, found that emotional centers of the brain were active when subjects were presented with moral dilemmas (e.g., "Would you kill one person in order to save five?"). Key areas were the superior temporal sulcus, posterior cingulate, and medial frontal gyrus. The authors found that these centers were especially active when subjects imagined themselves directly and physically harming another person, but emotional centers were engaged during all moral reasoning tasks. Moll et al. (2002) gave subjects a series of sentences describing events that were either morally significant, nonmoral but emotional, or neutral. The moral sentences, as compared to the neutral, caused greater activation in structures associated with emotional response (superior temporal sulcus, the temporal pole, and orbitofrontal cortex). The nonmoral emotional sentences caused activation in a different range of areas, but this may be a consequence of the fact that they elicited emotions that do not overlap significantly with the moral emotions evoked in the study. Many of the moral sentences concerned harms or injustices, whereas the nonmoral emotional sentences tended to concern things that are physically disgusting. On the CAD hypothesis, harm and injustice elicit anger, rather than disgust. In any case, the core finding of the study was clear. Moral cognition elicits activation in structures associated with emotion.

Future research is needed to determine which brain structures underlie which aspect of moral experience. The structures identified in the Moll et al. study overlap only partially with the structures identified by Greene et al. Different structures may be involved in different kinds of tasks. Careful work distinguishing different kinds of transgressions is also likely to reveal variable responses in the brain. These early studies support the view that emotions contribute to moral judgments.

Emotions Embodied

Hume endorsed the hypothesis that moral concepts are emotionally grounded. He claimed that it was consistent with empiricism. There is, however, an important objection that must be addressed. So far I have just been assuming that empiricists can regard emotions as primitive mental states on a par with perceptions and motor responses. The assumption is open to challenge. Many psychologists assume that emotions are actually cognitive in nature, comprised of complex, and highly structured appraisals (see review in Roseman et al., 1990). Some of these appraisals are even presumed to be moral in nature. For example, anger is associated with the appraisal that there has been an offense against me (Lazarus, 1991). Offense is a moral concept. An offense is a wrong or a violation of rights. If anger comprises a judgment pertaining to offense, then offensive cannot itself be defined in terms of anger. Moreover, empiricists cannot hope to accommodate abstract concepts by appeal to emotions if emotions themselves implicate abstract concepts. The attempt to reduce moral concepts to emotions presupposes that emotions are noncognitive in some sense.

Fortunately, I think that presupposition is defensible. I defend a noncognitive theory more fully elsewhere (Prinz, 2004). I argue that appraisal theories make it too difficult to have an emotion. They suppose that anger requires a concept of offense. It is unlikely that young children and animals have a concept of offense, and it is unlikely that brain structures involved in the elicitation of emotions harbor such concepts (Zajonc, 1984; LeDoux, 1996).

If emotions are not cognitive, what are they? The theory I prefer is a version of the James–Lange theory, which has also be defended by Damasio (James, 1884; Lange, 1885; Damasio, 1994; Prinz, 2004). On this approach, emotions are perceptions of changes in one's bodily state. When matters of concern arise our bodies change in systematic ways. The perception of a patterned bodily response is an emotion. In many cases, the bodily responses are triggered by simple perceptual cues. The response we call fear can be triggered by a loud noise or a sudden loss of support; anger can be triggered by a physical attack or even a glare; sadness can be caused by separation from a loved one; joy can be caused by achieving a goal; and so on. Over development, new emotion elicitors are learned, and they can become increasingly abstract, but in each case, I would maintain, the elicitor can be grounded in sensory states.

If emotions are perceptions of bodily changes caused by perceptions of things that concern us, then emotions are perceptions in a straightforward sense. To have an emotion is to perceive one's body. In this respect, emotions are just like sights, sounds, or smells. This is an improvement over Hume. He could never quite reconcile emotions with his contention that concepts have perceptual grounding. He thought that emotions were not perceptions, in the ordinary sense, but rather perceptions of perceptions. This is a rather obscure idea, and an inelegant feature of Hume's program. The James–Lange view brings emotions into line with other sensory states.

Emotions also have an intimate connection with action. The bodily patterns associated with the emotions are not arbitrary. In anger, fists tighten to facilitate acts of aggression. In fear, blood flows to the limbs, enabling a flight response. In sadness, the body tends to become heavy and prevents us from continuing activities that may be futile after a loss. In disgust, our bodies attempt to expel contaminants, and withdraw from sources of contamination. Even facial expressions may be regarded as instrumental actions. Most obviously, they communicate how we are disposed to act (Fridlund, 1994). They may also serve other purposes. Teeth bearing in anger allows biting. The wide eyes of surprise make it easier to see the source of surprise elicitation. In short, emotions are perceptions of the body's actions and preparations for action. Emotions are embodied in a very strong sense: they are perceptions of the body, and they bear a direct connection to action (for more on the embodied nature of emotions, see Glenberg et al., Chapter 6, this volume).

The relation between emotion and action may put some pressure on the traditional James–Lange view. Both James and Lange argue that actions precede emotions, and that emotions are perceptions of actions. This means that emotions are passive. They do not cause us to act. I think this picture may be correct, but it is tempting to put things the other way. Perhaps emotions are inner action commands, which orchestrate changes in the body. Emotional feelings would still be perceptions of bodily changes, on this view, but emotional feelings would be distinguished from the emotions themselves. The idea would be to identify emotions with action commands, and emotion feelings with perceptions of the bodily changes brought about by such commands. The picture is close to the ideas found in LeDoux's (1996) work. LeDoux emphasizes the role of the amygdala, which can be regarded as a body control center. The picture also relates to Ekman's (1972) proposal that emotions are "affect programs," and to Frijda's (1986) equation of emotions and "action tendencies."

If these authors are right, then the James–Lange theory gets things backwards. It emphasizes body perception, where it should emphasize body control. It's not clear how to decide between these options. Are emotions perceptions or commands? Inputs or outputs? Fortunately, such questions may be based on a false dichotomy. It is possible that emotions are both perceptions and commands. That is to say, there may be mental states that serve a dual function of regulating the body and perceiving changes in the body. There is good reason to think that perception and control are tightly coupled, in any case. In order to affectively regulate body change, the current state of the body must be registered. Regulation requires registration. Thus, input and output systems may be heavily connected. Moreover, the very same cell populations may be involved in both of these processes. The primate brain contains cells that are involved in both the perception and the control of molar actions, such as grasping (e.g., Gallese et al., 1996). These mirror neurons probably aren't involved in emotions, but emotions may be underwritten by cells that function in a similar way. It is possible that there are also cells that both perceive and control changes in our visceral organs, facial expressions, and other bodily states. There is preliminary evidence consistent with this possibility. Anterior cingulated cortex is active during both the perception and control of visceral organs (Critchley et al., 2000), and second somatosensory cortex is involved in both the perception and control of emotional expressions (Adolphs et al., 2000). We don't know yet if individual cells in these regions are doing double duty, but we do know that these regions are consistently implicated in neuroimaging studies of emotion (Damasio et al., 2000). If emotion circuits contain cells that behave like mirror neurons, the James–Lange theory will collapse into action control theory associated with other authors. Ruling in favor of this possibility is premature. In the remainder of this discussion, I will assume that that the James–Lange theory is correct, but I leave the more enactive theory on the table as a live possibility. Either way, emotion and action are closely related. Let me return now to the issue of emotions and morality.

If moral concepts are emotionally grounded, we should expect a link between moral judgment and behavior. Moral anger should be associated with aggression, moral disgust should be associated with withdrawal, and guilt should lead to a general reduction in behavioral activation. These connections stand in need of empirical investigation, but they enjoy immense anecdotal support. We aggress against those who violate our rights, we shun those who morally disgust us, and we become submissive when we feel guilty.

Good and Bad

The view that I have been sketching can be summarized as follows. The concepts of moral *good* and *bad* are sentiments; sentiments are dispositions to experience different emotions on different occasions; and emotions are perceptions of the body's preparation for action. This aligns with the empiricist theory of concepts outlined above. According to that theory, concepts are tools for tracking categories, they are highly variable, and they are stored records of perceptual-motor states. Let me consider these theses in reverse order.

The contention that moral concepts are perceptual-motor records follows immediately from the contention that moral concepts are emotionally grounded. Emotions are perceptual states. The contention that moral concepts are variable follows from the fact that they are sentiments. A sentiment is a disposition, but, on any particular occasion when a moral judgment is formed the disposition may be realized by one of its constitutive emotions. When I judge that it was bad of me to take the last cookie, I feel guilty. When I judge that it was bad of you to take the last cookie, I feel angry. Both of these affective responses are instances of the same concept. They are unified by the fact that they belong to the same underlying sentiment towards cookie hoarding. The sentiment itself can be implemented by a long-term memory structure that generates moral emotions in a context-sensitive way.

What about the first tenet of the brand of empiricism that I favor? Is there any sense in which emotionally grounded moral concepts can be regarded as tools for tracking categories? What categories might those be? The natural answer is that moral concepts track good and bad things. The category of good things consists of forms of conduct, character traits, individuals, and events that are good. Likewise for the category of bad things. Moral concepts have the function of tracking these categories. Someone with successful moral concepts will judge that some form of conduct is good in just those cases when the conduct in question really is good.

Here a philosophical question arises. What makes something good or bad? The answer that I favor is a version of what philosophers call a "sensibility theory" of value (Prinz, forthcoming; see also Wiggins, 1987; McDowell, 1985). Something is good (or bad) just in case we are disposed to have a positive (or negative) moral sentiment toward it upon careful reflection. The clause about careful reflection is important. We often develop moral sentiments toward things that would not elicit those sentiments if we had more information at our disposal. Attitudes toward the moral value of a particular foreign policy decision, for example, might change if we knew all the facts or if we had less personal interest in seeing our own nations prosper. When we judge that something is moral, we are expressing our sentiments, but we are also implying that those sentiments would remain after careful consideration. Once again, this is an informal observation of moral behavior, not an experimental result. It would be worth investigating in the lab. It seems that moral concepts are, in this respect, like concepts of natural kinds. We believe that we can be mistaken when we make a moral judgment. We can be duped by appearances. A case may appear morally bad on initial consideration, and then appear good on further reflection (or vice versa). If this analysis is correct, then moral concepts are in the business of tracking those things that evoke our moral emotions up reflection, rather than that those things that evoke our knee-jerk reactions.

The Role of Reason

The suggestion that reliable moral judgments depend on reflection may give the impression that morality is based on reason, rather than passion. That would be a mistake. Reason has an important role in moral judgment, but it is an auxiliary role. The story goes like this. Each of us has a set of basic moral values. These are things that we do not defend by proving reasons. They are things that we feel passionately about, and things that we find it difficult to question. The badness of killing or stealing or molesting may be examples. We do not believe that killing is bad for any reason. It is moral bedrock, implemented by our emotional responses. If we tried to defend our conviction, we would get flustered or we would generate reasons post hoc. But, in addition to our basic moral values, we have many derived moral values. These, I would argue, are dependent on reason. Suppose we believe that it is immoral to trade with a country that is guilty of human rights violations. This judgment is probably not basic. The alleged badness stems from the fact that trading with such a country promotes injustice in some way. But one can have a purely reason-based debate about whether it really does promote injustice. Emotions need not be involved.

On this model, much moral deliberation will be a two stage process. When we consider a case we must use reason to decide whether it involves something toward which we have a basic moral value. Then the basic moral value determines our moral response. We reason that a trade agreement promotes cruelty, and then our sentiments dictate that cruelty is morally bad. The role of careful reflection in moral judgment generally concerns the first stage of this process. On an empiricist account, this reasoning process will typically involve perceptual simulation and imagination. We may envision a novel scenario and judge how similar it is to a scenario that we have already formed a moral judgment about. In some cases, we may bypass perceptual simulation by means of verbal knowledge. Perhaps we read somewhere that trade embargoes against despotic nations has no statistical impact on human rights abuses. Reasoning verbally can help us draw a moral conclusion. This kind of reasoning, which is undoubtedly widespread, is a convenient shorthand for simulation. If asked what is a "despot," we would eventually have to translate the word into images of exemplars or characteristic despotic behaviors.

Where Do Moral Concepts Come From?

If basic moral values are the product of sentiment, rather than reason, then they probably originate in a process other than rational deliberation. Some basic moral values may have their seeds in biology. We may be innately empathetic towards members of our species, for example. But such innate sentiments fall short of true moral rules. We naturally squirm at the sight of another person in pain, but that does not mean we are innately programmed to feel guilt when we are cruel. Guilt may be a learned response. Rats are disturbed when they see other rats in distress, but they do not feel guilty, and they do not have moral rules (Church, 1959). One difference between us and rats is that we have the capacity to put our selves in others' shoes. When a rat sees another rat suffering, the misery it experiences is egocentric. When we see another person suffering, we become concerned *for that person*. At the collective level, this leads human societies to develop rules that protect self and other alike. These rules are transmitted through threat of punishment, including social ostracism. That threat leads us to feel guilt about doing harm to others, not just empathetic distress. Once created, moral rules take on a life of their own, and they can be used to regulate many different kinds of conduct.

On the picture that I am describing, morality is a human cultural artifact. It is a system that we have devised to coordinate behavior. This means that morality is culturally informed. We acquire moral sentiments as a result of moral training (love, withdrawal, punishment, and so on). The way we are trained reflects the values that have been developed within our culture. Any adequate study of moral cognition must therefore take culture into account.

Examples of cultural variation in morality are easy to come by. In ancient Greece and modern China, infanticide was considered acceptable. In contemporary Euro-American culture, it is treated as murder. In many societies polygamy has been norm. In ours, departures from monogamy are frowned on. In some most societies, brother-sister incest is a serious taboo. In Ptolemaic Egypt, as many as 20% of Greek immigrants may have been married to their siblings. In modern industrialized societies, cannibalism is considered among the most horrific of all possible crimes. In chiefdoms, it has been widely practices, and in Aztec Mexico, thousands of people were probably cannibalized every year. Various historical and material factors can contribute to explaining these substantive differences (Prinz, forthcoming).

Cultural variables are also reflected in the aforementioned work on Shweder's typology of moral rules. Some cultures evidently emphasize one class of rules over another. Our own culture tends to emphasize rules of autonomy. In Orrisa India, rules of divinity are much more entrenched (Shweder et al., 1997). Being pure, in the way proscribed by local religious customs, is a dominant moral value. The many subcultures found in the West tend also to have views about purity, but these may take on different forms and they may be less central in driving behavior and less powerful in eliciting emotional response.

These examples provide strong support for descriptive moral relativism: The thesis that cultures have distinct moral values. This is not the same as metaethical moral relativism: the view that no set of moral values has a unique claim to truth. Metaethical moral relativism does not follow from descriptive moral relativism. Perhaps, of the many moralities in the world, one is right and the others are wrong. I doubt this very much. If moral concepts are based on learned emotional responses, then it is hard to see what the criterion for correct application of moral concepts is beyond conformity to the local norms. On the face of it, this is a very disturbing picture that threatens deeply held moral convictions. Our most central values may be historical constructs. On the other hand, it opens up the door for moral improvement. If moral rules are artifacts, created by us to coordinate behavior, then we can revise them. We can come up with better ways (healthier, happier, more stable ways) of getting along. Morality is a work in progress, and received values can be revised. This possibility has proven to be very valuable over the course of the last century, in which attitudes toward women, religious and ethnic minorities, have transformed.

Other Moral Concepts

I have been presenting an analysis of the fundamental moral concepts, *good* and *bad*. To judge that something is *good* (or *bad*) is to believe that on reflection it would be recognized as an example of something toward which one harbors a context sensitive, culturally informed moral sentiment. In actual processing, such judgments are typically implemented by a more or less immediate emotional responses, but those responses can be modified, at an individual or cultural level, over time.

Good and *bad* are not the only moral concepts, of course. Other examples include: *right* and *wrong, justice, obligation, permission, entitlement,* and *responsibility* – just to name a few. There are also concepts that may not be initially recognized as moral, but have a moral dimension. The concept of *courage,* of being a *person,* and of *ownership* are all examples. I suspect that the forgoing analysis of *good* and *bad* will offer the resources needed to make progress on these concepts within an empiricist framework. This is not the place to analyze more moral concepts, but I want to conclude with a few brief remarks on *ownership* to illustrate the point.

Jackendoff (1992: chapter 3) offers an extended critique of those who attempt to show that abstract concepts can be derived from sensory-motor concepts. His main foil is Lakoff (1987), who characterizes abstract concepts as metaphorical extensions of spatial concepts. Jackendoff uses *ownership* as a test case. Verbs relating to ownership use adverbs and prepositions. We give things *away*, we take *from*, we have *in* our possession, and so forth. This might lead one to think that ownership is a metaphorical extension of these spatial concepts. Cognitive grammarians have also emphasized the notion of containment, which is thought to be represented using a schematic image of one object inside of another. Ownership might be regarded as a metaphorical extension of containment. Jackendoff argues that this is not the case. He notes that understanding spatial relations is not sufficient for understanding ownership. Something that belongs to me can be in your hands, for example. No combination of spatial primitives explains what it means to own something. Jackendoff concludes that *ownership* has no sensory basis. He says that some concept of *ownership* must be innate.

I agree that *ownership* is not a spatial concept (though spatial proximity is often a cue to who owns what). But that does not mean it lacks a sensory-motor foundation. The approach that I have been sketching offers a much more promising avenue for explaining *ownership* in empiricist terms. Observe some of the ways in which ownership relations are emotionally regulated. If I own an object, I may get angry at you if you use it without asking me first. I will not feel guilty about getting angry and I would expect others to get angry in the same situation. I will feel satisfied if you are punished for using the object, and I may get angry at bystanders who do not share my anger at you for what you have done. The pattern of emotions and practices of permission-giving distinguish owning an object from merely wanting an object. What I want to suggest is that the concept of ownership is not merely associated with patterns, it is constituted by such patterns.

Ownership involves two things. First, there is a set of behavioral practices in which one agent uses an object or resource freely, and any others who wish to use it must ask for permission. Second, there is a set of sentiments that enforce these practices. Our concept of ownership includes behavioral scenarios and underlying emotions. The concept can be explained in sensory-motor terms, and I see no reason for thinking that it must be innate. A caregiver may punish a child for using her sibling's toy without asking first. In this simple act, the caregiver teaches the child a practice and applies a moral sentiment to violations of that practice. This can provide a foundation for the concept of *ownership*, and it does not require nativist commitments. Jackendoff says that *ownership* is a good candidate for an innate concept, because it seems to be universal. It is important, however, to resist inferences from universality to innateness. All societies face distribution problems. It is valuable for all societies to develop emotionally enforced practices that determine who can use what. The emergence of ownership concepts across the globe is, therefore, hardly surprising.

These remarks are not intended as a complete account of the concept of ownership. They are intended as an advertisement for a promising strategy for explaining abstract concepts in the moral domain. Concepts that may seem hopeless distant from perceptual experience may have a perceptual basis in our patterns of emotional response.

CONCLUSIONS

This chapter began with an overview of an empiricist theory of concepts. Empiricism is having a resurgence because evidence from psychology and cognitive neuroscience suggest that concepts may be grounded in perceptual-motor states. But empiricism cannot get past the starting gate if it cannot accommodate abstract concepts. Abstract concepts come in many forms. My goal here has been to examine one class of examples. Moral concepts pose a serious challenge for empiricism. Goodness and badness do not seem to be observable properties. Two wrongs don't look alike. Hume's solution was to explain good and bad not by appeal to external perception, but by appeal to inner perception. Two wrongs are unified by the emotions that they incite in us. I have sketched an updated version of Hume's story. I recommended a Jamesian theory of emotion according to which emotions are perceptions of the body's preparation for action. I surveyed recent evidence for the claim that moral concepts are emotionally grounded. A complete elaboration and defense must be taken up elsewhere (Prinz, forthcoming). Hopefully, I have shown that such research is worth pursuing. Emotions may play some role in explaining other abstract concepts, especially evaluative concepts and concepts regulating social interaction. Other classes of abstract concepts must be explained using different resources (see Prinz, 2002, for some strategies). Mathematical concepts, for example, are unlikely to be grounded in emotion. If empiricism is to be fully defended, each class of abstract concepts must be grounded in perceptual-motor states. Every time a class is of abstract concept is explained in this way, a barrier in the path of empiricism is removed. In this chapter, hope to have contributed to eroding one of those barriers.[1]

---

[1] I owe thanks to Larry Barsalou for discussion of recent research on perceptual grounding and to Geoff-Sayre McCord for discussion of moral psychology. I am also very much indebted to the editors and to two anonymous referees.

References

Adolphs, R., Damasio, H., Tranel, D., Cooper, G., & Damasio, A. R. (2000). A role for somatosensory cortices in the visual recognition of emotion as revealed by three-dimensional lesion mapping. *Journal of Neuroscience 20*, 2683–2690.

Anderson, S. W., Bechara, A., Damasio, H., Tranel, D., & Damasio, A. (1999). Impairment of social and moral behaviour related to early damage in human prefrontal cortex. *Nature Neuroscience 2*, 1032–1037.

Barsalou, L. W. (1987). The instability of graded structure: Implications for the nature of concepts. In U. Neisser (Ed.), *Concepts and Conceptual Development: Ecological and Intellectual Factors in Categorization*. Cambridge: Cambridge University Press.

Barsalou, L. W. (1999). Perceptual symbol systems. *Behavioral and Brain Sciences 22*, 577–609.

Blair, R. J. R., & Cipolotti, L. (2000). Impaired social response reversal – A case of "acquired sociopathy." *Brain 123*, 1122–1141.

Chao, L. L., & Haxby, J. V., Martin, A. (1999). Attribute-based neural substrates in temporal cortex for perceiving and knowing about objects. *Nature Neuroscience 2*, 913–919.

Chao, L. L., & Martin, A. (2000). Representation of manipulable manmade objects in the dorsal stream. *NeuroImage 12*, 478–484.

Church, R. M. (1959). Emotional reactions of rats to the pain of others. *Journal of Comparative & Physiological Psychology 52*: 132–134.

Critchley H. D., Cornfield D. R., Chandler M. P., Mathias C. J., & Dolan R. J. (2000). Cerebral correlates of autonomic cardiovascular arousal: A functional neuroimaging investigation in humans. *Journal of Physiology 523*, 259–270.

Damasio, A. R. (1989). Time-locked multiregional retroactivation: A systems-level proposal for the neural substrates of recall and recognition. *Cognition 33*, 25–62.

Damasio, A. R. (1994). *Descartes' Error: Emotion Reason and the Human Brain*. New York: Gossett/Putnam.

Damasio, A. R., Grabowski, T. J., Bechara, A., Damasio, H., Ponto, L. L. B. Parvizi, J., & Hichwa, R. D. (2000). Subcortical and cortical brain activity during the feeling of self-generated emotions. *Nature Neuroscience 3*, 1049–1056.

Ekman, P. (1972). *Emotions in the Human Face*. New York: Pergamon Press.

Eisenberg, N. (2000). Emotion, regulation, and moral development. *Annual Review of Psychology 51*, 665–697.

Fodor, J. A. (2004). Having concepts: A brief refutation of the twentieth century. *Mind and Language*.

Fridlund, A. (1994). *Human Facial Expression: An Evolutionary View*. San Diego, CA: Academic Press.

Frijda, N. H. (1986). *The Emotions*. Cambridge: Cambridge University Press.

Gallese, V., Faddiga, L., Fogassi, L., & Rizzolatti, G. (1996). Action recognition in the premotor cortex. *Brain 119*, 593–609.

Gibson, J. J. (1979). *The Ecological Approach to Visual Perception*. Boston: Houghton Mifflin.

Greene, J., & Haidt, J. (2002). How (and where) does moral judgment work? *Trends in Cognitive Science 6*, 517–523.

Greene, J. D., Sommerville, R. B., Nystrom, L. E., Darley, J. M., & Cohen, J. D. (2001). An fMRI investigation of emotional engagement in moral judgment. *Science 293*, 2105–2108.

Haidt, J., Bjorklund, F., & Murphy, S. (in preparation). Moral dumbfounding: When intuition finds no reason.

Hoffman, M. L. (2000). *Empathy and Moral Development: Implications for Caring and Justice.* New York: Cambridge University Press.

Hume, D. (1739/1978). *A Treatise of Human Nature.* P. H. Nidditch (Ed.). Oxford: Oxford University Press.

Jackendoff, R. (1992). *Languages of the Mind.* Cambridge, MA: MIT Press.

James, W. (1884). What is an emotion? *Mind 9*, 188–205.

Lakoff, G. (1987). *Women, Fire, and Dangerous Things: What Categories Reveal about the Mind.* Chicago: Chicago University Press.

Lange, C. G. (1885). Om sindsbevaegelser: et psyko-fysiologisk studie. Kjbenhavn: Jacob Lunds. Reprinted in *The Emotions.* C. G. Lange & W. James (Eds.), I. A. Haupt (Trans.) Baltimore: Williams and Wilkins Company, 1922.

Lazarus, R. S. (1991). *Emotion and Adaptation.* New York: Oxford University Press.

LeDoux J. E. (1996). *The Emotional Brain.* New York: Simon and Schuster.

Martin, A., & Chao, L. L. (2001). Semantic memory and the brain: Structure and processes. *Current Opinion in Neurobiology 11*, 194–201.

McDowell J. (1985) Values and secondary qualities. In T. Honderich (Ed.), *Morality and Objectivity: A Tribute to J. L. Mackie* (pp. 110–129). London: Routledge.

Millikan, R. G. (2000). *On Clear and Confused Ideas: An Essay about Substance Concepts.* Cambridge: Cambridge University Press.

Milner, A. D., & Goodale, M. A. (1995). *The Visual Brain in Action.* Oxford: Oxford University Press.

Moll, J., de Oliveira-Souza, R., Eslinger, P. J., Bramati, I. E, Mourao-Miranda, J., Andreiuolo P., & Pessoa, L. (2002). The neural correlates of moral sensitivity: A functional magnetic resonance imaging investigation of basic and moral emotions. *Journal of Neuroscience 22*, 2730–2736

Murphy, G. L., & D. L. Medin (1985). The role of theories in conceptual coherence. *Psychological Review 92*, 289–316.

Pecher, D., Zeelenberg, R., & Barsalou, L. W. (2003). Verifying different-modality properties for concepts produces switching costs. *Psychological Science 14*, 119–124.

Prinz, J. J. (2002). *Furnishing the Mind: Concepts and Their Perceptual Basis.* Cambridge, MA: MIT Press.

Prinz, J. J. (2003). Imitation and moral development. In S. Hurley and N. Chater (Eds.), *Perspectives on Imitation: From Cognitive Neuroscience to Social Science.* Cambridge, MA: MIT Press.

Prinz, J. J. (2004). *Gut Reactions: A Perceptual Theory of Emotion.* New York: Oxford University Press.

Prinz, J. J. (forthcoming). The emotional construction of morals. Oxford: Oxford University Press.

Roseman, I. J., Spindel, M. S., & Jose, P. E. (1990). Appraisals of emotion-eliciting events: Testing a theory of discrete emotions. *Journal of Personality and Social Psychology 59*, 899–915.

Rozin, P., Haidt, J., & McCauley, C. R. (1993). Disgust. In M. Lewis & J. M. Haviland, *Handbook of Emotions*. New York: Guilford Publications.

Rozin, P., Lowery, L., Imada, S., & Haidt, J. (1999). The CAD triad hypothesis: A mapping between three moral emotions (contempt, anger, disgust) and three moral codes (community, autonomy, divinity). *Journal of Personality & Social Psychology 76*, 574–586.

Shweder, R. A., Much, N. C., Mahapatra, M., & Park, L. (1997). The "big three" of morality (autonomy, community, divinity), and the "big three" explanations of suffering. In A. Brandt & P. Rozin (Eds.), *Morality and Health*. (pp. 119–169). New York: Routledge.

Simmons, K., & Barsalou, L. W. (2003). The similarity-in-topography principle: Reconciling theories of conceptual deficits. *Cognitive Neuropsychology 20*, 451–486.

Simmons, W. K., Pecher, D., Hamann, S. B., Zeelenberg, R., & Barsalou, L. W. (2003). fMRI evidence for modality-specific processing of conceptual knowledge on six modalities. *Meeting of the Society for Cognitive Neuroscience*, New York, March.

Spivey, M., Tyler, M., Richardson, D., & Young, E. (2000). Eye movements during comprehension of spoken scene descriptions. *Proceedings of the 22nd Annual Conference of the Cognitive Science Society* (pp. 487–492). Mahwah, NJ: Erlbaum.

Warrington, E. K., & McCarthy, R. (1983). Category specific access dysphasia. *Brain 106*, 859–878.

Wiggins, D. (1987). A sensible subjectivism. In *Needs, Values, Truth*. Oxford: Blackwell.

Zajonc, R. B. (1984). On the primacy of affect. *American Psychologist 39*, 117–123.

6

Grounding Language in Bodily States

The Case for Emotion

Arthur M. Glenberg, David Havas,
Raymond Becker, and Mike Rinck

It has become increasingly clear over the past few years that the symbols used by language become meaningful through grounding. For example, Glenberg and Kaschak (2002) demonstrated that some linguistic constructions are grounded in literal action, and Pecher, Zeelenberg, and Barsalou (2003), as well as Stanfield and Zwaan (2001), showed how language is grounded in perceptual and imaginal states, respectively. In this chapter, we report initial results demonstrating how language may also be grounded in the bodily states that comprise emotions. We begin by discussing the logical and theoretical reasons for supposing that language is grounded in bodily states, and then we move to a brief review of the recent work demonstrating grounding in action and perceptual states. This introductory material is followed by the report of two experiments consistent with the claim that language about emotional states is more completely understood when those states are literally embodied during comprehension.

WHY LANGUAGE MUST BE GROUNDED OUTSIDE
THE LINGUISTIC SYSTEM

To ask how a symbol is grounded is to ask how it becomes meaningful by mapping it onto something else that is already meaningful. One hypothesis is that linguistic symbols (e.g., words and syntactic constructions) become meaningful only when they are mapped to nonlinguistic experiences such as actions and perceptions. A second hypothesis is that linguistic symbols can be grounded in other linguistic symbols. For example, words are often defined in terms of other words: That is exactly how most dictionaries work. In contrast to what is intuitive about the dictionary view of grounding, Searle's (1980) Chinese Room argument and Harnad's (1990) symbolic merry-go-round argument provide the contrary intuition that word meaning cannot result from defining words solely in terms of other words. In Harnad's argument, he asks us to imagine traveling to a country where we do not speak the language (e.g., China), and our only resource is a dictionary written solely in that language. When we arrive, we are confronted with a sign comprised of linguistic characters. Attempting to comprehend the sign, we look up the first symbol in the dictionary to be confronted with a definition (Definition 1) comprised of more symbols, none of which we understand. Undaunted, we look up the definition (Definition 2) of the first symbol contained in Definition 1, only to find that the symbols in Definition 2 are also meaningless to us. We continue to look up the definitions of symbols used in other definitions, but none of definitions provide any help. Apparently, no matter how many symbols we look up, if they are only defined in terms of other symbols, the process will not generate any meaning. That is, if we are to learn the meaning of the Chinese symbols, those symbols must be grounded in something other than additional Chinese symbols.

Although Harnad's argument seems compelling, traditional and contemporary theories of meaning proposed by cognitive psychologists suggest otherwise – that meaning of undefined and arbitrary symbols arises from definitions that are themselves comprised of more undefined and arbitrary symbols.[1] For example, the Collins–Loftus theory (1975) proposes that conceptual information arises from the pattern of relations among nodes in a network. Here, every node corresponds to an undefined word, and the set of nodes to which a particular node is connected corresponds to the words in the dictionary definition. Similarly, recently proposed theories based on the mathematics of high-dimensional spaces (e.g., Burgess & Lund, 1997; Landauer & Dumais, 1997) suggest that linguistic meaning can arise from defining linguistic symbols in terms of other linguistic symbols. For example, HAL (Burgess & Lund, 1997) is a computer program that combs the Internet for linguistic stimuli. It creates a matrix with both rows and columns corresponding to the words encountered. The entries into the cell defined by the intersection of a particular row and column denote the frequency with which the words appear together in pieces of text (e.g., word pairs, triplets, quadruplets, and so on). According to Burgess and Lund, the meaning of a word is given by a vector created by the (approximately) 70,000 numbers in the row corresponding to a particular word combined with the (approximately) 70,000 numbers in the column corresponding to the same word. That is, Burgess and Lund claim that finding enough other words with which a particular word co-occurs is sufficient to ground meaning.

---

[1] The symbols are arbitrary in the sense that there is no natural connection between the symbol and what it represents. For example, the word "chair" does not look, taste, feel, or act like a chair, and the word "eight" is not larger in any sense then the word "seven."

In fairness, many cognitive theorists recognize that during initial language acquisition cognitive symbols are associated with information derived from perception and action. Nonetheless, according to the theories, this perceptual and action information plays virtually no role in mature language use. That is, all thinking and all language comprehension (after initial perceptual processing) are based on the manipulation of arbitrary symbols. It is this claim that is questioned by many theories of embodied cognition that give a primary role to perception and action in linguistic processing.

In contrast to the dictionary-like theories of Collins and Loftus (1975), Burgess and Lund (1997) and many others (e.g., Anderson, Matessa, & Lebiere, 1997; Kintsch, 1988), recent theoretical (e.g., Barsalou, 1999; Glenberg, 1997) and empirical (Glenberg & Kaschak, 2002; Pecher et al., 2003; Stanfield & Zwaan, 2001) work within the embodiment framework has demonstrated how mature language use is grounded in bodily states of action and perception. Consider, for example, Pecher et al. (2003) who demonstrated a perceptual basis to property verification. Participants responded whether or not an object (e.g., a blender) has a particular property (e.g., loud). Pecher et al. found that when the perceptual dimension probed on the current trial (e.g., "LEAVES–rustle" probes the auditory dimension) was the same as the dimension probed on the previous trial (e.g., "BLENDER–loud" probes the auditory dimension), responding was faster than when the perceptual dimension probed on the previous trial was different (e.g., "CRANBERRIES–tart"). Apparently, understanding a concept presented linguistically calls on perceptual experience, not just arbitrary nodes.

Zwaan and his associates (e.g., Stanfield & Zwaan, 2001) asked participants to verify that a picture (e.g., of a pencil) depicted an object mentioned in a sentence (e.g., "The pencil is in a cup"). They found that pictures matching the implied orientation of the object (a pencil depicted vertically in this case) were responded to faster than pictures of the object in an orientation that mismatched the orientation implied by the sentence. Thus, understanding the sentence appears to call on experience with real pencils and real cups and the orientations that they can take, rather that just the association of nodes representing pencils and cups.

As another example of grounding in bodily states, Glenberg and Kaschak (2002) asked each participant to judge the sensibility of sentences such as "You gave Andy the pizza" or "Andy gave you the pizza" by moving the hand from a start button to a Yes button. Location of the Yes button required a literal movement either toward the body or away from the body. Responding was faster when the hand movement was consistent with the action implied by the sentence (e.g., moving away from the body to indicate "Yes" for the sentence, "You gave Andy the pizza") than when the literal movement was inconsistent with that implied by the sentence. Apparently, understanding these action sentences called on the same neural and bodily states involved in real action. Thus, in contrast to theories that claim language symbols are grounded solely in other symbols, these results imply that understanding language calls on bodily states involved in perception, imagery, and action.

This brief overview of embodied accounts of language comprehension suggests several questions. First, does the notion of grounding language in bodily states miss the distinction between "sense" and "reference?" Philosophers such as Frege have suggested that the meaning of a symbol is composed of the objects to which the symbol refers (reference), as well as a more formal definition (sense). The work in embodiment seems to demonstrate that people think of referents upon encountering a word (e.g., Stanfield and Zwaan's participants think of an image of a pencil upon reading the word "pencil"), but how can grounding in bodily states provide definitions? Within the embodiment framework, there are alternative ways of addressing this question, here we note just one. Barsalou (1999) has developed the ideas of perceptual symbols and simulators. The perceptual symbol corresponding to an object (e.g., the perceptual symbol for a gasoline engine) is abstracted (by selective attention) from experiences with the object and retains the format of the neural coding generated by the perceptual and action experiences. Thus, the perceptual symbol for how an engine looks uses the same neural format as visual perception, whereas the sound of the engine uses the format of audition. Perceptual symbols operate as simulators, that is, they can be modified to fit particular situations. The number of different ways in which a person can use a perceptual symbol in simulations is a measure of that person's knowledge about that object. Thus, a skilled mechanic can simulate the effects of many operations on an automobile engine and how those operations might affect the sound of the engine, its performance, and so on. Most of the rest of us can engage in only a limited number of simulations, such as how to start an automobile engine, or how to add oil. Because a perceptual symbol is derived from particular experiences and maintains the format of those experiences, it corresponds, at least roughly, to the philosopher's notion of reference. In contrast, the range of simulations corresponds to the notion of "sense." Thus, the skilled mechanic, by verbally describing her simulations, can provide a detailed definition of an engine.

A second question is whether all language can be grounded in bodily (that is, perception and action) experience. The data suggest that the answer is a qualified "yes." The qualification arises because some components of language are better characterized as instructions for manipulating (through simulation) grounded representations, rather than as grounded representations themselves. Whereas there are reasons to believe that even these instructions may be grounded in experience (cf. Lakoff, 1987), our current focus is on their role in guiding simulations. For example, Kaschak and Glenberg (2000) tested the notion that verb-argument constructions guide the embodied simulation of sentences. According to construction grammar (e.g., Goldberg, 1995), verb-argument constructions (corresponding to the syntax of simple sentences) convey meanings, and it is these meanings that Kaschak and Glenberg presumed to guide the simulations. For example, the syntax of the double-object construction (subject-verb-object 1-object 2) such as "Mike handed Art the apple" is claimed to carry the meaning that the subject transfers object 2 to object 1 by means of the verb. Kaschak and Glenberg inserted into the construction frame innovative denominal verbs, such as "to crutch," that have no standard verb meaning, hence any verb meaning must be coming from the construction itself. Kaschak and Glenberg demonstrated two effects. First, people readily interpreted sentences such as "Mike crutched Art the apple" as implying that Mike transferred the apple to Art by using the crutch. Second, this meaning only arose when the object named by the verb could be used to effect the transfer; experimental participants would reject as nonsense sentences such as "Mike paper-clipped Art the apple." Apparently, the double-object syntax directs a simulation making use of perceptual symbols in which the goal is to effect transfer. If people cannot figure out how to simulate that transfer (e.g., how a paper clip can be used to transfer an apple), then the sentence is rejected as nonsense.

A simulation account was also developed by De Vega, Robertson, Glenberg, Kaschak, and Rinck (in press) who investigated the interpretation of temporal adverbs such as "while" and "after." They proposed that temporal adverbs are instructions to the language system regarding the order and timing of simulations. For example, "while," as in "While painting a fence the farmer whistled a tune," is an instruction to simulate the two actions as occurring at the same time. De Vega et al. tested this claim by requiring participants to read sentences describing events that (in reality) are easy or difficult to perform at the same time. Events that are difficult to perform at the same time require the same motor system (e.g., painting a fence and chopping wood), and events that are easy to perform at the same time require different motor systems (e.g., painting a fence and whistling a tune). As predicted, participants rejected as nonsense sentences describing same motor system events conjoined with the temporal adverb "while" (e.g., "While painting a fence the farmer chopped the wood"), whereas the same events were readily accepted when conjoined with the adverb "after" (e.g., "After painting a fence the farmer chopped the wood"). Apparently, these adverbs are not simply symbols that are stuck into a representational structure. Instead, they direct the participant in how to think about, that is, simulate, the perception and action details of the situation, such as whether the motor actions can actually be performed as described.

GROUNDING LANGUAGE IN EMOTIONAL STATES

There are strong connections between language and emotion (see Barsalou, Neidenthal, Barbey, and Rupert, 2003, for a review of some of this literature from a different perspective). When reading or listening, we often find ourselves becoming sad, angry, afraid, happy, joyous, or aroused depending on the meaning of the language we are processing. It is likely that much of the pleasure we gain in reading and listening to narratives and poetry is directly related to an author's skill in producing these emotional states in us. In fact, language can be a reliable method for inducing emotional changes in experimental situations. To this effect, language has been used in the form of explicit verbal instructions (e.g., Velten cards or hypnotic suggestions, see Bower, 1981), and also implicitly by having participants read newspaper reports (Johnson & Tversky, 1983). Furthermore, there is formal evidence for the prominent role of emotions in language processing. For example, Haenggi, Gernsbacher, and Bolliger (1994) demonstrated that emotional inferences can be processed with greater facility than spatial inferences. That is, participants read target sentences that matched the emotional state of a character more quickly than target sentences that matched spatial states. Participants were also faster to notice incongruities between emotional states than between spatial states. Moreover, the emotional states of readers influence their judgments of, and memory for, fictional character traits (Erber, 1991; Laird, Wagener, Halal, & Szegda, 1982).

Thus, connections between language and emotion are strong and well-documented. In addition, the effects of emotions on cognitive processes such as attention, memory, and interpretation have been studied extensively, with induced emotions as well as naturally occurring emotions and clinical emotional disorders (for reviews, see Bower, 1981; or Williams, Watts, MacLeod, & Mathews, 1997). Nonetheless, researchers have rarely addressed the effects of emotional state on higher-level language processes (for exceptions, see Bower, 1981). In this chapter, we begin to address this question: How does emotional state influence language processing?

The embodied account begins to answer this question by making a strong claim regarding the grounding of emotional language. Namely, understanding of language about emotional states requires that those emotional states be simulated, or partially induced, using the same neural and bodily mechanisms as are recruited during emotional experiences. To state this claim differently, language about emotions is grounded in emotional states of the body, and simulating those states is a prerequisite for complete and facile understanding of the language about those states.

At this point, it is worth pausing to consider just what we mean by "emotional states of the body." A major component of these bodily states is current physiology, such as the levels of various hormones, nutrients, and oxygen in the blood as well as heart rate, vaso-constriction, configuration of the musculature, and so on. We also include brain states such as the balance in activation between the left and right frontal lobes and activation of the amygdala. Our major claim is that language about emotional states is grounded directly in this complex of bodily states rather than in abstract and arbitrary cognitive nodes.

According to the strong embodiment claim, part of understanding emotional language is getting the body into (or moving toward) the appropriate bodily state because that is what gives the words their meaning. Consequently, if bodily systems are already in (or close to) those appropriate states, then understanding should be facilitated, and if the bodily systems are in inappropriate states, those states should interfere with language understanding. More concretely, if we are reading about pleasant events, we should be faster to understand those sentences if we are in a happy state than if we are in an unhappy state. Conversely, if we are reading about unpleasant events, we should be faster to understand those sentences if we are in an unhappy state than if we are in a happy state. Note that these predictions are based on two assumptions. The first is a dimensional assumption, namely that the bodily states corresponding to happiness are further away from those corresponding to unhappiness than to a neutral state. The second assumption is a type of inertia. Because the body is literally a physical and biological system that cannot change states instantaneously, it will take longer to shift from a happy state to an unhappy state (states that are far away) than to shift from a happy state to a neutral state.

In seeming opposition to these predictions, Forgas and Bower (1987) demonstrated longer reading times for character descriptions corresponding in evaluative valence with participants' induced moods than for noncorresponding descriptions. However, this result may well reflect the demands of their task that requires participants to make evaluative judgments about the described characters. As Forgas and Bower speculate, this task may have encouraged associative elaboration well beyond that needed to comprehend the sentences.

To test the predictions from the strong embodiment claim, we need a means of reliably shifting the body into happy and unhappy states. Strack, Martin, and Stepper (1988) provide just such a methodology. They noted that holding a pen in one's mouth using only the teeth (and not the lips) forces a partial smile. In contrast, holding the pen using only the lips (and not the teeth) forces a partial frown.[2] Strack et al. demonstrated that these facial configurations differentially affected peoples felt emotions as well as their emotional assessment of stimuli: Participants rated cartoons as funnier when holding the pen in their teeth (and smiling) than when holding the pen in their lips (and frowning). This effect of facial configuration has

---

[2] Note that having the face in a particular configuration is part of the bodily state corresponding to a particular emotion.

TABLE 6.1. *Examples of Sentences Used in Experiments 1 and 2*

Pleasant sentences
The college president announces your name, and you proudly step onto the stage.
The cold air rushes past you as you race down the snowy slope.
Ready for a snack, you put the coins into the machine and press the buttons.
You and your lover embrace after a long separation.
You laugh as the merry-go-round picks up speed.

Unpleasant sentences
The police car rapidly pulls up behind you, siren blaring.
Your supervisor frowns as he hands you the sealed envelope.
You've made another error at shortstop, bringing the crowd to its feet.
Your debate opponent brings up a challenge you hadn't prepared for.
Your father collapses at the end of the annual road race.

---

been replicated numerous times (e.g., Berkowitz & Troccoli, 1990; Ohira & Kurono, 1993; Larsen, Kasimatis, & Frey 1992; Soussignan, 2002).

In our experiments, we used the Strack et al. (1988) procedure to manipulate bodily state while participants read and understood sentences describing pleasant and unpleasant events. We measured how long it took to read and understand the sentences. On the basis of the strong embodiment claim, we predict an interaction between the pen condition (Teeth or Lips) and the valence of the sentence (Pleasant or Unpleasant). That is, participants should read and judge pleasant sentences more quickly when holding the pen in their teeth than when holding the pen in their lips, and the converse should be found for unpleasant sentences.

Examples of the sentences are given in Table 6.1. The 96 sentences (48 pleasant and 48 unpleasant) were based on those constructed and normed by Ira Fischler (personal communication, 2003), although we made changes in a small number of them.[3] Each of the original sentences was rated by approximately 60 participants on a scale from 1 (most unpleasant) to 9 (most pleasant). The mean (and standard deviation) for the unpleasant sentences was 2.92 (.66), and the mean for the pleasant sentences was 6.50 (.58).

In the first experiment, each participant viewed a sentence on a computer screen by pressing the space bar on the computer keyboard (which also initiated a timer). The participant judged the valence of the sentence by pressing the "3" key on the keyboard, which was labeled with the letter "U," for unpleasant, or the "0" key, which was labeled with the letter "P," for pleasant. The left and right index fingers were used to make the Unpleasant and Pleasant responses, respectively. Half of the 96 participants began the experiment in the Teeth condition (holding the pen using

---

[3] We are very grateful to Ira Fischler who provided us with the stimulus sentences.

TABLE 6.2. *Reading Times in Milliseconds and Proportion Consistent Valence Judgments (in Parentheses) from Experiment 1*

First Half of the Experiment

Pen Condition	Sentence Valence	
	Pleasant	Unpleasant
Teeth (smiling)	2706 (.96)	2735 (.97)
Lips (frowning)	2828 (.97)	2690 (.97)

Second Half of the Experiment

Pen Condition	Sentence Valence	
	Pleasant	Unpleasant
Teeth (smiling)	2678 (.95)	2663 (.96)
Lips (frowning)	2661 (.96)	2623 (.97)

only their teeth), and half began in the Lips condition (holding the pen using only their lips). During the experiment, participants switched between holding the pen in their teeth and lips every 12 sentences. In each of these blocks of 12 sentences, half of the sentences were Pleasant and half Unpleasant. Participants were told that the purpose of the pen manipulation was to examine the effects of interfering with the speech articulators during reading.

Overall, the participants were highly accurate, that is, the judgments corresponded to the normative classification 96% of the time (range of 87% to 100%). Because of two worries, we decided to analyze the data including a factor of experiment half (First half or Second half). One of these worries was that the pen manipulation would become onerous and unpleasant in both the Teeth and Lips conditions as the musculature fatigued. The other worry was that the task was so simple (judging the valence of the sentences) that people would learn to make the judgment on the basis of a quick scan of a few words rather than reading and understanding the whole sentence.

The reading (and judgment) times for the two halves of the experiment are presented in Table 6.2. The means were computed only for those sentences judged correctly. Also, reading times were eliminated if they were more than 2.5 standard deviations from a participant's mean in any particular condition.

The critical interaction between Pen condition and Sentence valence was significant, $F(1,95) = 5.41$, $MSe = 80515$, $p = .02$. Although the triple interaction of Half of the experiment with Pen condition and Sentence condition was not significant ($p = .10$), it is clear from the data in Table 6.2 that the majority of the interaction comes from the first half of the

TABLE 6.3. *Reading Times in Milliseconds and Proportion "Easy" Judgments (in Parentheses) from Experiment 3*

First Half of the Experiment

	Sentence Valence	
Pen Condition	Pleasant	Unpleasant
Teeth (smiling)	3442 (.93)	3496 (.94)
Lips (frowning)	3435 (.94)	3372 (.91)

Second Half of the Experiment

	Sentence Valence	
Pen Condition	Pleasant	Unpleasant
Teeth (smiling)	3128 (.95)	3261 (.94)
Lips (frowning)	3256 (.95)	3127 (.97)

experiment. Note that the form of this interaction is just what was predicted on the basis of the strong embodiment claim. Namely, reading the pleasant sentences is 122 msec faster when holding the pen in the teeth (and smiling) than when holding the pen in the lips (and frowning), whereas reading of the unpleasant sentences is 45 msec slower when holding the pen in the teeth than when holding the pen in the lips.

Although the data are consistent with the strong embodiment claim, there is a possible problem with the experimental procedure, namely that the judgment draws the participants' attention to the valence of the sentences. Thus, a skeptic might argue that the bodily effects of the pen manipulation emerge only when people must explicitly judge emotional valence, and thus the effects are not reflective of basic understanding processes. To address this problem, we conducted a second experiment in which the task was to judge whether or not the sentences were easy or hard to understand. We told participants that we had written the sentences to be easy to understand, but that some difficult ones might have snuck through and that we needed their help in finding them. Thus, the great majority of their responses would be "Easy," but that there might be a few "Hard" responses. The participants were never informed that the sentences differed in valence. Furthermore, taking a cue from the social psychology literature, we asked participants after the experimental session if they had ever heard of the pen procedure or had suspected that we were attempting to manipulate their moods. We eliminated the data from four of the 42 participants who answered the latter question in the affirmative.

The 38 participants judged most of the sentences as easy to understand (94%, with a range of 60% to 100%). The reading time data are presented in Table 6.3. These data are based solely on sentences classified as "Easy," and reading times more that 2.5 standard deviations from the participant's mean for a particular condition were eliminated.

Overall, there was a significant interaction between Pen condition and Sentence valence, $F(1,37) = 6.63$, $MSe = 103382$, $p = .01$. However, the same interaction was significant for the judgments, $F(1,37) = 4.48$, $MSe = .003$, $p = .04$, indicating the possibility of some sort of judgment-by-reading speed tradeoff. Because the judgments seemed to have stabilized in the second half of the experiment, we also examined the data by halves of the experiment. Considering only the first half of the experiment, the critical interaction was significant for the judgments, $F(1,37) = 8.56$, $MSe = .002$, $p = .01$, but the interaction was not significant for the reading times, $p > .3$. The opposite pattern was obtained for the second half. Namely, the critical interaction was not significant for the judgments, $p > .3$, but was significant for the reading times, $F(1,37) = 4.89$, $MSe = 134316$, $p = .03$.[4] Thus, if we consider the data from both halves of the experiment or only the data from the second half, there is ample evidence for the critical interaction in the time needed to understand the sentence.

The data from the two experiments are clear and consistent: When reading and understanding sentences, judgments are facilitated when the suggested mood of the sentence is congruent with the mood induced by the pen manipulation. This finding is consistent with the predictions derived from the strong embodiment claim. As such, the data lend support to the general claim that language is grounded in bodily states, and the data lend support to the specific claim that language about emotions is grounded in emotional states literally produced by the body. Nonetheless, two issues will have to be addressed in further research.

The first issue concerns the prediction derived from the strong embodiment claim that relative to a neutral condition, both facilitation and interference should be observed. Our data might simply reflect facilitation (e.g., smiling speeds processing of pleasant sentences) with no interference for incongruent conditions (e.g., smiling may not interfere with processing of unpleasant sentences). Unfortunately, two pilot experiments designed to induce a neutral condition were failures. In the first pilot experiment, we implemented Strack et al.'s neutral condition of holding the pen in one hand rather than in the mouth. This necessitated a change in the response method from using the left and right index fingers to respond "Easy" and

---

[4] Why are the effects most apparent in the first half of Experiment 1 and the second half of Experiment 2? We think that the task used in Experiment 1 (judging valence of the sentence) was very easy, and eventually participants learned to make those judgments by quickly scanning the sentences for key words, thus obviating the effect in the second half. The task used in Experiment 2 (judging if the sentence was easy or hard to understand) was more difficult (note the slower times compared to Experiment 1). Importantly, there were no surface cues as to whether a sentence should be judged easy or hard, and hence the participants were forced to carefully consider each sentence throughout the experiment.

"Hard" respectively (as in Experiments 1 and 2), to using the right index finger to indicate "Hard" and the right middle finger to indicate "Easy." With this change, however, the critical interaction was no longer significant. We suspect that the interaction disappeared because responding with the index finger was actually easier than responding with the middle finger, leading to a conflict between the labels "Hard" and "Easy" and the difficulty of actually making the response. In the second pilot experiment, we used as a neutral condition holding the pen between the knees so that the two index fingers could once again be used to make the "Easy" and "Hard" responses. We obtained the critical interaction, but to our surprise, the pen-between-the-knees condition seemed to be a super-pleasant condition and not a neutral condition. That is, for the pleasant sentences, responding was fastest in the pen-between-the-knees condition, and for the unpleasant sentences, responding was slowest in this condition!

A second issue calling for caution is that the results portrayed in Tables 6.2 and 6.3 are consistent with other accounts in addition to the strong embodiment claim. Consider, for example, Bower's (1981) theory of the relation between cognition and emotion. In Bower's theory, bodily states influence cognition by activating nodes (e.g., a happy node) that can spread activation to associated nodes representing happy and pleasant words such as, from Table 6.1, "proudly," "lover," and "embrace." Because these nodes are already activated, the corresponding words are read faster, leading to the critical interaction between bodily state and reading time.[5] Although the Bower model and the embodied approach make similar predictions for the experiments reported here, there does seem to be an important difference between the accounts. Namely, in the Bower model, bodily states have an effect on cognition (including language comprehension) by activating the presumed emotion nodes which then activate other nodes corresponding to words. In this model, language understanding results from the manipulation of those other nodes. Thus, comprehension of emotional language is only indirectly grounded in the bodily states corresponding to emotions. In contrast, the strong embodiment claim is that language understanding is directly grounded in bodily states, that is, that language understanding requires the appropriate bodily states to derive meaning from the words. We are currently developing experimental procedures to differentiate between these accounts.

In conclusion, our results add an important new finding consistent with the claim that language is grounded in bodily states. Previous work has demonstrated that language is grounded in action, in perceptual states,

[5] It is not clear whether this conjoining of bodily states and AAA principles will be successful. Indeed, the representation of emotions as nodes in a network, just like any other type of node, has received considerable criticism from emotions researchers (cf. Williams, Watts, MacLeod, & Mathews, 1997).

and in images. These new experiments demonstrate how language about emotion-producing situations may well be grounded in bodily states of emotion.

ACKNOWLEDGMENTS

This work was supported by NSF grants BCS-0315434 and INT-0233175 to Arthur Glenberg and a grant from the German Academic Exchange Service (DAAD) to Mike Rinck. Any opinions, findings, and conclusions or recommendations expressed in this material are those of the authors, and do not necessarily reflect the views of the NSF. We thank Brianna Buntje, Sheila Simhan, Terina Yip, and Bryan Webster for fantastically efficient data collection and interesting discussion of these results. We are also very grateful to Gordon Bower whose insightful review of an initial version of this chapter resulted in a substantially improved final version. Requests for reprints may be directed to Arthur Glenberg at glenberg@wisc.edu.

References

Anderson, J. R., Matessa, M., & Lebiere, C. (1997). ACT-R: A theory of higher level cognition and its relation to visual attention. Human-Computer Interaction. Special Issue: *Cognitive Architectures and Human-Computer Interaction 12*, 4, 439–462.

Barsalou, L. W. (1999). Perceptual symbol systems. *Behavioral and Brain Sciences 22*, 577–660.

Barsalou, L. W., Niedenthal, P. M., Barbey, A., & Ruppert, J. (2003). Social embodiment. In B. Ross (Ed.), *The Psychology of Learning and Motivation*, Vol. 43. San Diego: Academic Press.

Berkowitz, L., & Troccoli, B. T. (1990). Feelings, direction of attention, and expressed evaluations of others. *Cognition and Emotion 4*, 305–325.

Bower, G. H. (1981). Mood and memory. *American Psychologist 36*, 129–148.

Burgess, C., & Lund, K. (1997). Modeling parsing constraints with high-dimensional context space. *Language and Cognitive Processes 12*, 177–210.

Collins, A. M., & Loftus, E. F. (1975). A spreading-activation theory of semantic processing. *Psychological Review 82*, 407–428.

De Vega, M., Robertson, D. A., Glenberg, A. M., Kaschak, M. P., & Rinck, M. (in press). On doing two things at once: Temporal constraints on actions in language comprehension. *Memory and Cognition*.

Erber, R. (1991). Affective and semantic priming: Effects of mood on category accessibility and inference. *Journal of Experimental Social Psychology 27*, 79–88.

Fischler, I. S. (July 23, 2003).

Forgas, J. P., & Bower, G. H. (1987). Mood effects on person-perception judgments. *Journal of Personality and Social Psychology 53*, 53–60.

Glenberg, A. M. (1997). What memory is for. *Behavioral and Brain Sciences 20*, 1–55.

Glenberg, A. M., & Kaschak, M. P. (2002). Grounding language in action. *Psychonomic Bulletin & Review 9*, 558–565.

Goldberg, A. E. (1995). *Constructions: A construction grammar approach to argument structure*. Chicago: University of Chicago Press.

Haenggi, D., Gernsbacher, M. A., & Bolliger, C. M. (1994). Individual differences in situation-based inferencing during narrative text comprehension. In H. van Oostendorp & R. A. Zwaan (Eds.), *Naturalistic text comprehension: Vol. LIII. Advances in discourse processing* (pp. 79–96). Norwood, NJ: Ablex.

Harnad, S. (1990). The symbol grounding problem. *Physica D 42*, 335–346.

Johnson, J. D., & Tversky, A. (1983). Affect, generalization, and the perception of risk. *Journal of Personality and Social Psychology 45*, 20–31.

Kaschak, M. P., & Glenberg, A. M. (2000). Constructing meaning: The role of affordances and grammatical constructions in sentence comprehension. *Journal of Memory and Language 43*, 508–529.

Kintsch, W. (1988). The role of knowledge in discourse comprehension: a construction-integration model. *Psychological Review 95*, 163–182.

Laird, J. D., Wagener, J. J., Halal, M., & Szegda, M. (1982). Remembering what you feel: Effects of emotion on memory. *Journal of Personality and Social Psychology 42*, 646–657.

Lakoff, George (1987). *Women, Fire, and Dangerous Things: What Categories Reveal about the Mind*. Chicago: University of Chicago Press.

Landauer, T. K., & Dumais, S. T. (1997). A solution to Plato's problem: The latent semantic analysis theory of acquisition, induction, and representations of knowledge. *Psychological Review 104*, 211–240.

Larsen, R. J., Kasimatis, M., & Frey, K. (1992). Facilitating the furrowed brow: An unobtrusive test of the facial feedback hypothesis applied to unpleasant affect. *Cognition & Emotion 6*, 5, 321–338.

Ohira, H., & Kurono, K. (1993). Facial feedback effects on impression formation. *Perceptual and Motor Skills 77*(3, Pt. 2), 1251–1258.

Pecher, D., Zeelenberg, R., & Barsalou, L. W. (2003). Verifying different-modality properties for concepts produces switching costs. *Psychological Science 14*, 119–124.

Searle, J. R. (1980). Minds, brains, and programs. *Behavioral and Brain Sciences 3*, 417–457.

Soussignan, R. (2002). Duchenne smile, emotional experience, and autonomic reactivity: A test of the facial feedback hypothesis. *Emotion 2*, 1, 52–74.

Stanfield, R. A., & Zwaan, R. A. (2001). The effect of implied orientation derived from verbal context on picture recognition. *Psychological Science 121*, 153–156.

Strack, F., Martin, L. L., & Stepper, S. (1988). Inhibiting and facilitating condition of facial expressions: A nonobtrusive test of the facial feedback hypothesis. *Journal of Personality and Social Psychology 54*, 768–777.

Williams, J. M. G., Watts, F. N., MacLeod, C., & Mathews, A. (1997). *Cognitive Psychology and Emotional Disorders*, Second edition. Chichester: John Wiley.

7

Situating Abstract Concepts

Lawrence W. Barsalou and Katja Wiemer-Hastings

Roughly speaking, an abstract concept refers to entities that are neither purely physical nor spatially constrained. Such concepts pose a classic problem for theories that ground knowledge in modality-specific systems (e.g., Barsalou, 1999, 2003a,b). How could these systems represent a concept like *TRUTH*?[1] Abstract concepts also pose a significant problem for traditional theories that represent knowledge with amodal symbols. Surprisingly, few researchers have attempted to specify the content of abstract concepts using feature lists, semantic networks, or frames. It is not enough to say that an amodal node or a pattern of amodal units represents an abstract concept. It is first necessary to specify the concept's content, and then to show that a particular type of representation can express it. Regardless of how one might go about representing *TRUTH*, its content must be identified. Then the task of identifying how this content is represented can begin.

The primary purpose of this chapter is to explore the content of three abstract concepts: *TRUTH, FREEDOM,* and *INVENTION.* In an exploratory study, their content will be compared to the content of three concrete concepts – *BIRD, CAR,* and SOFA – and also to three intermediate concepts that seem somewhat concrete but more abstract than typical concrete concepts – *COOKING, FARMING,* and *CARPETING.* We will first ask participants to produce properties typically true of these concepts. We will then analyze these properties using two coding schemes. Of particular interest will be the content of abstract concepts, and how it compares to the content of concrete and intermediate concepts.

We will not attempt to provide evidence that modality-specific systems represent abstract concepts. Once we have assessed their content, however,

---

[1] Italics will be used to indicate concepts, and quotes will be used to indicate linguistic forms (words, sentences). Within concepts, uppercase words will represent categories, whereas lowercase words will represent properties of categories.

we will speculate on how modality-specific systems could represent it. Notably, though, recent studies have obtained evidence for modality-specific representations in abstract concepts. Glenberg and Kaschak (2002) found that abstract concepts contain motor information, as did Richardson, Spivey, Barsalou, and McRae (2003). For evidence that other types of concepts are grounded in modality specific systems, see recent reviews by Barsalou (2003b), Barsalou, Niedenthal, Barbey, and Ruppert (2003), and Martin (2001).

RELATED ISSUES IN REPRESENTING ABSTRACT CONCEPTS

The issue of modal versus amodal representation is not the only important issue related to abstract concepts. Previous researchers have raised other important issues. In particular, previous researchers have suggested that situations, word associations, and metaphors are potentially important aspects of how abstract concepts are represented. We address each in turn.

Situation Availability[2]

In a series of studies, Schwanenflugel, Shoben, and their colleagues demonstrated that it is often difficult to think of a situation in which an abstract concept occurs (for a review, see Schwanenflugel, 1991). For example, what is a situation in which *TRUTH* occurs? Although a court trial might eventually come to mind, or a child confessing to a parent, it often takes a while to retrieve such situations. In contrast, situations seem to come to mind much more readily for concrete concepts. For *CHAIR*, situations like living rooms and classrooms come to mind quickly.

Schwanenflugel, Shoben, and their colleagues explored the role of situation availability across a variety of cognitive tasks. To do this, they first demonstrated the general advantage of concrete over abstract concepts (also see Paivio, 1986). Specifically, they showed that (1) lexical access is faster for concrete words than for abstract words (e.g., Schwanenflugel, Harnishfeger, & Stowe, 1988), (2) word comprehension is faster for concrete words than for abstract words (e.g., Schwanenflugel & Shoben, 1983; Schwanenflugel & Stowe, 1989), and (3) memory is better for concrete words than for abstract words (e.g., Wattenmaker & Shoben, 1987). Then, in the same studies, these researchers demonstrated that situation availability played a major role in these differences by manipulating the presence

---

[2] In the original work on this topic, Schwanenflugel and her colleagues referred to what we're calling "situation availability" as "context availability." We use "situation" instead, first, because the construct of a situation has played a central role in much of our recent work and in the work of other researchers (see Yeh and Barsalou, 2004, for a review), and second, because situations can be viewed as one possible form of context.

versus absence of a relevant situation. For example, participants might first read about a court trial before studying "truth" for a memory test, or first read about a living room before studying "chair." When relevant situations were present, abstract words were processed as well as concrete words. Participants accessed and understood both types of words equally quickly, and remembered them just as well.

These findings demonstrate two points about the processing of words. First, the meanings of words are not established in isolation. A word's meaning is typically not a stand-alone package of features that describes its associated category. Instead, words are typically understood and represented against background situations (cf. Murphy & Medin, 1985). When a situation is not available, a concept is difficult to process. Much early work on language comprehension reached this same conclusion (for reviews, see Bransford & Johnson, 1973; Bransford & McCarrell, 1974). Much recent work echoes this theme (e.g., Barsalou, 2003b; A. Clark, 1997; H. Clark, 1992; Yeh & Barsalou, 2004). In general, situations provide much useful information for understanding concepts. Understanding what *CHAIR* means relies not only on the physical properties of the object, but also on the settings in which it is found (e.g., classrooms) and the activities performed in them (e.g., attending lectures). Knowledge of chairs is inadequate if one does not know how they are used in relevant situations. For this reason, situations often appear central to the representation of concepts.

Second, retrieving situations for abstract concepts appears more difficult than retrieving situations for concrete concepts. At least the following two factors may be responsible. First, abstract concepts may be associated with a wider variety of situations than concrete concepts (Galbraith & Underwood, 1973). As a result of greater interference between competing situations, retrieving a single one may be more difficult than for a concrete concept. Second, when people process abstract concepts in the real world, there may typically be a relevant situation already in place. People may not typically entertain a concept like *TRUTH* unless a relevant situation is in place to which the concept applies. As a result, the conceptual system becomes oriented toward retrieving information about abstract concepts with relevant situations already in place. Conversely, because it is relatively unusual to process abstract concepts in situational vacuums, people draw blanks initially when receiving them out of context.

Word Association

People may not exactly draw a blank when processing abstract concepts in isolation. Instead, the word for an abstract concept may trigger highly associated words. Because no situation comes to mind immediately, other associated information becomes active. Because the memory cue is a word, other associated words come to mind, following the principle of encoding specificity (Tulving & Thomson, 1973). Note, however, that these words don't necessarily constitute conceptual meaning. Instead, as word associates become active, only their surface-level phonological forms are retrieved, accompanied by minimal meaning. Certainly, more semantic content could be retrieved on occasion. Nevertheless, meaning may often be processed minimally.

Several sources of evidence support the conjecture that abstract words encountered out of context initially activate superficial word associations. First, Glaser (1992) reviews much evidence that words in general often generate word associates, prior to the activation of conceptual information. Consider an example. Solomon and Barsalou (2004) found that participants used the strength of word associations in a property verification task when associative strength was a diagnostic cue for responding – they did not typically access conceptual knowledge. Participants adopted this strategy because the object and property words on true trials tended to be associated (e.g., "horse" – "mane"), whereas the object and property words on false trials tended to be unassociated (e.g., "chair" – "feathers"). Because word association strength predicted the correct response, participants did not need to access conceptual knowledge. Kan, Barsalou, Solomon, Minor, and Thompson-Schill (2003) reported fMRI evidence consistent with Solomon and Barsalou's behavioral findings. Glaser (1992) offers many such examples of surface-level word forms playing central roles in "conceptual" tasks. Together, these findings indicate that word associations can become activated quickly with minimal retrieval of conceptual information.

A second source of evidence further suggests that processing abstract concepts in isolation may initially produce word associations. As Pulvermüller (1999) reviews, lesion and neuroimaging studies have localized the processing of abstract concepts in left frontal areas. In these studies, participants usually receive isolated words for abstract concepts not linked to particular situations. Thus, retrieving situations should be difficult, and word associations could fill the conceptual void. Consistent with this account, left-frontal areas tend to be implicated with word generation processes (e.g., Thompson-Schill, D'Esposito, Aguirre, & Farah; 1997; Peterson, Fox, Posner, Mintus, & Raichle, 1989). The proximity of these areas to Broca's area further implicates word generation. To our knowledge, no neuroscience research has assessed the processing of abstract concepts in situations. It would be interesting to see if situational processing shifted brain activation outside word generation areas.

A third line of work also implicates word association in the processing of isolated abstract concepts. Krauth-Gruber, Ric, Niedenthal, and Barsalou (2004) had participants generate information about isolated abstract and concrete concepts under one of three instructional sets. One group produced word associations for the abstract and concrete concepts. A second group constructed an image of what each concept referred to and then described the image. A third group produced properties that are typically true of each concept. Of interest was whether property generation participants more resembled word association participants or imagery participants in the information produced. For concrete concepts, property generation participants produced essentially the same information as imagery participants, consistent with the conclusion that property generation participants used images to represent these concepts (also see Wu & Barsalou, 2004). For abstract concepts, however, property generation participants essentially produced the same information as word association participants, consistent with the conclusion that property generation participants initially accessed word associations for the isolated abstract words. When a background situation was not present, the initial information retrieved for the abstract concepts appeared to be word associations.

Finally, it is worth noting that the retrieval of word associations during initial lexical access is consistent with theories like LSA (Landauer & Dumais, 1997) and HAL (e.g., Burgess & Lund, 1997). According to these theories, a word becomes associated to other words it cooccurs with in texts, with associative strength reflecting frequency and proximity of cooccurrence. Subsequently, when a word is encoded, its network of word associates becomes active. According to LSA and HAL, these associates constitute the word's meaning. Alternatively, these associates may simply be word forms that point to underlying concepts.

Metaphor

Some theorists have argued that the meanings of abstract concepts are grounded in concrete domains (e.g., Gibbs, this volume; Lakoff & Johnson, 1980; Lakoff & Turner, 1989). For example, the abstract concept, *ANGER*, is grounded in concrete phenomena, such as boiling water exploding out of a closed pot. We agree that metaphors often augment the meanings of abstract concepts, and make certain aspects of their conceptual content salient (e.g., Boroditsky & Ramscar, 2002).

Nevertheless, direct experience of abstract concepts appears central to their content (Prinz, Chapter 5, this volume). One reason is that people have considerable amounts of direct experience with abstract concepts. Consider *ANGER*. People have much experience with the external situations that trigger anger, what anger feels like subjectively, and how one acts and looks when angry. Indeed, norms for emotion concepts like *ANGER* contain detailed features of this experience (e.g., Fehr & Russell, 1984). Notably, these norms don't contain much mention of metaphors.

Direct experience of abstract concepts is important for another reason. A concrete metaphor can not be mapped into an abstract concept, if the abstract concept doesn't have it's own structure (e.g., Murphy, 1997). If an abstract concept has no structure based on direct experience, the concrete metaphor would have nothing to map into. Certainly, metaphors may interpret direct experience and add new material to it. The point is, however, that metaphors complement direct experience of abstract concepts, which often appears extensive.

Thus, our focus will be on the direct knowledge that people have of abstract concepts. Later, when we report an exploratory study, we will focus exclusively on direct knowledge. Indeed, we found little mention of metaphors when people described the content of abstract concepts.

HYPOTHESES ABOUT CONCEPTUAL CONTENT

A common assumption is that abstract and concrete concepts have little, if anything, in common. With respect to their content, they constitute two completely different kinds of concepts. In contrast, we propose that concrete and abstract concepts share important similarities. In particular, we propose that they share common situational content (Hypothesis 1). Where concrete and abstract concepts differ is in their focus within background situations, with concrete concepts focusing on objects, and abstract concepts on events and introspections (Hypothesis 2). As a result of these different foci, the representation of abstract concepts is more complex, being less localized in situational content than the content of concrete concepts (Hypothesis 3). Finally, because the content of abstract concepts is grounded in situations, this content can be simulated in modality-specific representations (Hypothesis 4). We address each hypothesis in turn.

Hypothesis 1. Concrete and Abstract Concepts Share Situational Content

As reviewed earlier, situations appear important for accessing and representing both abstract and concrete concepts. Consider the concrete concept, *HAMMER*. If people only know the physical parts of *HAMMERS* (e.g., *head*, *handle*), they lack an adequate concept of the category. Instead, people must also know the settings where the objects are used, such as the presence of two boards and nails, along with an agent for using them. People also need to know the actions that the agent performs (e.g., swinging the hammer), and also the events that result from these actions (e.g., the hammer head driving the nail into the boards). Finally, people need to know about the mental states of the agent, including goals (e.g., bind two boards together) and affective reactions (e.g., satisfaction when the nail is pounded in correctly). Only when all of the relevant situational content about *HAMMERS* is known does someone approach a full understanding of the concept. For a detailed account of how situational knowledge underlies the semantics of artifacts and natural kinds, see Barsalou, Sloman, and Chaigneau (in press).

Situations appear even more central to abstract concepts. Consider Barsalou's (1999) semantic analysis of an everyday sense of *TRUE*, namely, the sense that an agent's claim about the world is accurate. To represent this sense requires a situation that contains the following event sequence. First, a speaker makes a verbal claim about some state of the world to a listener (e.g., it's raining outside). Second, the listener constructs a mental representation of the speaker's claim (e.g., what raining outside might look like). Third, the listener perceives the part of the world that the claim is about (e.g., the weather outside). Fourth, the listener determines whether the represented claim matches or doesn't match the current state of the world. Fifth, if the claim matches the world, the listener concludes that the speaker's claim has the property of being *TRUE*; otherwise, it's *FALSE*. As this example illustrates, a complex situation is necessary to represent the meaning of *TRUE*, including multiple agents (e.g., speaker, listener), physical events (e.g., communication, states of the world), and mental events (e.g., representing, comparing). Without a situation, it would be impossible to represent the meaning of this abstract concept. Barsalou (1999) provides additional examples of how situations underlie other abstract concepts, such as *OR*, and also ad hoc categories, such as *THINGS TO STAND ON TO CHANGE A LIGHT BULB*.

As these examples illustrate, situations appear central to both concrete and abstract concepts. Thus, there should be strong similarities between their content. When we ask participants to describe the content of concepts, we should observe extensive mention of situations for not only for abstract concepts, but also for concrete ones.

Hypothesis 2. Concrete and Abstract Concepts Differ in Situational Focus

Where we propose that concrete and abstract concepts differ is in their focus on situational content. For concrete concepts, attention should focus on the respective objects against their background situations. In representing *HAMMERS*, the focus should be on hammer objects in their situations of use. Even though information about events and introspections exists in the representation, attention focuses on the critical objects and their specific properties.

In contrast, the focus for abstract concepts should be distributed across other types of situational content. Specifically, abstract concepts should focus on event and introspective properties. One basis for this prediction is Barsalou's (1999) preliminary analyses of abstract concepts, where these two types of properties played central roles. Complex configurations of event and introspective properties generally appeared necessary to capturing the meaning of an abstract concept. Further bases for this prediction are empirical findings from Wiemer-Hastings and her colleagues. In one line of work, the similarity between the linguistic contexts in which abstract concepts occur predicted the similarity of the concepts' meanings (Wiemer-Hastings & Graesser, 2000; see also Wiemer-Hastings & Graesser, 1998). Because these contexts were defined as verbs and prepositions, this correlation supports the proposal that events and settings are central for abstract concepts. In another study, introspective properties were especially important for predicting the differential abstractness of abstract concepts (Wiemer-Hastings, Krug, & Xu, 2001).

Hypothesis 3. Abstract Concepts are More Complex Than Concrete Concepts

According to Hypothesis 2, concrete concepts focus on objects in situations, whereas abstract concepts focus on events and introspections. An implication of this proposal is that the representations of abstract concepts should be more complex than those of concrete concepts. For concrete concepts, the focus is on a relatively local, spatially circumscribed region of a situation. In a *HAMMER* situation, for example, the focus is on the region that the hammer occupies.

For abstract concepts, however, the focus is on multiple components that are not localized but distributed widely. In a *TRUE* situation, for example, the focus includes the speaker's claim, the listener's representation of the claim, and the listener's assessment of the claim. All these components, and the relations between them, must be represented and integrated to evaluate *TRUE's* focal content. We have increasingly come to believe that abstract concepts seem "abstract" because their content is distributed across situations. Another contributing factor may be the centrality of introspective information, which may be more subtle to detect than entity information. Thus, in the study to follow, we expected to see more complex representations for abstract concepts than for concrete ones.

Hypothesis 4. The Content of Abstract Concepts Could, in Principle, Be Simulated

All of the conceptual content that we have discussed so far could, in principle, be simulated in the brain's modality specific systems. It is well known from both imagery and neuroscience research that people construct images of objects, settings, and events (see Barsalou, 2003b; Martin, 2001). Thus, all of this situational content could in principle be simulated as people represent concrete and abstract concepts.

In contrast, little direct evidence bears on the representation of the introspective information central to abstract concepts (also important but backgrounded for concrete concepts). Nevertheless, it seems quite plausible that introspective content could be simulated in mental images (for specific proposals, see Barsalou, 1999, 2003a). It seems possible to simulate the introspective experiences of emotions (e.g., happiness), drive states (e.g., hunger), and cognitive operations (e.g., comparing two imagined objects). There is no empirical or theoretical reason for believing that introspective content could *not* be simulated as part of a conceptual representation. Thus, we will assume that the presence of introspective content in conceptual representations does not constitute evidence against embodied theories of knowledge.

AN EXPLORATORY STUDY

To assess these hypotheses, we asked college students to produce the properties of three abstract concepts, three concrete concepts, and three concepts intermediate in abstractness. Because we wanted to explore the content of these concepts in an open-ended manner, we did not constrain participants' protocols to any particular type of information. Thus participants were simply asked to describe the properties that they thought were characteristic of each concept. As will be seen, these probes led to a diverse collection of responses.

Two other factors besides concept abstractness were manipulated: situation availability (whether a concept was or was not preceded by the description of a situation) and concept form (whether a concept was presented as an entity, event, quality, etc.). These factors had little effect, so we do not report results for them. Because participants responded at their own pace for a full minute, they produced diverse content that obscured possible effects of these manipulations.

Analyses. To examine the content of participants' protocols, two coding schemes were applied. First, Wu and Barsalou's (2004) coding scheme established the amounts of taxonomic, entity, setting/event, and introspective content in the protocols (for additional applications of this coding scheme, see Cree & McRae, 2003; Krauth-Gruber et al., 2004; McRae & Cree, 2002). This coding scheme makes it possible to assess whether situational content occurs across all three concept types (Hypothesis 1). It also enables assessing whether different types of situational content are more important for concrete vs. abstract concepts (Hypothesis 2).

A second analysis established larger groups of properties in the protocols (e.g., extended descriptions of people, events, introspections, etc.). To capture these larger protocol units, a second coding scheme was developed. This scheme also captured the hierarchical relations that frequently integrated these larger units. As will be seen, analysis of these units and their hierarchical structure provides insight into the shared and distinctive properties of abstract, concrete, and intermediate concepts. Applying this scheme also allowed us to assess whether the representations of abstract concepts are more complex than those of concrete concepts (Hypothesis 3).

Finally, both analyses allow informed speculation about Hypothesis 4. Once these two analyses establish the content of abstract, concrete, and intermediate concepts, we can begin thinking about whether modality-specific systems could in principle simulate it.

Method

Materials. The critical materials included three abstract concepts, three concrete concepts, and three intermediate concepts. Each abstract concept took three forms: *TRUE, THE TRUTH, TRUTHFULNESS; A FREEDOM, TO FREE, FREELY; AN INVENTION, TO INVENT, INVENTIVENESS.* Similarly, each intermediate concept took three forms: *A COOK, TO COOK, SOMETHING THAT HAS BEEN COOKED; A FARM, TO FARM, SOMETHING THAT HAS BEEN FARMED; A CARPET, TO CARPET, SOMETHING THAT HAS BEEN CARPETED.* A single form was used for the three concrete concepts (*A BIRD, A SOFA, A CAR*), given that these concepts did not have similar variants. As described earlier, the form of concepts had no effect. Thus, we only report results collapsed across forms (e.g., results are combined for *A FREEDOM, TO FREE,* and *FREELY*).

Six lists of the nine critical items were constructed. Each contained one variant of each abstract concept, one variant of each intermediate concept, and all three of the fixed concrete concepts. One set of three lists was counter-balanced such that each variant of a concept occurred equally often, and also such that the variants of different concepts differed maximally within a given list. Each third of the list contained one abstract concept, one concrete concept, and one intermediate concept, in random orders. The entire counterbalancing process was performed twice, to produce a second set of three lists, so that a given concept's list position varied, along with its neighbors, in the respective third of the list.

A short paragraph was constructed for each concept that described a relevant situation. For variants of *TRUTH*, the paragraph described a boy telling his mom that he wasn't responsible for breaking a living room vase, and his mom believing him. Similarly, for *CAR*, a short paragraph described a woman using her car for commuting to work, and listening to music while doing so. As described earlier, the open-ended nature of the protocols obscured any effects of this manipulation, such that it receives no further discussion here.

Participants and Design. Initially, the study included 24 Emory undergraduates who participated for pay. Half received the words in isolation, and half received the words preceded by situations. Within each group, two participants received each of the six versions of the critical list.

Over the course of data analysis, three participants' data were lost due to computer problems (one situations subject and two no-situations subjects). For the remaining 21 participants, 4 of the 189 protocols (21 participants × 9 concepts) were also lost due to computer problems. No more than one protocol was ever lost per concept or participant, and these were distributed evenly across abstract, concrete, and intermediate categories. Because of this study's exploratory nature, these missing participants and protocols were not replaced. Because concept abstractness was manipulated within participants, every remaining participant's data could be assessed on this variable.

Procedure. Participants received the following open-ended instructions to produce the properties of concepts:

The general purpose of this experiment is to study people's knowledge about the world. Our specific purpose here today is to learn more about people's understanding of a few specific concepts. Before we go any further, let me stress that there are no correct responses to the questions that I am about to ask you. Thus, please don't worry about whether you've come up with the right answer or not. This is not an issue at all. Instead, what we're doing here is performing a scientific experiment, where the purpose of this experiment is to understand how normal people like yourself think about various concepts. Here's what you can do to help us learn more about this. In a moment, when I ask you about various concepts, please respond with the very first thoughts that come to mind, and then keep responding with the thoughts that continue to come to mind, until I ask you to stop.

Later in the instructions, participants practiced producing properties for *TREE, BRICK, PENCIL,* and *CAMERA* verbally. The instructions did not give any examples of possible properties that could be produced, so as to avoid biasing participants' responses. On every trial, participants received the following instruction:

Please report your thoughts as they come to mind.
What characteristics are typically true of the following concept: [concept name]

When ready, participants began producing characteristics verbally for a full 1 min. Whenever a participant paused for 5 sec, the experimenter stated, "Please continue to describe your thoughts as they come to mind." When participants were in the middle of describing a property at the 1 min point, they were allowed to complete the description. A digital video camera captured each protocol to a computer, with participants consenting to the recording process.

Prior to the nine critical trials, participants produced properties for six randomly ordered practice concepts, which they did not realize constituted practice. As for the critical materials, two concepts were abstract (*INTEGRITY, VAGUE*), two were concrete (*A ROSE, A BRUISE*), and two were intermediate (*TO HAMMER, SOMETHING THAT HAS BEEN PAINTED*).

Analysis 1: Establishing the Content of Protocol Elements

Each of the nine critical protocols for a given participant was transcribed and coded using the Noldus software for digital video coding. As a judge viewed a protocol, she transcribed each statement into a file and coded it with one of the 45 coding categories from the Wu and Barsalou (2004) coding scheme.[3] These 45 coding categories fell into 5 general groups: taxonomic, entity, setting/event,[4] introspective, and miscellaneous. A taxonomic code was applied to statements that mentioned a taxonomic category related to the target concept. An entity code was applied to statements that described a property of a physical object. A setting/event code was applied to statements that described a property of a setting or event. An introspective code was applied to statements that described the mental state of someone in a situation.

The specific taxonomic coding categories were synonym, ontological category, superordinate, coordinate, subordinate, and individual. The specific entity coding categories were external component, internal component, external surface property, internal surface property, substance/material, spatial relation, systemic property, larger whole, entity behavior, abstract entity property, and quantity. The specific setting/event coding categories were person, nonperson living thing, setting object, social organization, social artifact, building, location, spatial relation, time, action, event, manner, function, physical state, social state, and quantity. The specific introspective coding categories were affect/emotion, evaluation, representational state, cognitive operation, contingency, negation, and quantity. The specific miscellaneous coding categories were cue repetition, hesitation, repetition, and meta-comment. For definitions of these categories, see Wu and Barsalou (2004), Cree and McRae (2003),

---

[3] An updated version of the Wu and Barsalou (2004) scheme was used that incorporated additional categories found by McRae and Cree (2002) to be important.

[4] In Wu and Barsalou (2004), McRae and Cree (2002), and Cree and McRae (2003), "setting/event properties" were referred to as "situational properties." We refer to them as "setting/event properties" here because we use "situation" more generally to include introspective information, not just external information about settings and events in the world.

TABLE 7.1. *Proportions of Property Types for Different Concept Types from Analysis 1*

Concept type	Property type			
	Taxonomic	Entity	Setting/Event	Introspective
Concrete	.07	.26	.46	.21
Intermediate	.04	.22	.53	.22
Abstract	.05	.15	.52	.28
Average	.05	.21	.50	.24

McRae and Cree (2002), and Krauth-Gruber et al. (2004). Figure 7.1 presents a representative protocol coded with this scheme (also see Figure 7.2 later).

In analyzing the results, few differences of theoretical importance occurred at the level of the 45 specific codes. Instead, the interesting results appeared at the level of the general coding categories, aggregating across the specific codes within them. Thus, we only report results from the general level. To establish reliability, a second judge coded the statements for a single participant's nine concepts, and agreed with 95% of the codes given by the judge who coded all of the protocols. Similar levels of agreement using this scheme were reported in Wu and Barsalou (2004), where reliability averaged 90%.

Table 7.1 presents the proportions of protocol statements in the four general coding categories of interest: taxonomic, entity, setting/event, and introspective properties. For each of the 21 participants, the average proportion of properties was computed for each of the 4 general coding categories, once each across the 3 concepts for each of the 3 concept types. These proportions were subjected to an arcsin transformation that normalized variance (Winer, 1971), and then submitted to a mixed ANOVA having context, concept abstractness, and general coding category as factors. Unless noted otherwise, all reported tests were significant at the .05 level. Because the tests assessed a priori predictions, post hoc corrections were not employed. The large size of most F values further reduces the probability of a Type I error. *MSEs* are reported in arcsin units.

Overall Differences in Content. The proportions for the four general coding categories differed ($F(3,57) = 160.13$, $MSE = .02$ arcsin). As Table 7.1 illustrates, setting/event properties were produced most often in the protocols. Half of the properties produced, .50 overall, described aspects of settings and events. Notably, introspective properties were next most frequent (.24), followed by entity properties (.21), and taxonomic categories (.05). In statistical tests of the adjacent differences, setting/event properties were

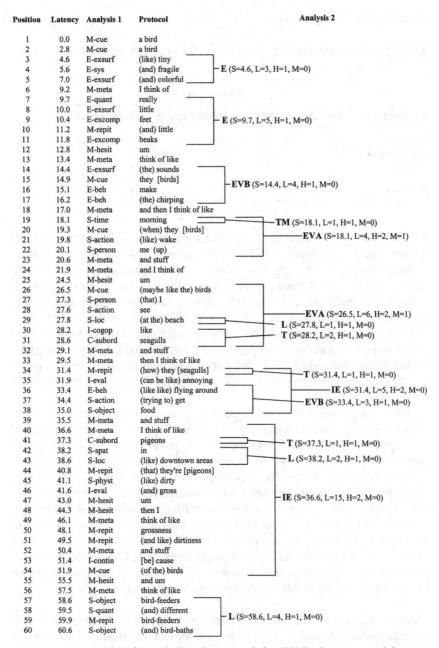

Position	Latency	Analysis 1	Protocol	Analysis 2
1	0.0	M-cue	a bird	
2	2.8	M-cue	a bird	
3	4.6	E-exsurf	(like) tiny	
4	5.6	E-sys	(and) fragile	E (S=4.6, L=3, H=1, M=0)
5	7.0	E-exsurf	(and) colorful	
6	9.2	M-meta	I think of	
7	9.7	E-quant	really	
8	10.0	E-exsurf	little	
9	10.4	E-excomp	feet	E (S=9.7, L=5, H=1, M=0)
10	11.2	M-repit	(and) little	
11	11.8	E-excomp	beaks	
12	12.8	M-hesit	um	
13	13.4	M-meta	think of like	
14	14.4	E-exsurf	(the) sounds	
15	14.9	M-cue	they [birds]	EVB (S=14.4, L=4, H=1, M=0)
16	15.1	E-beh	make	
17	16.2	E-beh	(the) chirping	
18	17.0	M-meta	and then I think of like	
19	18.1	S-time	morning	TM (S=18.1, L=1, H=1, M=0)
20	19.3	M-cue	(when) they [birds]	EVA (S=18.1, L=4, H=2, M=1)
21	19.8	S-action	(like) wake	
22	20.1	S-person	me (up)	
23	20.6	M-meta	and stuff	
24	21.9	M-meta	and I think of	
25	24.5	M-hesit	um	
26	26.5	M-cue	(maybe like the) birds	
27	27.3	S-person	(that) I	EVA (S=26.5, L=6, H=2, M=1)
28	27.6	S-action	see	
29	27.8	S-loc	(at the) beach	L (S=27.8, L=1, H=1, M=0)
30	28.2	I-cogop	like	
31	28.6	C-subord	seagulls	T (S=28.2, L=2, H=1, M=0)
32	29.1	M-meta	and stuff	
33	29.5	M-meta	then I think of like	
34	31.4	M-repit	(how) they [seagulls]	T (S=31.4, L=1, H=1, M=0)
35	31.9	I-eval	(can be like) annoying	IE (S=31.4, L=5, H=2, M=0)
36	33.4	E-beh	(like like) flying around	
37	34.4	S-action	(trying to) get	EVB (S=33.4, L=3, H=1, M=0)
38	35.0	S-object	food	
39	35.5	M-meta	and stuff	
40	36.6	M-meta	I think of like	
41	37.3	C-subord	pigeons	T (S=37.3, L=1, H=1, M=0)
42	38.2	S-spat	in	
43	38.6	S-loc	(like) downtown areas	L (S=38.2, L=2, H=1, M=0)
44	40.8	M-repit	(that) they're [pigeons]	
45	41.1	S-physt	(like) dirty	
46	41.6	I-eval	(and) gross	IE (S=36.6, L=15, H=2, M=0)
47	43.0	M-hesit	um	
48	44.3	M-hesit	then I	
49	46.1	M-meta	think of like	
50	48.1	M-repit	grossness	
51	49.5	M-repit	(and like) dirtiness	
52	50.4	M-meta	and stuff	
53	51.4	I-contin	[be] cause	
54	51.9	M-cue	(of the) birds	
55	55.5	M-hesit	and um	
56	57.5	M-meta	think of like	
57	58.6	S-object	bird-feeders	
58	59.5	S-quant	(and) different	L (S=58.6, L=4, H=1, M=0)
59	59.9	M-repit	bird-feeders	
60	60.6	S-object	(and) bird-baths	

FIGURE 7.1. Example of an analyzed protocol for *BIRD*. Position and latency (sec) for each coded statement in the protocol is shown. Text in parenthesis was produced in the protocol but not coded. Text in brackets was added by the coder to facilitate interpretation. The codes from Analyses 1 and 2 are also shown., along with the brackets used to indicate clusters in Analysis 2. For Analysis 1, C-* represents a taxonomic statement, E-* represents an entity statement, S-* represents a

significantly more likely than introspective properties ($F(1,57) = 44.15$, $MSE = .02$ arcsin); introspective properties did not differ from entity properties ($F(1,57) = .84$, $MSE = .02$ arcsin, $p > .25$); entity properties were significantly more likely than taxonomic properties ($F(1,57) = 30.24$, $MSE = .02$ arcsin).

These results offer support for Hypothesis 1, namely, background situational information is central to the representation of concepts. Properties that described settings and events were mentioned most often overall, and introspective properties were mentioned frequently as well. Entity properties were also mentioned, but overall, they only occurred at a rate of .21, whereas setting/event and introspective properties occurred at a combined rate of .74. Clearly situational information is central to the knowledge that people have about concepts.

Differences Between Concept Types. Are there departures from the overall trend at each level of concept abstractness? A significant interaction between concept abstractness and general coding category indicated that this ordering differed somewhat between concrete, intermediate, and abstract concepts ($F(1,57) = 15.18$, $MSE = .02$ arcsin). Although informative differences occurred between these concept types, as described shortly, the overall trend across types tended to occur for each individually. As Table 7.1 illustrates, setting/event properties were always most important, followed by introspection and entity properties (whose ordering differed slightly between types), with taxonomic properties always last. The interaction notwithstanding, it's clear that setting/event information is central for every category type.

The differences responsible for the interaction support Hypothesis 2, namely, concrete concepts focused on entity properties within situations, whereas abstract concepts focused on setting/event and introspection properties. A planned comparison to test this prediction used the following contrast weights: for concrete concepts, the means were weighted +2 (entity), −1 (setting/event), −1 (introspective); for abstract concepts, the means were weighted −2 (entity), +1 (setting/event), +1 (introspective). In support of Hypothesis 2, this comparison was significant ($F(1,57) = 16.94$, $MSE = .02$ arcsin). Although participants spent much time describing situations for all concepts, they focused more on entities for concrete concepts, and more on settings, events, and introspections for abstract concepts. Intermediate concepts fell in between, having

---

FIGURE 7.1 (*cont.*) setting/event statement, I-* represents an introspective statement, and M-* represents a miscellaneous statement. * represents the name of the specific code applied to the statement, which was not used in the analysis. See the text and the appendix for further detail on the coding schemes.

intermediate levels of the information distinctive for concrete and abstract concepts.

Analysis 2: Establishing Hierarchical Systems of Larger Protocol Units

The Wu and Barsalou (2004) coding scheme produces a micro-analysis of a protocol, parsing it into very small units and coding their individual content. Clearly, however, sets of these small units form larger groups, which the Wu and Barsalou scheme doesn't capture. Thus, this second analysis attempted to identify these groups. On the basis of examining the protocols, coding categories for these groups were developed and applied to the protocols. As the Appendix illustrates, larger groups of statements often described various types of entities, events, and introspections, along with taxonomic categories and social institutions. Figure 7.2 presents a representative protocol for an abstract concept coded with this scheme. For a representative example of a concrete concept, see Figure 7.1 presented earlier.

Coding Procedure. To establish the reliability of the coding scheme, a second judge independently coded all of the protocols. For clusters that both judges identified, they used the same code 88% of the time. The second judged failed to include 10% of the clusters that the first judge included, and added 2% additional clusters. Thus agreement on these clusters was reasonably high.

Several other aspects of each cluster were coded besides its content. First, the average latency to the beginning of each cluster was recorded. The cluster labels in Figures 7.1 and 7.2 provide the starting cluster latencies using "$S =$ ".

Second, the average length of each cluster was recorded (i.e., the number of Wu and Barsalou statements it contained). Note that we included clusters of only a single statement if that statement contained information for a particular cluster type in the analysis. Single-statement clusters were included so that every occurrence of each content type would be counted in this analysis, even when short. Figures 7.1 and 7.2 illustrate examples of single-statement clusters. The cluster labels in Figures 7.1 and 7.2 provide cluster length using "$L =$ ".

Third, the average hierarchical level of each cluster was recorded. As Figures 7.1 and 7.2 illustrate, clusters were often embedded within each other hierarchically. The lowest level clusters received values of 1. Clusters that contained at least one level-one cluster received values of 2. Clusters that contained at least one level-two cluster received values of 3, and so forth. The cluster labels in Figures 7.1 and 7.2 provide hierarchical level using "$H =$ ".

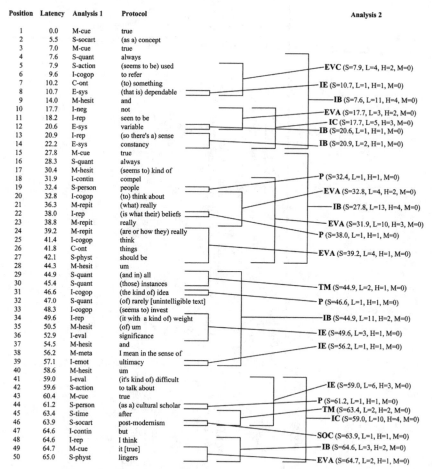

Position	Latency	Analysis 1	Protocol	Analysis 2
1	0.0	M-cue	true	
2	5.5	S-socart	(as a) concept	
3	7.0	M-cue	true	
4	7.6	S-quant	always	
5	7.9	S-action	(seems to be) used	EVC (S=7.9, L=4, H=2, M=0)
6	9.6	I-cogop	to refer	
7	10.2	C-ont	(to) something	IE (S=10.7, L=1, H=1, M=0)
8	10.7	E-sys	(that is) dependable	
9	14.0	M-hesit	and	IB (S=7.6, L=11, H=4, M=0)
10	17.7	I-neg	not	EVA (S=17.7, L=3, H=2, M=0)
11	18.2	I-rep	seen to be	IC (S=17.7, L=5, H=3, M=0)
12	20.6	E-sys	variable	IB (S=20.6, L=1, H=1, M=0)
13	20.9	I-rep	(so there's a) sense	IB (S=20.9, L=2, H=1, M=0)
14	22.2	E-sys	constancy	
15	27.8	M-cue	true	
16	28.3	S-quant	always	
17	30.4	M-hesit	(seems to) kind of	P (S=32.4, L=1, H=1, M=0)
18	31.9	I-contin	compel	
19	32.4	S-person	people	EVA (S=32.8, L=4, H=2, M=0)
20	32.8	I-cogop	(to) think about	
21	36.3	M-repit	(what) really	IB (S=27.8, L=13, H=4, M=0)
22	38.0	I-rep	(is what their) beliefs	
23	38.8	M-repit	really	EVA (S=31.9, L=10, H=3, M=0)
24	39.2	M-repit	(are or how they) really	P (S=38.0, L=1, H=1, M=0)
25	41.4	I-cogop	think	
26	41.8	C-ont	things	EVA (S=39.2, L=4, H=1, M=0)
27	42.1	S-physt	should be	
28	44.3	M-hesit	um	
29	44.9	S-quant	(and in) all	
30	45.4	S-quant	(those) instances	TM (S=44.9, L=2, H=1, M=0)
31	46.6	I-cogop	(the kind of) idea	
32	47.0	S-quant	(of) rarely [unintelligible text]	P (S=46.6, L=1, H=1, M=0)
33	48.3	I-cogop	(seems to) invest	
34	49.6	I-rep	(it with a kind of) weight	IB (S=44.9, L=11, H=2, M=0)
35	50.5	M-hesit	(of) um	
36	52.9	I-eval	significance	IE (S=49.6, L=3, H=1, M=0)
37	54.5	M-hesit	and	IE (S=56.2, L=1, H=1, M=0)
38	56.2	M-meta	I mean in the sense of	
39	57.1	I-emot	ultimacy	
40	58.6	M-hesit	um	
41	59.0	I-eval	(it's kind of) difficult	IE (S=59.0, L=6, H=3, M=0)
42	59.6	S-action	to talk about	
43	60.4	M-cue	true	P (S=61.2, L=1, H=1, M=0)
44	61.2	S-person	(as a) cultural scholar	TM (S=63.4, L=2, H=2, M=0)
45	63.4	S-time	after	IC (S=59.0, L=10, H=4, M=0)
46	63.9	S-socart	post-modernism	
47	64.6	I-contin	but	SOC (S=63.9, L=1, H=1, M=0)
48	64.6	I-rep	I think	IB (S=64.6, L=3, H=2, M=0)
49	64.7	M-cue	it [true]	EVA (S=64.7, L=2, H=1, M=0)
50	65.0	S-physt	lingers	

FIGURE 7.2. Example of an analyzed protocol for *TRUE*. Position and latency (sec) for each coded statement in the protocol is shown. Text in parenthesis was produced in the protocol but not coded. Text in brackets was added by the coder to facilitate interpretation. The codes from Analyses 1 and 2 are also shown., along with the brackets used to indicate clusters in Analysis 2. For Analysis 1, C-* represents a taxonomic statement, E-* represents an entity statement, S-* represents a setting/event statement, I-* represents an introspective statement, and M-* represents a miscellaneous statement. * represents the name of the specific code applied to the statement, which was not used in the analysis. See the text and the appendix for further detail on the coding schemes.

Cluster Content: Overview.

On the average, participants produced 23.50 clusters for concrete concepts, 24.40 for intermediate concepts, and 23.75 for abstract concepts. Table 7.2 presents the proportions of clusters falling into the 14 coding categories of Analysis 2 at each level of concept abstractness.

TABLE 7.2. *Proportion of Cluster Types Across Concept Types from Analysis 2*

		Space-Time		Entities				Event				Introspection			
Concept Type	Taxonomic Category	Location	Time	Object	Person	Characteristic Behavior	Non-Agent	Agentive	Communi-cation	Goal	Evaluation/Affect	Belief	Contingency/Complex Relation	Social Institution
Concrete	.12	.12	.03	.14	.06	.06	.02	.18	.01	.01	.12	.06	.06	.02
Intermediate	.06	.10	.03	.23	.07	.00	.00	.21	.00	.02	.11	.05	.08	.03
Abstract	.05	.02	.03	.05	.20	.00	.01	.18	.05	.02	.09	.11	.12	.08
Average[a]	.08	.08	.03	.14	.11	.02	.01	.19	.02	.02	.11	.07	.09	.04

Note: The total number of clusters was 1,436 for concrete concepts, 1,539 for intermediate concepts, and 1,346 for abstract concepts.
[a] Averages are weighted by the number of observations in each concept type x cluster type cell of the design.

Because one participant's data were lost prior to Analysis 2, only 20 participants were included, 10 with situations and 10 without. For these 20 participants, the average proportion of properties produced in each of the 14 coding categories was established across the 3 concepts at each level of concept abstractness. These proportions were subjected to an arcsin transformation that normalized variance, and were then submitted to a mixed ANOVA having context, concept abstractness, and coding category as factors. Unless noted otherwise, all reported tests were significant at the .05 level. Because all tests assessed a priori predictions, post hoc corrections were not employed. The large size of most F and t values further reduces the probability of a Type I error. MSEs are reported in arcsin units.

As Table 7.2 illustrates, the results from Analysis 2 converge on the same basic conclusions as Analysis 1. On the one hand, the distributions of cluster types are similar across concrete, intermediate, and abstract concepts, indicating that similar types of situation information underlie all three concept types (Hypothesis 1). On the other hand, differential emphasis exists on the different types of situational information for concrete vs. abstract concepts (Hypothesis 2). There is also evidence for greater complexity in abstract concepts (Hypothesis 3).

In the ANOVA, cluster type exhibited a main effect, indicating that some cluster types were more likely than others ($F(13,234) = 53.96$, $MSE = .007$ arcsin). Some of the more common cluster types included agentive events (.19), objects (.14), persons (.11), and evaluations/affects (.11). The importance of a given cluster type was often similar for the three concept types. For example, agentive events and evaluations/affects were important for all three, whereas times, non-agentive events, and goals were relatively unimportant for all three. Clearly, though, important differences occurred, as indicated by a significant interaction between concept type and cluster type ($F(26,234) = 16.84$, $MSE = .007$ arcsin). As will be seen, the specific differences underlying this interaction are consistent with Hypotheses 2 and 3.

Cluster Content: Dominant Cluster Types for Concrete Concepts. First we consider cluster types that tended to be more important for concrete concepts than for abstract ones (intermediate concepts will be included as relevant). As Table 7.2 illustrates, object clusters were more important for concrete and intermediate concepts than for abstract concepts (concrete vs. abstract, $F(1,234) = 11.57$, $MSE = .007$ arcsin; intermediate vs. abstract, $F(1,234) = 48.29$, $MSE = .007$ arcsin). This pattern supports the prediction that concrete and intermediate concepts both focus on physical objects in situations. Interestingly, more object clusters occurred for intermediate than for concrete objects ($F(1,234) = 11.57$, $MSE = .007$ arcsin). This contrasts with the finding from Analysis 1 that entity properties were produced equally often for both concept types. The analysis of cluster length, however, will show that object clusters were longer for concrete concepts than for intermediate ones (Table 7.3). This pattern suggests the following conclusion. For concrete concepts, a single object tends to be salient (e.g., SOFAS), such that participants describe it at length. For intermediate concepts, a *configuration* of objects is often salient, such that participants describe each of them briefly (e.g., TO COOK refers to a cook, food, a stove, utensils, etc.). As a result, more clusters occur for the intermediate concepts, albeit shorter.

Locations were also more important for concrete and intermediate concepts than for abstract ones (concrete vs. abstract, $F(1,234) = 14.29$, $MSE = .007$ arcsin; intermediate vs. abstract, $F(1,234) = 9.14$, $MSE = .007$ arcsin). Concrete and intermediate concepts did not differ. This pattern suggests that people often think of physical objects in particular physical locations. In contrast, abstract concepts appear less tied to particular settings, and more tied to particular types of events, as we will see.

Finally, characteristic behaviors were important only for the concrete concepts (concrete vs. abstract, $F(1,234) = 5.14$, $MSE = .007$ arcsin; concrete vs. intermediate, $F(1,234) = 5.14$, $MSE = .007$ arcsin). When describing these objects, participants often discussed the behaviors that these entities typically exhibit (e.g., for BIRDS, they fly, nest, etc.).

In summary, this pattern is consistent with Hypothesis 2. Although concrete concepts are associated with much of the same situational information as abstract concepts, concrete concepts focus more on the physical aspects of situations, including objects, locations, and typical behaviors. Intermediate concepts also tend to focus attention on objects and locations.

Cluster Content: Dominant Cluster Types for Abstract Concepts. We next consider cluster types that tended to be more important for abstract concepts than for concrete ones. As Table 7.2 illustrates, person clusters were more important for abstract concepts than for concrete and intermediate concepts (abstract vs. concrete, $F(1,234) = 51.57$, $MSE = .007$ arcsin; abstract vs. intermediate, $F(1,234) = 41.29$, $MSE = .007$ arcsin). This suggests that abstract concepts may often have a more social character than concrete concepts, drawing attention to the properties of people and the relations between them. Further evidence for this conclusion is the trend towards significance for communicative events. As Table 7.2 illustrates, descriptions of communication tended to be more likely for abstract concepts than for concrete and intermediate ones (abstract vs. concrete, $F(1,234) = 2.29$, $MSE = .007$ arcsin, $p < .25$; abstract vs. intermediate, $F(1,234) = 3.57$, $MSE = .007$ arcsin, $p < .10$). As Table 7.2 further illustrates, social institutions were mentioned most often for abstract concepts (abstract vs. concrete, $F(1,234) = 5.14$, $MSE = .007$ arcsin; abstract vs. intermediate, $F(1,234) = 3.57$, $MSE = .007$ arcsin, $p < .10$). Together, these three findings suggest that social

TABLE 7.3. *Average Cluster Length and Hierarchical Level for Cluster Types Across Concept Types from Analysis 2*

Concept Type	Taxonomic Category	Cluster Type												
		Space-Time		Entities		Characteristic Behavior	Event				Introspection			
		Location	Time	Object	Person		Non-Agent	Agentive	Communication	Goal	Evaluation/Affect	Belief	Contingency/Complex Relation	Social Institution
Average length														
Concrete	2.59	2.39	1.62	2.23	1.56	3.74	3.32	4.65	5.25	5.38	4.10	5.15	7.92	4.09
Intermediate	5.40	2.37	1.17	1.52	1.50	1.00	4.20	3.89	4.89	4.52	3.92	5.71	9.23	2.43
Abstract	3.48	1.53	1.51	1.21	1.38	1.00	2.44	3.68	3.59	3.64	2.78	6.15	8.82	1.96
Average¹	3.49	2.30	1.44	1.69	1.45	3.66	3.23	4.06	3.98	4.43	3.72	5.75	8.73	2.35
Average hierarchical level														
Concrete	1.14	1.07	1.00	1.09	1.00	1.29	1.42	1.63	1.25	1.67	1.40	1.74	2.16	1.50
Intermediate	1.47	1.12	1.00	1.06	1.04	1.00	1.80	1.66	1.67	2.08	1.50	1.95	2.53	1.23
Abstract	1.29	1.11	1.05	1.05	1.04	1.00	1.22	1.68	1.56	1.64	1.47	2.06	2.60	1.15
Average[a]	1.25	1.10	1.02	1.07	1.03	1.29	1.43	1.66	1.52	1.80	1.45	1.94	2.47	1.21

[a] Averages are weighted by the number of observations in each concept type x cluster type cell of the design.

situations may often be central to the content of abstract concepts. This is consistent with Hypothesis 2's prediction that abstract concepts focus attention on complex conceptual structures in background situations.

Abstract concepts were also most likely to exhibit two forms of introspection. First, beliefs tended to occur more often for abstract concepts than for the other two concept types (abstract vs. concrete, $F(1,234) = 3.57$, $MSE = .007$ arcsin, $p < .10$; abstract vs. intermediate, $F(1,234) = 5.14$, $MSE = .007$ arcsin). Processing abstract concepts often triggered a participant's opinion on these concepts. Second, contingency and other complex relations also tended to occur most often for abstract concepts (abstract vs. concrete, $F(1,234) = 5.14$, $MSE = .007$ arcsin; abstract vs. intermediate, $F(1,234) = 2.29$, $MSE = .007$ arcsin, $p < .25$). This finding is consistent with the conclusion that the conceptual content of abstract concepts is more complex than the content of concrete concepts. Because abstract concepts often depend critically on multiple pieces of information distributed across a situation, complex relations are needed to coordinate them.

Cluster Latency. The average latency across all clusters was 30.29 sec, which is what would be expected in a protocol that lasts about 60 sec. Notably, the average latencies did not vary substantially from this overall average, indicating that a given type of cluster could occur at just about any point in a protocol, for a given type of concept. There appeared to be little tendency for a particular type of cluster to occur early or late, with this flexibility holding equally for different concept types and for different cluster types.

Cluster Length. The top half of Table 7.3 presents the average lengths of clusters. Average cluster lengths did not differ significantly between concrete (3.67), intermediate (3.55), and abstract concepts (3.69). However, cluster lengths did vary considerably across cluster types. Cluster length increased from physical clusters (location, time, object, person), to event clusters (characteristic behavior, nonagentive, agentive, communicative), to introspective clusters (goal, evaluations/affects, belief, contingency/complex relations). Specifically, the average cluster length for event clusters (4.00) was longer than for physical clusters (1.75) ($t(2,613) = 18.51$, $SE = .12$). In turn, the average cluster length was longer for introspective clusters (5.90) than for events clusters (4.00) ($t(2,296) = 9.08$, $SE = .21$). One interpretation of this pattern is that physical components were relatively easy to describe, and therefore required short clusters. When clusters described events and introspective states, they become increasing complex conceptually, thereby requiring longer descriptions.

Hierarchical Level. The bottom half of Table 7.3 presents the average hierarchical level of clusters. As Hypothesis 3 predicts, the average hierarchical level of a cluster increased with concept abstractness, indicating greater organizational complexity in abstract concepts. Clusters for intermediate concepts (1.46) had higher hierarchical levels than clusters for concrete concepts (1.37) ($t(2,973) = 5.09$, $SE = .02$). In turn, clusters for abstract concepts (1.57) had higher hierarchical levels than clusters for intermediate concepts (1.46) (1.37) ($t(2,883) = 5.35$, $SE = .02$).

Hierarchical level also varied across cluster types. Specifically, hierarchical level increased from physical clusters (location, time, object, person), to event clusters (characteristic behavior, non-agentive, agentive, communicative), to introspective clusters (goal, evaluations/affects, belief, contingency/complex relations). The average hierarchical level for event clusters (1.62) was higher than for physical clusters (1.06) ($t(2,613) = 20.29$, $SE = .03$). In turn, the average level was higher for introspective clusters (1.93) than for event clusters (1.63) ($t(2,296) = 7.36$, $SE = .04$).

One interpretation of this pattern is as follows. Physical components are most primitive and therefore constitute the lowest level of description. In turn, events tend to build on physical components and thus establish higher-level clusters that include physical ones. Finally, introspective clusters tend to be highest because they often integrate lower- and intermediate-level clusters for physical components and events. Consistent with this account, contingency/complex relations (2.47), along with beliefs (1.94) and goals (1.80), tended to reside at the highest hierarchical levels.

One final aspect of hierarchical level concerns its relation to cluster length. As a cluster increases in level, it should tend to incorporate increasing numbers of Level 1 clusters, such that its overall length increases. To test this hypothesis, the overall averages for cluster length were correlated with the overall averages for cluster level. The resulting correlation was .97, indicating that hierarchical level played a major role in cluster length.

Episodic vs. Generic Memory. Because episodic memories were observed in the protocols, each cluster was coded for whether it appeared to be an episodic vs. generic memory. Clusters were coded as episodic when they obviously contained an autobiographical memory, or when they met Nelson's (1986) person, tense, and article criteria for being episodic. In Figures 7.1 and 7.2, $M = 0$ indicates generic status and $M = 1$ indicates episodic status.

Overall, episodic content occurred in 11% of the clusters, but increased with concreteness (8% for abstract concepts, 10% for intermediate concepts, 14% for concrete concepts). This trend is consistent with much research showing that concrete concepts are better cues for memory (e.g., Paivio, 1986), and also for analogy (e.g., Gentner, Ratterman, & Forbus, 1993; Ross & Kilbane, 1997). Nevertheless, all concept types accessed episodic information. Interestingly, the least likely clusters for a given concept type tended to produce the most episodic access. Thus, concrete object and location clusters were more likely to produce episodic memories for abstract concepts than for concrete concepts, whereas social and introspective clusters were more likely to produce episodic memories for concrete concepts. One possibility is that infrequently retrieved types of information aren't as automatized or generic as frequent types, and thus rely more on episodic memories for their content.

Summary of Analyses 1 and 2

Both analyses offer support for Hypothesis 1, namely, common situational content is produced across concrete, intermediate, and abstract concepts. Regardless of the concept, participants tended to describe background situations, including information about entities, settings, events, and introspections. In Analysis 1, 50% of protocol content described settings and events, 24% described introspections, and 21% described entities. Although these values varied somewhat by concept type, all concept types included significant amounts of each content type. Analysis 2 similarly found that clusters for physical settings (36%), events (24%), and introspections (29%) occurred consistently across concrete, intermediate, and abstract concepts.

Both analyses also offer support for Hypothesis 2, namely, the focus on situational content differs for concrete and abstract concepts, with intermediate concepts lying in between. In Analysis 1, the percentage of entity properties increased from abstract (15%) to intermediate (22%) to concrete (26%) concepts. Similarly, in Analysis 2, concrete concepts had higher percentages of objects (14%), locations (12%), and characteristic behaviors (6%) than did abstract concepts (5%, 2%, and 0%, respectively). These patterns suggest that concrete concepts focus more on objects, locations, and behaviors in situations than do abstract concepts.

Conversely, abstract concepts focus more on social aspects of situations, such as people, communication, and social institutions. Abstract concepts also focus more on introspections, especially beliefs and contingency/complex relations. In Analysis 1, the percentage of introspection properties was higher for abstract concepts (28%) than for concrete and intermediate concepts (21%, 22%). In Analysis 2, person clusters were higher for abstract concepts (20%) than for concrete concepts (6%), as were communicative events (5% vs. 1%), and social institutions (8% vs. 2%). Similarly, belief clusters were higher for abstract concepts (11%) than for concrete concepts (6%), as were complex/contingency relations (12% vs. 6%). Thus, both Analyses 1 and 2 indicate that concrete and abstract concepts emphasize different aspects of situational content.

Analysis 2 also offered support for Hypothesis 3, namely, that abstract concepts are more complex than concrete concepts, with intermediate concepts lying between. As concept abstractness increased, so did hierarchical complexity. Specifically, the average hierarchical level of clusters increased from concrete (1.37) to intermediate (1.46) to abstract concepts (1.57). As concepts became more abstract, the structures describing them included greater depths of nested clusters.

The following pattern across the different cluster measures brings out the nature of this increasing complexity. As Table 7.2 illustrates, abstract concepts were nearly twice as likely to have contingency/complex and belief clusters than were concrete concepts (23% vs. 12% overall). As Table 7.3 illustrates, contingency/complex and belief clusters were the two longest types of clusters observed (8.73 and 5.75 vs. values that ranged from 1.44 to 4.43 for the other cluster types). As Table 7.3 further illustrates, contingency/complex and belief clusters were also the highest hierarchically, along with goal clusters (2.47, 1.94, and 1.80 vs. values that ranged from 1.02 to 1.66 for the other cluster types). Putting all this together, abstract concepts were most likely to have the types of clusters that were especially long and especially high hierarchically. Consistent with Hypothesis 3, conceptual structures for abstract concepts were more complex than those for concrete concepts.

DISCUSSION

This exploratory study provides evidence for Hypotheses 1, 2, and 3. Clearly, though, this study only constitutes a preliminary attempt at establishing the representation of abstract concepts. Many issues remain unresolved, and much further research remains to be done.

Was the Particular Nature of the Task Responsible for the Results?

In the exploratory study reported here, diverse types of information were produced for both concrete and abstract concepts. Not only did participants produce information about objects and events, they produced considerable introspective information about idiosyncratic beliefs and complex contingencies. Furthermore, they produced episodic information along with generic information. Is this information typical of what people produce for concepts? Or was something unusual about this study responsible?

Perhaps the open-ended nature of our probe was a factor, namely, participants were told that there were no "correct" properties to produce, and that they should produce information as it came to mind. Participants were not asked to focus their responses in any particular manner, such as providing concept definitions. Furthermore, we required that participants respond for a full 1 min, which probably contributed further to the diverse content obtained.

Another set of factors concerns the particular concepts studied. First, only three concepts were studied for each type. Perhaps these particular samples of concepts biased responses. Second, concepts of very different types were mixed together. Perhaps carry-over effects occurred from one concept type to another (e.g., perhaps the introspections important for abstract concepts carried over to concrete concepts).

We agree that future studies should be aware of such factors, and that resolving their effects is important. Nevertheless, we do not believe that these factors distorted the results of this study. First, we believe that the open-ended nature of our probe is a desirable quality in exploring conceptual content. Problematically, when probes restrict responses, the responses obtained may be tailored online to the information requested. As a result, the responses may not provide a representative account of the underlying information in memory. For example, when researchers present a vertical column of short blanks on a page, and ask participants to list the defining features of a concept, this may produce online processing tailored to the constraints of the task. Participants may scan across many situations, and try to find common properties that fit in the short blanks. Even though participants may actually be retrieving a diverse collection of situations, the response method may not allow them to express it. Instead, the response format may more reflect the experimenter's a priori belief that feature lists represent concepts. We believe that open-ended response collection enables more direct measurement of the underlying information stored for a concept.

Second, the types of content observed here have been observed before. Previous studies using the Wu and Barsalou coding scheme have observed similar distributions of content (e.g., Cree & McRae, 2003; Krauth-Gruber et al., 2004; McRae & Cree, 2002; Wu & Barsalou, 2004). More recently, Wiemer-Hastings and Xu (2004) have found that situational properties are produced more often than entity and introspective properties in a larger sample of concrete and abstract concepts than explored here. Again, concrete concepts were more likely to produce entity properties, whereas abstract concepts were more likely to produce introspective properties (this pattern was more accentuated in their data than in ours). Notably, these distributions were produced in much shorter protocols than those collected here. Thus, increasing research converges on the distributions of content observed here for concrete and abstract concepts.

Third, we agree that it is important to study more than three concepts per concept type. Nevertheless, the concepts studied here are representative of their respective types. Clearly, *TRUTH, FREEDOM,* and *INVENTION* are abstract concepts, whereas *SOFA, CAR,* and *BIRD* are concrete. Although various subtypes of abstract and concrete concepts may exhibit somewhat different content, we suspect that the general trends observed here are likely to be observed.

Finally, it may well be true that carry-over effects occurred between concept types, and that different results would be found for a pure list of abstract or concrete concepts. Nevertheless, an important question to ask is what this would tell us. People don't normally process either concrete or abstract concepts in isolation. Instead, these concept types are almost always processed together, as a quick examination of any text will indicate. Thus, a mixed list may represent actual processing conditions better than a pure list. If carry-over effects are occurring, they may reflect a natural phenomenon that enters into the normal processing of concrete and abstract concepts.

Does the Conceptual Content Observed Here Constitute Core Knowledge?

In the concepts and categories literature, the representations studied are typically much simpler than the ones observed here. In category learning research, conceptual knowledge often consists of exemplars or prototypes defined by only a few physical properties. In work that focuses on concepts in higher cognition, even these representations are relatively simple, often taking the form of a single feature list, or a single relational structure. Not only is the amount of content vastly smaller in these standard representations, the content is also vastly restricted, excluding not only introspective information, but also much event information (cf. Markman & Ross, 2003). Clearly, idealization is a useful scientific strategy, and it has led to many important discoveries in the categorization literature. Nevertheless, it may be misleading to assume that these simpler representations constitute the content of conceptual knowledge. Conceptual knowledge may include much larger amounts of content, and also a much wider variety.

On the basis of our findings, a reader might be convinced that a concept contains larger amounts of more varied knowledge than usually assumed, but still argue that most of this knowledge is relatively peripheral to the concept's core content. This view, however, assumes not only that core knowledge exists for concepts, but also that it is most central. On this view, a concept is like a dictionary or encyclopedia entry that attempts to define a category with a centralized summary representation.

Since Wittgenstein (1953), however, empirical findings have not been kind to this view. Not only is it intuitively difficult to define most natural concepts, there appears to be little empirical evidence for such definitions (e.g., Hampton, 1979; McCloskey & Glucksberg, 1978; Rosch & Mervis, 1975). Furthermore, extensive research on exemplar models has suggested that diverse collections of exemplars can implement many conceptual functions (e.g., Medin & Schaffer, 1978).

Barsalou (2003a, 2003b) presents an alternative to the core knowledge view (also see Barsalou, Niedenthal et al., 2003). On this account, a concept generates a multitude of situational representations, each tailored to guiding goal-directed activity with a particular concept instance in a particular situation. For example, the concept for *CARS* produces diverse situational representations that guide various car activities, such as driving, fueling, washing, buying, etc. Furthermore, each of these situational representations contains entity, setting, event, and introspective information relevant to the respective goal-directed activity. On this view, learning a concept establishes the ability to completely represent a wide variety of situations relevant to interacting with the concept's instances. As a result, a concept becomes a large collection of situational representations.

This account explains the results of the exploratory study here. When people produce information about a concept in an unconstrained manner, they retrieve and describe a wide variety of situations in a relatively haphazard manner, regardless of whether the concept is concrete or abstract. Furthermore, these situations exhibit the diverse content observed here, including entity, setting, event, and introspective information. Finally, much personalized content is included, such as beliefs, opinions, and episodic memories, because this information supports individualized interactions with concept instances. Because people differ in the goals, values, and experiences associated with a concept's instances, their knowledge becomes tailored to optimize their particular interactions with them.

An important question is whether a core definition exists across situations. One possibility is that such definitions don't usually exist explicitly in memory. Instead, when people are asked to produce a definition, they sample from situations in memory, and produce an online definition that covers just these situations (e.g., Barsalou, 2003a, 2003b; Medin & Ross, 1989; Ross, Perkins, & Tenpenny, 1990). If a person performs this activity a lot, and thoroughly samples situations from memory, a core definition might become explicitly established. Nevertheless, this definition may still be relatively peripheral. As people encounter concept instances in the world, they may be more likely to retrieve a situational representation suited to interacting with it, rather than the definition, which may not be particularly useful.

If this account is correct, it suggests an important direction for future research. Rather than allowing people to produce the content of a concept in an unrestricted manner, it might be useful to have them produce content relevant to a specific situation. If the primary role of concepts is to serve situated action, then studying their actual use in situations may provide insights into them. Not only might this be true for abstract concepts, it may be equally true for concrete ones.

Can Embodied Theories Explain the Content of Abstract Concepts?

For most of this paper, we have focused on the content of abstract concepts, having little to say about embodiment. Establishing the content of abstract concepts, however, is an essential first step in explaining how embodied theories could represent them. We can only begin formulating embodied accounts once we have identified the content of these concepts. We believe that the importance of this first step constitutes an appropriate contribution for an edited volume on embodied cognition.

As we have seen, abstract concepts focus on social, event, and introspective content, while also including, less centrally, content about physical settings. How might embodied theories represent this situational content? One answer is that the conceptual system stores memories of situational perceptions, and then later simulates these memories to represent concepts (Yeh & Barsalou, 2004). To see this, consider the content of perception. At any given moment, people perceive the immediate space around them, including the setting, objects, agents, and events present. They also perceive current introspective states, including affects, drives, and cognitive operations. Most importantly, even when people focus attention on a particular entity or event in the situation, they continue to perceive the background situation – it does not disappear. If perceptual experience takes the form of a situation, and if a conceptual representation simulates perceptual experience, then the form of a conceptual representation should take the form of a perceived situation. When people construct a simulation to represent a category, they should tend to envision the category in a relevant perceptual situation, not in isolation. When people conceptualize *CHAIR*, for example, they should attempt to simulate not only a chair, but a more complete perceptual situation, including the surrounding space, along with any relevant agents, objects, events, and introspective states.

In principle, it seems possible that an embodied view could represent all of the content observed here for abstract concepts. Because all of this content is perceived in the situations that involve abstract concepts, this content could, in principle, be simulated later when representing these concepts. If these states existed at the time of processing an actual situation, there is no reason why they cannot be reenacted later. Clearly, though, much further research, aimed at addressing this particular proposal, is necessary.

APPENDIX CODING CATEGORIES FOR ANALYSIS 2

In the examples shown below for each coding category, the target concept is shown in lower case italics, and the coded information is shown in upper case.

Taxonomic Category (*T*)

A concept from the same taxonomy as the target concept, including superordinates, subordinates, coordinates, and individuals; for nonobjects, may be antonyms or other related concepts from the same taxonomic field, unless a dependency between them is stated; often contrastive; for personality traits, go with *P* if the focus is on the person, but go with *T* if the focus is on the taxonomy; also includes contrasts within a category across multiple types of things, discussing different kinds of things at high level, etc. (e.g. *bird*–ANIMAL, *truth*–LIE).

Space and Time

Location (L). A place where an entity or event occurs; may be an environmental setting, or a larger contextual object (e.g., *bird*–GEORGIA, *a carpet*–ON THE FLOOR).

Time (TM). A time when an entity or event occurs; may be a time of day, year, holiday, etc. (e.g., *sofa*–PRETTY SOON (I'M GETTING A COUCH); *to invent*–RIGHT NOW (WHAT WE HAVE IS THE RESULT OF INVENTIONS).

Entities

Object (O). An entity; a physical/structural property of a physical entity; not a person; can be a description of either a target entity or some other entity in a situation (e.g. *bird*–WINGS; *car*–WHEELS).

Person (P). A person; a property of a person, often an agent in a situation; typically a personality trait, ability, or mental capacity, although physical properties are possible, too; for personality traits, the focus is on the person, not on a taxonomy, in which case use T; do not include goals, which go in IG; etc. (e.g., *to cook*–A LOT OF MOTHERS; *true*–A CULTURAL SCHOLAR).

Events

Characteristic Behavior (EVB). The characteristic behavior of an entity described in an aggregate manner (e.g., *bird*–SINGS; *a farm*–GRASS GROWTH).

NonAgentive (EVN). A nonintentional event typically involving inanimate objects (e.g., *car*–AXELS ROT; *to carpet*–YOUR HOUSE GETS FLOODED).

Agentive (EVA). An event involving an agent; not typically an aggregate statement about the characteristic behavior of an entity (EVB); typically a event initiated by an agent that has an effect on a patient; nonhumans can be agents as long is the event is not an aggregate description of their characteristic behavior; (e.g. *to cook*–YOU HEAT SOMETHING UP ON THE STOVE; *true*–PEOPLE THINK ABOUT WHAT THEIR BELIEFS REALLY ARE).

Communication (EVC). Any act of communication (e.g., *true*–WHEN WHAT YOU'RE SAYING IS NOT A LIE; *freedom*–PEOPLE ON TV SAYING WHATEVER THEY WANT TO BE SAYING).

Introspections

Goal (IG). The goal or intention of an agent; often "the reason" for something (e.g. *true*–PEOPLE DON'T REALLY WANT TO KNOW WHAT'S GOING ON; *cook*–TO MAKE EXACTLY WHAT YOU WANT TO EAT).

Evaluation/Affect (IA). An evaluation or emotion (typically by the subject), (e.g., *pigeon*–DIRTY; *freedom*–INTERESTING TO ME).

Belief (IB). An at least somewhat tenuous belief (typically held by the participant); typically a claim about fact or the state of the world; not something obvious or known; not knowledge; instead, something that is contestable; often an opinion; when evaluation is salient, use IE; if a contingency is present, use IC; if the opinion is strong, stay with IB (e.g.; *justice*–BEAUROCRATIC; *sofa*–YOU DON'T SIT RIGID ON A SOFA).

Contingency/Complex Relation (IC). A contingency of some sort, a dependency, necessity, possession, part-whole relation, or some other complex relation; contingencies can be if-then relations, or dependencies, such as a concept depending on some property for its definition, where the relation is stated explicitly (could be a necessity); other complex relations may apply as well, such temporal relations, an agent possessing something, part-whole relations, etc.; typically the arguments of each relation should be coded as well with some other cluster code; other lexical signals include because, unless, only if, after, before, etc. (e.g., *true*–DIFFICULT TO DISCUSS AFTER POST MODERNISM; *freedom*–THE IDEA OF FREEDOM IMPLIES DIFFERENT KINDS OF FREEDOMS).

Social Institution or Artifact (SOC)

A culturally created object, institution, or concept (e.g. *bird*–TWEETY BIRD, *true*–POSTMODERNISM).

ACKNOWLEDGMENTS

The research in this article was supported by National Science Foundation Grants SBR-9905024 and BCS-0212134 to Lawrence W. Barsalou.

We are grateful to Courtney Emery, Rachel Robertson, Kyle Simmons, Christy Wilson, Melissa Armstrong, and Susan McManus for assistance with the study reported here. We are also grateful to Aron Barbey, Diane Pecher, Rolf Zwaan, and two anonymous reviewers for helpful comments. Address correspondence to Lawrence W. Barsalou, Department of Psychology, Emory University, Atlanta, GA 30322 (barsalou@emory.edu, http://userwww.service.emory.edu/~barsalou/).

References

Barsalou, L. W. (1999). Perceptual symbol systems. *Behavioral and Brain Sciences 22*, 577–609.

Barsalou, L. W. (2003a). Abstraction in perceptual symbol systems. *Philosophical Transactions of the Royal Society of London: Biological Sciences 358*, 1177–1187.

Barsalou, L. W. (2003b). Situated simulation in the human conceptual system. *Language and Cognitive Processes 18*, 513–562.

Barsalou, L. W., Niedenthal, P. M., Barbey, A., & Ruppert, J. (2003). Social embodiment. In B. Ross (Ed.), *The Psychology of Learning & Motivation, Vol. 43* (pp. 43–92). San Diego: Academic Press.

Barsalou, L. W., Sloman, S. A., & Chaigneau, S. E. (in press). The HIPE theory of function. In L. Carlson & E. van der Zee (Eds.), *Representing functional features for language and space: Insights from perception, categorization and development*. Oxford: Oxford University Press.

Boroditsky, L., & Ramscar, M. (2002). The roles of body and mind in abstract thought. *Psychological Science, 13*, 185–188.

Bransford, J. D., & Johnson, M. K. (1973). Considerations of some problems of comprehension. In W. G. Chase (Ed.), *Visual Information Processing*. New York: Academic Press.

Bransford, J. D., & McCarrell, N. S. (1974). A sketch of a cognitive approach to comprehension: Some thoughts about understanding what it means to comprehend. In W. B. Weimer & D. S. Palermo (Eds.), *Cognition and the Symbolic Processes* (pp. 377–399). Hillsdale, NJ: Lawrence Erlbaum Associates.

Burgess, C., & Lund, K. (1997). Modelling parsing constraints with high-dimensional context space. *Language and Cognitive Processes 12*, 177–210.

Clark, A. (1997). *Being There: Putting Brain, Body, and World Together Again*. Cambridge, MA: MIT Press.

Clark, H. H. (1992). *Arenas of Language Use*. Chicago: University of Chicago Press.

Cree, G. S., & McRae, K. (2003). Analyzing the factors underlying the structure and computation of the meaning of chipmunk, cherry, chisel, cheese, and cello (and many other such concrete nouns). *Journal of Experimental Psychology: General 132*, 163–201.

Fehr, B., & Russell, J. A. (1984). Concept of emotion viewed from a prototype perspective. *Journal of Experimental Psychology: General 113*, 464–486.

Galbraith, R. C., & Underwood, B. J. (1973). Perceived frequency of concrete and abstract words. *Memory and Cognition 1*, 56–60.

Gentner, D., Rattermann, M. J., & Forbus, K. D. (1993). The roles of similarity in transfer: Separating retrievability from inferential soundness. *Cognitive Psychology 25*, 524–575.

Glaser, W. R. (1992). Picture naming. *Cognition 42*, 61–106.

Glenberg, A. M., & Kaschak, M. P. (2002). Grounding language in action. *Psychonomic Bulletin and Review 9*, 558–569.

Hampton, J. A. (1979). Polymorphous concepts in semantic memory. *Journal of Verbal Learning and Verbal Behavior 18*, 441–461.

Kan, I. P., Barsalou, L. W., Solomon, K. O., Minor, J. K., & Thompson-Schill, S. L. (2003). Role of mental imagery in a property verification task: fMRI evidence for perceptual representations of conceptual knowledge. *Cognitive Neuropsychology 20*, 525–540.

Krauth-Gruber, S., Ric, F., Niedenthal, P. M., & Barsalou, L. W. (2004). The representation of emotion concepts: The role of perceptual simulation. Manuscript under review.

Lakoff, G., & Johnson, M. (1980). *Metaphors We Live By*. Chicago: University of Chicago Press.

Lakoff, G., & Turner, M. (1989). *More Than Cool Reason: A Field Guide to Poetic Metaphor*. Chicago: University of Chicago Press.

Landauer, T. K., & Dumais, S. T. (1997). A solution to Plato's Problem: The latent semantic analysis theory of acquisition, induction, and representation of knowledge. *Psychological Review 104*, 211–240.

Markman, A. B., & Ross, B. H. (2003). Category use and category learning. *Psychological Bulletin 129*, 592–615.

Martin, A. (2001). Functional neuroimaging of semantic memory. In. R. Cabeza & A. Kingstone (Eds.), *Handbook of Functional Neuroimaging of Cognition* (pp. 153–186). Cambridge, MA: MIT Press.

McCloskey, M., & Glucksberg, S. (1978). Natural categories: Well-defined or fuzzy sets? *Memory and Cognition 6*, 462–472.

McRae, K., & Cree, G. S. (2002). Factors underlying category-specific semantic deficits. In E. M. E. Forde & G. Humphreys (Eds.), *Category-specificity in mind and brain* (pp. 211–249). East Sussex, UK: Psychology Press.

Medin, D. L., & Ross, B. H. (1989). The specific character of abstract thought: Categorization, problem-solving, and induction. In R. J. Sternberg (Ed.) *Advances in the Psychology of Human Intelligence, Vol. 5*, (pp. 189–223). Hillsdale, NJ: Lawrence Erlbaum Associates.

Medin, D. L., & Schaffer, M. (1978). A context theory of classification learning. *Psychological Review 85*, 207–238.

Murphy, G. L. (1997). Reasons to doubt the present evidence for metaphoric representation. *Cognition 62*, 99–108.

Murphy, G. L., & Medin, D. L. (1985). The role of theories in conceptual coherence. *Psychological Review 92*, 289–316.

Nelson, K. (Ed.) (1986). *Event representations: Structure and Function in Development*. Mahwah, NJ: Erlbaum.

Paivio, A. (1986). *Mental Representations: A Dual Coding Approach*. New York: Oxford University Press.

Peterson, S. E., Fox, P. T., Posner, M. I., Mintus, M. A., & Raichle, M. E. (1989). Positron emission tomographic studies of the processing of single words. *Journal of Cognitive Neuroscience 1*, 153–170.

Pulvermüller, F. (1999). Words in the brain's language. *Behavioral and Brain Sciences 22*, 253–336.

Richardson, D. C., Spivey, M. J., Barsalou, L. W., & McRae, K. (2003). Spatial representations activated during real-time comprehension of verbs. *Cognitive Science 27*, 767–780.

Rosch, E., & Mervis, C. B. (1975). Family resemblances: Studies in the internal structure of categories. *Cognitive Psychology 7*, 573–605.

Ross, B. H., & Kilbane, M. C. (1997). Effects of principle explanation and superficial similarity on analogical mapping in problem solving. *Journal of Experimental Psychology: Learning, Memory and Cognition, 23*, 427–440.

Ross, B. H., Perkins, S. J., & Tenpenny, P. L. (1990). Reminding-based category learning. *Cognitive Psychology 22*, 460–492.

Schwanenflugel, P. J., Harnishfeger, K. K., & Stowe, R. W. (1988). Context availability and lexical decisions for abstract and concrete words. *Journal of Memory and Language 27*, 499–520.

Schwanenflugel, P. J. (1991). Why are abstract concepts hard to understand? In P. J. Schwanenflugel (Ed.), *The Psychology of Word Meaning* (pp. 223–250). Mahwah, NJ: Erlbaum.

Schwanenflugel, P. J., & Shoben, E. J. (1983). Differential context effects in the comprehension of abstract and concrete verbal materials. *Journal of Experimental Psychology: Learning, Memory, and Cognition 9*, 82–102.

Schwanenflugel, P. J., & Stowe, R. W. (1989). Context availability and the processing of abstract and concrete words in sentences. *Reading Research Quarterly 24*, 114–126.

Solomon, K. O., & Barsalou, L. W. (2004). Perceptual simulation in property verification. *Memory & Cognition 32*, 244–259.

Thompson-Schill, S. L., D'Esposito, M., Aguirre, G. K., & Farah, M. J. (1997). Role of left prefrontal cortex in retrieval of semantic knowledge: A reevaluation. *Proceedings of the National Academy of Science 94*, 14792–14797.

Tulving, E., & Thomson, D. M. (1973). Encoding specificity and retrieval processes in episodic memory. *Psychological Review 80*, 352–373.

Wattenmaker, W. D., & Shoben, E. J. (1987). Context and the recallability of concrete and abstract sentences. *Journal of Experimental Psychology: Learning, Memory, and Cognition 13*, 140–150.

Wiemer-Hastings, K., & Graesser, A. C. (1998). Contextual representation of abstract nouns: A neural network approach. *Proceedings of the 20th Annual Conference of the Cognitive Science Society* (pp. 1036–1042). Mahwah, NJ: Erlbaum.

Wiemer-Hastings, K., & Graesser, A. C. (2000). Representing abstract concepts with abstract structures. *Proceedings of the 22nd Annual Conference of the Cognitive Science Society* (pp. 983–989). Mahwah, NJ: Erlbaum.

Wiemer-Hastings, K., Krug, J., & Xu, X. (2001). Imagery, context availability, contextual constraint, and abstractness. *Proceedings of the 23rd Annual Conference of the Cognitive Science Society* 1134–1139. Mahwah, NJ: Erlbaum.

Wiemer-Hastings, K., & Xu, X. (2004). Content differences for abstract and concrete concepts. Manuscript under review.

Winer, B. J. (1971). *Statistical Principles in Experimental Design* (2nd ed.). New York: McGraw-Hill.

Wittgenstein, L. (1953). *Philosophical Investigations* (G. E. M. Anscombe, Trans.). New York: Macmillan.

Wu, L., & Barsalou, L. W. (2004). Perceptual simulation in property generation. Manuscript in review.

Yeh, W., & Barsalou, L. W. (2004). The situated character of concepts. Manuscript in review.

8

Dynamicity, Fictivity, and Scanning

The Imaginative Basis of Logic and Linguistic Meaning

Ronald W. Langacker

COGNITIVE SEMANTICS

The last quarter century has seen the emergence of what has come to be known as **cognitive semantics**. This collective endeavor has vastly expanded and profoundly altered our view of both meaning and its relation to grammar. It offers new solutions to classic problems. More fundamentally, it reshapes the entire conceptual landscape within which the problems themselves are posed and formulated.[1]

The most basic development is simply the unequivocal identification of meaning with **conceptualization**, i.e., the cognitive activity constituting our apprehension of the world (Langacker, 1987a, 2000; Talmy, 2000a, 2000b). Since the mind is part of the loop, linguistic semantics does not just reflect the external situations described, but inescapably incorporates particular ways of **construing** those situations and portraying them for linguistic purposes. It thus involves the full range of our mental capacities, as well as the elaborate conceptual structures we construct and manipulate. Included – being absolutely fundamental to cognition and language – are capacities reasonably called **imaginative**: metaphor (Lakoff & Johnson, 1980, 1999), metonymy (Kövecses & Radden, 1998), fictivity (Matsumoto, 1996a, 1996b; Talmy, 1996; Langacker, 1999b), mental space construction (Fauconnier, 1985; Fauconnier & Sweetser, 1996), and conceptual blending (Fauconnier, 1997; Fauconnier & Turner, 1998a, 1998b, 2002). These capacities are however grounded in everyday bodily experience: motion, perception, muscular exertion, etc. Basic experience of this sort is projected metaphorically onto other domains, and in abstracted form provides the skeletal organization of conceptual structure in general. This of course is **embodiment** (Johnson, 1987; Lakoff, 1987).

---

[1] An earlier version of this paper (Langacker, 2003) appeared in the journal *Korean Linguistics*. It is reprinted with the kind permission of the Association for Korean Linguistics.

The expressions in (1), for instance, represent four alternate construals of the same event, effected by the imaginative capacities of metaphor and metonymy.

(1)(a) *She read Hillerman's new novel in a single evening.* [neutral]
  (b) *She **devoured** Hillerman's new novel in a single evening.* [metaphor]
  (c) *She read the new **Hillerman** in a single evening.* [metonymy]
  (d) *She **devoured** the new **Hillerman** in a single evening.* [metaphor and metonymy]

The examples in (2)–(3) illustrate embodiment. Physical motion through space provides a means of apprehending change:

(2)(a)(i) *We went to the store.*
    (ii) *The situation went from bad to worse.*
  (b)(i) *She turned to face him.*
    (ii) *The weather turned cold.*

Modals are based on **force dynamics** (Talmy, 1988; Sweetser, 1982; Langacker, 1991: 6.3). For instance, *must* evokes an irresistible force, *should* a lesser force, and *may* the absence of a barrier, with respect to either social interaction ("root modals") or judgments of likelihood ("epistemic modals"):

(3)(a) *You {must/should/may} attend this protest rally.* [root modals]
  (b) *She {must/should/may} be home by now.* [epistemic modals]

Later, I will describe some abstract manifestations of such basic activities as perceptual scanning, putting objects into a group, matching one object against another, and selecting randomly from a set of objects.

An example of how cognitive semantics transforms the consideration of classic problems is Fauconnier's account of the specific/nonspecific contrast for indefinite articles (1985). The indefinite article in (4)(a) is ambiguous between a specific and a nonspecific interpretation, depending on whether a particular individual is being referred to. This ambiguity is resolved in (4)(b) and (4)(c) by adding *certain*, to force a specific reading, or shifting to *any*, for a nonspecific reading.

(4)(a) *Joe wants to meet **an actress**.* [ambiguous]
  (b) *Joe wants to meet **a certain actress**.* [specific]
  (c) *Joe wants to meet **an actress** – **any actress**.* [nonspecific]

Rather than positing two different senses for the indefinite article,[2] Fauconnier ascribes the semantic contrast to a difference in **mental space configuration**. Starting from the space representing the speaker's conception

---

[2] Positing two different senses would be inelegant if only because comparable pairs of meanings would be needed for other indefinite determiners.

(a) <u>Specific</u>   (b) <u>Nonspecific</u>

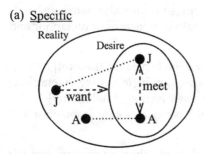
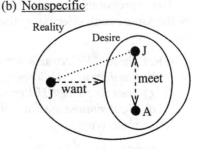

FIGURE 8.1. Specificity contrast.

of reality, the verb *want* (**a space builder**) sets up a space incorporating the
content of Joe's desire, as shown in Figure 8.1. Joe (J) plays a role in both
spaces, and on both interpretations an actress (A) occurs in the desire space.
The semantic contrast resides in whether this actress **corresponds** to one
in reality (dotted lines indicate correspondences). She does on the specific
interpretation. The nonspecific interpretation is merely the case where the
actress referred to is "conjured up" just to characterize the nature of Joe's
desire, and has no status outside the mental space created for this purpose.
It is thus a **fictive** entity, an **imagined instance** of the \ rather than an actual
individual.

The fictive nature of the actress referred to in (4)(c) is not a matter of the
nominal expression being nonreferential, in a linguistically relevant sense.
On both readings, the phrase *an actress* designates an instance of the *actress*
type. And as shown in (5), in both cases a discourse referent is established
which can subsequently be referred to by means of an anaphoric pronoun:

(5)(a) *Joe wants to meet **an actress**. **She** is very talented.* [specific]
   (b) *Joe wants to meet **an actress**. **She** has to be very talented, though.* [non-
       specific]

The contrast instead resides in the position of the nominal referent with
respect to the mental space configuration assumed, i.e., which mental
space(s) it occupies. The referents of the pronoun and the antecedent must
occupy the same mental space (Langacker, 1996a). In (5)(a), that space is
reality. In (5)(b), *have to* signals that the desire space continues to be the
focus of discussion.

In what follows, I will suggest the fundamental importance to linguistic
meaning of two basic notions of cognitive semantics: **dynamicity**, pertaining to the time course of a conceptualization, and **fictivity**, just illustrated.
I will then apply these notions to the characterization of certain elements
considered "logical" in nature, with special reference to quantifiers. It turns
out that conceptual and imaginative phenomena are especially crucial for
problems traditionally dealt with in logic and formal semantics.

DYNAMICITY

Because it resides in neurological activity, conceptualization is necessarily **dynamic** (Langacker 1997a, 1999a: ch. 12, 2001a). By this I mean that it emerges and develops through **processing time**. Moreover, this temporal dimension proves to be inherent and essential to the characterization of conceptual structure, with important and pervasive linguistic ramifications.

The most obvious cases of dynamicity are those correlated with word order. Due to the temporality of the speech stream, we can hardly avoid accessing facets of a complex conception in the order given by the sequencing of the words that symbolize them. Dynamicity is not however limited to this dimension. It is essential that we not oversimplify the manifest complexity of language processing by assuming that a single "left-to-right" pass through a sentence is all there is. Instead, we can reasonably presume that sequenced processing occurs simultaneously in multiple dimensions and on different time scales. Simultaneously, for example, we have to keep track of discourse strategies, clause structure, and the conceptions evoked by individual lexical items, as well as the fine details of articulatory phonetics. In addition to following the order of presentation, we are able – by means of short-term memory – to backtrack and thus to reexamine and reanalyze material already encountered (e.g. in processing "garden-path" sentences). We can further hold analysis in abeyance until a sufficient amount of material has accumulated and is available for resolution within a single window of attention. Moreover, sequential processing is not invariably in the focus of attention and may not even be subject to conscious awareness, especially at smaller time scales. We are more likely to be aware of it at the level of discourse or clause structure than, say, as part of the internal semantics of a lexical item.

Word order is of course exploited for grammatical purposes, e.g. to identify subject and object. It can also be used iconically, as in (6), to suggest the sequence of events:

(6)(a) *She quit her job and got married.*
   (b) *She got married and quit her job.*

My concern, though, is with another class of examples, where the sequence of expression induces a conceptual ordering which actually **constitutes** the meaning conveyed. I have in mind, for instance, the contrasting variants of the "nested locative" construction, exemplified in (7):

(7)(a) *Your camera is upstairs, in the bedroom, in the closet, on the top shelf.*
   (b) *Your camera is on the top shelf, in the closet, in the bedroom, upstairs.*

The "zooming in" and "zooming out" varieties are conceptually quite distinct, despite containing the same elements and describing the same complex spatial configuration. The alternative sequences of mental access afforded by the constructional variants are pivotal to the expressions' semantic value.

Presenting an especially clear example of dynamicity are pairs of expressions like those in (8), which describe the same objective situation. Their semantic contrast resides exclusively in the conceptualizer's **direction of mental scanning** in building up to a full apprehension of the spatial configuration. It is not a difference in conceptual content, but rather of the order in which the configuration is mentally accessed.

(8)(a) *A scar extends from his ankle to his knee.*
 (b) *A scar extends from his knee to his ankle.*

In this case the conceptual ordering is not just a function of word order, but reflects the lexical meanings of *from* and *to*. The two motivations coincide: in (8)(a), for instance, we are prompted by word order to start our mental scanning at the ankle, thus reinforcing the instruction given lexically by the phrase *from his ankle*. This is the first of many cases we will see where a conceptual sequencing is established independently of word order (which is only one factor inducing it, albeit an important and pervasive one). What happens when word order and lexical meaning are in conflict, instead of reinforcing one another? Though generally considered grammatical, sentences like (9) present a certain awkwardness. Based on their meanings, the prepositional phrases are telling us to trace a mental path starting at the ankle, yet on the basis of linear order we must first evoke the knee.

(9) *?A scar extends to his knee from his ankle.*

We can handle this noncongruence, but it does require extra processing effort. Let me suggest that it requires an additional processing step, amounting to a **reconceptualization** of the configuration being described. Through linear processing, we first encounter *to his knee*, which induces us to construct a partial configuration comprising only what is being portrayed as the endpoint of the spatial path. This is the first transition depicted in Figure 8.2, where a dashed arrow indicates direction of mental scanning, and the solid arrow labeled T represents processing time. We then encounter the phrase *from his ankle*, which focuses on the origin of the spatial path. The final transition in Figure 8.2 comprises the mental scanning required to complete the path, i.e., to conceptualize its extension from beginning to end. I believe that we do have to reconceptualize the path, by starting over and tracing through it in proper sequence from beginning to end, in order to properly apprehend it and establish it as a coherent conception. With the order in (9) the path is, if you like, a kind of garden path, since after focusing on its termination we have to back up and scan through it again in the proper sequence. With the order in (8)(a) this extra

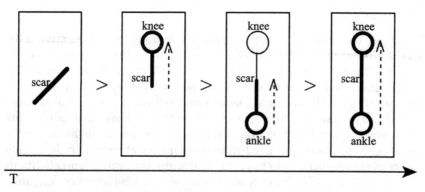

FIGURE 8.2. Scanning and reconceptualization.

step is not required. Nor in (8)(b), where we scan only once along the path but in the opposite direction. But in all cases the scar itself is static – the spatial path reflects our dynamic **construal** of the static situation.

Directed mental scanning of this sort is not limited to spatial configurations. In precisely analogous fashion we scan through time, or along any kind of scale.[3] The same effects are observed when the order of expression forces us to reconceptualize the situation to fully apprehend it:

(10)(a) *The rainy season starts in December and runs through March.*
  (b) *??The rainy season runs through March and starts in December.*
  (c) *They raised tuition from $15,000 to $20,000.*
  (d) *?They raised tuition to $20,000 from $15,000.*

A linguistically important manifestation of dynamicity, one **not** inherently tied to word order, are phenomena involving the use of conceptual **reference points** (Langacker, 1993). We commonly invoke the conception of one entity as a reference point in order to establish mental contact with another, i.e., to mentally access one entity via another. A case in point is the ubiquitous phenomenon called **metonymy**, where the entity an expression would normally designate – which in cognitive grammar is called its **profile** – is used instead as a reference point providing mental access to what it is actually understood as referring to. For instance, the name for a place is often used to evoke an associated event (as in *Chernobyl was a great tragedy*). Other phenomena best analyzed in reference point terms include possessives (Langacker, 1995) and topic constructions (Langacker, 1999c; Kumashiro, 2000). Van Hoek (1995, 1997) provides a detailed reference point account of pronominal anaphora. I have further argued extensively for a reference point characterization of subject and object (Langacker, 1999d, 2001b).

---

[3] This is not to deny that spatial metaphor may be involved.

FICTIVITY

Language has long been viewed primarily as a vehicle for describing the world around us. Canonically, therefore, nominal expressions would be used for the direct description of actual individuals, and sentences for the direct description of actual events and situations they participate in. Yet this view may not be accurate. Departures from the supposed canon are so varied and prevalent as to suggest a fundamental revision in how we think about language and the functions it serves. Such cases are not limited to the kinds of nonactuality involved in making false statements, in describing future events (which might not actually eventuate), or in creating fictitious worlds (as in a novel). Indeed, one has to be struck by how very common it is that **fictitious** entities are invoked and **directly** described even when our concern is with **actuality**. Surprisingly often, our characterization of actual situations is effected only indirectly, through the mediation of **fictive** or **virtual** entities conjured up for that purpose.

Note first that, by itself, a lexical noun (e.g., *cat, oxygen*) merely specifies a **type** of **thing**, not any particular **instance** of that type. Likewise, a lexical verb (e.g., *chase, love*) merely specifies a type of event or situation – i.e., it profiles what I call a **process** – not any particular process instance. The entity (thing or process) designated by a type specification is fictive in nature; it does not per se refer to an actual individual or an actual process. It is only at the level of a full **noun phrase** (e.g., *this cat, some oxygen*), or a full **finite clause** (e.g., *I chased it, She may love him*), that reference is made to particular instances of a thing or process type. A noun phrase or finite clause incorporates what I call a **grounding** element, which singles out an instance of a type and locates it with respect to the **ground**, i.e., the speech event and its participants. Nominal grounding elements include articles, demonstratives, and certain quantifiers. Modals and tense are the clausal grounding elements of English (Langacker, 1991: Chapter 6).

A type is a fictive entity, not an actual individual. It represents an abstraction from actuality which captures the commonality inherent across a set of actual instances. Using the metaphor of **planes** to indicate abstraction (equivalently, we could speak of **tiers** or **mental spaces**), the relation between a type (t) and instances of a type ($t_{i,j,k}$) is depicted in Figure 8.3. A thing or process type corresponds to any number of instances of that type, distinguished by their position in the instance plane (which I also refer to as the **domain of instantiation** – see Langacker, 1991). But while the type projects to all its instances, per se it does not occupy any particular position in that plane. It is important to keep in mind how types (and other kinds of virtual entities) are connected to actuality, as well as how they arise from it. Types arise as a kind of **generalization** over actual occurrences, such that sets of occurrences are perceived as being alike in significant respects.

Thus every lexical noun or verb evokes a fictive entity, the thing or process type it designates. It is only in the context of a larger syntactic

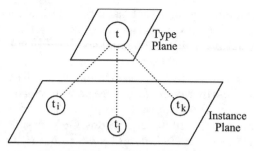

FIGURE 8.3. Type vs. instance.

configuration, a full noun phrase or a finite clause incorporating ground-ing, that reference to an actual individual is achieved. Thus (11)(a) makes reference to an actual instance of loving involving an actual cat. However, nouns and verbs are often used alone, without grounding. This is usual, for example, in both compounding and morphological derivation. In (11)(b), no particular cat is being referred to, and no particular instance of loving. Linguistic reference to these entities remains at the type level. Still, the sen-tence is a statement about actuality, where Sarah supposedly does engage in the process of loving with respect to actual cats. While the statement is concerned with actuality, the entities it refers to **directly** for this purpose – namely *cat* and *love* – are **virtual** in nature (types). To grasp the expres-sion's overall import, we must apprehend not only what is directly coded linguistically, but also how the virtual entities invoked are connected to actuality.

(11)(a) *Sarah **loves this cat**.*
   (b) *Sarah is a **cat-lover**.*

Note that the lower plane in Figure 8.3 is labeled the "instance plane" rather than the "actual plane." I use this label because the type/instance distinction is not the same as the virtual/actual distinction. It is true that types are virtual entities, but instances do not have to be actual – they can either be actual or virtual. We have already seen this in regard to the in-definite article, in (4) and Figure 8.1. In (4) [*Joe wants to meet an actress*], the actress is described linguistically by means of a full noun phrase, incorpo-rating a grounding element (the article). The phrase *an actress* designates an instance of the *actress* type. This is common to both the specific and the nonspecific interpretations.[4] The contrast resides in where the instance is located – whether it only occurs in the mental space representing Joe's desire, or whether it also occurs in reality (which for our purposes is equiva-lent to what I am calling actuality). Thus, on the nonspecific interpretation the actress referred to is a **virtual** or **fictive** instance of the actress type,

---

[4] By contrast, *Joe has an actress fetish* makes reference to *actress* only at the type level.

whereas on the specific interpretation it is an **actual** instance. A virtual instance of a type can be characterized as a nonactual instance "conjured up" for a special purpose, with no status outside the mental space (or plane) constructed for that purpose.

Linguistic reference to virtual instances of a type is extremely prevalent. Suppose, for example, that in my class there were three occasions in which a student asked a question which turned out to be quite insightful. Three different students were involved, and three different questions. One possible description of this scenario is (12)(a), where *students* and *questions* naturally occur in the plural, since multiple students and multiple questions figured in the events reported. This is a fairly direct description of the actual occurrences, summarized over the three specific events. However, I could also describe exactly the same scenario using (12)(b). What is striking here is that *student* and *question* occur in the singular, even though I am reporting on a complex occurrence involving three of each. How can that be?

(12)(a) *Three times, students asked intelligent questions.*
  (b) *Three times, a student asked an intelligent question.*

The answer, I suggest, is that we capture a generalization over the three occurrences and describe it by means of a fictive event representing the commonality of the three actual events. The student directly referred to in (12)(b) is not any one of the actual students involved, but a fictive student conjured up to make the generalization. The question described in (12)(b) is likewise a virtual question rather than any of the actual ones, and the profiled event of asking is also virtual. It is this fictive event involving virtual instances of the *student* and *question* types that is directly coded linguistically. How this virtual event maps onto actuality is specified by the initial adverbial expression, *three times*. The overall meaning of the sentence comprises both the fictive event described and the nature of its connection to actuality, so specified. In Figure 8.4, the fictive profiled event is shown as occupying what is termed a **generalization** plane. The label reflects the nature of its origin: it is abstracted from actuality as a generalization over

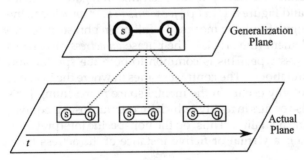

FIGURE 8.4. Fictive referents in a generalization.

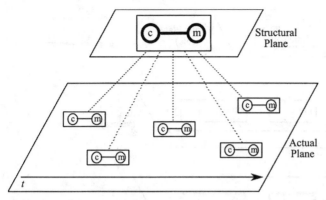

FIGURE 8.5. Generic statement.

several actual occurrences. How it is conceived as deriving from actuality is part of the semantic value of such sentences.

Virtual structures derive from actuality in a variety of ways, so there are numerous kinds of virtual planes. The type plane in 8.3 and the generalization plane in Figure 8.4 both represent generalizations, but generalizations of different sorts. Yet another kind of generalization leads to **generic** expressions. There are of course numerous kinds of generic statements (Langacker, 1997b), including some employing universal quantifiers (considered later). All involve fictivity, but I will only mention the kind that uses singular nouns, e.g., (13):

(13) *A cat plays with a mouse it has caught.*

A singular generic is quite analogous to the fictive statement in (12)(b), except that the generalization expressed by the directly coded virtual event is a **global** generalization, pertaining to what is conceived as the world's stable **structure** (cf. Goldsmith & Woisetschlaeger, 1982), whereas (12)(b) is a **local** generalization capturing what is common to just a few occurrences, not construed as being characteristic of the world's inherent nature. I thus describe the virtual event – involving a virtual cat and a virtual mouse – as inhabiting the **structural** plane, as seen in Figure 8.5. The genericity is not specifically coded, but inheres in the nature of the conceived relationship between actuality and the plane in which the profiled event is found. Owing to the different nature of the abstraction, vis-à-vis the one in Figure 8.4, here the number of actual instances corresponding to the virtual event is indeterminate.[5] The virtual event projects to actuality in an open-ended way, with the possibility of instantiation at any time and any place, pending the availability of a cat and a mouse. Actuality is being

---

[5] Five instances are shown, but merely for diagrammatic purposes.

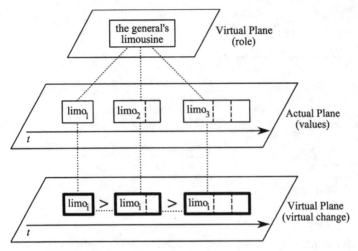

FIGURE 8.6. Fictive change.

described – the statement pertains to the world's actual nature – but no actual event is directly mentioned.

Various sorts of virtuality fall under the rubric of **fictive change** (Matsumoto, 1996a; Sweetser, 1997). One kind of fictive change is exemplified by (14):

(14) *The general's limousine keeps getting longer.*

On the relevant interpretation, no actual limousine changes in length. There is only the fiction of change, hinging on the distinction made by Fauconnier between **roles** and **values** of those roles. *The general's limousine* is a role description: it describes a role filled by different particular vehicles at different times, each then being a value of that role. Like a type, a role per se is a fictive entity.[6] You may be able to drive a Rolls, but you cannot drive a role, which is not an actual, individual object. Reference to a role is only one of three levels of virtuality that figure in this example. A second level is the general type (e.g., *limousine*) that the role instantiates. Beyond this, we view a number of distinct values instantiating the role – a number of different actual limousines – *as if* they were all the same entity. This yields the conception of a single, albeit virtual object whose length at different times can be compared. Such comparison with respect to a single entity is required for a coherent conception of change. The resulting change, profiled in Figure 8.6, constitutes a third level of virtuality.

---

[6] They are different in that a role is itself a virtual instance of some type, in this case the *limousine* type. Note that the role description is a full noun phrase and incorporates grounding.

A special case of fictive change is **fictive motion** (Langacker, 1986; Matsumoto, 1996a; Talmy, 1996). Of the various kinds of fictive motion, I will only consider examples like (15)(b)–(c). Paths are usually immobile – they do not actually move, as suggested by a verb like *rise* or an adverb like *quickly*. Yet we describe them with dynamic language that normally pertains to actual motion. We need to distinguish and characterize three distinct uses. In (15)(a) the motion is actual. Virtual motion can either be **perfective**, as in (15)(b), or **imperfective**, as in (15)(c).

(15)(a) *The balloon rose quickly.* [actual motion]
   (b) *The path is rising quickly as we climb.* [perfective virtual motion]
   (c) *The path rises quickly near the top.* [imperfective virtual motion]

Being perfective, the verb *rise* in (15)(b) indicates a change through time. It is shown to be perfective by occurrence in the progressive, which in English only occurs on verbs construed perfectively (Langacker, 1987b). But if the subjects of these verbs are static entities and do not move, where is the change?

Such uses do involve motion on the part of the subject, but the motion is virtual rather than actual. Though imagined, the motion has an experiential basis, reflecting what a person experiences while moving along the expanse of the path. In (15)(b), the movers and the motion are mentioned explicitly in the adverbial clause. This type of sentence is infelicitous when, as in (16), the object in question is too small to imagine someone traveling along it. Of course, as noted by Elena Dapremont, it becomes acceptable in a special context where we can indeed imagine this, e.g., for a party of hikers climbing Mt. Rushmore.[7]

(16) **His forehead is rising less steeply near the hairline.*

As shown in Figure 8.7(a), I analyze these perfective cases of fictive motion in terms of a viewer (*V*) who moves along the path-like entity coded by the subject. Through time (*t*), the moving viewer occupies different positions along this spatial path. The area around the viewer at a given moment – perhaps to be identified with the immediate field of view – is given as a rectangle. What counts as the *path* (or the *forehead*, etc.) for purposes of these expressions is that portion of the overall entity which falls within that area, hence in actuality it differs referentially from moment to moment. As in Figure 8.6, these distinct entities are fictively construed as if they were a single entity. Construed in this fashion, the path (identified as the portion of the path we see right now) is experienced as itself moving through space, hence rising. Such instances of fictive motion on the part

---

[7] Mt. Rushmore is a mountain in South Dakota on which are carved giant heads of four American presidents.

(a) Perfective Virtual Motion

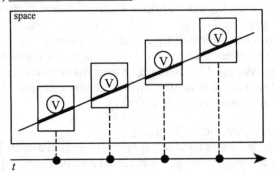

(b) Imperfective Virtual Motion

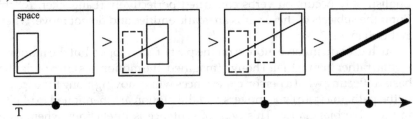

FIGURE 8.7. Fictive motion.

of a fictive mover are generated by the viewing experience of someone actually moving along the extended object.[8]

The key to this kind of fictive motion is a **local view** generated by moving along an extended object, such that only a portion of that object is subtended by the field of view at any one instant. Closely related are fictive motion expressions like (15)(c), which take a **global view** of the object in question. These expressions are imperfective, i.e., the situation they profile is construed as stable and temporally unbounded. In English, occurrence in the simple present tense is diagnostic of imperfectivity. These imperfectives are generalized statements, describing the global configuration observable at any time by any viewer. They do not in any salient way evoke a viewer moving along the path or depend on such a viewer to generate the change suggested by the motion verb. Instead, this sense of change resides in the **conceptualizer's mental scanning** through the global scene in building up to its full conceptualization, as sketched in Figure 8.7(b). The time involved

---

[8] We can further describe such cases in terms of whole-for-part metonymy, in regard to the subject, and conceptual blending whose constitutive elements are the conception of actual motion and of a static scene. These characterizations are all consistent with one another.

is thus **processing** time (T), i.e., time as the **medium** of conception, rather than **conceived** time (t), where time functions as an **object** of conception. By mentally scanning along its expanse, in building up to its full conception, the conceptualizer experiences the path as "growing" in a particular direction. The full configuration thus arrived at is portrayed as being stable through time, and since this is the profiled relationship, the resulting sentences are imperfective.

This is the kind of scanning previously illustrated in (8)–(9) and Figure 8.2. Nothing actually moves, neither the subject nor any viewer. What motivates the use of a motion verb is a **subjective** counterpart of actual motion, namely mental scanning along a spatial path in the course of building up the full conception of a global configuration (Langacker, 1990, 1999e). A sense of motion remains, as reflected in the motion verb as well as directional phrases (e.g., *from his ankle to his knee*), however it becomes less salient as one goes from actual motion, to perfective virtual motion, to imperfective virtual motion. The use of motion verbs despite such attenuation is a linguistic manifestation of embodiment. The bodily experience is that of moving around in space, and observing other objects doing so. Linguistic elements whose prototypical values are grounded in such experience are extended to other situations where we are able to discern a virtual and/or subjective analog of the actual entities they designate.

FICTIVE SCANNING

Once we have made the transition from actual motion to mental scanning through processing time, we are no longer limited to the spatial domain. Indeed, I have already smuggled in an example. Consider a portion of the previous paragraph, viewing it as a linguistic expression: *as one goes from actual motion, to perfective virtual motion, to imperfective virtual motion.* This expression itself is a case of imperfective virtual motion. Probably it caused you no problem, since we resort to such scanning all the time – it is a perfectly normal feature of everyday language use. Here are a few more examples:

(17)(a) *From one restaurant to the next, prices vary greatly.*
 (b) *Through the centuries, we have had many great leaders.*
 (c) *As body size increases, the average gestation period gets longer.*
 (d) *Reliability improves with the more expensive models.*
 (e) *When you think of our options, each one seems worse than the last.*
 (f) *From the brightest student in the class to the dumbest, they all work very hard.*

These sentences describe static overall situations in dynamic terms. While they do not use motion verbs, they certainly do induce us to mentally scan in a certain order through a range of alternatives. This scanning is prompted in various ways: by prepositional phrases specifying source (*from X*), path (*through Y*), and goal (*to Z*); by expressions of fictive change (*improves, increases*); by comparatives (*gets longer, worse than the last*); and so on. While I am not prepared to offer a detailed description of such expressions, I believe a correct characterization of their conceptual import has to incorporate abstract mental scanning as a basic organizing feature.

Observe, moreover, that even this mental scanning exhibits a kind of fictivity. For instance, apprehending (17)(f) invokes the idea of mentally accessing the students in the class in the order of their ranking for intelligence, but obviously we do not actually do so – we can understand the sentence without knowing the individual students or even how many there might be. Similarly, while (17)(c) invokes the notion of sequentially examining species in accordance with their body size, in actuality we need not direct our attention to any particular species. Instead, we simply imagine the requisite kind of scanning experience. We conjure up a small-scale model of the sequenced alternatives, limited in number and represented only schematically, and simulate the scanning experience by mentally running through these fictive entities. That is, I believe we employ **mental models**, in the sense of Johnson-Laird (1983), as well as mental **simulation**, in the sense of Barsalou (1999).

These mental gymnastics are really quite pedestrian. They are not unlike what we do, for example, in handling large numbers that we cannot really grasp directly. Suppose I tell you that three million people visited the San Diego Zoo last year. You are likely to apprehend this statement by conjuring up the image of people going through the turnstiles, but the number of individuals you mentally observe in this fashion will be far less than three million – you will imagine just a few people, characterized only schematically, and take them as representative of a larger whole.

The scanning invoked in (17)(f) is sketched in Figure 8.8. The dashed arrow indicates sequence of mental access. Arranging the students in order of descending intelligence, and scanning through them in this sequence,

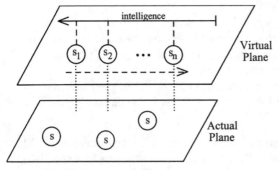

FIGURE 8.8. Fictive scanning.

is something that happens only fictively, hence it is shown as taking place in the virtual plane. The students evoked correspond to actual students, but precisely how they map onto actual students is unspecified – even if we know who the actual students are, we do not necessarily know which ones are the brightest, the dumbest, etc. Hence the dotted correspondence lines merely indicate that the students scanned correspond to students in the actual plane, without indicating which particular individuals they correspond to. The situation evoked pertains to actuality, and is abstracted from actuality, but the explicit conceptual content is mostly virtual.

The claim, then, is that many fairly mundane expressions, like those in (17), incorporate fictive mental scanning as a central facet of their conceptual semantic value. This imagined scanning through a virtual range of alternatives combines fictivity with dynamicity, often as a means of apprehending an actual situation that would not be easy to grasp or describe directly. Evidence that we do in fact resort to fictive scanning – that it is not just a figment of my own imagination – comes from otherwise peculiar uses of certain temporal adverbs, notably *still* and *already* (cf. Michaelis, 1991, 1993, 1996):

(18)(a) *You won't get very far with a contribution of $10,000, or even $25,000. And $50,000 is **still** not enough for a private interview with the president.*

(b) *Forget about calculus – elementary algebra is **already** too difficult for him.*

Prototypically, *still* indicates that some activity continues past a potential stopping point, and *already*, that something happens earlier than expected:

(19) *Jack is **still** writing his dissertation, but Jill has **already** finished hers.*

In (18), however, nothing is happening. There is no actual activity or event to characterize in terms of its temporal distribution. I suggest that *still* and *already* are nonetheless employed in (18) with something approximating their usual values. What is special about them is simply that the activity in question is not the situation explicitly described by the clause ($50,000 not being enough for an interview; elementary algebra being too difficult), but rather an otherwise covert process of fictive mental scanning. In (18)(a), there is scanning along a scale representing the possible size of political contributions. *Still* indicates that, when scanning reaches the $50,000 mark, one has not yet arrived at the amount necessary for a presidential interview. In (18)(b), mental scanning proceeds through a range of mathematical subjects, ordered in terms of increasing difficulty. Here the scanning is more obviously fictive, since we are unlikely to actually think of particular subjects other than the two explicitly mentioned. In

(a)

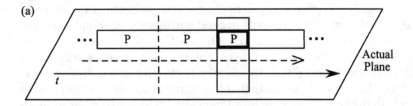

(b)

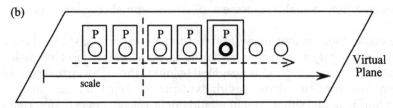

FIGURE 8.9. Fictivity with temporal expressions.

any case, *already* specifies that, in scanning along this scale, one encounters a subject that is too difficult sooner than might be anticipated.

Such uses of *still* and *already* are overt symptoms of the type of scanning proposed, or perhaps they themselves prompt us to engage in this mental construction. They have their usual values, except that they now pertain to the distribution of a **conceptual** activity through **processing** time, as opposed to an **actual** activity through **conceived** time.[9] They pertain to the very activity of dynamically accessing the ordered elements of a fictive mental construct.

The actual and virtual uses of *still* are depicted in Figure 8.9. In diagram (a), representing *still* in expressions like (19), a bar represents the continuation through conceived time of the situation in question, labeled *P*. A rectangle indicates the span of time being singled out for examination, i.e., its **immediate temporal scope**. The segment of the ongoing situation that falls within this scope is the portion in focus, i.e., it is profiled by the clause. What *still* contributes is a scanning through time (dashed arrow), tracing through *P*'s temporal extension, with the specification that *P* continues beyond a potential cut-off point (vertical dashed line) and obtains during the focused temporal interval.

Contrast this with Figure 8.9(b), representing *still* in a sentence like (18)(a). Here the mental scanning is fictive in nature, so it inheres in the virtual plane and occurs only through processing time, not conceived time. Moreover, the entities sequentially accessed are alternatives of some kind (in this case sums of money), shown diagrammatically as circles. These

---

[9] The activity, in other words, is subjectively rather than objectively construed, as defined in Langacker 1990 and 1999e.

entities are arranged along a scale (such as a quantity scale), along which mental scanning occurs. As each entity is accessed in its turn, it proves to have the property labeled *P* (in this case, being insufficient to merit an interview with the president). *Still* indicates that finding property *P* associated with the accessed entity continues past a potential cut-off point and is characteristic of the entity currently in focus. In both 8.9(a) and 8.9(b), *still* has the experiential import of continuing to encounter property *P* longer (in processing time) than might be expected during the process of mental scanning. The difference is that, in the actual examples, this subjective process of mental scanning proceeds along the axis of conceived time (*t*), whereas in the fictive examples it proceeds along some scale.

We can take this one step further (fictively speaking). When the temporal adverbs in question specify frequency, comparable mental scanning provides a means of quantifying over the entities thus encountered. Consider the examples in (20):

(20)(a) *A professional basketball player is **usually** tall.*
   (b) *A professor is **always** arrogant.*
   (c) *Theoretical linguists are {**often/frequently/commonly**} obtuse.*
   (d) *Politicians are {**seldom/rarely/never**} honest.*

On the relevant (and more likely) interpretation, these sentences are taken as quantifying over sets of individuals, specifying which proportion of them exhibit a certain property. Thus (20)(a) effectively indicates that **most** professional basketball players are tall, (20)(b) that **all** professors are arrogant, (20)(c) that **many** linguistic theorists are obtuse, and (20)(d) that **few if any** politicians are honest.

Once we appreciate the prevalence and naturalness of fictive mental scanning, these uses are straightforward. Once more, the temporal adverbs are employed with something approximating their normal values. What is special is simply the conceptual configuration to which they apply. We invoke the fictive conception of moving through the world and encountering multiple instances of a certain type (*professional basketball player, professor, theoretical linguist, politician*). The adverbs pertain to this tacit, fictive process of exploration and specify the frequency of events in which an encountered individual of the type in question exhibits the property in question. Granted the assumption that the individuals fictively encountered are representative, the frequency of events in which they exhibit the property translates into the proportion of type instances exhibiting the property.

This is sketched in Figure 8.10. The sequential examination of instances occurs in the virtual plane, as a mental simulation representing what is purported to be the nature of actual experience. A certain proportion of the instances fictively examined turn out to exhibit the property in question, *P*. The temporal adverb specifies the frequency of such events. The individual meanings of these adverbs pose interesting problems, but here

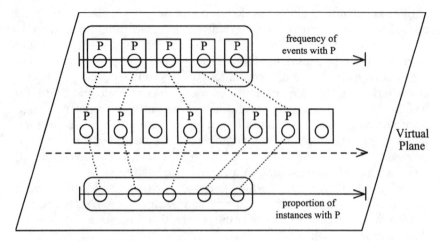

FIGURE 8.10. Fictivity with frequency expressions.

I have merely indicated, in generalized fashion, that the set of events where *P* is encountered falls somewhere along a scale whose expanse is given by the totality of events. However, since each examining event resides in the examination of an instance of the type, the frequency of events where *P* is encountered correlates exactly with the proportion of instances exhibiting *P*. It is the frequency of events that the adverb explicitly encodes, yet from the fictive scenario evoked we can "read off" the proportion of instances. It is not the case that the temporal adverbs have the import of nominal quantification as their meaning per se – rather, we conventionally employ them, with fictive temporal value, as part of a mental construction from which such quantification can be inferred.

We use sentences like those in (20) to say something about what the world is actually like, but the entities directly mentioned or alluded to are virtual: e.g., no particular politicians are encountered, and the process of wandering the globe to encounter and examine them is imaginary. Hence the semantic problem of describing the quantificational use of temporal adverbs is not one of nominal quantification per se. Basically it reduces to the problem of characterizing the mental construction invoked and how we dynamically access it.

"LOGICAL" ELEMENTS

Fictively, we have already wandered into the traditional territory of logic and formal semantics. Of prime concern in these disciplines have been such matters as quantification, negation, and implication. In cognitive semantics, even so-called "logical" elements like these are naturally considered manifestations of our imaginative capacities.

We can start with the claim by Johnson (1987) and Lakoff (1987, 1990) that abstract **image schemas** are fundamental components of conceptual structure. Examples include such notions as *container-content, center-periphery, part-whole, source-path-goal, linkage, force, balance*, etc. Abstracted from everyday bodily experience involving perception, motion, and muscular exertion, these schematic notions are projected metaphorically to other domains of experience. The manipulation of image schematic structure is even claimed – quite correctly, I believe – to underlie mental constructions usually thought of as formal and disembodied, such as logical deduction and mathematics (Lakoff & Núñez, 1998, 2000).

To take a simple example, Lakoff (1987, 272) explicates the deduction pattern known as *modus ponens* in terms of the inherent logic of the *container-content* image schema, based on the metaphor that sets or classes are containers for their members. Lakoff's claim is that we carry out this reasoning pattern via **image schema transformation**, as illustrated in Figure 8.11. Each premise has an image schematic representation, employing the container metaphor for sets. We combine these via the image schema transformation of **superimposition**. From the resulting composite image, we derive the conclusion by means of the image schema transformation of **fading out**. In short, once we properly characterize the conceptual structures being invoked and manipulated, the logical deduction is simply a matter of "reading off" the results, apparent by simple (mental) inspection. Of course, all these structures are fictive in nature, even though the reasoning pertains to actuality (George Lakoff is an actual linguist, and an actual mammal).

(21) **Modus ponens** Premise$_1$:   *All linguists are mammals.*
                   Premise$_2$:   *George Lakoff is a linguist.*
                   Conclusion: *Therefore Lakoff is a mammal.*

Let me very briefly consider two other "logical" elements: the conditional *if* (used in implicational statements) and negation. I will then discuss quantifiers at greater length.

In mental space theory, *if* is treated as a **space builder**, setting up a hypothetical mental space in which a certain situation (*P*) holds (Fauconnier,

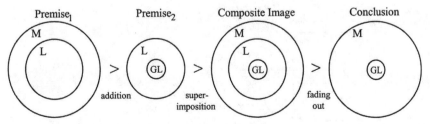

FIGURE 8.11. An imagistic account of *modus ponens*.

if P (then) Q

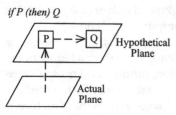

FIGURE 8.12. Conditionals.

1985, 1996, 1997; Sweetser, 1996; Dancygier & Sweetser, 1997). The import of a conditional construction *if P (then) Q* is that, upon examining the space containing *P*, one will also encounter *Q*. In other words, the construction incorporates a kind of mental scanning, sketched in Figure 8.12: starting from an imagined situation where *P* is observed, further inspection of the same situation leads to the observation of *Q*. The occurrence in this construction of *then*, whose basic value is temporal, can thus be related to the temporality of the scanning process (as noted previously for *still* and *already*).

It is generally accepted that a negative sentence presupposes the consideration of its positive counterpart. We can describe this in terms of the relation between a virtual and an actual plane, as sketched in Figure 8.13. The positive situation is given as **X [F] Y**, *F* being the focus of negation, i.e., the element that fails to correspond to actuality. This positive situation is not only explicitly coded, but even functions as the expression's profile. Nonetheless, it is virtual in nature, being conjured up just for purposes of describing actuality. Negation serves to specify how this virtual situation maps onto actuality: namely, the actual situation is obtained by cancelling out substructure *F*. This operation of mental cancellation is inherently dynamic, as indicated by the arrows. It is only by first evoking the virtual situation that one can cancel out *F* to arrive at the actual one.

In some cases, e.g., (22)(a), the entire proposition is focused and thus cancelled, so that nothing is left (hence *X* and *Y* are vacuous). In others,

not

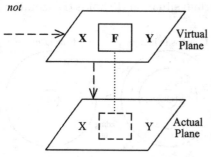

FIGURE 8.13. Negation.

only a portion of the profiled situation constitutes the focus (or "target") of negation, generally marked in English by unreduced stress (small caps):

(22)(a) *It didn't rain last night.*
   (b) *I didn't eat the ZUCCHINI.*
   (c) *She didn't PASSIONATELY embrace me.*

Since the uncancelled portion is not specifically excluded from actuality, if conceptually coherent it can be taken as real. Thus (22)(b) cancels the notion of zucchini from the description of my eating, but it leaves open the possibility that I did eat something. And in (22)(c), the absence of passion is still compatible with her having given me a friendly hug. Indeed, limitation of the focus of negation to the elements in question suggests that the remainder is in fact valid.

We turn now to a classic issue in logic and formal semantics, namely **quantifier scope**. This too is a matter of conceptual structure in which fictive entities play a crucial role (Langacker, 1991, 3.3, 1999b). Let us take just one example, which is ambiguous between a scopal and a non-scopal interpretation:

(23) *Three boys lifted two chairs.*

On the nonscopal interpretation, (23) simply profiles an interaction between a group consisting of three boys and a group consisting of two chairs, all construed as actual individuals.[10] This is diagrammed in Figure 8.14(a).

Of more interest here is the scopal interpretation. Under normal circumstances the quantifier on the subject is interpreted as having **wide scope**, and that on the object, **narrow scope** (i.e., *three* has *two* "in its scope").[11] This is where fictivity enters the picture, since, on this reading, direct reference is made to three actual boys, but not to any actual chairs. As shown in Figure 8.14(b), the import is rather that each of the three actual boys participated in one instance of the **event type** *boy lift two chairs*. That is, the two chairs referred to are virtual chairs, conjured up to characterize an event type (*boy lift two chairs*), one instance of which is ascribed to each actual boy.[12]

On the scopal interpretation, no actual chairs are directly mentioned, although it can be inferred that between 2 and 6 actual chairs were involved. Note the infelicity of (24)(a), where by default the second sentence is taken as describing actuality. The problem is that the antecedent *two chairs*

---

[10] There is vagueness about how many atomic lifting events there were, and how many members of each set participated in each atomic event, but that is not pertinent here.

[11] In formal logic, the contrast is represented by different nestings of quantifiers in a logical formula.

[12] On the less likely interpretation where *two* has wide scope, reference is instead made to two actual chairs, each of which participates in one occurrence of the event type *three boys lift chair*.

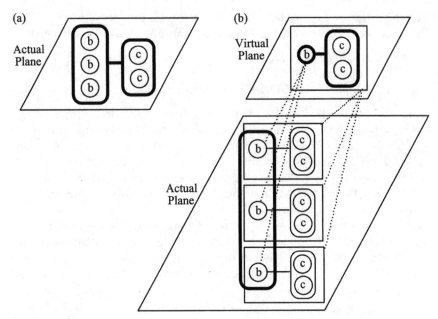

FIGURE 8.14. Quantifier scope.

occupies the virtual plane, whereas the anaphoric *both* is actual – since no actual chairs were directly mentioned, anaphoric reference to them is conceptually inconsistent (see Langacker, 1996a). However, we can rescue the discourse by making it clear that the second sentence also pertains to the type description (*boy lift two chairs*), as in (24)(b). Here the antecedent and the anaphor are both construed as referring to virtual entities.

(24)(a) *Three boys each lifted **two chairs**. ***Both** were metal.*

   (b) *Three boys each lifted **two chairs**. In each case, **both** were metal.*

Obviously, this is not a full account of logical scope, but only an example of an approach to it. I believe, however, that it is basically the correct approach and that the phenomenon hinges crucially on the evocation of fictive entities. This also proves to be the case when we examine the meanings of individual quantifiers (Langacker, 1991, 3.2).

QUANTIFIER MEANINGS

Whereas logicians have often been content to posit a single universal quantifier (∀), English, quite strikingly, has no less than six means of quantifying over all members of a class:

(25)(a) *All cultures are worth preserving.*

   (b) *Cultures are worth preserving.*

(c) *A culture is worth preserving.*
(d) *Every culture is worth preserving.*
(e) *Each culture is worth preserving.*
(f) *Any culture is worth preserving.*

It is also striking that some universally quantified nominals are singular, despite their apparent reference to a class with indefinitely many members. From the cognitive semantic perspective, this variation is obviously symptomatic of different ways of conceptualizing the process of making generalizations reaching to all members of a set. These conceptual differences constitute different linguistic meanings and in large measure account for differences in form and grammatical behavior.

These kinds of universal quantification represent alternate strategies for making and expressing generalizations by means of fictive entities. A first observation is that the generalization in question need not be truly universal, applying globally to all instances of a type, but can also apply locally to a restricted set of instances relevant in a particular context. The statements in (26), for instance, apply just to the students attending the campus in question:

(26)(a) *On this campus, all students are encouraged to think independently.*
(b) *On this campus, students are encouraged to think independently.*
(c) *On this campus, a student is encouraged to think independently.*
(d) *On this campus, every student is encouraged to think independently.*
(e) *On this campus, each student is encouraged to think independently.*
(f) *On this campus, any student is encouraged to think independently.*

There are, then, limitations on the scope of the generalizations made, with fully generic statements constituting the extreme case where no restrictions whatever are imposed. This parameter has to be distinguished from the meanings of the quantifiers per se. Rather it pertains to the conceptual configuration with respect to which the quantifiers are employed. In terms of the previous discussion, it pertains to the nature of the plane (or mental space) constructed to represent the generalization, and how the structure represented on that plane maps onto actuality.

Consider first the indefinite articles in (25)(c) and (26)(c). These are simply cases of evoking a virtual instance of a type in order to make a local or global generalization, as previously exemplified in (12)–(13). In (12)(b) [*Three times, a student asked an intelligent question*], diagrammed in Figure 8.4, the generalization made is local in character, so the plane bearing the fictive profiled event is constructed on an ad hoc basis just for that purpose. In (13) [*A cat plays with a mouse it has caught*], diagrammed in Figure 8.5, the fictive event occurs in a plane conceived as representing the world's inherent nature, its stable structure; this is how I will understand the term **generic**. But the indefinite article in these examples – (12)(b), (13), (25)(c), and (26)(c) – has its normal value. What is special is simply that the thing instance it evokes is virtual, occurring in a virtual plane constructed by abstraction from actuality to capture a generalization valid within some range.

Universal quantification with a zero determiner, as in (25)(b) and (26)(b), is quite similar. The zero determiner is the mass-noun counterpart of the indefinite article *a* (mass nouns include plurals as a special case). Hence the contrast is primarily a matter of whether the mental model conjured up to represent this generalization contains just a single virtual instance of a type (the minimum needed to capture the regularity) or multiple instances (reflecting more directly the multiplicity of instances all exhibiting the property in question).[13]

That leaves us with the true quantifiers *all, every, each,* and *any.* They divide into two groups, which I call **proportional** and **representative instance** quantifiers. *All* belongs in the first group, along with the non-universal *most* and *some.* One distinguishing property of this group is their occurrence with plurals (*all cats, most cats, some cats*). Naturally, *all* occurs as well with nonplural mass nouns (*all beer*). The representative instance quantifiers are *every, each,* and *any,* which combine with singular nouns (*every cat, each cat, any cat*). Additionally, *any* quantifies both plural and nonplural masses (*any cats, any beer*).

I refer to *all, most,* and *some* as **proportional** quantifiers because they designate some proportion of the relevant instances of the type in question. For a given type (t), we can speak of the contextually relevant **extension**, E_t, consisting of the maximal set of instances invoked for some purpose, notably as a basis for generalization.[14] A proportional quantifier – like the quantified nominal it derives – profiles a subpart of this extension (the type being determined by the quantified noun and its modifiers). As shown in Figure 8.15(a), *all* profiles a set coextensive with the maximal extension. Hence only one ellipse shows up in the diagram, since the profile, P, coincides with the maximal extension, E_t. The two are distinct in the case of *most,* which profiles a set that comes close to exhausting E_t without actually doing so. *Some* profiles a set of indeterminate size, being specified as nonempty. If we represent the full expanse of E_t as a scale, in the manner of Figure 8.15(d), then *all* falls at the positive endpoint of the scale, *most* lies in the vicinity of the endpoint, and *some* can be anywhere else (except at the zero point).

What should be noticed about this characterization is that everything is fictive. Consider (27):

(27) *Most cats are lazy.*

---

[13] For more details, and for some consequences of this difference, see Langacker 1996b, 1997b.
[14] In Langacker (1990) I called this the **reference mass** for the type.

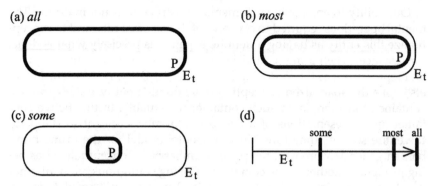

FIGURE 8.15. Proportional quantifiers.

While intended as a generalization about actuality, the entities directly invoked and described are virtual in nature, as sketched in Figure 8.16. First, E_c is the set of all cats (the maximal extension of the *cat* type). But there is no such object in the world – at least none of any measurable or determinate expanse, to which another can be compared in the manner of Figure 8.15. It is rather a mental construction, a fictive entity conjured up to make a generalization. Likewise, the profiled subset, the referent of *most cats*, is virtual rather than actual. Even if we accept (27) as a true description of actuality, such that the members of the profiled subset all exhibit laziness, we still do not know which **actual** cats are lazy and which ones not. For this reason the correspondences in Figure 8.16 are not connected to any particular cat instances in the actual plane. While pertaining to actuality, a statement like (27) describes it only indirectly – the entities it specifically invokes and directly describes are virtual, i.e., mental constructions.

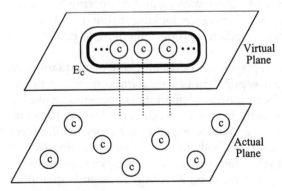

FIGURE 8.16. Most cats.

Our ability to engage in such mental construction is not in doubt. The mental operations required to conceive of the set of all cats, and to conceptualize this entity as having a definite expanse, is precisely what is done, for instance, when a mathematician speaks of the set of prime numbers and represents it as the following formula: $\{1, 2, 3, 5, 7, 11, \ldots\}$. The brackets evoke the spatialized conception of a bounded entity, a metaphorical container, but there is no such container in actuality. In this fictive container are representations of a few prime numbers, meant to stand for the entire set, i.e., they function as a mental model for the prime numbers in general. Moreover, the prime numbers are conceptualized as being grouped together in the container, as being contiguous, with all other numbers (nonprimes) excluded from it. But of course, even if we accept numbers as existing in reality, the primes are not contiguous in the sequence.

This fictivity is a clear example of embodiment, reflecting various aspects of our everyday experience in dealing with the physical world. We often move through our surroundings looking for objects of a certain type, or assemble objects to form a spatial group. Obviously, we perceive an object as having a certain spatial expanse, typically bounded, and very often we lay one object on top of another for purposes of comparison or measurement.

Fictively, then, in conceptualizing E_c (the set of all cats) we search exhaustively through our surroundings looking for cats, collect those we find, and put them together in one location to form an object conceptualized as having a bounded expanse. We carry out the analogous mental operations in conceptualizing the set profiled by *most* or *all*, and take the further step of fictively putting this set, P, on top of E_c to compare their sizes. In the case of *all cats*, we see that they match. In the case of *most cats*, we find that the boundaries of P approach those of E_c but do not quite reach them.

What about *some*, and for that matter *no* (as in *some cats, no cat(s)*)? Here I suspect that the experience of superimposing and comparing is less important than another common occurrence: looking inside a container to see what is there. *Some* corresponds to finding something in it, and *no* to finding it empty.

Let us turn now to the representative instance universal quantifiers, namely *every*, *each*, and *any*. Despite their universal import, these combine with singular nouns. Like the proportional quantifiers, these too invoke the maximal extension of a type as the basis for their characterization. Hence all the aforementioned aspects of embodied experience are pertinent, except that of laying one object on top of another for purposes of comparison or measurement. In contrast to *all*, which profiles a set conceived as a bounded entity that is matched against E_t, a representative instance quantifier

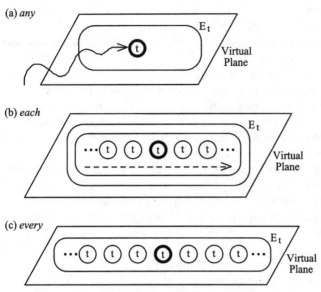

FIGURE 8.17. Representative instance quantifiers.

profiles just a single instance of type t. It is of course a fictive instance, as seen in (28):

(28) **A**: {*Every/each/any*} *cat is lazy.*
     B: **Which one?*

It is a virtual instance of the type conjured up for purposes of making a generalization. Reference to a single instance is sufficient for this purpose provided that this instance is somehow taken as being **representative** of the class as a whole. It is through such representativeness that a property ascribed to a single (fictive) instance is inferred as being universally applicable to class members.

The semantic contrast among *every, each,* and *any* resides in the way the profiled instance achieves its representativeness. This results from fictive mental operations, analogous to the superimposition and comparison fictively carried out in the case of *all*. For *any*, the operation is one of **random selection**. It is the abstract conceptual analog of reaching into a bag of candy and taking a piece at random, or selecting a card as part of a magic trick (where the magician says: *Pick a card, **any** card*). This is sketched in Figure 8.17(a), where the wavy arrow indicates the making of a random choice. Note that only the selected, profiled instance of the type is specifically evoked. Analogously, when reaching into a bag of candy to take out a piece, we may not see any of the pieces except the one we wind up extracting from inside the container.

By contrast, *each* invokes a number of instances in addition to the one put in profile as its fictive referent. I suggest that *each* involves the fictive operation of **sequential examination** – individually looking at the members of a group, one by one, until they have all been examined (like checking a stack of letters to make sure they all have stamps). The profiled individual lies somewhere in this sequence, with nothing to distinguish it from the others. This lack of any distinguishing properties, hence the arbitrariness of the choice, assures representativeness.[15]

Each has one other characteristic feature, indicated diagrammatically by the inner ellipse in Figure 8.17(b). Usually if not always, *each* quantifies over a contextually delimited set taken as being just part of the maximal extension E_t. If I say, for instance, that *each cat is lazy*, I am probably describing a particular set of cats (e.g., those in my house), not making a fully generic statement about domestic felines.[16] It is tempting to speculate that this property of *each* is a consequence of the fictive sequential examination it hinges on: it is easier to envisage sequential examination of a limited set of entities than one extending to all possible members of a class.

That brings us to *every*, which is the most difficult to characterize.[17] Perhaps it is best described as being like *each*, except that it lacks the fiction of sequential examination, hence applies to E_t as a whole (rather than just a delimited subset). In any case, it evokes the image of the members of E_t being simultaneously visible and available for examination (like the members of a chorus or the rows of colors in a box of crayons). Once again, there is nothing to distinguish the profiled instance from the others, hence its representativeness.

I have offered a characterization of the four universal quantifiers – *all*, *any*, *each*, and *every* – that has several important advantages: (i) it specifies how they are different, and thus provides a rationale for there being so many; (ii) at the same time, it accounts for their universal force; (iii) the mechanisms it relies on have been independently justified as cognitively available and linguistically relevant; and (iv) as a speaker, I find it intuitively satisfying. I believe I am not unrepresentative in this respect. I have exposed numerous groups of speakers (with varying degrees of linguistic

---

[15] Perhaps we should see *each* as incorporating the random selection that is central to *any*, but if so it is backgrounded, the notion of sequential examination being more salient. We might even posit another level of fictivity, such that the profiled entity exhibiting the property in question constitutes a generalization over the entities sequentially examined; in this respect it would be analogous to the fictive student conjured up in (12)(b).

[16] This is not so obvious in cases like (25)(e) [*Each culture is worth preserving*], though I suspect it is still in some sense valid. It may reflect the mental operation of delimiting the set of cultures actually manifested, out of all those that could potentially occur.

[17] I believe it is also the quantifier for which it is hardest to find equivalents in other languages.

sophistication) to diagrams like those in Figure 8.16, and none has ever had any difficulty accepting these spatialized representations. More pointedly, I have asked such groups about the contrast in (29). Not a few people have volunteered the judgment that *each* involves sequentiality in viewing the stars, and *every* simultaneity. Even more people see *any* as invoking random choice (whichever star you choose, you can see it tonight).

(29) *Tonight you can see {every/each/any} star in the Milky Way.*

Still, the strongest grounds for adopting such characterizations come from their ability to account for differences in distribution and grammatical behavior. A context like (29) is one that, in terms of **actual** viewing, lends itself to any of the **fictive** modes of access evoked by the quantifiers. We can indeed shift our gaze from one star to the next (as for *each*), or randomly choose one to look at (as for *any*). We can also see many stars simultaneously, standing out as individuals (as with *every*), but also see them as mass-like, with lesser individuation (as with *all*, which can also be used in this context). It stands to reason that a particular quantifier will tend to be employed when the actual situation in question, and usual ways of accessing it, **harmonize** with the kind of virtual access the quantifier evokes as part of its meaning.

Other such evidence is easily found. First, the characterizations of the universally quantifying *every*, *each*, *any*, and *all* correctly predict their distributions with respect to singular count nouns, plurals (which I treat as a subtype of mass nouns), and nonplural mass nouns. Because *every* and *each* profile single, discrete entities, they only occur with count nouns, as seen in (30)(a). By contrast, *all* profiles a fictive expanse whose boundary coincides with that of another mass, the maximal extension E_t. Nothing intrinsic to *all* specifies whether or not this mass consists of discrete entities, so *all* is compatible with either plural or nonplural mass nouns, as seen in (30)(b). It is not however compatible with a singular count noun. *Any* occurs with all three subtypes, as in (30)(c). This is because it is based on random selection. Random choice can be made regardless of whether the mass selected from is continuous or composed of discrete individuals. In the latter case, moreover, one can randomly pull out either a single object or a handful.

(30)(a) *{every/each} {coin/*coins/*money}*
   (b) *all {coins/money/*coin}*
   (c) *any {coin/coins/money}*

CONCLUSION

That we are endowed with certain imaginative capacities has long been recognized. The inherently dynamic nature of mental activity is also quite apparent. Generally not realized, however, is how utterly pervasive these factors are in cognition and how fundamental they are to linguistic semantics. Once they are recognized and fully accommodated, myriad problems of meaning and grammar become susceptible to natural and (I believe) insightful resolution. As they gradually emerge, I fully expect these solutions to provide increasing levels of empirical support for the basic principles of conceptual semantics and cognitive linguistics, one of these being embodiment.

References

Barsalou, L. W. (1999). Perceptual symbol systems. *Behavioral and Brain Sciences 22*, 577–660.

Dancygier, B., & Sweetser, E. (1997). Then in conditional constructions. *Cognitive Linguistics 8*, 109–136.

Fauconnier, G. (1985). *Mental Spaces: Aspects of Meaning Construction in Natural Language*. Cambridge, MA, and London: MIT Press/Bradford.

Fauconnier, G. (1996). Analogical counterfactuals. In G. Fauconnier and E. Sweetser, *Spaces, Worlds, and Grammar* (pp. 57–90). Chicago and London: University of Chicago Press.

Fauconnier, G. (1997). *Mappings in Thought and Language*. Cambridge: Cambridge University Press.

Fauconnier, G., & Sweetser, E. (Eds.), (1996). *Spaces, Worlds, and Grammar*. Chicago and London: University of Chicago Press.

Fauconnier, G., & Turner, M. (1998a). Conceptual integration networks. *Cognitive Science 22*, 133–187.

Fauconnier, G., & Turner, M. (1998b). Principles of conceptual integration. In J. P. Koenig (Ed.), *Spaces, Worlds, and Grammar* (pp. 269–283). Chicago and London: University of Chicago Press.

Fauconnier, G., & Turner, M. (2002). *The Way We Think: Conceptual Blending and the Mind's Hidden Complexities*. New York: Basic Books.

Goldberg, A. E. (Ed.), (1996). *Conceptual Structure, Discourse, and Language*. Stanford: CSLI Publications.

Goldsmith, J., & Woisetschlaeger, E. (1982). The logic of the English progressive. *Linguistic Inquiry 13*, 79–89.

Johnson, M. (1987). *The Body in the Mind: The Bodily Basis of Meaning, Imagination, and Reason*. Chicago and London: University of Chicago Press.

Johnson-Laird, P. N. (1983). *Mental Models*. Cambridge, MA: Harvard University Press.

Koenig, J. P. (Ed.), (1998). *Spaces, Worlds, and Grammar*. Chicago and London: University of Chicago Press.

Kövecses, Z., & Radden, G. (1998). Metonymy: Developing a cognitive linguistic view. *Cognitive Linguistics 9*, 33–77.

Kumashiro, T. (2000). *The Conceptual Basis of Grammar: A Cognitive Approach to Japanese Clausal Structure*. San Diego: University of California doctoral dissertation.

Lakoff, G. (1987). *Women, Fire, and Dangerous Things: What Categories Reveal about the Mind*. Chicago and London: University of Chicago Press.

Lakoff, G. (1990). The invariance hypothesis: Is abstract reason based on image-schemas? *Cognitive Linguistics 1*, 39–74.

Lakoff, G., & Johnson, M. (1980). *Metaphors We Live By*. Chicago and London: University of Chicago Press.

Lakoff, G., & Johnson, M. (1999). *Philosophy in the Flesh: The Embodied Mind and Its Challenge to Western Thought*. New York: Basic Books.

Lakoff, G., & Núñez, R. (1998). Conceptual metaphor in mathematics. In J. P. Koenig (Ed.), *Spaces, Worlds, and Grammar* (pp. 219–237). Chicago and London: University of Chicago Press.

Lakoff, G., & Núñez, R. (2000). *Where Mathematics Comes From: How the Embodied Mind Brings Mathematics into Being*. New York: Basic Books.

Langacker, R. W. (1986). Abstract motion. *Proceedings of the Annual Meeting of the Berkeley Linguistics Society 12*, 455–471.

Langacker, R. W. (1987a). *Foundations of Cognitive Grammar, Vol. 1, Theoretical Prerequisites*. Stanford: Stanford University Press.

Langacker, R. W. (1987b). Nouns and verbs. *Language 63*, 53–94.

Langacker, R. W. (1990). Subjectification. *Cognitive Linguistics 1*, 5–38.

Langacker, R. W. (1991). *Foundations of Cognitive Grammar, Vol. 2, Descriptive Application*. Stanford: Stanford University Press.

Langacker, R. W. (1993). Reference-point constructions. *Cognitive Linguistics 4*, 1–38.

Langacker, R. W. (1995). Possession and possessive constructions. In J. R. Taylor and R. E. MacLaury (Eds.), *Language and the Cognitive Construal of the World* (pp. 51–79). Trends in Linguistics Studies and Monographs 82. Berlin and New York: Mouton de Gruyter.

Langacker, R. W. (1996a). Conceptual grouping and pronominal anaphora. In B. Fox (Ed.), *Studies in Anaphora* (pp. 333–378). Typological Studies in Language 33. Amsterdam and Philadelphia: John Benjamins.

Langacker, R. W. (1996b). A constraint on progressive generics. In Goldberg, A. E. (Ed.), *Conceptual Structure, Discourse and Language* (pp. 289–302). Stanford: CSLI Publications.

Langacker, R. W. (1997a). A dynamic account of grammatical function. In J. Bybee, J. Haiman, & S. A. Thompson (Eds.), *Essays on Language Function and Language Type Dedicated to T. Givón* (pp. 249–273). Amsterdam and Philadelphia: John Benjamins.

Langacker, R. W. (1997b). Generics and habituals. In A. Athanasiadou and R. Dirven (Eds.), *On Conditionals Again* (pp. 191–222). Current Issues in Linguistic Theory 143. Amsterdam and Philadelphia: John Benjamins.

Langacker, R. W. (1999a). *Grammar and Conceptualization*. Cognitive Linguistics Research 14. Berlin and New York: Mouton de Gruyter.

Langacker, R. W. (1999b). Virtual reality. *Studies in the Linguistic Sciences 29*, 2, 77–103.

Langacker, R. W. (1999c). Double-subject constructions. In Sung-Yun Bak (Ed.), *Linguistics in the Morning Calm 4* (pp. 83–104). Seoul: Hanshin.

Langacker, R. W. (1999d). Assessing the cognitive linguistic enterprise. In T. Janssen and G. Redeker (Eds.), *Cognitive Linguistics: Foundations, Scope, and Methodology* (pp. 13–59). Cognitive Linguistics Research 15. Berlin and New York: Mouton de Gruyter.

Langacker, R. W. (1999e). Losing control: Grammaticization, subjectification, and transparency. In A. Blank and P. Koch (Eds.), *Historical Semantics and Cognition* (pp. 147–175). Cognitive Linguistics Research 13. Berlin and New York: Mouton de Gruyter.

Langacker, R. W. (2000). Why a mind is necessary: Conceptualization, grammar and linguistic semantics. In L. Albertazzi (Ed.), *Meaning and Cognition: A Multidisciplinary Approach* (pp. 25–38). Converging Evidence in Language and Communication Research 2. Amsterdam and Philadelphia: John Benjamins.

Langacker, R. W. (2001a). Dynamicity in grammar. *Axiomathes 12*, 7–33.

Langacker, R. W. (2001b). Topic, subject, and possessor. In H. G. Simonsen and R. T. Endresen (Eds.), *A Cognitive Approach to the Verb: Morphological and Constructional Perspectives* (pp. 11–48). Cognitive Linguistics Research 16. Berlin and New York: Mouton de Gruyter.

Langacker, R. W. (2003). Dynamicity, fictivity, and scanning: The imaginative basis of logic and linguistic meaning. *Korean Linguistics 18*, 1–64.

Matsumoto, Y. (1996a). How abstract is subjective motion? A comparison of coverage path expressions and access path expressions. In Goldberg, A. E. (Ed.), *Conceptual Structure, Discourse and Language.* (pp. 359–373). Stanford: CSLI Publications.

Matsumoto, Y. (1996b). Subjective-change expressions in Japanese and their cognitive and linguistic bases. In G. Fauconnier and E. Sweetser (Eds.), *Spaces, Worlds, and Grammar* (pp. 124–156). Chicago and London: University of Chicago Press.

Michaelis, L. A. (1991). Temporal priority and pragmatic ambiguity: The case of already. *Proceedings of the Annual Meeting of the Berkeley Linguistics Society 17*, 426–438.

Michaelis, L. A. (1993). "Continuity" within three scalar models: The polysemy of adverbial still. *Journal of Semantics 10*, 193–237.

Michaelis, L. A. (1996). Cross-world continuity and the polysemy of adverbial still. In G. Fauconnier and E. Sweetser (Eds.), *Spaces, Worlds, and Grammar* (pp. 179–226). Chicago and London: University of Chicago Press.

Sweetser, E. (1982). Root and epistemic modals: Causality in two worlds. *Proceedings of the Annual Meeting of the Berkeley Linguistics Society 8*, 484–507.

Sweetser, E. (1996). Mental spaces and the grammar of conditional constructions. In G. Fauconnier and E. Sweetser (Eds.), *Spaces, Worlds, and Grammar* (pp. 318–333). Chicago and London: University of Chicago Press.

Sweetser, E. (1997). Role and individual interpretations of change predicates. In J. Nuyts and E. Pederson (Eds.), *Language and Conceptualization* (pp. 116–136). Language, Culture and Cognition 1. Cambridge: Cambridge University Press.

Talmy, L. (1988). Force dynamics in language and cognition. *Cognitive Science 12*, 49–100.

Talmy, L. (1996). Fictive motion in language and "ception." In P. Bloom et al. (Eds.), *Language and Space* (pp. 211–276). Cambridge, MA, and London: MIT Press/Bradford.

Talmy, L. (2000a). *Toward a Cognitive Semantics, Vol. 1, Concept Structuring Systems.* Cambridge, MA: MIT Press/Bradford.

Talmy, L. (2000b). *Toward a Cognitive Semantics, Vol. 2, Typology and Process in Concept Structuring.* Cambridge, MA: MIT Press.

van Hoek, K. (1995). Conceptual reference points: A cognitive grammar account of pronominal anaphora constraints. *Language 71*, 310–340.

van Hoek, K. (1997). *Anaphora and Conceptual Structure.* Chicago and London: University of Chicago Press.

9

The Emergence of Grammar from Perspective

Brian MacWhinney

Successful communication rests not just on shared knowledge and reference (Clark & Marshall, 1981), but also on a process of mutual perspective taking. By giving clear cues to our listeners about which perspectives they should assume and how they should move from one perspective to the next, we maximize the extent to which they can share our perceptions and ideas. When language is rich in cues for perspective taking and perspective shifting, it awakens the imagination of the listener and leads to successful sharing of ideas, impressions, attitudes, and narratives. When the process of perspective sharing is disrupted by interruptions, monotony, excessive complexity, or lack of shared knowledge, communication can break down.

Although we understand intuitively that perspective taking is central to communication, few psycholinguistic or cognitive models assign it more than a peripheral role. Linguistic theory typically views perspective as a secondary pragmatic filter (Kuno, 1986; O'Grady, in press) that operates only after hard linguistic constraints have been fulfilled. This paper explores the hypothesis that, far from being peripheral or secondary, perspective taking is at the very core of language structure and higher-level cognition. This approach, which I call the Perspective Hypothesis, makes the following basic claims:

1. Perspective taking operates online using images created in five systems: direct experience, space/time deixis, plans, social roles, and mental acts.
2. Language uses perspective taking to bind together these five imagery subsystems.
3. Grammar emerges from conversation as a method for supporting accurate tracking and switching of perspective.
4. By tracing perspective shifts in language, children are able to learn the cognitive pathways and mental models sanctioned by their culture.

This hypothesis builds on recent advances in cognitive linguistics, embodied cognition, cognitive neuroscience, anthropology, and developmental psychology. The Perspective Hypothesis represents a particular case of a more general type of analysis called "emergentism" (MacWhinney, 1999b, 2002). The general emergentist framework views emergence as operative on five time levels. The current article focuses on the online emergence of perspective during conversational processing, as highlighted in point (3). Developmental aspects of the emergence of perspective marking are discussed elsewhere (MacWhinney, 1999a).

The articulation of a theory of perspective is central to the theory of embodied cognition. It forces a fundamental rethinking of the dynamics of mental models, the nature of sentence processing, the functional grounding of grammatical structures, the shape of language acquisition, and the co-evolution of language and cognition. This rethinking is fundamental, because perspective serves as a common thread that links together the cognitive systems governing direct experience, space-time deixis, causal plans, social roles, and mental acts. Because perspective interacts with imagery constructed on each of these levels, it provides a general rubric for knitting together all of cognition. Consider a sentence, such as "Last night, my sister's friend reminded me I had dropped my keys under the table behind the garage." Here, we see how a single utterance integrates information about time (last night), social relations (sister's friend), mental acts (remind), space (under, behind), objects (keys, table, garage), and events (drop). Within each of these informational levels, there are perspectives, including those of the sister, the friend, the speaker, and the various locations. Although this information may be elaborated in different regions of the brain, language achieves an integration of this information across all of these domains. According to the Perspective Hypothesis, it does this by specifying shifts of perspective across each of the five levels.

Consider how it might that we would understand the sentence, "the cat licked herself." In the basic superficial mode of processing, which I call the depictive mode, we see a movie of the cat raising her paw to her mouth and licking the fur with her tongue. In a deeper, more embodied level of processing, which I call the enactive mode, we take the stance of the cat by mapping her paw to our hand and her tongue to our tongue. Most people would say that they are unlikely to employ the enactive mode, when the sentence is presented by itself outside of context. However, if we embed the sentence in a larger discourse, we are more inclined to process enactively. Consider this passage:

The cat spotted a mockingbird perched on the feeder. She crouched down low in the grass, inching closer and closer with all her muscles tensed. Just as she pounced, the bird escaped. Disappointed, she lept up to a garden chair, raised her paw to her tongue, and began licking it.

Here, each clause links to the previous one through the perspective of the cat as the protagonist. As we chain these references together, we induce the listener to assume a single enactive perspective. The longer and more vivid our descriptions, the more they stimulate enactive processes in comprehension.

LEVEL 1: DIRECT EXPERIENCE

Language codes direct experience through words for objects such as "banana" or "finger." Our basic mode of interaction with objects is through direct experience and direct perception. Direct perceptions involve vision, touch, smell, taste, kinesthesia, and proprioception. These interactions take advantage of the affordances (Gibson, 1977) that objects provide for both perception and action. As we use our arms, legs, and bodies to act upon objects, we derive direct feedback from these objects. This feedback loop between action and perception does not rely on symbols, perspective, or any other form of cognitive distancing. Instead, it is designed to give us immediate contact with the world in a way that facilitates quick adaptive reactions. Because this system does not need to rely on memory, imagery, perspective, or other cognition systems (Gibson, 1977), it can remain fully grounded.

Consider the ways in which we perceive a banana. When we see a banana, we receive nothing more than an image of a yellow curved object. However, as we interact directly with the banana, additional perceptions start to unfold. When we grab a banana, our hands experience the texture of the peel, the ridges along the peel, the smooth extensions between the ridges, and the rougher edges where the banana connects with other bananas into a bunch. When we hold or throw a banana, we appreciate its weight and balance. When we peel a banana, we encounter still further sensations involving the action of peeling, as well as the peel itself. With the peel removed, we can access new sensations from the meat of the banana. An overripe banana can assault us with its pungent smell. When we eat a banana, our whole body becomes involved in chewing, swallowing, and digestion. All of these direct interactions in vision, smell, taste, touch, skeletal postures, kinesthesia, proprioception, and locomotor feedback arise from a single object that we categorize as a "banana." It is this rich and diverse set of sensations and motor plans that constitutes the fullest grounding for our understanding of the word "banana."

Imagery and Decoupling

The direct grounding of perception is limited and elaborated in three important ways. First, it is clear that we know things that do not derive from direct perception. Consider again the case of the banana. We know that bananas are rich in potassium and Vitamin E, that they are grown in Central America by United Fruit cooperatives, and so on. These are declarative facts (Paivio, 1971; Tabachneck-Schijf, Leonardo, & Simon, 1997) that elaborate the primary notion of a banana that we derive from direct embodied perception.

Second, direct perception is revised and redirected by decoupling through mental imagery. Direct experience can be captured and replayed through the system of mental imagery. When we imagine a banana, we call up images of its shape, taste, and feel, even when it is not physically present. Imagery serves a variety of cognitive functions in the areas of planning, memory, dreams, and perspective taking. We might be hungry and think of a banana as a possible food source, or we might detect a smell that would lead us to construct a visual image of a banana. Recent research in neurophysiology has shown that, when we imagine objects and actions in this way, we typically activate the same neuronal pathways that are used for direct perception and direct action. For example, when we imagine performing bicep curls, there are discharges to the biceps (Jeannerod, 1997). When a trained marksman imagines shooting a gun, the discharges to the muscles mimic those found in real target practice. When we imagine eating, there is an increase in salivation. Neuroimaging studies by Parsons et al. (1995) and Martin, Wiggs, Ungerleider, and Haxby (1996) and Cohen et al. (1996) have shown that, when subjects are asked to engage in mental imagery, they use modality-specific sensorimotor cortical systems. For example, in the study by Martin et al., the naming of tool words specifically activated the areas of the left premotor cortex that control hand movements. The imagery system relies on the cognitive creation of a body map (Damasio, 1999; Kakei, Hoffman, & Strick, 1999). This body map then functions as an internal homunculus that can be projected to track the actions of others through the system of motor neurons (Rizzolatti, Fadiga, Gallese, & Fogassi, 1996).

Imagery works together with memory, planning, dreaming, and projection to allow us to decouple thought from direct experience. Together, these processes allow us to move beyond a direct linkage to object and actions and to imagine potential actions and their possible results. In effect, imagery facilitates the partial decoupling of cognition from direct perception. At the same time, the decomposable nature of perceptual symbol systems (Barsalou, 1999) allows us to reestablish partial grounding for the purposes of comprehension, planning, and memory. However, the fact that cognition can become partially decoupled through imagery should not be construed as meaning that it is fully decoupled (Burgess & Lund, 1997).

Finally, there is evidence that top-down influences from memory can redirect the nature of direct perception. Phenomena such as the McGurk effect, apparent motion, amodal completion, and repetition priming all

indicate that our intake of new perceptual material can be biased by concurrent perceptions or images derived from memory.

The Language of Direct Experience

The mapping of direct experiences onto linguistic form is confined in
English to the level of individual words, including nouns, verbs, and adjectives. The noun "banana" packages together all our experiences with
this object into a single unanalyzed whole. Verbs encode images of direct
action, often in relation to movements of the body. When we hear the word
"walk," we immediately activate the basic elements of the physical components of walking (Narayanan, 1997). These include alternating motions of
the legs, counterbalanced swinging of the arms, pressures on the knees and
other joints, and the sense of our weight coming down on the earth. Adjectives such as "green" or "round" encode largely perceptual dimensions
of direct experiences.

Polysynthetic languages can express more complex direct perceptions
in single words. For example, in Navajo, a chair is "bikáá'dah'asdáhí" or
"on-it-one-sits." To take a more familiar example, many languages refer
to a corkscrew as a "cork puller." Languages can also capture aspects of
direct experience through the projection of the body image. In English, we
speak of the hands of a clock, the teeth of a zipper, and the foot of the
mountain. In Apache, this penchant for body part metaphors carries over
to describing the parts of an automobile. The tires are the feet of the car,
the battery is its heart, and the headlights are its eyes. Adjectives encode
images of direct perceptions for attributes such as weight, color, or smell.

Much of the current work on embodied cognition focuses on the interpretation of language referring to direct perceptions. For example, Stanfield
and Zwaan (2001) found that, when given sentences such as "John pounded
the nail into the floor," subjects construct interpretations with a nail pointing downwards. In these tests, subjects must develop full images of the
relevant sentences. However, the actual dependent measures in the studies are limited to the imagined direct perceptions linked to the position of
specific objects, such as the "nail" in this example.

LEVEL 2: SPACE AND TIME

Perspective taking in space and time depends on a different set of cognition mechanisms. For direct experience, perspective taking involves the
projection of the body image onto the body and motions of other agents.
For space, perspective taking involves the projection of a deictic center
and mapping onto the position of another agent. Deictic centers (Duchan,
Bruder, & Hewitt, 1995) can be constructed in three frameworks: egocentric,

allocentric, and geocentric. Positions in these frames are coded through locative adverbs and prepositions.

Egocentric deixis directly encodes the perspective of the speaker. The spatial position of the speaker becomes the deictic center or "here." Locations away from this deictic center are "there." In face-to-face conversation, the deictic center can include both speaker and listener as a single deictic center. In this case, "here" can refer to the general position of the speaker and listener, and "there" can refer to a position away from the speaker and listener. Other terms that are grounded in the self's position and perspective include "forward," "backward," "up," "down," "left," and "right."

The second spatial frame is the allocentric frame, sometimes called the object-centered or intrinsic frame. This frame is constructed by projecting the deictic center onto an external object. To do this, the speaker assumes the perspective of another object and then judges locations from the viewpoint of that object. The basic activity is still deictic, but it is extended through perspective taking. For example, "in front of the house" defines a position relative to a house. In order to determine exactly where the front of the house is located, we need to assume the perspective of the house. We can do this by placing ourselves into the front door of the house where we would face people coming to the front door to "interact" with the house. Once its facing is determined, the house functions like a secondary human perspective, and we can use spatial terms that are designed specifically to work with the allocentric frame such as "under," "behind," or "next to." If we use these terms to locate positions with respect to our own bodies as in "behind me" or "next to me," we are treating our bodies as the centers of an allocentric frame. In both egocentric and allocentric frames, positions are understood relative to a figural perspective that is oriented like the upright human body (Clark, 1973; Bryant, Tversky, & Franklin, 1992).

The third deictic reference system, the geocentric frame, enforces a perspective based on fixed external landmarks, such as the position of a mountain range, the sun, the North Star, the North Pole, or a river. These landmarks must dominate a large part of the relevant spatial world, since they are used as the basis for a full-blown Cartesian coordinate system. The Guugu Yimithirr language in northeast Queensland (Haviland, 1996) makes extensive use of this form of spatial reference. In Guugu Yimithirr, rather than asking someone to "move back from the table," one might say, "move a bit to the mountain." We can use this type of geocentric reference in English too when we locate objects in terms of compass points. However, our uncertainty about whether our listener shares our judgments about which way is "west" in a given microenvironment makes use of this system far less common. On the other hand, we often make use of Cartesian grids centered on specific local landmarks in English. For example, we can describe a position as being "fifty yards behind the school." In this case, we are adopting an initial perspective that is determined either by our own location (e.g., facing the school) or by the allocentric perspective of the school for which the entry door is the front. If we are facing the school, these two reference frames pick out the same location. When we describe the position as being located "fifty yards toward the mountain from the school," we are taking the perspective of the mountain, rather than that of the speaker or the school. We then construct a temporary Cartesian grid based on the mountain and perform allocentric projection to the school. Then we compute a distance of 50 yards from the school in the direction of the mountain.

Shifts in spatial perspective can lead to strange alternations of allocentric reference. For example, if we are lying down on our backs in a hospital bed, we might refer to the area beyond our feet as "in front of me," even though the area beyond the feet is usually referred to as "under me." To do this, we may even imagine raising our head a bit to correct the reference field, so that at least our head is still upright. We may also override the normal shape of the allocentric field by our own egocentric perspective. For example, when having a party in the back yard of a house, we may refer to the area on the other side of the house as "in back of the house," thereby overriding the usual reference to this area as "the front of the house." In this case, we are maintaining our current egocentric position and perspective as basic and locating the external object within that egocentric perspective.

Temporal Perspective

In many ways, we conceive of time as analogous to space. Like space, time has an extent through which we track events and objects in terms of their relation to particular reference moments. Just as spatial objects have positions and extents, events have locations in time and durations. Time can also be organized egocentrically, allocentrically, or globally. When we use the egocentric frame, we relate events to event times (ET) that have a location in relation to our current speaking time (ST) (Vendler, 1957). Just as there is an ego-centered "here" in space, there is an ego-centered "now" in time. Just as we can project a deictic center onto another object spatially, we can also project a temporal center onto another time in the past or future. In this case, the central referent is not speaking time, but another reference time (RT). We can track the position of events in relation to either ST or RT or both using linguistic markings for tense. We can also encode various other properties of events such as completion, repetition, duration, and so on, using aspectual markers.

Just as we tend to view events as occurring in front of us, rather than behind us, we also tend to view time as moving forwards from past to future. As a result, it is easier to process sentences like (1) with an iconic temporal order than ones like (2) with a reversed order. However, sentences like (3) which require no foreshadowing of an upcoming event, are the most natural of all.

1. After we ate our dinner, we went to the movie.
2. Before we went to the movie, we ate our dinner.
3. We ate our dinner and then we went to the movie.

Temporal reference in narrative assumes a strict iconic relation between the flow of the discourse and the flow of time. Processing of sequences that violate temporal iconicity by placing the consequent before the antecedent is relatively more difficult (Zwaan, 1996). However, in practice, it is difficult to describe events in a fully linear fashion and we need to mark flashbacks and other diversions through tense, aspect, and temporal adverbials.

Formal methods for calculating time also allow us to construct the temporal analog to the geocentric frame. For example, we can use moments such as New Year's Day, the birth of Christ, noon, and midnight as absolute reference points from which we compute time forward and backward. At with the geocentric spatial frame, we can shift between these calendrocentric frames by telescoping from minutes, to hours, days, months, years, and centuries.

LEVEL 3: EVENTS

The basic unit of cognition on Level 3 is the event. Events are chained together to encode long event sequences or plans. Events and plans involve the linkage of a variety of actions on objects. For example, we might devise a plan to clean up the house that will involve a variety of operations using brooms, vacuums, sponges, and fluids. In addition, our plans may involve other people with whom we work in parallel and in cooperation. The execution and tracking of these complex plans requires not only perspective taking, but also perspective shifting. These shifts involve new combinations of actors, actions, and objects. Representing perspective shifts requires a method for representing and accessing competing plans, resolving the competition, and developing optimal sequences of the components (Sacerdoti, 1977).

Complex plans are composed of individual events, each organized from a particular perspective. Even when we maintain a single overall causal perspective across a series of events, we still make brief shifts to secondary perspectives. When describing how to assemble a bench, we might say, "Take the long segment of the rear fence guard and insert the black plastic guide screw until it is parallel to the bottom of the guard; then align the guard perpendicular to the right edge of the moveable brace." Here, we first take the perspective of the person doing the assembly, while shifting secondary attention first to the rear fence guard and then the guide screw. Then the guide screw itself becomes the perspective for a moment, until we then shift back to the perspective of the person doing the assembly, for the verb "align." Note that the shift of perspective to the guide screw was prepared by its receipt of secondary attention as the object of "insert." In other contexts, we may make even stronger shifts between actors, as when a football announcer describes a play by first taking the perspective of the quarterback, then the rusher, then the receiver, and finally the defense tackler.

In order to segment reality into separate events, language and cognition provide us with a system that orders nouns into role slots constellated around verbs. We use verbs to segment the flow of reality into bite-size actions and events. Then we flesh out the nature of the events by linking actors and objects to the verbs, as fillers of role slots. Item-based grammars (Hudson, 1984; MacWhinney, 1988; Hausser, 1999; Kay & Fillmore, 1999) derive syntactic structure from the ways in which individual words or groups of words combine with others. For example, the verb "fall" can combine with the perspective of "glass" to produce "the glass fell." In this combination, we say that "fall" has an open slot or valency for the role of the perspective and that the nominal phrase "the glass" is able to fill that slot and thereby play the role of the perspective. In item-based grammars, this basic slot-filling mechanism is used recursively to produce the full range of human language. The specific phrasal structures of various languages emerge as a response to the process of combining words into appropriate role slots as we listen to sentences in real time (Hawkins, 1999).

Item-based patterns are the building blocks of larger clauses. Using item-based patterns, adjectives and other modifiers combine with nouns to form noun phrases. These phrases then attach to each other and to verbs using prepositions and other operators. Conjunctions, complementizers, and relativizers then combine clauses into complex sentences. In order to track shifts and flows of perspective through these complex structures, language provides us with a wide array of grammatical structures and cues including passivization, clefting, dislocation, coreference, reflexivity, obviation, possession, quantification, scope, ergativity, relativization, subordination, ellipsis, coordination, agreement, case marking, and word order placement. These systems are primarily sensitive to Level 3 causal chains, but they also encode Level 2 space-time structures, as well as some of the role and mental act structures we will discuss in the final two sections. The next five subsections focus on examining how five specific syntactic processes are shaped by the impact of perspective shifting. The five processes are ambiguity, relativization, pronominal co-reference, reflexivization, and clitic assimilation. I am selecting these five processes as illustrations because they are easily accessible and have figured heavily in both the linguistic and psycholinguistic literature. However, the analyses I offer here can be developed equally well for all major grammatical constructions.

Ambiguity

Syntactic ambiguities and garden paths arise from competition (MacWhinney, 1987; MacDonald, Pearlmutter, & Seidenberg, 1994) between alternative perspectives. Consider the example of sentence (4) below. In this sentence, we tend to assume the first noun is the perspective of the participial "visiting," yielding the interpretation that "if relatives visit you, they can be a nuisance." At the same time, we are also able to imagine that some unspecified person is the perspective of "visit" with the relatives as the object, yielding the interpretation that "it can be a nuisance to pay a visit to one's relatives." In (5), on the other hand, the pronoun "they" prepares us to adopt the shifted perspective. In example (6), because the verb "cry" is intransitive, the only possible interpretation is the one with "babies" as the perspective of "crying."

4. Visiting relatives can be a nuisance.
5. If they arrive in the middle of a workday, visiting relatives can be a nuisance.
6. Crying babies can be a nuisance.

In (7), the initial perspective resides with "Brendan" and the shift to the perspective of "Grand Canyon" is difficult because it is inanimate and immobile. The shift to the perspective of "the dogs" is easier in (8), although again we can maintain the perspective of "Brendan" if we wish.

7. Brendan saw the Grand Canyon flying to New York.
8. Brendan saw the dogs running to the beach.

In cases of prepositional phrase attachment competitions, such as (9), we can maintain the perspective of the starting point or shift to the direct object. If we identify with "the women," then we have to use the beach as the location of their discussion. If we shift perspective to "the dogs" then we can imagine the women looking out their kitchen window and talking about the dogs as they run around on the beach.

9. The women discussed the dogs on the beach.
10. The women discussed the dogs chasing the cats.

In (10), on the other hand, we have a harder time imagining that the women, instead of the dogs, are chasing the cats.

The starting point or initial nominal phrase (if there is one) is always the default perspective. In most English sentences, this means that the perspective is the subject of the verb. In transitive sentences, there is always some attentional shift to the object, but this shift can be amplified, if there are additional cues, as in (8) and (10). In some syntactic contexts in English, it is possible to shift perspective even more abruptly by treating the verb as intransitive and the following noun as a new subject. Examples (11)–(13) illustrate this effect:

11. Although John frequently jogs, a mile is a long distance for him.
12. Although John frequently jogs a mile, the marathon is too much for him.
13. Although John frequently smokes, a mile is a long distance for him.

Detailed self-paced reading and eye-movement studies of sentences like (11), with the comma removed, show that subjects often slow down just after reading "a mile." This slow down has been taken as evidence for the garden-path theory of sentence processing (Mitchell, 1994). However, it can also be interpreted as reflecting what happens during the time spent in shifting to a new perspective when the cues preparing the processor for the shift are weak. Examples, such as (5) and (11–13), show that perspectival shifting is an integral part of online, incremental sentence processing (Marslen-Wilson & Tyler, 1980).

Perspectival ambiguities also arise from competitions between alternative interpretations of quantifier scopes. Consider these two examples:

14. Someone loves everyone.
15. Everyone is loved by someone.

If we take the perspective of "someone" in (14), we derive an interpretation in which it is true of some person that that person loves all other people. However, if we take the perspective of "everyone," we derive an interpretation in which everyone is loved by at least one person. This second interpretation is much more likely in (15), because in that sentence "everyone" is the starting point. However, both interpretations are potentially available in both cases, because it is always possible to switch perspective away from the starting point to subsequent referents in a sentence, given additional processing time and resources. Further examples of this type include perspective shifts in numerical quantification, such as (16) and (17):

16. Two students read three books.
17. Three books are read by two students.

In (16) assumption of the perspective of the starting point allows us to imagine that the two students are reading the same three books. If, on the other hand, we process the quantifier scoping by assuming the perspective of the books, then we can imagine that there would be a total of six students reading the books.

Perspective shift theory also allows us to understand why (18) is acceptable and (19) is not. In (18) the perspective of every farmer is distributed so that each of the farmers ends up owning a well-fed donkey. In this perspective, there are many donkeys. Sentence (19), on the other hand, forces us to break this distributive scoping and to think suddenly in terms of a single donkey, which violates the mental model set up in the main clause.

18. Every farmer who owns a donkey feeds it.
19. *Every farmer who owns a donkey feeds it, but will it grow?

Relativization

Restrictive relative clauses provide further evidence of the impact of perspective shifting on sentence processing difficulty. Processing these structures can require us to compute multiple shifts of perspective. Consider these four types of restrictive relative clauses:

SS:	The dog that chased the cat kicked the horse.	0 switches
OS:	The dog chased the cat that kicked the horse.	1 − switch
OO:	The dog chased the cat the horse kicked.	1 + switch
SO:	The dog the cat chased kicked the horse.	2 switches

In the SS type, the perspective of the main clause is also the perspective of the relative clause. This means that there are no true perspective switches in the SS relative type. In the OS type, perspective flows from the main clause subject (dog) to the main clause object (cat) in accord with the general principle of partial shift of perspective to the object. At the word "that" perspective then flows further to "the cat" as the subject of the relative clause. This perspective shift is made less abrupt by the fact that "cat" had already received secondary focus before the shift was made. In the OO type, perspective also switches once. However, in this case, it switches more abruptly to the subject of the relative clause. In the SO relative clause type, there is a double perspective shift. Perspective begins with the main clause subject (dog). When the next noun (cat) is encountered, perspective shifts once. However, at the second verb (kicked), perspective has to shift back to the initial perspective (dog) to complete the construction of the interpretation.

The perspective account predicts this order of difficulty: SS > OO = OS > SO. Studies of both acquisition (MacWhinney, 1982) and adult processing (MacWhinney & Pléh, 1988) have provided support for these predictions. For example, a reaction time study of Hungarian relative clause processing by MacWhinney and Pléh (1988) shows how the processing of perspective operates in a language with highly variable word order. In Hungarian, all six orders of subject, object, and verb are grammatical. In three of these orders (SOV, SVO, and VSO), the subject is the topic; in the three other orders (OSV, OVS, and VOS), the object is the topic. When the main clause subject is the topic, the English pattern of difficulty appears (SS > OO = OS > SO). However, when the object is the topic, the opposite order of difficulty arises: OO > OS = SO > SS. These sentences illustrate this contrast in Hungarian, using English words and with the relative clause in parentheses and NOM and ACC to mark the nominative subject and the accusative object:

> S (SV) OV: The boy-NOM (he chased car-ACC) liked girl-ACC. "The boy who chased the car liked the girl."
>
> O (OV) SV: The boy-ACC (car-NOM chased him) girl-NOM liked. "The girl like the boy the car chased."

The S(SV)OV pattern is the easiest type for processing in the SOV word order. This processing follows the English pattern observed above. The O(OV)SV pattern is the easiest type to process in the OSV word order. Here the consistent maintenance of an object perspective through the shift from the main to the relative clause is easy, since the processor can then smoothly shift later to the overall sentence perspective. This contrast illustrates the fundamental difference in the way topic-centered languages manage the processing of perspective.

Sentences with multiple center embeddings have even more switches. For example, "the dog the cat the boy liked chased snarled" has four difficult perspective switches (dog -> cat -> boy -> cat -> dog). Sentences that have as much perspective shifting as this without additional lexical or pragmatic support are incomprehensible, at least at first hearing. But note that the mere stacking of nouns by itself is not enough to trigger perspective shift overload. Consider the sentence, "My mother's brother's wife's sister's doctor's friend had a heart attack." Here, we do not really succeed in taking each perspective and switching to the next, but some form of sloppy comprehension is still possible. This is because we just allow ourselves to skip over each perspective and land on the last one mentioned. In the end, we just know that someone's friend had a heart attack.

Pronominal Co-reference

Perspective taking also plays a central role in shaping the grammar of pronominal co-reference. Consider sentences (20) and (21). Coreference between "he" and "Bill" is possible in (21), but blocked in (20).

> 20. *He$_i$ says Bill$_i$ came early.
> 21. Bill$_i$ says he$_i$ came early.

Note that the pronoun "he" in (20) and (21) can refer to someone mentioned outside of the sentence such as "Tom." What is specifically blocked in (20) is coreference between "he" and "Bill" as indicated by their subscripts. The theory of Government and Binding (Reinhart, 1981; Chomsky, 1982; Grodzinsky & Reinhart, 1993) seeks to explain this phenomenon and a wide variety of related phenomena in pronominal coference in terms of structural relations in a phrase-marker tree. Principle C of the binding theory holds that a pronoun can only be bound to a referent in the clause through a c-command relationship. An element is said to c-command another element if it stands in a direct chain above it in a phrase tree. In (20), "Bill" is too low in the tree to c-command the pronoun. As a result, Principle C excludes a coreferential reading for (20), but not for (21). In (21) "Bill" c-commands the pronoun because it stands in a direct chain of dominance above it in the tree. As a result, the pronoun can be bound to the referent "Bill" in (21).

The Perspective Hypothesis attributes the unavailability of the coreferential reading of (20) to a very different set of forces. The initial claim of the perspective hypothesis is that starting points must be fully referential (MacWhinney, 1977). Gernsbacher (1990) has discussed this requirement in terms of the theory of "structure building." The idea is that listeners attempt to build up a sentence's interpretation incrementally. To do this, they need to have the starting point fully identified, since it is the basis for the rest of the interpretation. In dozens of psycholinguistic investigations, Gernsbacher has shown that the initial nominal phrase has the predicted "advantage of first mention." This advantage makes the first noun more memorable and more accessible for further meaningful processing. In (20), the listener must relate the initial pronoun to some already established discourse entity. Since "Bill" is not yet available, the listener is forced to assume that "he" refers to some previously mentioned actor. In the case of (21) on the other hand, "Bill" is available as a referent and therefore "he" can corefer to "Bill."

The blockage of coreference in (20) is not a simple matter of linear order, since coreference between a pronoun and a following noun is possible, when the pronoun is in an initial subordinate clause. Consider the contrasts between these four sentences, where the asterisk on (24) indicates that "he" cannot be co-referential with "Lester."

22. Lester$_i$ started to feel dizzy, when he$_i$ drank the vodka.
23. When he$_i$ drank the vodka, Lester$_i$ started to feel dizzy.
24. *He$_i$ started to feel dizzy, when Lester$_i$ drank the vodka.
25. When Lester$_i$ drank the vodka, he$_i$ started to feel dizzy.

In (22) and (23), "Lester" c-commands the pronoun, since the subordinate clause is a branch of the VP. As a result, coreference is possible, even if the subordinate clause occurs at the beginning of the sentence, as in (23). In (24) and (25), on the other hand, "Lester" no longer c-commands the pronoun, and coference should be blocked. However, the acceptability of (25) is a problem for this version of binding theory. Reinhart (1983) explains the anomaly by arguing that coreference in (25) is supported by discourse constraints.

The Perspective Hypothesis offers a somewhat different account for this pattern. It attributes the acceptability of coreference in (22) and (25) to the fact that the reference "Lester" has already been mentioned before the pronoun is encountered. It attributes the acceptability of coreference in (23) to the fact that the subordinating conjunction "when" gives the processor instructions that a subsequent NP can be used for coreference to "he." In (24), no such instructions are available and coreference is blocked by the fact that the pronoun appears in initial position, as in (20). We can state these two principles in the following form:

26. Perspective Referentiality: Each clause needs to be organized from the viewpoint of a perspective. In English, the perspective is given by the first nominal. If that nominal is a pronoun, it must be bound to a noun previously mentioned in the sentence or discourse and is not available for binding to following nominal referents. This requirement applies in somewhat weaker form to direct and indirect objects.

27. Cues for Cataphora: Cues that emphasize backgrounding or ongoing relevance allow an perspectival pronoun to maintain its candidacy for cataphoric binding (i.e., binding to following nominal referents).

The Perspective Referentiality Requirement also applies in a somewhat weakened form to the direct and indirect objects of verbs. Van Hoek (1997) shows how availability for coreference is determined by position in the argument chain (Givón, 1976). Although attention is first focused on the subject or trajector, it then moves secondarily to the object or other complements of the verb that are next in the "line of sight" (Langacker, 1995). This gradation of the perspectival effect as we move through the roles of subject, direct object, adjunct, and possessor is illustrated here:

28. *He_i often said that $Bill_i$ was crazy.
29. ? John often told him_i that $Bill_i$ was crazy.
30. ? John often said to him_i that $Bill_i$ was crazy.
31. His_i new dog licked $Bill_i$.
32. The students who studied with him_i enjoyed $John_i$

By the time we reach elements that are no longer in the main clause, as in (31) and (32), cataphora is not blocked, since elements in a subordinate clause are not crucial perspectives for the structure building process. This gradient pattern of acceptability for increasingly peripheral clausal participants matches up with the view that the process of perspective taking during structure building requires core participants to be referential.

Principle C of the binding theory can account for some of these patterns. For example, the acceptability of (32) above is in conformity with the fact that there is no c-command relation between "him" and "John." However, the acceptability of (31) is not. Because both the binding theory and the

Perspective Hypothesis provide a central role for the perspective/subject, it is not surprising to find that their predictions are often similar. The two accounts differ most clearly for patterns that are outside of the scope of core syntactic patterning. Consider this pair:

33. She$_i$ had just come back from vacation, when Mary$_i$ saw the stack of unopened mail piled up at her front door.
34. *She$_i$ came back from vacation, when Mary$_i$ saw the stack of unopened mail piled up at her front door.

The presence of "had just" in (33) works to generate a sense of ongoing relevance that keeps the first clause in discourse focus long enough to permit co-reference between "she" and "Mary." This is a further instance of the principle of Cues for Cataphora.

Preposed prepositional phrases have often presented problems for binding theory accounts (Kuno, 1986). Consider these examples:

35. *Near John$_i$, he$_i$ keeps a laser printer.
36. Near John's$_i$ computer desk, he$_i$, keeps a laser printer.
37. *He$_i$ keeps a laser printer near John$_i$.
38. *He$_i$ keeps a laser printer near John's$_i$ computer desk.

In (36) we have enough conceptual material in the prepositional phrase to enactively construct a temporary perspective for "John." In (35) this is not true, and therefore "John" is not active enough to link to "he." The binding theory attempts to explain patterns of this type by referring to the "unmoved" versions of the sentences in (37) and (38) above. Co-reference is clearly blocked in (37) and (38), despite the fact that it is possible in (36). This indicates that linear order is important for the establishment of perspective and that (36) does not "derive" in any direct sense from (38). These examples motivate a third principle of the Perspective Hypothesis account for co-reference.

39. Perspective Promotion: A nominal in a backgrounded prepositional phrase is so low in perspective that it cannot be a co-referent. However, additional cues of current relevance and perspectival action can elevate its status to allow it to become a candidate co-referent.

These sentences from Reinhart (1983) provide further examples of aspectual effects on perspective taking.

40. In Carter's$_i$ hometown, he$_i$ is still considered a genius.
41. ? In Carter's$_i$ hometown, he$_i$ is considered a genius.

Although both of these sentences can be given coreferential readings, it is relatively easier to do so for (40), because "still" serves as a cue for cataphora that forces perspective promotion in the preposed prepositional phrase. Just as markers of ongoing relevance such as "had just" or "still" can promote the candidacy of a pronoun in a main clause for cataphora, so indefinite marking on a nominal can decrease its candidacy for co-reference, as indicated by the comparison of (42) with (43).

42. While Ruth argued with the man$_i$, he$_i$ cooked dinner.
43. ? While Ruth argued with a man$_i$, he$_i$ cooked dinner.
44. While Ruth was arguing with a man$_i$, he$_i$ was cooking dinner.

The functionalist literature has long recognized the fact that when a new nominal is first introduced as indefinite, it is a poor candidate for coreference. The addition of an aspectual marker of current relevance in (44) overcomes the effect of indefiniteness in (43), making "man" available as a coreferent for "he." Gradient patterning of this type provides further evidence that pronominal co-reference is under the control of pragmatic factors (Kuno, 1986). In this case, the specific pragmatic factors involve interactions between definiteness and perspective. The more definite the referent, the easier it is to assume its perspective. These effects illustrate the following two principles:

45. Givenness: Indefinite nominals are relatively poor candidates for coreference. However, their candidacy can be promoted by cues for ongoing relevance and perspectival focusing.
46. Cue Summation: In accord with the Competition Model (McDonald & MacWhinney, 1989) account, the candidacy of a noun for coreference is the product of the cues in favor of its candidacy over the product of all cues present.

Strong crossover (Postal, 1971) sentences provide further illustrations of these basic principles. In these sentences, the initial wh-word (who) indicates the presence of information that needs to be identified. In (47) the listener has to set up "who" as an item that must be eventually bound to some argument slot. At the same time, the listener has to use "he" as the perspective for structure building. The wh-word is not a possible candidate for the binding of the crucial subject pronoun, so it must be bound to some other referent. However, when the pronoun is not in the crucial subject role, co-reference or crossover between the wh-word and the pronoun is possible, as in (49) and (50).

47. *Who(m)$_i$ does he$_i$ like most?
48. Who$_i$ likes himself$_i$/*him$_i$ most?
49. Who$_i$ thought that Mary loved him$_i$?
50. Who$_i$ likes his$_i$ mother most?

In (48) co-reference is possible for "himself" but not "him" in accord with the principles of perspective flow in reflexives discussed in the next section.

Reflexivization

The original claim of the binding theory was that non-reflexive personal pronouns such as "he" or "him" are bound primarily to referents in higher clauses, whereas reflexive pronouns such as "himself" are bound to other elements within the same clause. Two decades of further research (Zribi-Hertz, 1989; Tenny & Speas, 2002) have called this initial characterization into question without providing a satisfactory alternative. However, the Perspective Hypothesis provides a promising way of understanding the wide range of phenomena related to reflexivization. The analysis I will present here, as well as my selection of example sentences, depends heavily on input from my colleague Carol Tenny whose analysis in Tenny and Speas (2002) agrees in most regards with what I am presenting here.

We should begin by noting that the core claim of the binding theory – that clausemates much be reflexivized, does a good job of accounting for the contrasts such as (51) and (52).

51. *John$_i$ kicked him$_i$.
52. John$_i$ kicked himself$_i$.

Despite the success of this basic principle, there are many structures, even within a single clause, that permit coreference without reflexivization. Consider the following examples:

53. Phil hid the book behind him/himself.
54. Phil ignored the oil on him/himself*.

In (53), both anaphoric and reflexive coreference are possible. In (54) anaphoric reference is possible, but reflexive reference is more difficult. The Perspective Hypothesis accounts for this difference in terms of the principle of Perspective Flow. In (53), once the act of hiding is completed, our perspective shifts back to "Phil" allowing us to view him still as the perspective and a candidate for reflexivization. In (54), on the other hand, once our attention has shifted to the "oil," we have no particular reason to refocus on "Phil." The effect of perspective flow on reflexives can be summarized in the following two principles:

55. Perspective Flow and Short Distance Reflexives: Within a clause, coreference to the principle perspective must be marked by a reflexive. Anaphoric reference is possible if intervening introduction of a secondary perspective blocks the domination of the initial perspective.
56. Perspective Flow and Long Distance Reflexives: Outside a clause, reflexive coreference is possible if the clause-external referent is still highly foregrounded and perspectival.

Let us consider some further examples of these effects. One clause-internal domain that permits both reflexive and anaphoric coreference is the domain of complex noun phrases with representational nouns such as "picture," "story," or "report." These nouns shift perspective from the main clause to the representation of the referent in the embedded noun phrase, as in (57). Because perspective has been shifted, anaphoric coreference with "him" becomes possible, since "John" is no longer a totally commanding perspective. However, (58) illustrates how this shift of perspective also depends on the shape of the activity in the main clause. In (58) the action of telling is more dynamic than the action of hearing in (57). As a result, anaphoric reference is blocked in (58).

57. John$_i$ heard a story about him$_i$/himself$_i$.
58. Max$_i$ told a story about *him$_i$/himself$_i$.

The facilitation of anaphoric reference in (57) is not simply a function of placement of the pronoun in a prepositional phrase, as (59) illustrates. In this example, anaphoric coreference is blocked by the fact that the head of the noun phrase "Mary" has itself become perspectival.

59. John talked to Mary$_i$ about *her$_i$/herself$_i$.

The presence of intervening perspectives facilitates the use of short distance pronouns that would otherwise be blocked by reflexives. Consider some further examples:

60. John$_i$ saw a snake near him$_i$/himself$_i$.
61. Jessie$_i$ stole a photo of her$_i$/herself$_i$ out of the archives.

In the classic example (60) from Lakoff (1974), the shift of perspective to the "snake" is enough to permit anaphoric coreference, although reflexive coreference is also possible. In (61) a similar shift is induced by the representational noun "photo." However, it is not always the case that an intervening noun will shift perspective enough to permit anaphoric reference, as examples (62)–(65) illustrate.

62. Bill$_i$ dragged the box behind him$_i$/himself$_i$.
63. Bill$_i$ dragged the box toward him$_i$/himself$_i$.
64. Bill$_i$ dragged the box to *him$_i$/himself$_i$.
65. Bill$_i$ dragged the box on *him$_i$/himself$_i$.

In (62) the preposition "behind" identifies Bill as a location, thereby causing enough perspective shift to license the short distance pronoun. In (63), the preposition "toward" activates the role of Bill as goal, again establishing a new perspective. In (64) and (65), on the other hand, the prepositions "to" and "on" simply specify the shape of the action and fail to refocus perspective enough to license the short distance pronouns.

In Examples (57)–(65) there is an intervening noun that can facilitate the shift of perspective. However, in (66) and (67) the licensing of anaphoric coreference occurs without this shift.

66. John$_i$ signaled behind him$_i$/himself$_i$ to the pedestrians.
67. Bill$_i$ pointed next to him$_i$/himself$_i$ at the mildew on the roses.

In these sentences, the verbs themselves trigger a strong shift of perspective away from the subject, drawing attention to other objects through the acts of signaling and pointing.

We also need to consider another group of predicates that, like (58) and (64) fail to license anaphoric coreference. These are illustrated in sentences (68) and (69).

68. Max twisted the knife into *him/himself.
69. Margaret pinned the nametag to *her/herself.
70. Mary painted a portrait of *her/herself.

In these examples, the perspective continues to maintain active control of the action, despite the presence of an intervening object. Because of this, there is not enough shift in perspective to permit anaphoric coreference. However, if attention is shifted away from the causor to the path itself, as in (71), anaphoric coreference is possible.

71. Max twisted the knife partway into him/himself.

Finally, let us consider a set of constructions in which perspective shift is induced by the presence of other refocusing devices. These devices can include evaluative adjectives such as "beloved" or "silly" as illustrated in (72) and (73), definite markers as in (74) and (75), and further specification of the complex noun phrase as in (76) and (77).

72. Jessie stole a photo of *her/herself out of the archives.
73. Jessie stole a silly photo of her/herself out of the archives.
74. Anna hid a snapshot of *her/herself under the linoleum.
75. Anna hid the snapshot of *her/herself under the linoleum.
76. Lucie talked about the operation on *her/herself.
77. Lucie talked about the operation on her/herself that Dr. Edward performed.

Clitic Assimilation

As a final example of the impact of perspective taking on grammar, let us consider the process of clitic assimilation. In English, the infinitive "to" often assimilates with a preceding modal verb to produce contractions such as "wanna" from "want to" in cases such as (79). However, this assimilation is blocked in environments like the one in (80), making (81) unacceptable.

78. Why do you want to go?
79. Why do you wanna go?
80. Who(m) do you want to go?
81. *Who(m) do you wanna go?

According the binding theory (Chomsky, 1981), the blocking of the assimilation in (80–81) is due to the presence of the trace of an empty category in the syntactic tree. However, there is reason to believe that the environment in which assimilation is favored is determined not by syntactic forces, but by perspective flow. According the Perspective Hypothesis, cliticization is possible in (79) because the perspective of the higher clause is maintained as the perspective of the complement. In (81), on the other hand, perspective undergoes a forced processing shift from "who(m)" to "you" and then back to "who(m)." These perspective shifts block cliticization.

Perspective can also shift to implicit external controllers. Compare examples (82) and (83) below in which the infinitive does not cliticize with (84) where it does.

82. I get ta go. (Privilege)
83. I got ta go. (Privilege)
84. I gotta go. (Obligation)

In the case of (84), the first person subject has an immediate obligation to fulfill, whereas in (82) and (83), the fact that the subject receives the privilege of going is due presumably to the intercession of an outside party. Thus, the perspective continuation is less direct in (82) and (83), than it is in (84). According to the Perspective Hypothesis, cliticization occurs when a motivated subject engages directly in an action. When there is a shift to another actor, or a conflict of perspectives, cliticization is blocked.

LEVELS 4 AND 5: SOCIAL ROLES AND MENTAL ACTS

Our analysis in this paper has focused on the grammar of the clause, as reflected in basic structures governing perspective identification in direct experience, space-time deixis, and clausal action. Examples such as (78–84) show that even core grammatical structures can reflect social role relations and aspects of the theory of mind. Because of space limitations, we cannot analyze the effects of these higher levels on grammar in detail here. However, it may be useful to draw a bit of attention to some of the more obvious ways in which social roles and mental acts impact grammar and discourse.

First, it is import to note that single lexical items characterize many complex social roles and mental acts. Items like "libel," "Internet," or "solidarity," encode social scenarios organized about the perspective of social actors (Barsalou & Wiemer-Hastings, Chapter 7, this volume). Let us take the noun "libel" as an example. When we speak of some communication as being "libelous," we mean something like the following. The person using the word "libel" is taking the perspective of an "accused" person who declares to some general audience that the (purported) libeler has asserted that the accused has engaged in some illegal or immoral activity. Moreover, the accused wishes to convince the general audience that the libeler's claims are false and designed to make the audience think poorly of the accused in ways that influence the his or her ability to function in public life involving the general audience. In fact, the full legal characterization of libel is more complex than this, but the everyday use of the word "libel" has roughly this basic form. This single word conveys a complex set of interacting and shifting social perspectives. To evaluate whether or not a statement is libelous, we have to assume the perspective of the accused, the purported libeler, and the audience to evaluate the various claims and possible counterclaims. All of this requires continual integration and shifting of social roles and mental acts.

Second, language makes extensive use of kinship terms, appellations, and pronouns to characterize social roles. The decision about whether to call someone "you," "your Honor," "Mary," or "Mrs. Smith" depends on a complex system of role evaluation. In other languages, these distinctions can extend to influencing a wide range of grammatical structures, such as in the Japanese verb sets that mark three levels of honorific relations.

Third, verbs like "promise," "forgive," "admire," and "persuade" encode multiple relations of expectation, benefit, evaluation, and prediction between social actors. To evaluate the uses of these verbs requires flexible perspective taking and coordination. Within this larger group of mental state verbs, one dimension of contrast is known as "explicit causality." Sentence (85) illustrates the use of the experiencer-stimulus verb "admire"; whereas sentence (86) illustrates the use of a stimulus-experiencer verb like "apologize."

85. John admired Mary, because she was calm under stress.
86. John apologized to Mary, because he had cracked under stress.

McDonald and MacWhinney (1995) asked subjects to listen to sentences like (85–86), while making a crossmodal probe recognition judgment. Probe targets included old nouns (John, Mary) new nouns (Frank, Jill), old verbs (admire, apologize), and new verbs (criticize, resemble). The probes were placed at various points before and after the pronoun ("he" and "she"). The task was to judge whether the probe was old or new. McDonald and MacWhinney found that stimulus-experiencer verbs like "apologize" in (86) tend to preserve the reaction time advantage for the first noun (John) as a probe throughout the sentence. In terms of the perspective hypothesis, this means that perspective is not shifted away from the starting point in these sentences. However, experiencer-stimulus verbs like "admired" in (85) tend to force a shift in perspective away from the starting point (John) to the stimulus (Mary) right at pronoun. This leads to a period of time around the pronoun during which "Mary" has relatively faster probe recognition times. However, by the end of the sentence in (86), the advantage of the first noun reappears. The fact that these shifts are being processed immediately on-line is evidence in support of the perspective taking account of sentence processing.

The implicit perspectives in verbs also influence the grammar of complementation. Smyth (1995) found that children in the age range between 5 and 8 have problems understanding co-reference in sentences like (87–91).

87. Minnie told Dorothy that she knew Superman.
88. Minnie told Dorothy that Superman knew her.
89. Minnie asked Dorothy if she knew Superman.
90. Minnie reminded Dorothy that she knew Superman.
91. Minnie told Dorothy that she made Superman cry.

Adults are able to maintain the viewpoint of the initial subject (Gernsbacher, 1990) even in the complement clause. However, children (Franks & Connell, 1996) process (87–91) in a very different way, being more likely to shift to the perspective of Dorothy. Adults reason that it makes little sense for Minnie to tell Dorothy about what she knows, since Dorothy should already have a pretty good view of the contents of her own mind. These social perspectives are nicely encoded in verbs such as "tell," "ask," or "remind." For example, it does make sense to remind Dorothy about her knowledge, since reminding implies the possibility of forgetting. These various speech act verbs thus serve as models to the child of ways of structuring social interactions and theories of mind (Bartsch & Wellman, 1995).

CONCLUSION

In this paper we have examined the ways in which the Perspective Hypothesis can offer new explanations for a variety of patterns in grammar and sentence processing. Elsewhere (MacWhinney, 1999a, 2002, 2003), I have discussed how this hypothesis offers a new way of understanding the linkage between language, society, and the brain. In this new formulation, communication is viewed as a social interaction that activates mental processes of perspective taking. Because perspective taking and shifting are fundamental to communication, language provides a wide array of grammatical devices for specifically marking perspective and perspective shift. Language allows us to integrate information from the domains of direct experience, space/time, plans, roles, and mental acts. Across each of these dimensions, we assume and shift between perspectives in order to construct a fully human, unified conscious awareness.

References

Barsalou, L. W. (1999). Perceptual symbol systems. *Behavioral and Brain Sciences 22*, 577–660.

Bartsch, K., & Wellman, H. (1995). *Children Talk about the Mind*. New York: Oxford University Press.

Bryant, D. J., Tversky, B., & Franklin, N. (1992). Internal and external spatial frameworks for representing described scenes. *Journal of Memory and Language 31*, 74–98.

Burgess, C., & Lund, K. (1997). Modelling parsing constraints with high-dimension context space. *Language and Cognitive Processes 12*, 177–210.

Chomsky, N. (1981). *Lectures on Government and Binding*. Cinnaminson, NJ: Foris.

Chomsky, N. (1982). *Some Concepts and Consequences of the Theory of Government and Binding*. Cambridge, MA: MIT Press.

Clark, H., & Marshall, C. (1981). Definite reference and mutual knowledge. In B. W. A. Joshi & I. Sag (Eds.), *Elements of Discourse Understanding*. Cambridge, MA: Cambridge University Press.

Clark, H. H. (1973). Space, time, semantics, and the child. In T. E. Moore (Ed.), *Cognitive Development and Language Acquisition* (pp. 28–63). New York: Academic Press.

Cohen, M. S., Kosslyn, S. M., Breiter, H. C., DiGirolamo, G. J., Thompson, W. L., Anderson, A. K., et al. (1996). Changes in cortical activity during mental rotation. A mapping study using functional MRI. *Brain 119*, 89–100.

Damasio, A. (1999). *The Feeling of What Happens: Body and Emotion in the Making of Consciousness*. New York: Harcourt Brace.

Duchan, J. F., Bruder, G. A., & Hewitt, L. E. (1995). *Deixis in Narrative: A Cognitive Science Perspective*. Hillsdale, NJ: Lawrence Erlbaum Associates.

Franks, S. L., & Connell, P. J. (1996). Knowledge of binding in normal and SLI children. *Journal of Child Language 23*, 431–464.

Gernsbacher, M. A. (1990). *Language Comprehension as Structure Building*. Hillsdale, NJ: Lawrence Erlbaum.

Gibson, J. J. (1977). The theory of affordances. In R. E. Shaw & J. Bransford (Eds.), *Perceiving, Acting, and Knowing: Toward an Ecological Psychology* (pp. 67–82). Hillsdale, NJ: Lawrence Erlbaum.

Givón, T. (1976). Topic, pronoun, and grammatical agreement. In C. Li (Ed.), *Subject and Topic* (pp. 149–188). New York: Academic Press.

Grodzinsky, J., & Reinhart, T. (1993). The innateness of binding and coreference. *Linguistic Inquiry 24*, 187–222.

Hausser, R. (1999). *Foundations of Computational Linguistics: Man–machine Communication in Natural Language*. Berlin: Springer.

Haviland, J. (1996). Projections, transpositions, and relativity. In J. Gumperz & S. Levinson (Eds.), *Rethinking Linguistics Relativity* (pp. 271–323). New York: Cambridge University Press.

Hawkins, J. A. (1999). Processing complexity and filler-gap dependencies across grammars. *Language 75*, 244–285.

Hudson, R. (1984). *Word grammar*. Oxford: Blackwell.

Jeannerod, M. (1997). *The Cognitive Neuroscience of Action*. Cambridge, MA: Blackwell.

Kakei, S., Hoffman, D. S., & Strick, P. L. (1999). Muscle and movement representations in the primary motor cortex. *Science 285*, 2136–2139.

Kay, P., & Fillmore, C. J. (1999). Grammatical constructions and linguistic generalization: The "what's X doing Y?" construction. *Language 75*, 1–33.

Kuno, S. (1986). *Functional Syntax*. Chicago: University of Chicago Press.

Lakoff, G. (1974). Syntactic amalgams. In R. F. M. LaGaly & A. Bruck (Eds.), *Papers from the Tenth Regional Meeting*. Chicago: Chicago Linguistic Society.

Langacker, R. (1995). Viewing in grammar and cognition. In P. W. Davis (Ed.), *Alternative Linguistics: Descriptive and Theoretical Models* (pp. 153–212). Amsterdam: John Benjamins.

MacDonald, M. C., Pearlmutter, N. J., & Seidenberg, M. S. (1994). Lexical nature of syntactic ambiguity resolution. *Psychological Review 101* 4, 676–703.

McDonald, J. L., & MacWhinney, B. (1989). Maximum likelihood models for sentence processing research. In B. MacWhinney & E. Bates (Eds.), *The Crosslinguistic Study of Sentence Processing* (pp. 397–421). New York: Cambridge University Press.

McDonald, J. L., & MacWhinney, B. J. (1995). The time course of anaphor resolution: Effects of implicit verb causality and gender. *Journal of Memory and Language 34*, 543–566.

MacWhinney, B. (1977). Starting points. *Language 53*, 152–168.

MacWhinney, B. (1982). Basic syntactic processes. In S. Kuczaj (Ed.), *Language Acquisition: Vol. 1. Syntax and Semantics* (pp. 73–136). Hillsdale, NJ: Lawrence Erlbaum.

MacWhinney, B. (1987). Toward a psycholinguistically plausible parser. In S. Thomason (Ed.), *Proceedings of the Eastern States Conference on Linguistics*. Columbus: Ohio State University.

MacWhinney, B. (1988). Competition and teachability. In R. Schiefelbusch & M. Rice (Eds.), *The Teachability of Language* (pp. 63–104). New York: Cambridge University Press.

MacWhinney, B. (ed.), (1999b). *The Emergence of Language*. Mahwah, NJ: Lawrence Erlbaum Associates.

MacWhinney, B. (1999a). The emergence of language from embodiment. In B. MacWhinney (Ed.), *The Emergence of Language* (pp. 213–256). Mahwah, NJ: Lawrence Erlbaum.

MacWhinney, B. (2002). Language emergence. In P. Burmeister, T. Piske & A. Rohde (Eds.), *An Integrated View of Language Development – Papers in Honor of Henning Wode* (pp. 17–42). Trier: Wissenschaftlicher Verlag Trier.

MacWhinney, B. (2003). The gradual evolution of language. In B. Malle & T. Givón (Eds.), *The Evolution of Language*. Philadelphia: Benjamins.

MacWhinney, B., & Pléh, C. (1988). The processing of restrictive relative clauses in Hungarian. *Cognition 29*, 95–141.

Marslen-Wilson, W. D., & Tyler, L. K. T. (1980). The temporal structure of spoken language understanding. *Cognition 8*, 1–71.

Martin, A., Wiggs, C. L., Ungerleider, L. G., & Haxby, J. V. (1996). Neural correlates of category-specific knowledge. *Nature 379*, 649–652.

Mitchell, D. C. (1994). Sentence parsing. In M. Gernsbacher (Ed.), *Handbook of Psycholinguistics*. San Diego, CA: Academic Press.

Narayanan, S. (1997). Talking the talk is like walking the walk. *Proceedings of the 19th Meeting of the Cognitive Science Society 55–59*.

O' Grady, W. (in press). *Syntactic carpentry*. Mahwah, NJ: Lawrence Erlbaum Associates.

Paivio, A. (1971). *Imagery and Verbal Processes*. New York: Rinehart and Winston.

Parsons, L. M., Fox, P. T., Downs, J. H., Glass, T., Hirsch, T. B., Martin, C. C., et al. (1995). Use of implicit motor imagery for visual shape discrimination as revealed by PET. *Nature 375*, 54–58.

Postal, P. (1971). *Cross-Over Phenomena*. New York: Holt, Rinehart, and Winston.

Reinhart, T. (1981). Definite NP anaphora and c-command domains. *Linguistic Inquiry 12*, 605–635.

Reinhart, T. (1983). *Anaphora and Semantic Interpretation*. Chicago: University of Chicago Press.

Rizzolatti, G., Fadiga, L., Gallese, V., & Fogassi, L. (1996). Premotor cortex and the recognition of motor actions. *Cognitive Brain Research 3*, 131–141.

Sacerdoti, E. (1977). *A Structure for Plans and Behavior*. New York: Elsevier Computer Science Library.

Smyth, R. (1995). Conceptual perspective-taking and children's interpretation of pronouns in reported speech. *Journal of Child Language 22*, 171–187.

Stanfield, R. A., & Zwaan, R. A. (2001). The effect of implied orientation derived from verbal context on picture recognition. *Psychological Science 12*, 153–156.

Tabachneck-Schijf, H. J. M., Leonardo, A. M., & Simon, H. A. (1997). CaMeRa: A computational model of multiple representations. *Cognitive Science 21*, 305–350.

Tenny, C., & Speas, P. (2002). Configurational properties of point of view roles. In A. DiSciullo (Ed.), *Asymmetry in Grammar*. Amsterdam: John Benjamins.

van Hoek, K. (1997). *Anaphora and Conceptual Structure*. Chicago: University of Chicago Press.

Vendler, Z. (1957). Verbs and times. *Philosophical Review 56*, 143–160.

Zribi-Hertz, A. (1989). Anaphor binding and narrative point of view: English reflexive pronouns in sentence and discourse. *Language 65* 4, 695–727.

Zwaan, R. A. (1996). Processing narrative time shifts. *Journal of Experimental Psychology: Learning, Memory & Cognition 22*, 1196–1207.

10

Embodied Sentence Comprehension

Rolf A. Zwaan and Carol J. Madden

There are two views of cognition in general and of language comprehension in particular. According to the traditional view (Chomsky, 1957; Fodor, 1983; Pylyshyn, 1986), the human mind is like a bricklayer, or maybe a contractor, who puts together bricks to build structures. The malleable clay of perception is converted to the neat mental bricks we call words and propositions, units of meaning, which can be used in a variety of structures. But whereas bricklayers and contractors presumably know how bricks are made, cognitive scientists and neuroscientists have no idea how the brain converts perceptual input to abstract lexical and propositional representations – it is simply taken as a given that this occurs (Barsalou, 1999).

According to an alternative and emerging view, there are no clear demarcations between perception, action, and cognition. Interactions with the world leave traces of experience in the brain. These traces are (partially) retrieved and used in the mental simulations that make up cognition. Crucially, these traces bear a resemblance to the perceptual/action processes that generated them (Barsalou, 1999) and are highly malleable. Words and grammar are viewed as a set of cues that activate and combine experiential traces in the mental simulation of the described events (Zwaan, 2004). The main purpose of this chapter is to provide a discussion of this view of language comprehension. To set the stage for this discussion we first analyze a series of linguistic examples that present increasingly larger problems for the traditional view. Consider the following sentences.

(1) The exterminator checked the room for bugs.
(2) The CIA agents checked the room for bugs.

It is clear that the bug in (1) is not the same as the bug in (2). In other words, "bug" is a homonym. The traditional view has no problem accounting for these two different interpretations of "bug" because it simply assumes that the sentential context disambiguates the homonym such that the correct meaning is selected (although the incorrect meaning may be briefly activated, e.g., Swinney, 1979). Thus, in these cases, one might assume a stronger lexical association between "exterminator" and the "insect" meaning of "bug" than between "CIA agent" and that meaning and vice versa for the "microphone" meaning of bug. The following two sentences already present more of a challenge to the traditional view.

(3) Fred stole all the books in the library.
(4) Fred read all the books in the library.

It is clear that "all the books" means two slightly different things in these two sentences. For example, (3) implies that Fred stole all 12 copies of *War and Peace*, whereas (4) in the most likely interpretation means that Fred read only one copy of *War and Peace*. But both words refer to the same thing: a physical object consisting of written pages, bound together and in a cover. This presents a problem for the traditional view of compositionality according to which concepts have atomic meanings that should remain unchangeable across contexts. However, the traditional view can be amended to account for interpretations such as these. Pustejovsky (1995) has proposed that words have different qualia, that is different interpretations, and that these interpretations are selected by other words in the sentence. For example, a book can be both a physical object and a source of information. Stealing typically involves physical objects (although one can steal glances, kisses, or ideas) and thus "steal" selects the physical-object quale of "book." Reading, on the other hand, involves information (even when reading facial expressions, tracks in the snow, or passes in a soccer game), and therefore "read" selects the information-source meaning of "book." In this sense, the bricklayer metaphor can be extended to that of a child playing with legos (a metaphor used in many linguistics courses). Some pieces, like wheels, have different shapes and different sites for attachment. For example, an axle fits into a flange on the inside of the wheel and a little square block fits on the hub. Similarly, some verbs select one quale of a noun, whereas other verbs will select another.

However, it is not clear whether this lego-extended view of comprehension can account for the following sentences.

(5) John pounded the nail into the wall.
(6) John pounded the nail into the floor.

Here, both sentences use the same verb, and in both sentences, this verb selects the same quale of the noun, "nail"; it is a slender usually pointed and headed fastener designed to be pounded in. What is different in the two sentences is the nail's orientation. There is nothing in the traditional view to suggest that the nail's orientation should be part of the comprehender's mental representation. For example, a common way to represent sentences (5) and (6) is (e.g., Kintsch & van Dijk, 1978):

(7) [POUNDED[JOHN, NAIL]], [IN[NAIL, FLOOR]]
(8) [POUNDED[JOHN, NAIL]], [IN[NAIL, WALL]]

Nothing in these propositional representations says anything about the nail's orientation, yet empirical evidence shows that comprehenders routinely represent this orientation (Stanfield & Zwaan, 2001). A similar point can be made about the shape of objects.

(9) He saw the eagle in the sky.
(10) He saw the eagle in the nest.

According to the traditional view the words in these sentences form the building blocks of meaning out of which the comprehender builds a structure that reflects his or her interpretation of the sentence. But how would this work for sentences (9) and (10)? Surely the eagle in (9) cannot be the same lego brick as the eagle in (10). In (9) the eagle has its wings stretched out, whereas the eagle in (10) most likely has its wings drawn in. Again, there is empirical evidence that comprehenders are sensitive to these differences (Zwaan, Stanfield, & Yaxley, 2002) and again, this is not predicted by the traditional view. The traditional view also does not seem to have a straightforward account for how the following sentences are interpreted.

(11) Jack looked across the room to see where the whisper/explosion came from.
(12) Jack looked across the valley to see where the whisper/explosion came from.

Clearly, whisper is a better fit for (11) and explosion for (12). But how does the traditional theory account for this? The Merriam-Webster dictionary defines "whisper" as follows: "to speak softly with little or no vibration of the vocal cords especially to avoid being overheard." Nothing in this definition points directly to the distance over which a whisper can be heard by the human ear. Similarly, nothing in the definition of valley – "an elongate depression of the earth's surface usually between ranges of hills or mountains" according to Merriam-Webster – provides explicit information about the typical width of a valley. It might be argued that both terms contain information that can be used to infer the respective distances (e.g., "softly," "overhear," and "mountain"). But if one looks up "mountain," for example, the most relevant meaning to be found is "a landmass that projects conspicuously above its surroundings and is higher than a hill." Of course, this does little to alleviate the interpretation problem. This is an example of what has become known as the Chinese Room Problem (Searle, 1980). Given that dictionary meanings are not grounded in perception and action, the comprehender who has to rely on a dictionary is given a perpetual runaround (see also Glenberg, 1997).

Finally, consider the following pair of sentences.

(13) The pitcher hurled the baseball to you.
(14) You hurled the baseball at the batter.

There is nothing different about the intrinsic properties of the baseball in (13) and (14), such as shape or orientation. The only difference between the baseball in (13) and that in (14) is the direction of motion. Although the traditional view would not predict any differences in the mental representations of baseballs formed during comprehension of these two sentences (and may even have trouble explaining it post-hoc in an elegant manner), there is evidence that the direction of motion is incorporated into the representations of the two baseballs, yielding distinct simulations (Zwaan, Madden, Yaxley, & Aveyard, 2004). We will discuss this evidence and other relevant evidence in more detail later.

In the rest of this chapter, we propose the beginnings of a theory of sentence comprehension that accounts for these findings in a straightforward way.

INTERCONNECTED EXPERIENTIAL TRACES

In our proposed theory, we assume that all mental representations are experiential. Within the category of experiential representations, we distinguish between referent representations and linguistic representations (see also Sadoski & Paivio, 2001). Referent representations are traces laid down in memory during perceptions of and interactions with the environment. These traces are multimodal (i.e., combining multiple senses).[1] Because of attentional limitations, these traces are schematic (Barsalou, 1999). The second subcategory of experiential traces consists of linguistic traces. These traces are laid down as linguistic information is being received or produced. For example, there are perceptual traces of hearing, reading, seeing, and feeling (as in Braille) linguistic constructions. As well, there are motor representations of saying, signing, typing, and handwriting linguistic constructions. Not only are these constructions interconnected, they are also connected to referent representations, which are also interconnected (see Figure 10.1).

How are these interconnections established? The main mechanism is co-occurrence (e.g., Hebb, 1949). Certain entities in the environment tend

---

[1] Damasio (1999, p. 160) describes object representations as stored in "dispositional form." Dispositions are records, which are dormant, rather than active and explicit, as images are. Dispositions include: records of sensory aspects, records of the motor adjustments necessary to gather sensory signals, obligate emotional reaction.

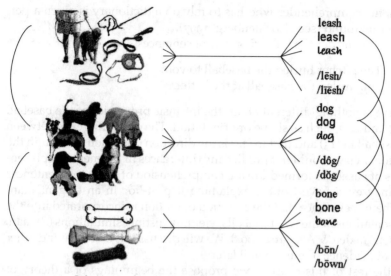

FIGURE 10.1. Schematic depiction of experiential (visual) traces of leashes, dogs, and bones, and of the visual and sound patterns associated with them, as well as the links between these traces.

to co-occur. Ducks are generally found in or near ponds or lakes, monitors on desks, pacifiers in babies' mouths, clouds in the sky, and branches above roots. Events may co-occur or follow in close sequence. For example, a scratchy sound accompanies the action of striking of a match, and a flame typically follows it, along with a sulfuric smell, which we may find pleasurable. Because of these spatio-temporal co-occurrences, combinations of entities, actions, events, and bodily states become part of the same experiential trace.

Similarly, linguistic constructs co-occur and may therefore develop associations between themselves. First proposed by associationists such as Hume and Locke, but eschewed by transformational grammarians, the analysis of linguistic co-occurrences has made a recent comeback in the form of sophisticated computational linguistic analyses involving large corpora, such as latent semantic analysis (LSA, Landauer & Dumais, 1997).[2] This idea that associations between representations are formed through co-occurrence of linguistic constructions is central to the current theory. For example, the words "nurse" and "doctor" often co-occur in language. As a result, the experiential traces for these linguistic units are associated, just as the words "peace" and "treaty" and the names Lennon and McCartney. Often sets of more than two words co-occur, as in "hail Mary pass," "internal revenue service," and "everything but the kitchen sink." As a

---

[2] These analyses actually go significantly beyond co-occurrences by assessing the degree to which words occur in similar contexts, but this is not relevant to the current argument.

result, entire sequences of words can be treated as constructions (Goldberg, 1995, 2003).

The connections that are established between experiential traces for referents and experiential traces for linguistic constructions are of critical importance to the grounding of language in perception and action (see also Goldstone, Yeng, & Rogosky, Chapter 12, this volume). The initial mechanism by which these connections are forged is co-occurrence. When children learn to speak, parents and others point out objects to them in the environment. Moreover, even when children are not attending to the entity in question, they can use mentalistic cues such as the speaker's eye gazes and facial expressions to form associations between constructs and referents (Bloom, 2000). As a result, children learn to associate an experience of a referent with a particular sound pattern. In fact, children are surprisingly adept at learning word meaning this way, often needing only a few exposures (Carey & Bartlett, 1978).

Children do not only learn to associate constructs with objects, but also with actions and properties. For example when parents say, "give me the ball," the child will associate an action – grasping a ball, extending the arm, and then releasing the ball into the grasp of a parent – with a linguistic construction (and with encouraging sounds and facial expressions on the part of the parent). In fact, the child learns something more fundamental, namely that this syntactic construction can be applied in many other contexts – for instance, "throw me the ball," and even "tell me a story." As such, the syntactic structure can be thought of as a linguistic construction that conveys meaning (Goldberg, 1995, 2003). The meaning of this construction, the double-object construction, is that an object or something more abstract moves from the agent to a recipient. This is what the different contexts in which the expression is used have in common. Importantly, however, this is only part of the meaning of an expression. For example, "throw me the ball" is associated with a different motor program than "give me the ball" and it is also associated with the salient pattern of an object getting smaller in one's visual field as it moves away from the thrower. On the other hand "tell me a story" is associated with cognitive effort and speech motor programs, as well as with certain encouraging or puzzled facial expressions on the part of the listener. As Hockett (1959) noted, one important feature of language – called displacement – is that it allows us to convey situations that are not part of our immediate environment. The connections between linguistic and referent traces enable this feature. For example, if we have never seen a zebra before and it is described to us as a "horse with black-and-white stripes," then we can form a new referent representation by combining the perceptual traces for horses, for stripes, and for black-and-white, based on their associations with the corresponding words (Harnad, 1990). This virtual experiential trace, constructed from a combination of other visual traces can now be stored in long-term memory. Along with it, an association is formed between the sound pattern of "zebra" and the new visual trace. This uniquely human way of learning about the environment through linguistic scaffolding significantly augments what we can learn by interacting directly with the environment.

One consequence of the development of connections between the two classes of experiential symbols is that co-occurrences in one domain will produce co-occurrences in the other. These effects are bidirectional. Just as the spatio-temporal proximity of certain objects or events enhances the likelihood that the linguistic constructions denoting them will co-occur, the co-occurrence of linguistic constructions will strengthen the connections between their referents. As a result, although there generally is not an analog first-order mapping between linguistic constructions and their referents, there is a strong second-order mapping. If the link between two constructs is strong, then it is very likely that the link between the corresponding referents is also strong (see Figure 10.1). This is one reason why techniques such as LSA are often surprisingly successful in capturing meaning. However, as we will show later, many experiential factors are not captured by linguistic co-occurrences.[3]

CONSTRUAL

Along with several other researchers, we conceive of language as a set of cues by which the speaker or writer manipulates the listener's or reader's attention on an actual or fictional situation (e.g., Langacker, 1987; Tomasello, 2003). The units in which this process takes place are attentional frames (Langacker, 2001). Attentional frames map onto intonation units, which are speech segments bounded by pauses or intonation shifts (Chafe, 1994). Because written language follows spoken language phylogenetically as well as ontogenetically, the segmentation of spoken language provides the grounding for the segmentation of written language. We define construal as the mental simulation of an experience conveyed by an attentional frame. This mental simulation uses the experiential traces that are activated by the linguistic constructions in the intonation unit.

Figure 10.2 (from Zwaan, 2004) shows the components of construal. Each construal necessarily includes:

* a *time* at which the simulated situation occurs (as related to the moment of utterance, to the previously simulated event, and sometimes to some reference point);
* a *spatial region* in which the described event takes place;
* a *perspective* (spatial and psychological) from which the situation is experienced;
* a *focal entity*;
* a *background entity*.

[3] There is much more to be said about this issue, but this is beyond the scope of this chapter.

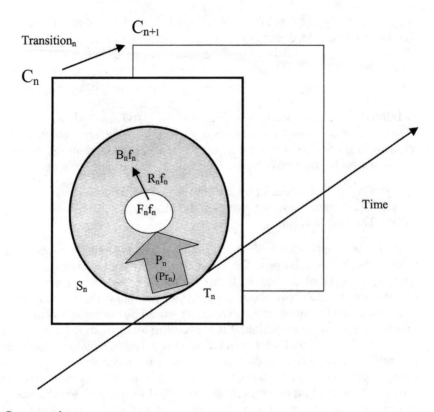

C = construal

T = time

S = spatial region (personal, action, vista)

P = perspective

F = focal entity

R = relation

B = background entity

f = feature

FIGURE 10.2. The components of construal (from Zwaan, 2004).

In addition, the focal entity, relation, and background entity can have features (e.g., size, color, intensity, speed).

Here, our focus is on the process of construal. An important component of construal is the establishment of a focal entity and background entity. Language provides many cues for this, including syntactic, morphemic, and paralinguistic information. In English, for example, the focal entity is usually the first entity described (Langacker, 1987). This means that in active sentences the entity performing an action is the focal entity, whereas in passive constructions the entity undergoing the action is the focal entity. This means that passivization is not without semantic consequences, so that a passive sentence is not really a paraphrase of its active counterpart.

Intonation units typically describe what linguists have traditionally analyzed as events, processes, and states (e.g., Vendler, 1967; Ter Meulen, 1995). Viewing language comprehension as the modulation of attention compels us to treat each as a type of event. Consider the following sentences.

(15) The car pulled out of the driveway.
(16) The car was zooming along on the interstate.
(17) The car was blue.

Punctate events such as (15) are perhaps the most easily conceptualized as mental simulations. The focal entity (the car) initiates an event (pulling out of) that changes its location relative to the background entity (the driveway). But how about (16)? For all we know, the car may keep zooming along for many hours to come. It would be preposterous to claim that we keep our mental simulations zooming along with it for a similar duration. The notion of attentional frame provides an elegant solution to this problem. The situation conveyed by (16) can be conceptualized as the event of perceiving a car zooming along (either from inside or outside of the car). A perceptual event such as this would only take a short amount of time. Along similar lines, a static description like (17) can simply be understood as the event of seeing a blue car rather than as a mental tour de force in which the color blue is continuously being simulated.[4]

In an experiential representation, the perspective of the observer or agent vis à vis the described situation needs to be represented. This is illustrated in (18).

(18) The red squirrel jumped into the tree.

It is easy to see that the linguistic constructs in (18) by themselves do not provide sufficient perspectival constraints. For instance, is the squirrel jumping from left to right or from right to left? Our working assumption is that in case of underspecification, people will use default expectations, which may depend on environmental constraints, handedness, the direction of reading, or other cultural conventions.[5]

---

[4] Often, a speaker or writer will insert a sentence later in the narrative to remind the listener/reader that the car is still in motion. When the reader's attention is directed back to the car, it should still be represented as zooming along.

[5] For example, right-handers recognize objects more quickly when lit from top-left than when lit from other angles. Presumably this has to do with the fact that under this angle, their right

In many cases, however, perspective is automatically produced as part of the mental simulation. Activating relevant perceptual memory traces of experience with words and referents creates a simulation. As a result, the simulation will automatically adopt the perspective of the most frequent (or perhaps most recent) relevant memory traces. For example, clouds are most often seen from below. Therefore, most traces of seeing clouds will be from below. As a result, comprehenders of the sentence: "The farmer looked at the clouds" are likely to simulate clouds from below. In many cases, entity features and the range of the human sensory apparatus jointly place constraints upon the observer's distance from it. For example, human hearing is such that a whisper can only be heard from a relatively short distance. That is why a whisper in (10) sounds odd. Another illustration is (19), a sentence used by Morrow and Clark (1988).

(19) A mouse/tractor approached the fence.

This example not only shows that the interpretation of "approach" depends on the size of the focal entity – i.e., people place the mouse closer to the fence than they do the tractor (Morrow & Clark, 1988) – it also suggests that the observer is closer to the scene in the case of the mouse than in the case of the tractor. The main constraint here is the mouse's size, which makes that we can see mice only from relatively short distances. Importantly, this constraint is not just imposed by the mouse's size, but also by the limits of human vision. Hawks, for instance, are able to see mice from much longer distances than humans. In other words, our auditory traces of whispers and our visual traces of mice and tractors already contain relevant perspectival information grounded in human sensation and perception. It may therefore not be farfetched to say that perspective is part of the meaning of some words (Talmy, 2000a, 2000b; Zwaan, 2004). There already is some evidence that comprehenders interpret perspective in verbs such as "come" and "go" and "bring" and "take" (Black, Turner, & Bower, 1979). For example, "come" implies movement toward the observer while "go" implies movement away from the observer. In some cases, perspective is explicitly stated. This is the case in a sentence like (20), where the putative default perspective of "cloud" must be overridden.

(20) From the mountaintop, the clouds below looked like big balls of cotton.

hand does not cast a shadow over manipulated objects. Left-handers also have a left bias, though less strong than right-handers, presumably because they live in a world dominated by right-handers (Sun & Perona, 1998, see also Mamassian & Goutcher, 2001). Consistent with this left bias, pictures with a left-to-right directionality are judged as more aesthetically pleasing than pictures with a right-to-left directionality (Christman & Pinger, 1997). Recent evidence suggests that bias may be culturally determined (Maass & Russo, 2003).

To summarize, rather than simply constructing mental representations of who-did-what-to-whom out of mental Lego blocks, we perform experiential simulations that necessarily imply a spatio-temporal perspective on the described situation. The typical experiential perspective on the entity denoted by a linguistic construction plays a key role in establishing a perspective.

As noted earlier, experiential representations consist of multitudes of traces and are stored by the brain in what Damasio (1999) calls "dispositional form." Usually, they will only be partly relevant to the current context. Of particular importance therefore is the idea that traces activated by different words constrain each other during construal. For example, the feature "red" of the focal entity "squirrel" in (18, reprinted below) initially activates a range of traces of visual experiences of the color red.

(21) The red squirrel jumped into the tree.

Most of these traces turn out not to be relevant in the context of the sentence, but that does not become clear until the first noun is processed.[6] Red squirrels are a particular kind of red (brownish red rather than fire truck red). So the noun will constrain what traces are relevant in the current context. But this is only the beginning. Just as red squirrels are a particular kind of red, they are a particular kind of squirrel. Unlike the gray squirrels typically found in North America, they have ear tufts (instead of mouse-like ears) and are smaller. In other words, the two concepts, "red" and "squirrel," constrain each other's representation. One way of conceptualizing this is that all the traces that make up a dispositional representation receive some degree of activation from the associated word, but that only one or a few of them will be activated above threshold and thus become incorporated in the mental simulation. In the next cycle, "jumped" provides further constraints on the ongoing simulation. For one, it provides some articulation of the shape of the squirrel; it is stretched out, rather than sitting on its hind legs, for example.[7]

During construal, the information is being integrated with previous construals, which form part of the context for the current construal in the comprehension of connected discourse. This is where the remaining two components of construal come into play: time frame and spatial region. When two construals pertain to the same time interval, they can be integrated more easily than when they pertain to two different intervals (Zwaan, 1996). To a certain extent, this is also true for spatial regions (see

---

[6] As evidence shows, comprehension is incremental, rather than postponed until certain linguistic boundaries are reached (e.g., Chambers et al., 2001).

[7] Also note that "squirrel" constrains the interpretation of "jumped." After all, the way a squirrel jumps is different from the way a human or an antelope jumps.

Zwaan & Radvansky, 1998, for a discussion). The topic of integration is beyond the scope of the present chapter, but is discussed in Zwaan (2004).

EMPIRICAL EVIDENCE

What empirical evidence do we have for our claims? In this section we review the research from our lab; further relevant evidence is reviewed in other chapters in this volume. In most experiments, we used the same methodology. Subjects are exposed to linguistic materials and are then presented with one or more pictures. Their task consists in comprehending the sentences and performing speeded judgments on the pictures. The rationale is that sentence comprehension will involve a construal in which visual traces are activated and used that either match or mismatch the visual traces created by the pictures. 'Match' and 'mismatch' should be thought of in relative terms only. In our interactions with the environment there will probably never be a perfect match between a new visual trace and one already in memory. For example, we rarely if ever see objects under identical angles and lighting conditions and against identical backgrounds on different occasions. As a result, all visual traces are slightly different from each other. Some theories of object recognition account for this by assuming that some amount of interpolation between visual traces in memory occurs in order to obtain a match with the visual input (e.g., Bülthoff & Edelman, 1992; Tarr, 1995). In the context of our experiments, the claim is simply that the match condition provides a stronger match between construal and picture traces than the mismatch condition. We should also note that in our experiments, subjects are often not directly relating the picture to the sentence. In that sense, it cannot be argued that the subjects' responses are due to special imagery strategies.

Here is a list of claims we have made about construal:

1. Comprehenders represent perceptual aspects of referents or situations;
2. Comprehenders represent spatial relations between object parts;
3. Comprehenders represent dynamic aspects of events;
4. Comprehenders represent perspective.

How do these claims hold up against empirical scrutiny? Let's revisit sentences (3) and (4), which are included below as (22) and (23).

(22) John pounded the nail into the wall.
(23) John pounded the nail into the floor.

Our contention is that these sentences lead to different mental representations. Specifically, we predict that comprehenders will represent the orientation of the nail. In order to test this prediction, Stanfield and Zwaan (2001) presented subjects with sentences such as (22) and (23), followed by a line drawing of an object. The subjects simply decided whether the picture depicted a word mentioned in the sentence. Two things are important to note. First, a picture of a nail, irrespective of its orientation, should yield a "yes" response. Second, a picture of a horizontal nail would match a construal of (22) and one of a vertical nail would match a construal of (23). Stanfield and Zwaan found that responses were significantly faster in the match than in the mismatch condition. One suboptimal feature of these experiments was that the direction in which the nail points is indeterminate in case of the wall – it could point to the left or to the right (for obvious reasons, we don't have this problem with the floor). As mentioned earlier, it may be that people use a default assumption in cases such as these. But this means that the direction of the nail would in some cases mismatch that of the nail in the construal. Our counterargument is that the match condition still provides a better match than the mismatch condition because the visual trace of a horizontal nail, regardless of its orientation, provides a better match than a picture of a vertical nail.[8]

In a later series of experiments, we tested the claim that construal necessarily includes a representation of the shape of a focal entity (Zwaan, Stanfield, & Yaxley, 2002). Using the same logic as in our earlier experiments, we had subjects read sentences and then presented them with pictures. The sentences were of the type of (9) and (10) or as (24) and (25).

(24) He saw the lemon in the bowl.
(25) He saw the lemon in the glass.

In addition to a recognition task, we also employed a naming task. In a naming task, the subject sees a picture and simply names it. We used a naming task because it provides a more implicit measure than a recognition task. The recognition task calls for the subject to compare the picture with the sentence. Not so in the naming task-naming the picture does not directly involve reference to the sentence. Nonetheless, in both experiments we found that the match condition yielded faster responses than the mismatch condition. These findings suggest that comprehenders routinely represent the shape of the focal entity mentioned in a sentence.

In a more recent experiment, we investigated whether comprehenders form perceptual representations of described motion (Zwaan, Madden, Yaxley, & Aveyard, 2004). Subjects listened to sentences such as (26) or (27) over headphones.

(26) The shortstop hurled the softball at you.
(27) You hurled the softball at the shortstop.

---

[8] MacWhinney (Chapter 9, this volume) points out that the orientation of the nail is only part of the mental simulation, not the whole simulation. We concur. It is, however, a diagnostic part of the simulation and as such is amenable to an empirical test.

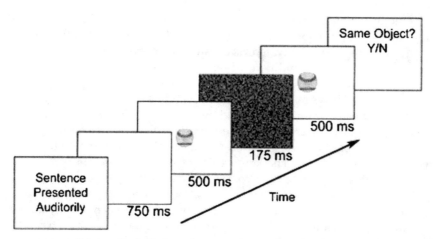

FIGURE 10.3. Schematic depiction of an experimental trial in Zwaan et al. (2004).

After each sentence, they saw two pictures each presented briefly and sep-
arated by a mask (see Figure 10.3). On critical trials, the depicted object was
mentioned in the sentence (e.g., a softball). Crucially, the second picture
was either bigger or smaller than the first one, thus suggesting movement
toward or away from the viewer. The size changes were very subtle. Subjects judged whether the two pictures were the same. On trials requiring
"no" responses, the two pictures were of different objects (e.g., a basketball and a snowmobile). In other words, the picture-judgment task was
extremely easy. Nonetheless, the subjects' responses were influenced by
the content of the sentences, exactly as predicted by our construal theory. Picture sequences in which the second ball was bigger than the first
were judged significantly faster when the sentence implied movement
toward the protagonist (e.g., as in (26)) than when the sentence implied
movement away from the protagonist (as in (27)). And the reverse was
true for sequences in which the second ball was smaller than the first.
Given that the sentence content was irrelevant to the picture-judgment
task, these results support the idea that comprehenders spontaneously
represent motion.

We explain this pattern by assuming that over the course of their lives,
people have stored numerous traces in memory of objects moving toward
them – and occupying an increasingly larger segment of their visual field –
or away from them – and occupying an increasingly smaller segment of
their visual field. These traces are dynamic representations (Freyd, 1987;
Wallis & Bülthoff, 1999) in that they extend and change over time. In accordance with Wallis and Bülthoff, among others, we assume that dynamic
mental object representations are the result of spatiotemporal associations
between visual patterns acquired during experience of our environment.

The picture sequence activates these traces as does construal of the preceding sentences. As a consequence, in the match condition the relevant visual traces are already activated via construal before the picture sequence is seen. In the mismatch condition, a dynamic trace is activated by the linguistic stimuli that is the reverse of the one activated by the picture sequence.

Another claim we made is that comprehenders represent the spatial relations between referents. We found evidence for this using a paradigm that was slightly different from the paradigms discussed before. In this paradigm, subjects made speeded semantic-related judgments to word pairs, e.g., branch-root. The key feature of the manipulation was in the locations of the words on the computer screen. In the match condition, the words were presented in a manner that was consistent with the relative positions of their referents. For instance, branches are canonically above roots and so the word branch was presented above root in the match condition. In the mismatch condition, the positions of the words were reversed, so that the word denoting the top referent was now presented below the word denoting the bottom referent. If people simply use lexical associations to make these judgments, the relative positions of the words on the screen should not make a difference. However, if people rely on perceptual representations to make these judgments, the match condition should yield faster responses than the mismatch condition. And this was exactly what we found (Zwaan & Yaxley, 2003; Experiments 1 and 3). Importantly, the effect disappeared when the words were presented horizontally, ruling out that it was caused by the order in which the words were read (Experiments 2 and 3). In a later study, using a visual-field manipulation, we found that the mismatch effect only occurred when the word pairs were briefly flashed to the left visual field and thus processed by the right hemisphere (Zwaan & Yaxley, 2003). This is consistent with the well-known fact that the right hemisphere is more involved in processing spatial relations than the left hemisphere.

Our account for these findings is straightforward. Parts of objects, such as branches, wheels, or elbows are typically not seen in isolation. In fact, they derive their meaning from context. For example, by itself "elbow" means nothing. It derives its meaning from being part of an arm. In perceptual terms it can be conceptualized as the focal part of an attended object (Langacker, 2001). When a word like "branch" is read or heard, visual traces of trees with branches as the focal part will be activated. And when "root" is read or heard, visual traces of trees with roots as the focal part will be activated. The spatial positions of the referents relative to the larger entities (landmarks) are part of the activated representation. The positioning of the words on the screen produces its own visual trace. This is either consistent or inconsistent with the composite visual traces of the referents thus producing the mismatch effect (see Figure 10.4).

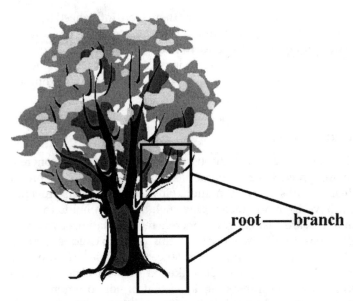

FIGURE 10.4. The relations between perceptual traces of roots and branches and between the lexical constructions associated with them.

We are not claiming that the semantic-relatedness judgments are exclusively based on visual traces of the words' referents. As pointed out in the introduction and as shown in Figure 10.1, experiential traces of referents are connected to experiential traces of linguistic constructs, which are interconnected based on co-occurrence in the linguistic input and output streams. Semantic-relatedness judgments are presumably based both on lexical and on referent associations. The left hemisphere data in Zwaan and Yaxley (2003) support this idea. The relative positions of the words on the screen did not affect the subjects' judgments, but these judgments were still accurate (i.e., the words were seen as related), implicating lexical associations.

We have reviewed several experiments from our lab that collectively have produced evidence in support of the view that construals involve visual representations. However, it is important to note that visual aspects are only one type – albeit a very important one – of experiential representations. Research currently underway in our lab focuses on auditory information as well.

A central claim of our theory concerns perspective. As yet, we have not conducted any specific studies on this topic, although the experiments on dynamic mental representations and on resolution are broadly relevant. The former demonstrate that the comprehenders had taken the perspective of the protagonist, given how their responses to picture sequences implying movement of an object toward or away from them were influenced by their correspondence with the movement described in the sentence, i.e., toward or away from the protagonist. We clearly need to have more extensive research on whether and how perspective is established during sentence comprehension. One important approach is described by MacWhinney (Chapter 9, this volume).

ABSTRACT REPRESENTATIONS

The empirical evidence we have discussed so far pertains to concrete situations. A common criticism of embodied theories is that they are ill equipped to deal with abstract information. However, several approaches to this problem have been advanced. One such approach holds that abstract representations are created from concrete representations by way of (metaphorical) extension (Gibbs, Chapter 4, this volume; Goldberg, 1995; Lakoff, 1987). Indeed, there is empirical evidence for this view (Boroditsky & Ramscar, 2002). Langacker (1987) has likened the abstraction process to superimposing multiple transparencies. What is not common across transparencies will become blurred, but commonalities will become well defined. For example, children often hear expressions such as "Put the ball on the floor," "Put the cup on the table." The only thing that is constant across all instances is that the child uses his or her hands to move an object to a location and then release it. This commonality then becomes schematized in action and language as "Put X" (Tomasello, 2003). Talmy (1996) assumes that a similar abstraction process underlies the meaning of locative prepositions such as "across."[9]

At first sight, a notion like negation presents a major problem for embodied accounts of meaning. How does one mentally simulate an entity, event or feature that is not present? Cognitive linguists have proposed to view negation as a sequence of simulations. We first simulate the situation that is negated and then the actual situation (Fauconnier, 1985). Thus, the meaning of "not" is captured by a sequence of construals rather than by a dictionary definition. We tested the first part of the negation hypothesis – that people initially represent the negated situation – by modifying the sentences from Zwaan et al. (2002). We simply converted the affirmative sentences into negative sentences, such as (30).

(30) The eagle was not in the tree.

If comprehenders first construe the negated situation, then they should initially show the same mismatch effect as the subjects in Zwaan et al. (2002). For example, (30) should first give rise to a construal of an eagle

---

[9] The point here is not that the embodied account of abstraction is unique. Rather, the point is that there exist embodied accounts of abstraction.

in a tree (wings drawn in). We did indeed obtain this effect in three experiments (Kaup, Yaxley, Madden, & Zwaan, unpublished manuscript). Obviously, the same mismatch effect would have occurred if our subjects had simply ignored the negation operator. However, we included comprehension questions (e.g., "Was the eagle in the nest?"), which prompted the subjects to pay attention to the negation. Most subjects answered these questions accurately. Moreover, the mismatch effect was still present when we analyzed the data from subjects with accuracy greater than 90% only. In other words, we can be confident that the subjects did indeed process the negation.

These findings demonstrate that comprehenders first construe the negated situation. But this is only part of the story, of course. It is now important to demonstrate that they will end up construing the actual situation. This will probably require the use of different items, as the actual situation is not strongly constrained by our materials. For instance, if the eagle is not in the nest, it doesn't mean that it is in the sky. It could be in a tree or perched on a rock, in both of which cases it would not have its wings outstretched. Nevertheless, this initial foray into finding empirical evidence for an experiential account of a rather abstract concept like negation is promising (see Kaup, Zwaan, & Lüdtke, in press, for a more thorough discussion). Other approaches to an embodied account of abstractions are being discussed in other chapters in this book (Barsalou & Wiemer-Hastings, Chapter 7, this volume; Gibbs, Chapter 4, this volume; Prinz, Chapter 5, this volume).

CONCLUSION AND OUTLOOK

We started this chapter by comparing two perspectives on cognition in general and on language comprehension in particular. According to the traditional perspective, language comprehension involves the activation and integration of discrete and abstract building blocks of meaning. These building blocks are most commonly represented as propositions or equivalently in semantic networks (in which a pair of nodes are the arguments and the link between them the predicate). We have demonstrated that this general view cannot account for a range of recent findings about language comprehension obtained in our experiments and in experiments by others. According to the alternative view, cognition in general and language comprehension in particular involve the activation and integration of experiential traces in the construal of a situation. These traces are activated by linguistic constructs, which are experiential representations in their own right. Language can be viewed as a sequence of cues modulating the comprehender's attention to a referential world, which is simulated by integrating experiential traces. As we have shown, this view can account for the recent findings we have discussed in this chapter. Moreover, it generates a volley of testable predictions regarding language comprehension, for example about the role of perspective in language comprehension.

However, it is clear that the view we have attempted to outline here is in need of further articulation. The challenge for researchers adopting an experiential perspective is to further articulate the theoretical frameworks, keeping them consistent with what is known about the brain, and test them in elegant and convincing experiments. We are optimistic that these goals are within our reach.

Our focus has been on the role of visual representations in language comprehension. This is because our empirical research thus far has focused on this phenomenon, primarily because it was motivated in part by the goal to show the limitations of amodal propositional representations. However, it is clear that embodied language comprehension involves more than just visual representations. For example, there is behavioral evidence that language comprehension may involve the activation of motor programs (Glenberg & Kaschak, 2002). The sympathetic activation of neurons in the premotor cortex, first observed in monkeys, is thought to underlie action understanding and therefore to mediate language comprehension (Rizzolatti & Arbib, 1998). MacWhinney (Chapter 9, this volume) provides an extension of these ideas. A full-fledged theory of embodied language comprehension should include both perceptual and action simulations. Moreover, it should be capable of explaining their relations (do they occur simultaneously, are they integrated into a coherent representation or are they independent, how is their construal cued by linguistic constructs).

The claims made by proponents of embodied comprehension, for example about the activation of visual representations during language comprehension, may at the same time seem trivial and counterintuitive. They will seem trivial to the lay person, or even to people with great expertise in the use of language, such as novelists and poets. Of course, words can be used to conjure up images in the reader's mind! However, these same claims will seem counterintuitive to researchers trained in traditional cognitive science. To them, the claim that meaning can be captured by experiential representations does not make sense. For one, the claim opens the door to the homunculus problem, and thus to an infinite regress. If there are pictures in the head, then there must be a little person in there looking at the pictures. And if so, who's in that person's mind? There are two responses to this criticism. First, this problem also seems to apply to the amodal view. After all, where is the little person reading all those quasi-linguistic propositions entering and leaving the revolving door of working memory? Second, and more importantly, the claim is not that there are pictures in the mind. Rather, the claim is that traces of visual and other experiences are (partly) reactivated and recombined in novel ways by associated words (Barsalou, 1999). In this sense, language comprehension is the vicarious experiencing of events. Speakers and writers carefully orchestrate linguistic constructs so that experiential traces in their audience's minds can be recombined in novel ways to produce novel experiences.

ACKNOWLEDGMENTS

We thank Diane Pecher and two anonymous reviewers for helpful feedback on an earlier version of this manuscript. The research reported here was supported by grant MH-63972 from the National Institutes of Health. The chapter was written while the first author was a Fellow at the Hanse Institute for Advanced Study in Delmenhorst, Germany. Please address all correspondence regarding this paper to: Rolf A. Zwaan, Department of Psychology, Florida State University, Tallahassee, FL 32306–1270. Email may be sent to: zwaan@psy.fsu.edu.

References

Barsalou, L. W. (1999). Perceptual Symbol Systems. *Behavioral and Brain Sciences 22*, 577–660.
Black, J. B., Turner, E., & Bower, G. H. (1979). Point of view in narrative comprehension memory. *Journal of Verbal Learning and Verbal Behavior 18*, 187–198.
Bloom, L. (2000). Pushing the limits on theories of word learning. *Monographs of the Society for Research in Child Development 65*, 124–135.
Boroditsky, L., & Ramscar, M. (2002). The roles of body and mind in abstract thought. *Psychological Science 13*, 185–188.
Bülthoff, H., & Edelman, S. (1992). Psychophysical support for a two-dimensional view interpolation theory of object recognition. *Proceedings of the National Academy of Sciences, USA 89*, 60–64.
Carey, S., & Bartlett, E. (1978). Acquiring a single new word. *Papers and Reports on Child Language Development 15*, 17–29.
Chafe, W. (1994). *Discourse, Consciousness, and Time: The Flow and Displacement of Conscious Experience in Speaking and Writing.* Chicago: University of Chicago Press.
Chambers, C. G., Tanenhaus, M. K., Eberhard, K. M., Filip, H., & Carlson, G. N. (2001). Circumscribing referential domains in real-time language comprehension. *Journal of Memory and Language 47*, 30–49.
Chomsky, N. (1957). *Syntactic Structures.* The Hague: Mouton.
Christman, S., & Pinger, K. (1997). Lateral biases in pictorial preferences: pictorial dimensions and neural mechanisms. *Laterality 2*, 155–175.
Damasio, A. R. (1999). *The Feeling of What Happens: Body and Emotion in the Making of Consciousness.* Harcourt Brace & Company.
Fauconnier, G. (1985). *Mental Spaces: Aspects of Meaning Construction in Natural Language.* Cambridge, MA: MIT Press.
Fodor, J. A. (1983). *The Modularity of Mind: An Essay on Faculty Psychology.* Cambridge, MA: MIT Press.
Freyd, J. J. (1987) Dynamic mental representations. *Psychological Review 94*, 427–438.
Glenberg, A. M. (1997). What memory is for. *Behavioral and Brain Sciences 20*, 1–55.

Glenberg, A., & Kaschak, M. (2002). Grounding language in action. *Psychonomic Bulletin and Review 9, 558–565.*

Goldberg, A. E. (1995). *Constructions: A Construction Grammar Approach to Argument Structure.* Chicago: University of Chicago Press.

Goldberg, A. E. (2003). Constructions: A new theoretical approach to language. *Trends in Cognitive Science 7, 219–224.*

Harnad, S. (1990). The Symbol Grounding Problem. *Physica D 42, 335–346.*

Hebb, D. O. (1949). *The Organization of Behavior: A Neuropsychological Theory.* New York: Wiley.

Hockett, C. F. (1959). Animal "languages" and human language. *Human Biology 31,* 32–39.

Kaup, B., Yaxley, R. H., Madden, C. J., & Zwaan, R. A. (May, 2004). Perceptual Simulation of Negated Text Information.

Kaup, B., Zwaan, R. A., & Lüdtke, J. (in press). The experiential view of language comprehension: How is Negation Represented? In F. Schmalhofer & C.A. Perfetti (Eds.), *Higher Language Processes in the Brain.* Mahwah, NJ: Erlbaum.

Kintsch, W., & van Dijk, T. A. (1978). Toward a model of text comprehension and production. *Psychological Review 85, 363–394.*

Lakoff, G. (1987). *Women, Fire, and Dangerous things: What Categories Reveal about the Mind.* Chicago: University of Chicago Press.

Landauer, T. K., & Dumais, S. T. (1997). A solution to Plato's problem: The latent semantic analysis theory of acquisition, induction, and representation of knowledge. *Psychological Review 104, 211–240.*

Langacker, R. (1987). *Foundations of Cognitive Grammar, Vol. 1.* Stanford, CA: Stanford University Press.

Langacker, R. W. (2001). Discourse in cognitive grammar. *Cognitive Linguistics 12,* 143–188.

Maass, A., & Russo, A. (2003). Directional bias in the mental representation of spatial events: nature or culture? *Psychological Science 14, 296–301.*

Mamassian, P., & Goutcher, R. (2001). Prior knowledge on the illumination position. *Cognition 81, B1–B9.*

Morrow, D. G., & Clark, H. H. (1988). Interpreting words in spatial descriptions. *Language and Cognitive Processes 3, 275–291.*

Pustejovsky, J. (1995). *The Generative Lexicon.* Cambridge, MA: MIT Press.

Pylyshyn, Z. W. (1986). *Computation and Cognition: Toward a Foundation for Cognitive Science.* Cambridge, MA: MIT Press.

Rizzolatti, G., & Arbib, M. A. (1998). Language within our grasp. *Trends in Neurosciences 21, 188–194.*

Sadoski, M., & Paivio, A. (2001). *Imagery and text: A dual coding theory of reading and writing.* Mahwah, NJ: Erlbaum.

Searle, J. R. (1980). Minds, brains, and programs. *Behavioral & Brain Sciences 3, 417–457.*

Stanfield, R. A., & Zwaan, R. A. (2001). The effect of implied orientation derived from verbal context on picture recognition. *Psychological Science 12, 153–156.*

Sun, J., & Perona, P. (1998). Where is the sun? *Nature Neuroscience 1, 183–184.*

Swinney, D. (1979). Lexical access during sentence comprehension: (Re)consideration of context effects. *Journal of Verbal Learning and Verbal Behavior 18,* 645–660.

Talmy, L. (1996). Fictive motion in language and "ception." In P. Bloom, L. Nadel, & M. A. Peterson (Eds.), *Language and Space* (pp. 211–276). Cambridge, MA: MIT Press.

Talmy, L. (2000a). *Toward a Cognitive Semantics, Vol. 1, Concept Structuring Systems.* Cambridge, MA: MIT Press.

Talmy, L. (2000b). *Toward a Cognitive Semantics, Vol. 2, Typology and Process in Concept Structuring.* Cambridge, MA: MIT Press.

Tarr, M. (1995). Rotating objects to recognize them: A case study on the role of viewpoint dependency in the recognition of three-dimensional objects. *Psychonomic Bulletin and Review 2,* 55–82.

Ter Meulen, A. G. B. (1995). *Representing Time in Natural Language: The Dynamic Interpretation of Tense and Aspect,* Cambridge, MA: MIT Press.

Tomasello, M. (2003). *Constructing a Language. A Usage-Based Theory of Language Acquisition.* Cambridge, MA: Harvard University Press.

Vendler, Z. (1967). *Linguistics in Philosophy.* Ithaca, NY: Cornell University Press.

Wallis, G., & Bülthoff, H. (1999). Learning to recognize objects. *Trends in Cognitive Sciences 3,* 22–31.

Zwaan, R. A. (1996). Processing narrative time shifts. *Journal of Experimental Psychology: Learning, Memory, and Cognition 22,* 1196–1207.

Zwaan, R. A. (2004). The immersed experiencer: Toward an embodied theory of language comprehension. In B. H. Ross (Ed.), *The Psychology of Learning and Motivation, Vol. 44.* (pp. 35–62). New York: Academic Press.

Zwaan, R. A., Madden, C. J., Yaxley, R. H., & Aveyard, M. (2004). Moving words: Language comprehension produces representational motion. *Cognitive Science 28,* 611–619.

Zwaan, R. A., & Radvansky, G. A. (1998). Situation models in language comprehension and memory. *Psychological Bulletin 123,* 162–185.

Zwaan, R. A., Stanfield, R. A., & Yaxley, R. H. (2002). Do language comprehenders routinely represent the shapes of objects? *Psychological Science 13,* 168–171.

Zwaan, R. A., & Yaxley, R. H. (2003). Spatial iconicity affects semantic-relatedness judgments. *Psychonomic Bulletin & Review 10,* 954–958.

Zwaan, R. A., & Yaxley, R. H. (2003). Hemispheric differences in semantic-relatedness judgments. *Cognition 87,* B79–B86.

11

On the Perceptual-Motor and Image-Schematic Infrastructure of Language

Michael J. Spivey, Daniel C. Richardson,
and Monica Gonzalez-Marquez

Language is not a module. Well, at least, it is not a feedforward encapsulated domain-specific perceptual input system in the way that Fodor (1983) imagined. To be sure, there are regions of cortex that are conspicuously specialized for language-like processes (e.g., Gazzaniga, 2000; Kuperberg, Holcomb, Sitnikova, Greve, Dale, & Caplan, 2003; Ojemann, 1983), but when cognitive neuroscientists refer to these cortical areas as "modules," they certainly do not imply solely feedforward synaptic projections or encapsulation from neighboring cortical areas. The vast and recurrent interconnectedness between anatomically and functionally segregated cortical areas (e.g., Douglas, Koch, Mahowald, Martin, & Suarez, 1995; Haxby, Gobbini, Furey, Ishai, Schouten, & Pietrini, 2001; Van Orden, Jansen op de Haar, & Bosman, 1997) unavoidably compromises any assumptions of information encapsulation, and can even wind up blurring the distinction between feedback and feedforward signals.

What this means is that we should expect language processes to function in concert with other perceptual, cognitive, and motor processes, not independently of them. For example, McGurk's famous and compelling demonstration of visual perception of mouth shape influencing the immediate percept of a spoken phoneme (McGurk & MacDonald, 1976) is emblematic of the intense degree to which speech perception and visual perception pay close attention to one another. More recently, visual perception has also been shown to play a strong role in spoken word recognition, syntactic processing, and reference resolution (Tanenhaus, Spivey-Knowlton, Eberhard, & Sedivy, 1995). As one begins to seriously consider the claim that language, perception, and action are interdependent, one is naturally encouraged to explore the theoretical developments taking place in cognitive linguistics, especially those involving image schemas as linguistic entities that are rooted in a spatial format of representation (e.g., Langacker, 1987; Talmy, 1983). This chapter reviews the psycholinguistic motivations for taking these claims seriously, and describes some recent experiments that provide empirical evidence for the psychological reality of the spatial and image-schematic underpinnings of language.

INTERACTION BETWEEN LANGUAGE AND VISION

In headband-mounted eyetracking experiments, participants often look briefly at an object that is initially considered relevant for action, and then quickly re-fixate their eyes on another object that becomes the actual target of the action. Essentially, the threshold for executing an eye movement is lower than the threshold for executing an overt reaching movement. Thus, by recording eye movements, one can obtain a measure of the partially active representations or decisions that compete against one another as the system settles on a single particular action (e.g., Gold & Shadlen, 2000; Schall, 2000). This vacillation between saccade targets, and thus between potential action targets, takes place on the scale of a few hundred milliseconds, and is typically unavailable to introspective awareness. For example, when sitting in front of a display of objects on a table (including a candle, bag of candy, a pencil, and a spoon), and instructed to "Pick up the candy," about one third of the time participants will fixate the *candle* for a couple hundred milliseconds (because, as a "cohort" [Marslen-Wilson, 1987] of the word/candy/, it shares several phonemes with it), then they fixate the bag of candy and pick it up (Spivey-Knowlton, Tanenhaus, Eberhard, & Sedivy, 1998). If you ask them whether they noticed having looked at the candle, they will deny having done so.

This kind of brief interference between similar sounding object names occurs not just for cohorts but also for rhymes (Allopenna, Magnuson, & Tanenhaus, 1998), as well as for novel words from an artificial lexicon (Magnuson, Tanenhaus, Aslin, & Dahan, 2003), and even for words that sound similar across different languages (Marian & Spivey, 2003; Spivey & Marian, 1999). It appears that the acoustic uptake of spoken input is continuously mapped onto visually relevant lexical representations, such that partial phonological matches to the names of multiple visual objects induces competition between partially active representations (something like interactive processing in the TRACE connectionist model of spoken word recognition, McClelland & Elman, 1986; see also Elman & McClelland, 1988, and Magnuson, McMurray, Tanenhaus, & Aslin, 2003).

A similar influence of visual context is observed with temporary ambiguities that arise *across* words, in the syntax of a sentence. When presented with a display containing an apple on a towel, another towel, and an empty box, and then instructed to "Put the apple on the towel in the box," participants often looked briefly at the irrelevant lone towel near the end of the spoken instruction before returning their gaze to the apple, grasping it, and then placing it inside the box (Spivey, Tanenhaus, Eberhard, & Sedivy, 2002; Tanenhaus et al., 1995). (With unambiguous control sentences, such as "Put the apple that's on the towel in the box," they almost never looked at the irrelevant lone towel.) In this case, the syntax is ambiguous as to whether the prepositional phrase "on the towel" is attached to the verb "put" (as a movement destination) or to the noun "apple" (as a modifier). Given the actions afforded by the display, the latter syntactic structure is the correct one. However, people tend to have a bias toward interpreting an ambiguous prepositional phrase as attached to the verb (Rayner, Carlson, & Frazier, 1983), at least when it is an action verb like "put" (cf. Spivey-Knowlton & Sedivy, 1995). Thus, the brief fixation of the irrelevant lone towel indicates a temporary partially activated incorrect parse of the sentence. To demonstrate the influence of visual context on this syntactic ambiguity resolution process, the display was slightly altered to include a second apple (resting on a napkin). In this case, the *visual copresence* (Clark's, 1992) of the two potential referents for the phrase "the apple" should encourage the listener to interpret the ambiguous prepositional phrase "on the towel" as a modifier (in order to determine which apple is being referred to) rather than as a movement destination (cf. Altmann & Steedman, 1988; Crain & Steedman, 1985; Spivey & Tanenhaus, 1998). And, indeed, with this display, participants rarely fixated the irrelevant lone towel, indicating that visual context had exerted an immediate influence on the incremental syntactic parsing of the spoken sentence (Spivey et al., 2002; Tanenhaus et al., 1995; see also Knoeferle, Crocker, Scheepers, & Pickering, 2003).

The word-by-word interfacing between spoken language and visual perception is also evidenced by reference resolution with complex noun phrases. Eberhard, Spivey-Knowlton, Sedivy, and Tanenhaus (1995) presented participants with a display of blocks of various shapes, colors, and markings, and gave them instructions like "Touch the starred yellow square." When the display contained only one starred block, participants often fixated on the target block before the head noun of the noun phrase had even been spoken. Fixation of the target block was slightly later when the display contained another starred block that was not yellow, and later still when the display also contained a starred yellow block that was not a square. This result shows that even before hearing the noun that refers to the object being described, listeners are processing the prenominal adjectives as they are heard and mapping their meaning onto the options available in the visual context. Such incremental reference resolution is also affected by the presence of minimally contrastive pairs in the display (Sedivy, Tanenhaus, Chambers & Carlson, 1999) as well as by object-to-object affordances in the display, i.e., containers of appropriate or inappropriate size (Chambers, Tanenhaus, Eberhard, Filip, & Carlson, 2002).

As these results from headband-mounted eye-tracking in language processing tasks began to acquire a little bit of notoriety, some psycholinguists would at times react somewhat grumpily at being told that visual perception is tightly coupled with language processing and that it can sometimes "tell language what to do." In contrast, when vision researchers became aware of these kinds of results, they were not surprised a bit. To them, it was perfectly expected that the visual system would be strong enough and important enough to occasionally "tell language what to do."

But it's a two-way street. Since any synaptic pathway between two cortical areas (mediated through a third area or not) is comprised of bi-directional information flow, one should also expect language to occasionally be able to "tell vision what to do" as well. For example, since the processing of spoken adjectives is continuous and incremental (Eberhard et al., 1995), one ought to predict that hearing a spoken instruction for a visual search task, while viewing the search display, could essentially convert a "serial" conjunction search (for "a red vertical bar") into something like a nested pair of "parallel" single-feature searches (first for the red things, since that is heard and processed first, and then for the vertical one among them). And, indeed, that is exactly what happens. When the search display is visible during the instruction (e.g., "Is there a green horizontal?"), the search slopes drop from about 20 ms/item to around 7 ms/item (Spivey, Tyler, Eberhard, & Tanenhaus, 2001; Tyler & Spivey, 2001).

It seems clear that the continuity in information flow between language processing and visual perception is substantially greater than was predicted by modular accounts of mind. The question that arises, then, is how do these highly-permeable "neural modules" for language and vision (and perhaps other faculties as well) communicate with one another so smoothly? Are there "interface modules" that perform the necessary translation between fundamentally incompatible formats of representation, e.g., amodal digital symbols in language and modal analog distributed representations in perception (cf. Jackendoff, 2002)? Or is it perhaps more likely that, deep down, both language and vision are using formats of representation that already have a substantial amount in common? Thus, not only would there be continuity in information flow, but also continuity in representational format. The theme of this chapter is that spatial representations may be a likely candidate (in addition to other analog and embodied candidates) for such a common format.

INTERACTION BETWEEN LANGUAGE AND SPACE

The set of findings described above provides strong support for models of visuolinguistic integration in which early continuous interaction between the two subsystems is crucial (e.g., Hildebrandt, Moratz, Rickheit, & Sagerer, 1999; Roy & Mukherjee, in press; Spivey-Knowlton, 1996). However, most of these findings and models are limited to language that makes reference to scenes and objects that are co-present with the spoken utterance (cf. Altmann & Kamide, 2004). Clearly, this is a subset of the range of circumstances in which language is used. Many other circumstances of language use, e.g., descriptions of far away scenes, gossip about people who are absent, discussions of abstract concepts, do not involve explicit reference to visible elements of the situational context of the conversation. Will scanning of the visuo-spatial backdrop that is available to a listener be at all relevant during comprehension of language that refers to things that are not copresent? Is space as important to language as the objects that fill it up?

In another headband-mounted eyetracking experiment, Spivey and Geng (2001, Experiment 1; see also Spivey, Tyler, Richardson, & Young, 2000) recorded participants' eye movements while they listened to spoken descriptions of spatiotemporally dynamic scenes and faced a large white projection screen that took up most of their visual field. For example, "Imagine that you are standing across the street from a 40 story apartment building. At the bottom there is a doorman in blue. *On the 10th floor, a woman is hanging her laundry out the window. On the 29th floor, two kids are sitting on the fire escape smoking cigarettes. On the very top floor, two people are screaming.*" While listening to the italicized portion of this passage, participants made reliably more upward saccades than in any other direction. Corresponding biases in spontaneous saccade directions were also observed for a downward story, as well as for leftward and rightward stories. (A control story, describing a view through a telescope that zooms in closer and closer to a static scene, elicited about equal proportions of saccades in all directions.) Thus, while looking at ostensibly nothing, listeners' eyes were doing something similar to what they would have done if the scene being described were actually right there in front of them. Instead of relying solely on an internal "visuospatial sketchpad" (Baddeley, 1986) on which to illustrate their mental model of the scene being described, participants also recruited the external environment as an additional canvas on which to depict the spatial layout of the imagined scene.

Although eye movements may not be required for vivid imagery (Hale & Simpson, 1970; but cf. Ruggieri, 1999), it does appear that they often naturally accompany it in one way or another (e.g., Antrobus, Antrobus, & Singer, 1964; Brandt & Stark, 1997; Demarais & Cohen, 1998; Laeng & Teodorescu, 2002; Neisser, 1967; see also Hebb, 1968). But what is it that the eyes are trying to do in these circumstances? Obviously, it is not the case that the eyes themselves can actually externally record this internal information. When the eyes move upward from the imagined 10th floor of the apartment building to the imagined 29th floor, no physical mark is left behind on the external location in the environment that was proxying for that 10th floor.

Rather than a physical mark, perhaps what they "leave behind" is a deictic pointer, or spatial index (Richardson & Spivey, 2000; Spivey, Richardson, & Fitneva, 2004). According to Ballard, Hayhoe, Pook, and Rao (1997; see also Pylyshyn, 1989, 2001), deictic pointers can be used in visuomotor routines to conserve the use of working memory. Instead of storing all the detailed properties of an object internally, one can simply store an address, or pointer, for the object's location in the environment, via a pattern of activation on an attentional/oculomotor salience map in parietal cortex (e.g., Duhamel, Colby, & Goldberg, 1992), along with a spatial memory salience map in prefrontal cortex (e.g., Chafee & Goldman-Rakic, 1998, 2000; Goldman-Rakic, 1993). If this spatial pointer is associated with some kind of coarse semantic information, e.g., a pattern of activation in one of the language cortices, or auditory cortex, or even visual cortex, then the spatial pointer can be triggered when sensory input activates that semantic information. Such pointers allow the organism to perceptually access relevant properties of the external world when they are needed (rather than storing them all in memory).

In the case of Spivey and Geng's (2001) eye movements during imagery, a few pointers allocated on a blank projection screen will obviously not make reference to any external visual properties, but they can still provide perceptual-motor information about the relative spatial locations of the *internal* content associated with the pointers. If one is initially thinking about *x* (e.g., the 10th floor) and then transitions to thinking about *y* (e.g., the 29th floor), then storing in working memory the relation *above* (*y,x*) may not be necessary if the eye movements, and their allocation of spatial indices, have embodied that spatial relationship already (cf. Pylyshyn, 1989). In this way, a "low-level" motor process, such as eye movements, can actually do some of the work involved in the "high-level" cognitive act of visual imagery elicited by linguistic input.

Results like these provide a powerful demonstration of how language about things not copresent is interfaced with perceptual-motor systems that treat the linguistic referents *as if they were copresent*. However, this still does not address what is often held (next to complex grammar) as the *piece d'resistance* of human language: Communication of abstract concepts and properties. In the same way that we, in Barsalou's (1999) words, "perceptually simulate" concrete (albeit, absent) objects that are being described to us, do we also somehow perceptually simulate abstract concepts that are being described to us?

IMAGE SCHEMAS AFFECT METALINGUISTIC JUDGMENTS

Why do we look up to some people, but look down on others? Perhaps it is because those we deem worthy of respect, our superiors, are somehow "above" us, and those we deem unworthy are somehow "beneath" us. But why does respect (or a lack of it) run along a vertical axis – or any spatial axis, for that matter? Much of our language is rich with such spatial talk. Concrete actions such as a push or a lift clearly imply a vertical or horizontal motion, but so too can more abstract concepts. Arguments can go "back and forth," and hopes can get "too high."

It is often claimed that there is a spatial component to language. The motivations for this claim include capturing subtle asymmetries and nuances of linguistic representation in a schematic spatial format (Langacker, 1987, 1990; Talmy, 1983), explaining the infant's development from sensorimotor to cognitive reasoning (Mandler, 1992), the difficulties in implementing a purely amodal, symbolic system (Barsalou, 1999), and a more general account of the mind as an embodied, experiential system (Lakoff & Johnson, 1999). Although they are construed differently by various theorists, there appears to be a good case for the conclusion that, at some level, image schemas represent "fundamental, persuasive organizing structures of cognition" (Clausner & Croft, 1999). If so, then one would expect a consistent pattern of image schemas to be produced not just by trained linguists and psychologists, but also by naïve subjects.

Recent work in psychology has documented the mapping between subjects' spatial linguistic terms and their mental representation of space (Carlson-Radvansky, Covey, & Lattanzi, 1999; Hayward & Tarr, 1995; Schober, 1995). Although there are consistencies in the ways in which spatial language is produced and comprehended (Hayward & Tarr, 1995), the exact mapping appears to be modulated by such factors as visual context (Spivey et al., 2002), the common ground between conversants (Schober, 1995) and the functional attributes of the objects being described (Carlson-Radvansky et al., 1999).

When language refers directly to explicit spatial properties, locations, and relationships in the world, it is quite natural to expect those linguistic representations to have at least some degree of overlap in their format. Spatial language terms appear to be grounded, at least somewhat, in perceptual (rather than purely amodal) formats of representation. In modelling the acceptability judgments for examples of the spatial term "above," Regier and Carlson (2001) found that the best fit to the data was provided by a model that was independently motivated by perceptual mechanisms such as attention (Logan, 1994) and population coding (Georgopoulos, Schwartz, & Kettner, 1986). However, an important component of the work presented herein involves testing for this representational format in an arena of language that does *not* exhibit any literal spatial properties: abstract verbs (such as *respect* and *succeed*). Work in cognitive linguistics has in fact argued that many linguistic and conceptual representations (even abstract ones) are based on metaphoric extensions to spatially laid out image schemas (Gibbs, 1996; Lakoff, 1987; Langacker, 1987; Talmy, 1983). This work suggests that if consistency across subjects is observed for spatial depictions of *concrete* verbs, then one should also expect a similar consistency for *abstract* verbs.

There are various old and new results suggesting that there is some consistency among speakers in the visual imagery associated with certain ideas and concepts. For example, Scheerer and Lyons (1957) asked subjects

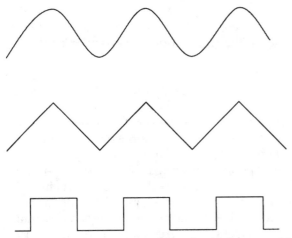

FIGURE 11.1. Schematic images based on Scheerer and Lyons (1957), shown to exhibit surprising agreement among participants when matched to the labels of *gold*, and *silver*, and *iron*.

to match the words "gold," "silver," and "iron" to three drawings which had previously been produced by other naive subjects. At least one set of these drawings (which resembled sine, saw tooth, and square waves, respectively, as in Figure 11.1), were consistently matched in that order by 85% of the subjects. Lakoff (1987) offers anecdotal evidence that when asked to describe their image of an idiom such as 'keeping at arms length' people have a considerable degree of commonality in their responses, including details such as the angle of the protagonist's hand. Similarly, Gibbs, Ström and Spivey-Knowlton (1997) carried out empirical work querying subjects about their mental images of proverbs such as "a rolling stone gathers no moss" and found a surprising degree of agreement – even about fine details such as the stone bouncing slightly as it rolled.

The approach we take here extends beyond the visual properties of a concept, toward more schematic or spatial representations of verbs. Barsalou's (1999) perceptual symbol system theory endorses the view held by several theorists (Gibbs, 1996; Lakoff, 1987) that to some degree abstract concepts are represented by a metaphoric extension to more concrete domains. For example, it is argued that the concept of *anger* draws on a concrete representation of "liquid in a container under pressure."

There is ample evidence to suggest that spatial information plays an important role in many aspects of language processing, from prepositional phrases (Regier & Carlson, 2001) to conceptual metaphors (Lakoff, 1987). However, the cognitive domains of language and space may have a particularly special 'point of contact' at the level of lexical representation. If we accept the idea that there is a spatial or perceptual basis to the core representation of linguistic items, it would be reasonable to assume that there is some commonality between these representations across different speakers, since we experience the same world, have similar perceptual systems, and by and large communicate successfully. Therefore, we might expect that there would be a consensus among subjects when we ask them to select or draw schematic diagrams representing words. Theorists such as Langacker (1987) have produced large bodies of diagrammatic linguistic representations, arguing that they are constrained by linguistic observations and intuitions in the same way that "well formedness" judgements inform more traditional linguistic theories. One approach would be to add to this body of knowledge by performing an analysis of a set of words using the theoretical tools of cognitive linguistics. However, it remains to be seen whether naïve subjects share these intuitions and spatial forms of representation. Therefore, in the same way that psycholinguists use norming studies to support claims of preference for certain grammatical structures, Richardson, Spivey, Edelman, and Naples (2001) surveyed a large number of participants with no linguistic training to see if there is a consensus amongst their spatial representations of words.

Richardson et al. (2001) empirically tested the claim that between subjects there is a coherence to the imagistic aspects of their linguistic representations. To this end, they addressed two questions: (1) Do subjects agree with each other about the spatial components of different verbs? and (2) Across a forced-choice and an open-ended response task, are the same spatial representations being accessed? It would be of further interest if the subjects' diagrams bore resemblance to those proposed by theorists such as Langacker (1987). However, as with more standard norming studies, the real value of the data was in generating prototypical representations that could be used as stimuli for subsequent studies of *online* natural language comprehension.

Richardson et al. (2001) first collected forced-choice judgments of verb image schemas from 173 Cornell undergraduates. Thirty verbs were divided into high and low concreteness categories (based on the MRC psycholinguistic database, Coltheart, 1981), and further into three image schema orientation categories (vertical, horizontal, and neutral). This latter division was based solely on linguistic intuitions, and as such, proved somewhat imperfect, as will be shown later. The verbs were inserted into rebus sentences as in Figure 11.2 (in some cases prepositions or verb particles were necessary).

The participants were presented with a single page, containing a list of the 30 rebus sentences and four pictures, labeled A to D. Each one contained a circle and a square aligned along a vertical or horizontal axis, connected by an arrow pointing up, down, left or right (see Figure 11.2). For each sentence, subjects were asked to select one of the four sparse images that best depicted the event described by the sentence, as shown

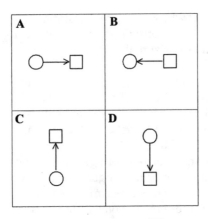

1. ○ argued with □.
2. ○ respected □.
3. ○ succeeded.

...

FIGURE 11.2. The four image schemas, along with some example rebus sentences, used by Richardson, Spivey, Edelman, and Naples (2001, Experiment 1).

in Figure 11.2. (Most of the verbs were used transitively in their rebus sentences, but some had to be used intransitively. The intransitive rebus sentences were roughly equally distributed across the six conditions of the experiment, and their results did not differ substantially from the transitive sentences.)

Results came out resoundingly in favor of consistent image-schematic intuitions among the naïve judges. All 10 of the horizontal verbs had a horizontal image schema as their majority selection, and all but one of the vertical verbs (*obey* was the exception) had a vertical image schema as their majority selection. As it turned out, the neutral group was actually more of a mixed bag of horizontals and verticals, rather than a homogeneously non-spatially-biased set of verbs. (So much for the experimenters' trained linguistic intuitions.) As one quantitative demonstration of consistency among subjects, the particular image schema that was most popular, for any given verb on average, was chosen by 63% of the subjects. The second most popular was chosen by 21%, the third by 10% and the fourth by 5%.

To compute a single index for the primary axis of each verb's image schema, Richardson et al. (2001) collapsed the leftward and rightward images into one "horizontal" category, and the upward and downward images into one "vertical" category, by converting the forced choice data into "axis angles." The leftward and rightward image schemas were assigned an angle of 0, and the upward and downward image schemas an angle value of 90°. An average axis angle between 0 and 90° was calculated, weighted by the proportion of participants who selected that orientation of image schema. The five concrete vertical verbs produced an overall mean axis angle of 81°, while the five concrete horizontal verbs produced an overall mean axis angle of 10°. Similarly, albeit less dramatically, the five abstract vertical verbs produced an overall mean axis angle of 55°, while the five abstract horizontal verbs produced an overall mean axis angle of 25°. (Item-by-item results appear in Figure 11.6, where the average axis angle for each verb, based on these forced-choice data, is depicted as a dashed line somewhere between vertical and horizontal.)

The results of this forced-choice experiment are encouraging for proponents of an image-schematic infrastructure supporting language. However, it could be argued that the pattern of results in this experiment mainly reflects the artificial and limited nature of the forced-choice task, in which the restricted and conspicuous set of given image schema choices could be accused of "leading the witness," as it were.

In their next experiment, Richardson et al. (2001) removed the constraints of a forced choice among a limited set of options, and allowed subjects to create their own image schemas in an open-ended response task. Participants were asked to create their own representation of the sentences using a simple computer-based drawing environment. The aim was to elicit quite abstract, or sparse, schematic representations. The custom computer interface allowed Richardson et al. to limit the participants to using a few different circles, a few different squares, and a few extendable and freely-rotated arrows. On each trial, the bottom of the screen presented a rebus sentence (using the same verbs from the forced-choice experiment), and the participant spent about a minute depicting a two-dimensional rendition of it with the few simple shapes at their disposal. Participants were instructed to "draw a diagram that represents the meaning of the sentence." When they finished a diagram, they clicked a "done" button and were presented with the next rebus sentence and a blank canvas.

Figures 11.3 and 11.4 show a representative set of participants' drawings of the concrete verb *argued with* and the abstract verb *respected*. As hoped, most of the 22 participants attempted to represent the verbs schematically. However, there were a few subjects who, despite the limitations of the drawing toolbox, attempted to *pictorially* represent the verbs. For example, in the drawing on the bottom left corner of Figure 11.4 (as well as in the drawing three frames to the right of it), one can see that the subject has drawn humanoid figures, using the arrows as arms. Indeed, since they were the only items that could be rotated and resized, the arrows were often used as generic lines to form a pictorial drawing. For this reason, Richardson et al. (2001) decided to ignore the arrows in their analysis, and focus on the relative positions of objects.

Similar to the "axis angle" computed in the previous experiment, Richardson et al. (2001) used the coordinates of objects within the canvas

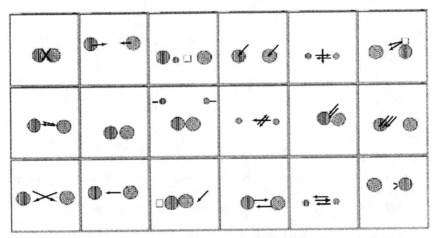

FIGURE 11.3. A representative sample of free-form drawings produced by naïve participants for the verb "argued with" (Richardson, Spivey, Edelman, & Naples, 2001, Experiment 2).

frame to define the "aspect angle" as a value between 0 and 90° to reflect the horizontal versus vertical extent of each drawing. If one imagines a rectangle drawn to include the centroids of all objects in a picture, the aspect angle is the angle of a diagonal line connecting the lower-left and upper-right corners of the rectangle. If the objects are perfectly aligned on a horizontal axis, the aspect angle would be 0. If the objects are perfectly aligned on a vertical axis, the aspect angle would be 90°. Figure 11.5 shows

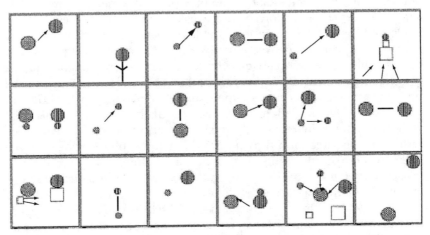

FIGURE 11.4. A representative sample of free-form drawings produced by naïve participants for the verb "respected" (Richardson, Spivey, Edelman, & Naples, 2001, Experiment 2).

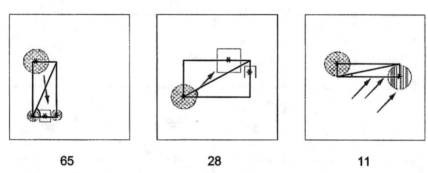

65   **28**   **11**

FIGURE 11.5. Example calculations of "aspect angle," an index of verticality or horizontality of the image, for the free-form drawings in Richardson, Spivey, Edelman, and Naples (2001, Experiment 2), such as those in Figures 11.3 and 11.4.

some example measurements of the aspect angle. Note that the aspect angle collapses left-right and top-bottom mirror reflections of a drawing. Richardson et al. used this measure because they were primarily interested in the horizontal vs. vertical aspect of each drawing, and less so its directionality. (As some of the verbs were used with an intransitive argument structure, they would sometimes elicit images containing only one object – thus rendering this aspect angle calculation impossible. These cases, which amounted to 17% of the data, were treated as missing data points.)

Figure 11.6 graphically represents the aspect angle data in what Richardson et al. (2001) termed "radar plots." Each verb's mean aspect angle (solid line) is shown together with its standard error (shaded fan area). The means for each condition are shown in the rightmost column of Figure 11.6. For comparison to the previous experiment, the mean axis angle of each verb in the forced-choice task is drawn as a dashed line.

Despite the free-form nature of the task, there was a reasonably high degree of agreement between participants. Moreover, there was also considerable agreement between the forced-choice experiment and the drawing experiment. By comparing each verb's mean axis angle in the first experiment to its mean aspect angle in the second experiment, via a pointwise correlation, Richardson et al. (2001) found that there was considerable item-by-item consistency between the forced-choice results and the free-form drawing results, with a robust correlation between mean axis angle and mean aspect angle for the verbs in the two tasks; $r = 0.71, p < .0001$. Importantly, the correlation was statistically significant for all the abstract verbs alone ($r = .64, p < .0001$), as well as for all the concrete verbs alone ($r = .76, p < .0001$). Thus, the two measures appear to be accessing the same internal representations, i.e., image schemas that are stable across the different tasks and across different subjects.

These findings provide compelling support for the image-schematic approach to language endorsed by cognitive linguistics (e.g., Langacker, 1987;

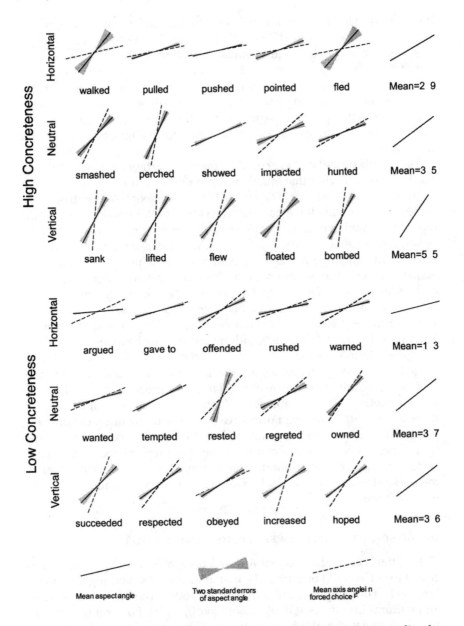

FIGURE 11.6. "Radar plots" indicating degree of verticality or horizontality for the derived image schemas of each of the 30 verbs used by Richardson, Spivey, Edelman, and Naples (2001).

Talmy, 1983). However, Figure 11.6 reveals some informative cases where the experimenters' "trained linguistic intuitions" were refuted by the participants. For example, in the neutral condition, both *perched* and *rested* were consistently given a vertical interpretation by participants in both tasks. Additionally, the average image schema for *obeyed* was considerably more horizontal than had been expected. These observations highlight the importance of using normative methodologies from psychology to accompany traditional introspective methodologies from linguistics (cf. Gibbs & Colston, 1995).

The results described here could be taken as further evidence challenging the "classical" view that linguistic representations are amodal, symbolic entities (e.g., Marcus, 2001; Dietrich & Markman, 2003). Alternatively, one could maintain that all we have shown is that such hypothetical, amodal representations have easy access to spatial information in a way that is consistent across users of a language. Given that language is learned and used in a spatially extended world that is common to all of us, then of course participants will find consistent relations between certain spatial dimensions and certain words. This could happen whether the underlying linguistic representations were multimodal 'perceptual simulations' (Barsalou, 1999), or amodal entries in a symbolic lexicon. Thus, the spatial consistency revealed by metalinguistic judgments may not be inherent to *linguistic* representations, but instead may be part of some other body of knowledge that can be deliberatively accessed from an amodal lexical entry.

What is required is a measure of language processing that does not involve metacognitive deliberation. If these kinds of spatial representations become active during normal real-time comprehension of language, and can be revealed in a concurrent but unrelated perceptual task, then it becomes much more difficult to argue that they are secondary representational appendices, separate from the core linguistic symbols, that are merely strategically accessed when some psychology experimenter overtly requests them.

IMAGE SCHEMAS AFFECT PERCEPTION AND MEMORY

The spatial representations that Richardson et al.'s (2001) participants ascribed to verbs could be part of the metaphoric understanding that underlies much of our language use, and may be rooted in embodied experiences and cultural influences (Gibbs, 1996; Lakoff, 1987). For example, respect may be associated with an upwards direction because as children we look up to our taller and wiser elders. Alternatively, perhaps these spatial elements are more like idioms, or linguistic freezes – historical associations that are buried in a word's etymology but are not part of our core understanding of the concept (Murphy, 1996). In fact, it has been argued that understandings based on metaphorical extensions (spatial or otherwise) happen only with unconventional expressions that require deliberative reasoning to understand, and that more conventional expressions – which are understood more automatically – do not employ metaphorical extensions for their comprehension (Keysar, Shen, Glucksberg, & Horton, 2000). This issue forms the central question of the next set of experiments to be described. Are the spatial representations associated with certain verbs merely vestigial and only accessible meta-cognitively, or are they automatically activated by the process of comprehending those verbs?

Richardson, Spivey, Barsalou, and McRae (2003) operationalized this question by presenting participants with sentences and testing for spatial effects on concurrent perceptual tasks. An interaction between linguistic and perceptual processing would support the idea that spatial representations are inherent to the conceptual representations derived from language comprehension (e.g., Barsalou, 1999). The interactions predicted were specific to the orientation of the image schema associated with various concrete and abstract verbs. Richardson and colleagues used the empirically categorized set of verbs from the norming studies of Richardson et al. (2001). Because it was assumed that image-schematic spatial representations bear some similarity to visuospatial imagery (albeit a weak or partially active form), they predicted that it would interact with perceptual tasks in a similar fashion.

Evidence of visual imagery interfering with visual perception was discovered at the turn of the century (Kuelpe, 1902; Scripture, 1896), and rediscovered in the late 1960s (Segal & Gordon, 1969). In demonstrations of the "Perky effect" (Perky, 1910), performance in visual detection or discrimination is impaired by engaging in visual imagery. In some cases, imagery can also facilitate perception (Farah, 1985; Finke, 1985). It is not certain what mechanisms produce these differing effects (Craver-Lemley & Reeves, 1992). For the present purposes, it suffices to note that facilitation only occurs when there is a relatively precise overlap in identity, shape or location between the imaginary and the real entity (Farah, 1985). In the more general case of generating a visual image and detecting or discriminating unrelated stimuli, imagery impairs performance (Craver-Lemley & Arterberry, 2001). Richardson et al.'s (2003) first experiment tested the hypothesis that nonspecific imagery activated by verb comprehension would *interfere* with performance on a visual task.

In this dual-task experiment, 83 participants heard and remembered short sentences, and identified briefly flashed visual stimuli as a circle or square in the upper, lower, left, or right sides of the computer screen. The critical sentences contained the verbs for which Richardson et al. (2001) had collected image schema norms. The data from these two norming tasks were combined and the result used to categorize the verbs empirically as either horizontal or vertical (instead of relying on experimenters' intuitions). Richardson et al. (2003) predicted an interaction between the linguistic and

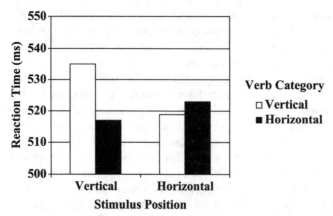

FIGURE 11.7. Reaction times to an unrelated visual stimulus as a function of the primary axis of orientation of the image schema belonging to a verb just heard (Richardson, Spivey, Barsalou, & McRae, 2003). Results reveal an interaction whereby the spatial extent of the image schema's layout interferes with perception in corresponding regions of the visual field.

visual tasks. That is, after comprehending a sentence with a vertical verb, and presumably activating a vertically extended image schema in some spatial arena of representation, participants' discrimination would thus be inhibited when an unrelated visual stimulus appeared in the top or bottom locations of the screen. Likewise, after a horizontal verb, the left and right positions should be inhibited.

The original 30 verbs were placed in present-tense sentences with typical agents and patients (plus some filler sentences), and were recorded by an experimenter speaking in a flat intonation and saved as mono mp3 sound files. The visual stimuli consisted of a central fixation cross, and a black circle and square that flashed for 200 ms above, below, or to the left or right of the fixation cross. Participants were instructed to identify the stimulus as quickly as possible, pressing one key to indicate a circle and another to indicate a square.

Reaction time results are shown in Figure 11.7. The four stimulus positions were collapsed into vertical and horizontal categories, since the norming data only distinguished verbs by their primary axes. As predicted, verb category interacted with stimulus position. Visual stimuli were identified faster in the vertical positions when preceded by a horizontal verb, and faster in the horizontal positions when preceded by a vertical verb. Interactions with concreteness did not approach significance, indicating that the effect was not significantly different for concrete and abstract verbs.

This result provides a first indication that comprehending a verb, whether concrete or abstract, automatically activates a visuospatial representation that (in its orientation of the primary axis, at least) resembles the image schema associated with the meaning of that verb. Moreover, because the verbs modulated perceptual performance in a spatially-specific manner predicted by the norming data, this suggests that Richardson et al.'s (2001) results were not an artefact of tasks requiring deliberate spatial judgments.

In a second experiment with the same set of sentences, Richardson et al. (2003) investigated how language comprehension interacts with a memory task. It has been robustly shown that imagery improves memory (Paivio, Yuille, & Smythe, 1966). Also, visual stimuli are remembered better when they are presented in the same spatial locations at presentation and test (Santa, 1977). Thus, it was hypothesized that spatial structure associated with a verb would influence the encoding of concurrent visual stimuli, which could then be measured later during retrieval.

During each block of study trials, 82 participants heard six sentences while line drawings of the corresponding agent and patient were presented sequentially in the center of the screen. During the test phase, the pictures were presented simultaneously in either a horizontal arrangement (side-by-side) or vertical arrangement (one above the other). Participants were instructed to indicate by button press whether the two pictures had been shown together as part of a sentence or not. In half of the test trials, the two pictures were taken from different sentences; in the other half (the critical trials) the pictures were from the same study sentence. It was predicted that the picture pairs would later be recognized faster if they were presented in an orientation consistent with the verb's image schema.

Results are shown in Figure 11.8. As predicted, verb category interacted with the orientation of the test stimuli. Pictures in a vertical arrangement were responded to faster if they were associated with a vertical verb, and

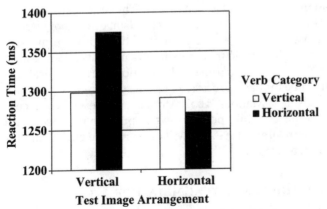

FIGURE 11.8. Reaction times to a related memory probe image as a function of the primary axis of orientation of the image schema belonging to a previously heard verb (Richardson, Spivey, Barsalou, & McRae, 2003). The interaction reveals that when the spatial arrangement of the probe images corresponded to the image schema's orientation, recall was faster.

pictures in a horizontal arrangement were responded to faster if they were associated with a horizontal verb. As before, interactions with concreteness did not approach significance, indicating that the effect was not significantly different for concrete and abstract verbs.

Thus, verb comprehension influenced how visual stimuli were encoded, in that recognition times were faster when the stimuli were tested in an orientation congruent with the verb's image schema. In contrast to the interference effect found in visual perception, image schemas facilitated performance in this memory task. One interpretation is that during study, verb comprehension activated an image schema. The spatial element of this image schema was imparted to the pictures, as if the verb image schema was acting as a scaffold for the visual memory. The pictures were then encoded in that orientation, and hence identified faster when presented at test in a congruent layout (e.g., Santa, 1977).

This set of findings with these 30 verbs constitutes persuasive evidence for spatially arranged image schemas being automatically activated as core components of linguistic meaning. And most recently, results from an offline forced choice experiment suggest that placing a verb in different syntactic frames can alter the orientation of the image schema's primary axis (Kako, Richardson, & Spivey, 2004). For example, although naive participants tended to select a vertically arranged image schema for a sentence like "The circle respected the square", they tended to select a horizontally arranged image schema for a sentence like "The circle and the square respected each other." Ongoing experiments are testing this syntactic modulation of the image schema's orientation in perception and memory tasks.

In addition to the theoretical and empirical advances provided by this work, there exists a methodological lesson as well. The series of offline and online experiments (Richardson et al., 2001; Richardson et al., 2003) stands as a powerful demonstration of the benefits of collecting norms from naïve language users of one's linguistic materials in advance, and then testing whether these aggregated meta-linguistic observations have implications for automatic real-time language processing (see also Bergen, Narayan, & Feldman, 2003; Coulson & Matlock, 2001; Matlock, in press). While cognitive linguistics should certainly be expected to provide the theoretical *framework a priori*, the theoretical *specifics* will often require empirical normative exploration in advance.

PERCEPTUAL SPACE AND CONCEPTUAL METAPHOR

We have recently been extending this empirical normative exploration of image-schematic influences to the topic of conceptual metaphors of space in verb meaning and linguistic aspect. The relationship between space and time in language has been the subject of intensive investigation for several decades. However, there are linguistic problems that, though they may appear superficially to be an instantiation of the conceptual relationship between space and time (a pattern observed regularly in language; cf. Lakoff, 1987), might be more parsimoniously explained as an illustration of the conceptual relationship between perceptual space and the linguistic instantiation of its properties, with no necessary appeal to a temporal explanation. Two examples discussed in this section are the Spanish copula verb/estar/and grammatical aspect.

The embodiment of spatial cognition is a central concern of cognitive linguistics. The behavior of the Spanish copula/estar/, notoriously difficult to account for by most linguistics theories, is easily explained within the cognitive linguistics paradigm as an example of how spatial cognition manifests itself in language. /Estar/has been traditionally considered one of a pair of copulas occurring in modern Spanish, typically translated into English, along with/ser/, as "to be". Any student who suffered through high school Spanish probably has dark tales to tell of receiving an apparently clear cut explanation of the function of these verbs, most commonly that/estar/was for temporary attributes and/ser/for permanent ones, only to be confronted with eternal lists of exceptions. If/estar/is for temporary attributes, why do we say/el está muerto/(he is dead) using/estar/and not/ser/? How can anyone be dead temporarily, barring the supernatural? If/ser/is for permanent attributes, why do we say/ ella es estudiante/(she is a student) using/ser/and not/estar/when people are not normally students for more than a temporary period of their lives (we would hope!)? Language scholars have been no less perplexed. Countless theories have been postulated to account for the dichotomy's less than predictable behavior. The most common of these can be divided into three categories; (1) temporary vs. permanent (stated above); (2) perfective vs imperfective; and (3) innate vs. noninnate (Delbecque, 1997.) These latter two theories run into similar inconsistencies as temporary vs. permanent. For (2) the explanation is borrowed from grammatical aspect where aspect is defined as "the internal temporal structure of an event." As such, an imperfective event is one unbounded in time and a perfective one is bounded. Examples from English are the sentence pairing (a)"John went to the store" vs. (b) "John was going to the store." Sentence (a) is bounded such that its beginning, middle and end are all encompassed in the temporal perspective of the speaker. Sentence (b) is unbounded in that the speaker is focused in the event's "ongoing" property. The verb/estar/is supposed to be the perfective copula in that it marks attributes that are "bounded" in time, while/ser/is supposed to mark those that are "unbounded." This explanation is especially productive for situations in which an attribute can appear with both verbs as in (c)/Elisa es triste/vs. (d)/Elisa está triste/. Both translate into (Elisa is sad). The difference is supposed to be that in (c) Elisa's sadness is unbounded in time, meaning that she is a sad person by constitution, while in (d) her sadness is bounded in time, meaning that she is sad because she just broke up with her boyfriend. Problems emerge when confronted with our original examples. It is quite difficult to construe being dead as a perfective event or being a student as an imperfective one. In fact, if anything, the opposite would appear more appropriate. The innate/non-innate theory transparently and predictably runs into similar problems. Though one is a woman innately,/soy mujer/, categorizing being a student as such is simply incorrect. Categorizing "being tired" as a non-innate attribute is not controversial. However, attempting to do the same with "being dead," is inadequate at best.

Reconceptualizing the so-called ser/estar copula problem using cognitive linguistics has a powerfully clarifying effect. By rejecting the classical notion that copulas are semantically colorless morphemes whose purpose is to serve as syntactic connectors between nouns and attributes (cf. Horton, 1995; Langacker, 1991), and instead analyzing these two verbs with the understanding that they are meaningful, motivated rather than arbitrary, as well as historical products, yields two hypotheses. The first is that the verbs are not a complementary copula system. The second, central to the present discussion, is that/estar/is a locative verb used in metaphoric extension, a phenomenon common to the world's languages.

Space and topic considerations are such that the discussion of why the two verbs are not actually a copula system, as traditionally construed, will not be elaborated upon here. Full details will be available in Gonzalez-Marquez and Spivey (2004). An elaborate exposition of copulas in general can be found in Pustet (2003).

Cognitive linguistics naturally postulates that/estar/is a locative verb now used in metaphorical extension. Accordingly, it is unsurprising that/estar/appears with equal ease in utterances such as 'Elisa está en la escuela' (Elisa is at school) and in 'Elisa está triste' (Elisa is sad). The latter utterance is thought to be an instantiation of metaphoric extension, i.e., Elisa is situated in the metaphoric space of sadness. This behavior is unsurprising because/estar/stems from the Latin 'stare'/to stand/and it is an etymological fact that verbs such as/to stand/and/to sit/tend to become location markers that sometimes are also used in metaphoric extension. Scandinavian languages such as Danish present a similar phenomenon in the verb 'stå'/to stand/ where it is used in utterances such as 'Maden står på bordet'/the food stands on the table/meaning "the food is on the table." Incidentally, the verb shares the same etymological origin as/estar/. An example from English is "From where I stand, that seems like a great deal." The behavior of "stand" is also more akin to the behavior of/estar/in that "stand" undergoes two metaphoric extensions. The first is that the act of standing is elaborated into a physical location, i.e. "from where I stand" that is then extended from a concrete physical location to the abstract, in the form of a reasoning perspective. A final example, also from English

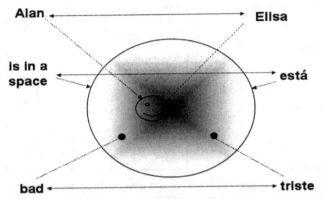

FIGURE 11.9. The verb/estar/can be understood as delineating a region of (in this case, emotional) state-space in which the Subject of the sentence is located, and attributing to that region the property denoted by the adjective.

that clearly illustrates the behavior of/estar/is the idea of being in a good or a bad space./Elisa está triste/"Elisa is sad" maps to the utterance "Alan is in a bad space" such that/estar/is the functional equivalent of "is in a space" and thus "Elisa" and "triste," and "Alan" and "bad" share parallel relationships with each other (see Figure 11.9).

The verb/estar/is in effect a grammaticalized instantiation of the idea of "being in a space." As such, attributes that are inferable about 'being in a space' are inferable about the use of the verb. Temporariness is predictable because that an object should be in a space does not imply permanence. Perfectivity is predictable given the temporariness implied in "being in a space," i.e., the act of being in the target space is assumed to be bounded in time or having a contained duration. Noninnateness is predictable because it is not assumed that an entity that can be moved in and out of a space has anything other than an arbitrary relationship to that space. Though a parsimonious explanation, the challenge comes in testing the hypothesis that/estar/is about space.

In our experiment (Gonzalez-Marquez & Spivey, 2004), subjects matched a spoken sentence with one of four image-schema options, two of which were filler stimuli to reduce the chances of participants developing strategies. The sentences referred to the objects depicted in the images. For example, stimulus sentences for the images below were 'La luna es arrugada' and 'La luna está arrugada,' both of which mean that the moon is wrinkled. (The copula/ser/was used here in the first sentence in the 3rd-person singular, i.e./es/as a control condition because it carries no spatial or locative implications.) The two key image schemas were designed so that one (Figure 11.10, left panel) showed an object in isolation without spatial reference and the other (Figure 11.10, right panel) showed the object in a space that contained the given attribute, in this case wrinkledness.

FIGURE 11.10. A schematic example rendition of the images used in Gonzalez-Marquez and Spivey's (2004) image-schema experiment with the Spanish verb/estar/. The left image treats the wrinkledness of the moon as an intrinsic property of the object, whereas the right image treats the moon's wrinkledness as the result of it being located in an attribute-space of wrinkledness.

Due to the spatial properties inherent to the verb/estar/, we predicted that subjects would choose the image in the right panel of Figure 11.10 for sentences containing/estar/, and the image in the left panel of Figure 11.10 for those containing the control verb/ser/. We expected the two other filler images to be rarely selected with these verbs.

Results from 356 participants show that the prediction was supported. With the verb/estar/, the metaphoric "attribute-space" image (e.g., right panel of Figure 11.10, for the case of a wrinkledness attribute) was chosen 51% of the time (see Figure 11.11). With the control verb/ser/, it was chosen only 21% of the time. These results suggest that/estar/is sensitive to a

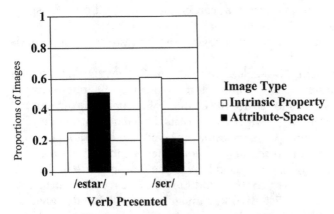

FIGURE 11.11. Proportions of critical images (from Figure 11.9) selected to best characterize sentences with/ser/and with/estar/. (Filler images were typically selected less than 20% of the time.)

spatial configuration in which the entity in question is located within an unbounded space qualified with the target attribute.

With/estar/, the metaphorical use of the spatial property of location may suffice to explain the verb's behavior. However, grammatical aspect is considerably more complex. Grammatical aspect, we suggest, may well present a variation on this same theme, albeit with an additional set of bells and whistles. Like previous analyses of/estar/, one of the most common problematizations of aspect has involved time. The definition of aspect as "the internal temporal structure of an event" (e.g., Chung & Timberlake, 1985; Li & Shirai, 2000) is commonly accepted and has produced countless volumes with time as the cornerstone of the analyses. The goal of most of these analyses, however, has been to describe the manifestation of the phenomena in a language or set of languages, and not to account for its occurrence as a cognitive manifestation. Langacker (1987), Narayanan (1997), and Janda (2004) have made important strides in this latter direction. Langacker postulated that aspect was grounded in our understanding of count versus mass nouns. Narayanan suggested that it was based on motion, and Janda on substances versus objects. It would be unwise to dismiss these different analyses out of hand and simply attempt yet another analysis that was independent of them. A more useful route, instead, is to take what they have in common as a point of departure.

A survey of languages (Li & Shirai, 2000) quickly reveals the virtual universality of marking events as either completed or ongoing, a distinction sometimes grammaticized as perfectivity vs. imperfectivity. Comparing the accounts mentioned above (Janda, 2004; Langacker, 1991; Narayanan, 1997) with the marking of events as completed or ongoing reveals a broad commonality in the form of a perceptual dichotomy: boundedness versus unboundedness. This virtual universality implies that this dichotomy is very likely to be grounded in the human cognitive apparatus (also implied in the above models), which in turn is fed by sensory perception. The question then becomes "Where and when in perception would such foundational physical manifestations of this dichotomy appear?" The answer we suggest is that they occur repeatedly in at least three modalities: vision, audition and touch. See Table 11.1.

Janda's (2004), Langacker's (1991), and Narayanan's (1997) models of aspect are very compelling, and they are compelling precisely because

TABLE 11.1. *Examples of Boundedness vs. Unboundedness in Three Modalities*

	Bounded	Unbounded
Vision	Looking at a rock	Looking at the sky
Touch	Grasping a baby bottle	Dipping a hand in water
Audition	The sound of a glass hitting the floor	The sound of the wind

they all tap into the bounded/unbounded perceptual dichotomy. Their one weakness comes in assuming that the patterns found in aspect are only mirrored in the theorist's chosen manifestation. Parrill (2000, p. 4) states "The claim that aspect is grounded in the motor programs responsible for bodily movement is based on the assumption that when two systems have identical organizational structure, principles of parsimoniousness dictate that they are likely to share much of their physical (neural) structure." This same argument can be used in support of a model of a sensorimotor grounding for aspect that includes but is not limited to motor programs, count vs. mass nouns or substances vs. objects. Sound, for example, shares many of the qualities described as proper to motion. Birds chirping comprise an iterative event. The sound of the ocean's roar is an ongoing event. Speech sounds that end abruptly (as happens when a child encounters adults having a conversation not meant for his ears) are telic events. The point is that these properties are not solely to be found in one perceptual or motor modality. They are, in fact, found in many places.

In a series of experiments that have been designed to test these hypotheses in different modalities, we are beginning to explore not how language influences perception but how perception influences language. We will limit our discussion to the tactile experiment as it is now in progress and the rather encouraging preliminary data warrant a brief report. Eight verbs were chosen that describe obviously concrete events (i.e., *walk, drive, dance,* and *sleep*) as well as less concrete ones (i.e., *think, enjoy, hope,* and *wait*). All were about open-ended events with no marked beginning or end, and all seemed natural in both perfective and imperfective form. During the experiment, participants were blindfolded and told that they would be asked to touch something for about 30 seconds, after which they would be given a noun and a bare verb (e.g., "man and walk") with which to make a sentence. The tactile stimuli were of two types, bounded objects such as a soap dish or unbounded substances such as sand. We predicted that bounded stimuli would prime speakers for perfective sentences and that unbounded stimuli would prime them for imperfective sentences.

Results from nine participants show a marked difference in the aspectual marking of the sentences produced (see Figure 11.12). When a participant manipulated a bounded stimulus, such as a small glass sculpture, she was slightly more likely to produce a perfective sentence (e.g., "The woman thought about her life.") than an imperfective one (e.g., "The woman was thinking about her life."). In contrast, when a participant manipulated an unbounded stimulus, such as water in a large bucket, she was more likely to produce an imperfective sentence than a perfective one. (No substantial differences between concrete and abstract verbs have been observed at this point.) Though certainly preliminary, this result hints at a relationship between sensorimotor processing and grammatical aspect that behooves

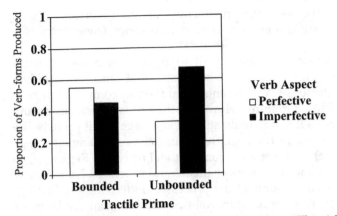

FIGURE 11.12. Proportion of perfective sentences (e.g., "The girl drank the milk.") and imperfective sentences (e.g., "The girl was drinking the milk.") produced by participants tactilely primed with bounded objects and with unbounded substances.

further exploration. We suggest that, as indicated by the/estar/ experiment, there may be conceptual metaphorical uses of spatial frames of reference (e.g., LOCATION IS ATTRIBUTE OWNERSHIP, PROXIMITY IS SIMILARITY, BOUNDEDNESS IS TEMPORAL DELIMITATION, UNBOUNDEDNESS IS TEMPORAL LIMITLESSNESS) that cross-cut language and the rest of perception, action, and cognition (e.g., Gibbs, 1996; Lakoff, 1987) and occasionally allow temporal properties to "piggyback" on spatial formats of representation (e.g., Boroditsky, 2000, 2001).

GENERAL DISCUSSION

We have presented evidence that metalinguistic judgments from linguistically naïve participants, as well as real-time verb comprehension and production, interacts with perceptual-spatial processes – at least with verbs that imply literal or metaphorical spatial relationships. In one study, the verbs were normatively categorized as having either horizontal or vertical image schemas (Richardson et al., 2001). Then the spatial orientation of these verbs' image schemas was shown to exert influences on spatial perception and memory, interfering with performance on a visual discrimination task, and facilitating performance in the encoding of a visual memory (Richardson et al., 2003). In additional studies, the conceptual metaphorical use of spatial location as an indicator of attribute ownership was shown to underlie the meaning of the Spanish verb/estar/, thus fundamentally differentiating it from its putative partner-copula/ser/(Gonzalez-Marquez & Spivey, 2004). Moreover, we reported preliminary evidence for the sensorimotor spatial properties of boundedness and unboundedness being related to the aspectual distinction between perfective verb forms (e.g., "Jerry ate.") and imperfective verb forms (e.g., "Jerry was eating.").

When one considers the ubiquity of topographical maps in cortex (cf. Swindale, 2001), it should not be surprising that much of cognition, even language, functions via representational formats comprised of two-dimensional map-like structures. However, the precise mechanisms and processes that carry out this spatialization of language is still yet to be determined. Future work in the cognitive neuroscience of language (e.g., Pulvermüller, 2002) and computational modeling (e.g., Regier, 1996) promises to reveal some of those mechanisms and processes. Nonetheless, even without explicit accounts of the processes underlying the findings reported herein, there are some important conclusions that can be made from this evidence for the role of continuous metric spaces in cognition and language.

These findings of linguistic processing relying so heavily on visual and other spatially laid out formats of representation point toward some profound implications looming on the horizon. From a broad perspective, topographic layouts for cognitive representations pose a significant problem for traditional symbol-minded accounts of both language in particular and cognition in general. True digital symbol manipulation would require a kind of neural architecture that is very different from the analog two-dimensional maps that might implement image-schematic representations (cf. Regier, 1996) and that we know populate much of cortex (e.g., Churchland & Sejnowski, 1992; Swindale, 2001). Individual neurons devoted to individual concepts were once considered as a possible neural mechanism of symbolic thought (cf. Lettvin, 1995; Rose, 1996), but such a representational scheme is now considered highly unlikely (e.g., Barlow, 1972; Pouget, Dayan, & Zemel, 2000). Thus, the future of cognitive science may hold for us a popular view of perception and cognition in which much of it is implemented in the two-dimensional spatial formats of representation that we know exist in the brain, without the use of discrete symbolic representations that we have yet to witness.

From a more focused perspective, the offline and online experimental results described herein have important implications for research in cognitive linguistics and psycholinguistics. First, they provide experimental evidence that converges with linguistic theory (Lakoff, 1987; Langacker, 1987; Talmy, 1983) and norming data (Gibbs, 1996) in support of the cognitive psychological reality of image schemas and the rich relationship between perceptual space and linguistic conceptual space (Gibbs & Colston, 1995). Second, a subset of the experiments demonstrate that linguistic representations are automatically linked with sensorimotor mechanisms (and not just metacognitive deliberations) in that they influence real-time performance in a perceptual task and a delayed memory task.

For traditional, as well as many conventional, theoretical frameworks in cognitive psychology and linguistics, language processing and spatial perception are not expected to be tightly coupled. These perspectives view language as an encapsulated system of amodal symbol manipulation, functioning independently from what is typically viewed as perceptual processing and the computation of knowledge regarding how entities and objects interact in the world (Chomsky, 1965; Fodor, 1983; Markman & Dietrich, 2000). This modular view certainly would not predict such interactions between language and perception.

However, several strands of behavioral research serve to buttress these observations of automatic cross-modal activation taking place during language processing. For example, the headband-mounted eyetracking studies, discussed in the introduction, provide several examples of the incremental comprehension of language being rapidly integrated with visual processing (e.g., Spivey-Knowlton et al., 1998; Tanenhaus et al., 1995). Moreover, priming studies have shown that at the moment of verb comprehension, typical agents, patients and instruments of that verb become activated (Ferretti, McRae, & Hatherell, 2001). It is argued that such thematic role information might be part of generalized situational knowledge that is rapidly activated during online language comprehension. It seems plausible that, at least with certain verbs, spatial information might be part of such generalized knowledge, and that the process of integrating this knowledge might involve perceptual mechanisms. A similar interplay between linguistic and perceptual processes was demonstrated by Kaden, Wapner, and Werner (1955),who found that subjective eye level can be influenced by the spatial components of words. Subjects sat in a dark room and saw luminescent words at their objective eye level. Subjects then had the words moved up or down, until they were at their subjective eye level. Words with an upward connotation ("climbing," "raising") had to be placed slightly lower to be perceived as being at eye level, whereas words with a downward component ("falling," "plunging") had to be placed slightly above the objective eye level.

It has been claimed that generating a representation of a text engages visuo-spatial processing, even when the text does not involve any description of spatial relations (Fincher-Kiefer, 2001), and that picture-story comprehension has many of the features of text comprehension at the level of neural activation (Robertson et al., 1999). Two recent studies have shown that reading a sentence can prime responses to depictions of items described in the sentence, specific to their orientation (Stanfield & Zwaan, 2001) and shape (Zwaan, Stanfield, & Yaxley, 2002), even though these attributes were only implied in the text. For example, after reading "John hammered the nail into the wall," participants saw a picture of a nail and verified that the object was featured in the sentence. Response times were faster when the nail was depicted in a horizontal rather than vertical orientation. The reverse was true if the sentence was "John hammered the nail into the floor." These results suggest that, during comprehension, readers generate some form of perceptual simulation that represents attributes implicit in the text. Similarly, a perceptual simulation appears to be generated during concept property verification tasks (Kan, Barsalou, Solomon, Minor, & Thompson-Schill, 2003; Solomon & Barsalou, 2001).

There is evidence that some form of *motor* simulation may also accompany language comprehension. For example, Glenberg and Kaschak (2002) had participants judge the sensibility of actions described in a sentence (e.g., "Close the drawer" vs. "Boil the air"). Judgments were made by a response that involved a hand movement either away or toward the body. Glenberg and Kaschak found what they termed an "action-sentence compatibility effect": participants were faster to make their response if they had to make a physical action (toward/away from the body) that was in the same direction as the described action ("Close/open the drawer"). Interestingly, as predicted by Richardson et al.'s (2003) results with abstract verbs, this effect also held for the transfer of abstract entities, as in "Liz told you the story" vs. "You told Liz the story."

These recent findings in the literature, as well as the results of the experiments detailed in the previous sections of this chapter, form a contiguous fabric of empirical support for the assertion, often made by cognitive linguistics, that certain characteristics of word meaning and grammar, both literal and metaphoric, are comprised of spatial representations. Moreover, the results endorse perceptual-motor theories of cognitive representation in general (e.g., Barsalou, 1999; Mandler, 1992) because these spatial representations are automatically activated during language comprehension and production, and they appear to be tightly coupled with concurrent perception, action, and cognition. We hope to see future research in this general area continue the interweaving of in-depth theoretical development (e.g., Talmy, 1983; see also Coulson, 2001) with normative treatment of linguistic materials (Gibbs, 1996) and real-time perceptual/cognitive experimentation (Richardson et al., 2003).

ACKNOWLEDGMENTS

Much of the work described herein was supported by NIMH grant #RO1-63691 to the first author and by Cornell Sage Fellowships to the second and third authors. The authors are grateful to Ulric Neisser, Seana Coulson, Irene Mittelberg, Rick Dale, Florencia Reali, and Ben Hiles for comments on the work, and to Elizabeth Goulding, Kola Ijaola, Pete Ippel, and Ji Sook Moon for assistance with stimulus construction and data collection.

References

Allopenna, P. D., Magnuson, J. S., & Tanenhaus, M. K. (1998). Tracking the time course of spoken word recognition using eye movements: Evidence for continuous mapping models. *Journal of Memory and Language 38*, 419–439.

Altmann, G., & Kamide, Y. (2004). Now you see it, now you don't: mediating the mapping between language and the visual world. In J. Henderson & F. Ferreira (Eds.), *The Interaction of Vision, Language, and Action*. Academic Press.

Altmann, G., & Steedman, M. (1988). Interaction with context during human sentence processing. *Cognition 30*, 191–238.

Antrobus, J. S., Antrobus, J. S., & Singer, J. L. (1964). Eye movements accompanying daydreaming, visual imagery, and thought suppression. *Journal of Abnormal and Social Psychology 69*, 244–252.

Baddeley, A. D. (1986). *Working memory*. Oxford: Oxford University Press.

Ballard, D. H., Hayhoe, M. M., Pook, P. K., & Rao, R. P. N. (1997). Deictic codes for the embodiment of cognition. *Behavioral and Brain Sciences 20*, 723–767.

Barlow, H. (1972). Single units and sensation: A neuron doctrine for perceptual psychology. *Perception 1*, 371–394.

Barsalou, L. W. (1999). Perceptual symbol systems. *Behavioral and Brain Sciences 22*, 577–660.

Bergen, B., Narayan, S., & Feldman, J. (2003). Embodied verbal semantics: Evidence from an image-verb matching task. In R. Alterman & D. Kirsh (Eds.), *Proceedings of the 25th Annual Conference of the Cognitive Science Society*. Boston: Cognitive Science Society.

Boroditsky, L. (2000). Metaphoric structuring: Understanding time through spatial metaphors. *Cognition 75*, 1–28.

Boroditsky, L. (2001). Does language shape thought? Mandarin and English speakers' conceptions of time. *Cognitive Psychology 43*, 1–22.

Brandt, S. A., & Stark, L. W. (1997). Spontaneous eye movements during visual imagery reflect the content of the visual scene. *Journal of Cognitive Neuroscience 9*, 27–38.

Carlson-Radvansky, L. A., Covey, E. S., & Lattanzi, K. M. (1999). What effects on "where": Functional influences on spatial relations. *Psychological Science 10* (6), 516–521.

Chafee, M. V., & Goldman-Rakic, P. S. (1998). Matching patterns of activity in primate prefrontal area 8a and parietal area 7ip neurons during a spatial working memory task. *Journal of Neurophysiology 79*, 2919–2940.

Chafee, M. V., & Goldman-Rakic, P. S. (2000). Inactivation of parietal and prefrontal cortex reveals interdependence of neural activity during memory-guided saccades. *Journal of Neurophysiology 83*, 1550–1566.

Chambers, C. G., Tanenhaus, M. K., Eberhard, K. M., Filip, H., & Carlson, G. N. (2002). Circumscribing referential domains during real-time language comprehension. *Journal of Memory & Language 47*, 30–49.

Chomsky, N. (1965). *Aspects of the Theory of Syntax*. Cambridge, MA: MIT Press.

Chung, S., & Timberlake, A. (1985). Tense, aspect and mood. In T. Shopen (Ed.), *Language, Typology and Syntactic Description. Volume 3: Grammatical Categories and the Lexicon* (pp. 202–258). Cambridge: Cambridge University Press.

Churchland, P. S., & Sejnowski, T. J. (1992) *The Computational Brain*. Cambridge, MA: MIT Press.

Clark, H. (1992). *Arenas of Language Use*. Chicago: University of Chicago Press.

Clausner, T. C., & Croft, W. (1999). Domains and image schemas. *Cognitive Linguistics 10*, 1–31.

Coltheart, M. (1981). The MRC psycholinguistic database. *Quarterly Journal of Experimental Psychology 33A*, 497–505.

Coulson, S., & Matlock, T. (2001). Metaphor and the space structuring model. *Metaphor and Symbol 16*, 295–316

Coulson, S. (2001). *Semantic Leaps: Frame-Shifting and Conceptual Blending in Meaning Construction*. New York: Cambridge University Press.

Crain, S., & Steedman, M. (1985). On not being led up the garden path. In D. R. Dowty, L. Kartunnen, & A. M. Zwicky (Eds.), *Natural Language Parsing*. Cambridge: Cambridge University Press.

Craver-Lemley, C., & Arterberry, M. E. (2001). Imagery-induced interference on a visual detection task. *Spatial Vision 14*, 101–119.

Craver-Lemley, C., & Reeves, A. (1992). How visual imagery interferes with vision. *Psychological Review 89*, 633–649.

Delbecque, N. (1997). The Spanish copulas SER and ESTAR. In M. Verspoor, K. D. Lee, & E. Sweetser (Eds.), *Lexical and Syntactical Constructions and the Construction of Meaning* (pp. 247–270). Amsterdam/Philadelphia: J. Benjamins.

Demarais, A. M., & Cohen, B. H. (1998). Evidence for image scanning eye movements during transitive inference. *Biological Psychology 49*, 229–247.

Dietrich, E., & Markman, A. B. (2003). Discrete thoughts: Why cognition must use discrete representations. *Mind and Language 18*, 95–119.

Douglas, R. J., Koch C., Mahowald, M., Martin K. A., & Suarez, H. H. (1995). Recurrent excitation in neocortical circuits. *Science 269*, 981–985.

Duhamel, J., Colby, C., & Goldberg, M. (1992). The updating of the representation of visual space in parietal cortex by intended eye movements. *Science 255*, 90–92.

Eberhard, K., Spivey-Knowlton, M., Sedivy, J., & Tanenhaus, M. (1995). Eye movements as a window into real-time spoken language comprehension in natural contexts. *Journal of Psycholinguistic Research 24*, 409–436.

Elman, J. L., & McClelland, J. L. (1988). Cognitive penetration of the mechanisms of perception: Compensation for coarticulation of lexically restored phonemes. *Journal of Memory and Language 27*, 143–165.

Farah, M. J. (1985). Psychophysical evidence for a shared representational medium for mental images and percepts. *Journal of Experimental Psychology 114*, 91–103.

Ferretti, T. R., McRae, K., & Hatherell, A. (2001). Integrating verbs, situation schemas, and thematic role concepts. *Journal of Memory and Language 44*, 516–547.

Fincher-Kiefer, R. (2001). Perceptual components of situation models. *Memory and Cognition 29*, 336–343.

Finke, R. A. (1985). Theories relating mental imagery to perception. *Psychological Bulletin 98*, 236–259.

Fodor, J. A. (1983). *The Modularity of Mind*. Cambridge, MA: MIT Press.

Gazzaniga, M. (2000). Cerebral specialization and interhemispheric communication: Does the corpus callosum enable the human condition? *Brain 123*, 1293–1326.

Georgopoulos, A. P., Schwartz, A. B., & Kettner, R. E. (1986). Neuronal population coding of movement direction. *Science 223*, 1416–1419.

Gibbs, R. W. (1996). Why many concepts are metaphorical. *Cognition 61*, 309–319.

Gibbs, R. W., & Colston, H. L. (1995). The cognitive psychological reality of image schemas and their transformations. *Cognitive Linguistics 6*, 347–378.

Gibbs, R. W., Ström, L. K., & Spivey-Knowlton, M. J. (1997). Conceptual metaphors in mental imagery for proverbs. *Journal of Mental Imagery 21*, 83–109.

Glenberg, A., & Kaschak, M. (2002). Grounding language in action. *Psychonomic Bulletin & Review 9*, 558–565.

Gold, J. I., & Shadlen, M. N. (2000). Representation of a perceptual decision in developing oculomotor commands. *Nature 404*, 390–394.

Goldman-Rakic, P. S. (1993). Working memory and the mind. In *Mind and brain: Readings from Scientific American magazine* (pp. 67–77). New York: W. H. Freeman.

Gonzalez-Marquez, M., & Spivey, M. J. (2004). Mapping from real to abstract locations: Experimental evidence from the Spanish verb ESTAR. Unpublished manuscript.

Hale, S. M., & Simpson, H. M. (1970). Effects of eye movements on the rate of discovery and the vividness of visual images. *Perception and Psychophysics 9*, 242–246.

Haxby, J. V., Gobbini, M. I., Furey, M. L., Ishai, A., Schouten, J. L., & Pietrini, P. (2001). Distributed and overlapping representations of faces and objects in ventral temporal cortex. *Science 293*, 2425–2430.

Hayward, W. G., & Tarr, M. J. (1995). Spatial language and spatial representation. *Cognition 55*, 39–84.

Hebb, D. O. (1968). Concerning imagery. *Psychological Review 75*, 466–477.

Hildebrandt, B., Moratz, R., Rickheit, G., & Sagerer, G. (1999). Cognitive modelling of vision and speech understanding. In G. Rickheit & C. Habel (Eds.), *Mental Models in Discourse Processing and Reasoning. Advances in Psychology 128* (pp. 213–236). Amsterdam, The Netherlands: Elsevier Science Publishers.

Horton, B. (1995). What Are Copula Verbs? In E. Casad (Ed.), *Cognitive Linguistics in the Redwoods: The Expansion of a New Paradigm in Linguistics* (pp. 319–346). Berlin, Germany: Walter de Gruyter & Co.

Jackendoff, (2002). *The Foundations of Language.* Oxford/New York: Oxford University Press.

Janda, L. (2004). A metaphor in search of a source domain: the categories of Slavic aspect. Unpublished manuscript.

Kaden, S. E., Wapner, S., & Werner, H. (1955). Studies in physiognomic perception: II. Effect of directional dynamics of pictured objects and of words on the position of the apparent horizon. *Journal of Psychology 39*, 61–70.

Kako, E., Richardson, D., & Spivey, M. (2004). Effects of syntactic context on the spatial orientation of verb image schemas. Unpublished manuscript.

Kan, I. P., Barsalou, L. W., Solomon, K. O., Minor, J. K., & Thompson-Schill, S. L. (2003). Role of mental imagery in a property verification task: fMRI evidence for perceptual representations of conceptual knowledge. *Cognitive Neuropsychology 20*, 525–540.

Keysar, B., Shen, Y., Glucksberg, S., & Horton, W. (2000). Conventional language: How metaphorical is it? *Journal of Memory and Language 43*, 576–593.

Knoeferle, P., Crocker, M., Scheepers, C., & Pickering, M. (2003). Actions and roles: Using depicted events for disambiguation and reinterpretation in German and English. In R. Alterman & D. Kirsh (Eds.), *Proceedings of the 25th Annual Conference of the Cognitive Science Society.* Boston: Cognitive Science Society.

Kuelpe, O. (1902). Ueber die objectivirung und subjectivirung von sinnesein-drucken [On objective and subjective sensory impressions]. *Philosophische Studien 49*, 508–556.

Kuperberg, G. R., Holcomb, P. J., Sitnikova, T., Greve, D., Dale, A. M., & Caplan, D. (2003). Distinct patterns of neural modulation during the processing of concep-tual and syntactic anomalies. *Journal of Cognitive Neuroscience 15*, 272–293.

Laeng, B., & Teodorescu, D. S. (2002). Eye scanpaths during visual imagery reenact those of perception of the same visual scene. *Cognitive Science 26*, 207–231.

Lakoff, G. (1987). *Women, Fire, and Dangerous things: What Categories Reveal about the Mind.* Chicago: University of Chicago Press.

Lakoff, G., & Johnson, M. (1999). *Philosophy in the Flesh: The Embodied Mind and Its Challenge to Western Thought.* New York: Basic Books.

Langacker, R. W. (1987). *Foundations of Cognitive Grammar: Theoretical Prerequisites.* Stanford, CA: Stanford University Press.

Langacker, R. W. (1990) *Foundations of Cognitive Grammar, Vol. 2: Descriptive Appli-cations Prerequisites.* Stanford, CA: Stanford University Press.

Langacker, R. W. (1991). *Concept, Image, Symbol: The Cognitive Basis of Grammar.* Berlin-New York: Mouton de Gruyter.

Lettvin, J. Y. (1995). J. Y. Lettvin on grandmother cells. In M. Gazzaniga (Ed.), *The Cognitive Neurosciences* (pp. 434–435). Cambridge, MA: MIT Press.

Li, P., & Shirai, Y. (2000). *The Acquisition of Lexical and Grammatical Aspect.* Berlin: Mouton de Gruyter.

Logan, G. D. (1994). Spatial attention and the apprehension of spatial relations. *Journal of Experimental Psychology: Human Perception and Performance 20*, 1015–1036.

Magnuson, J. S., McMurray, B., Tanenhaus, M. K., & Aslin, R. N. (2003). Lexical ef-fects on compensation for coarticulation: The ghost of Christmash past. *Cognitive Science 27*, 285–298.

Magnuson, J. S., Tanenhaus, M. K., Aslin, R. N., & Dahan, D. (2003). The time course of spoken word learning and recognition: Studies with artificial lexicons. *Journal of Experimental Psychology: General 132*, 202–227.

Mandler, J. M. (1992). How to build a baby: II. Conceptual primitives. *Psychological Review 99*, 587–604.

Marcus, G. F. (2001). *The Algebraic Mind: Integrating Connectionism and Cognitive Science.* Cambridge, MA: MIT Press.

Marian, V., & Spivey, M. (2003). Bilingual and monolingual processing of competing lexical items. *Applied Psycholinguistics 24*, 173–193.

Markman, A., & Dietrich, E. (2000). Extending the classical view of representation. *Trends in Cognitive Science 4*, 470–475.

Marslen-Wilson, W. (1987). Functional parallelism in word recognition. *Cognition 25*, 71–102.

Matlock, T. (in press). Fictive motion as cognitive simulation. *Memory and Cognition*.

McClelland, J. L., & Elman, J. L. (1986). The TRACE model of speech perception. *Cognitive Psychology 18*, 1–86.

McGurk, H., & MacDonald, J. W. (1976). Hearing lips and seeing voices. *Nature 264*, 746–748.

Murphy, G. (1996). On metaphoric representation. *Cognition 60*, 173–204.

Narayanan, S. (1997). Talking the talk is like walking the walk: A computational model of verbal aspect. In M. G. Shafto and P. Langley (Eds.), *Proceedings of the 19th Annual Conference of the Cognitive Science Society*. Mahwah, NJ: Erlbaum.

Neisser, U. (1967). *Cognitive psychology*. Englewood Cliffs, NJ: Prentice Hall.

Ojemann (1983). Brain organization for language from the perspective of electrical stimulation mapping. *Behavioral and Brain Sciences 6*, 189–230

Paivio, A., Yuille, J. C., & Smythe, P. C. (1966). Stimulus and response abstractness, imagery, and meaningfulness, and reported mediators in paired-associate learning. *Canadian Journal of Psychology 20*, 362–377.

Parrill, F. (2000). *Hand To Mouth: Linking Spontaneous Gesture and Aspect*. Unpublished B.A. Honors Thesis, Department of Linguistics, University of California, Berkeley. (http://mcneilllab.uchicago.edu/pdfs/parrill.pdf)

Perky, C. W. (1910). An experimental study of imagination. *American Journal of Psychology 21*, 422–452.

Pouget, A., Dayan, P., & Zemel, R. S. (2000). Inference and computation with population codes. *Annual Review of Neuroscience 26*, 381–410.

Pulvermüller, F. (2002). *The Neuroscience of Language: On Brain Circuits of Words and Serial Order*. New York: Cambridge University Press.

Pustet, R. (2003). *Copulas: Universals in the Categorization of the Lexicon*. Oxford: Oxford University Press.

Pylyshyn, Z. W. (1989). The role of location indexes in spatial perception: A sketch of the FINST spatial index model. *Cognition 32*, 65–97.

Pylyshyn, Z. W. (2001). Visual indexes, preconceptual objects, and situated vision. *Cognition 80*, 127–158.

Rayner, K., Carlson, M., & Frazier, L. (1983). The interaction of syntax and semantics during sentence processing: Eye movements in the analysis of semantically biased sentences. *Journal of Verbal Learning and Verbal Behavior 22*, 358–374.

Regier, T. (1996). *The Human Semantic Potential: Spatial Language and Constrained Connectionism*. Cambridge, MA: MIT Press.

Regier, T., & Carlson, L. A. (2001). Grounding spatial language in perception: An empirical and computational investigation. *Journal of Experimental Psychology: General 130*, 273–298.

Richardson, D. C., & Spivey, M. J. (2000). Representation, space and Hollywood Squares: Looking at things that aren't there anymore. *Cognition 76*, 269–295.

Richardson, D. C., Spivey, M. J., Barsalou, L. W., & McRae, K. (2003). Spatial representations activated during real-time comprehension of verbs. *Cognitive Science 27*, 767–780.

Richardson, D. C., Spivey, M. J., Edelman, S., & Naples, A. D. (2001). "Language is spatial": Experimental evidence for image schemas of concrete and abstract verbs. *Proceedings of the 23rd Annual Conference of the Cognitive Science Society* (pp. 845–850) Mahwah, NJ: Erlbaum.

Robertson, D. A., Gernsbacher, M. A., & Guidotti, S. J. (1999). FMRI investigation of the comprehension of written vs. picture narratives. Paper presented at the Cognitive Neuroscience Society Annual Meeting, Washington, DC.

Rose, D. (1996). Some reflections on (or by?) grandmother cells. *Perception 25*, 881–886.

Roy, D., & Mukherjee, N. (in press). Visual context driven semantic priming of speech recognition and understanding. *Computer Speech and Language.*

Ruggieri, V. (1999). The running horse stops: The hypothetical role of the eyes in imagery of movement. *Perceptual and Motor Skills 89*, 1088–1092.

Santa, J. L. (1977). Spatial transformations of words and pictures. *Journal of Experimental Psychology: Human Learning and Memory 3*, 418–427.

Schall, J. D. (2000). Decision making: From sensory evidence to a motor command. *Current Biology 10*, R404–R406.

Scheerer, M., & Lyons, J. (1957). Line drawings and matching responses to words. *Journal of Personality 25*, 251–273.

Schober, M. F. (1995). Speakers, addressees, and frames of reference: whose effort is minimized in conversations about locations? *Discourse Processes 20*, 219–247.

Scripture, E. W. (1896). Measuring hallucinations. *Science 3*, 762–763.

Sedivy, J. C., Tanenhaus, M. K., Chambers, C. G., & Carlson, G. N. (1999). Achieving incremental semantic interpretation through contextual representation. *Cognition 71*, 109–147.

Segal, S., & Gordon, P. E. (1969). The Perky Effect revisited: Blocking of visual signals by imagery. *Perceptual and Motor Skills 28*, 791–797.

Solomon, K. O., & Barsalou, L. W. (2001). Representing properties locally. *Cognitive Psychology 43*, 129–169.

Spivey, M. J., & Geng, J. J. (2001). Oculomotor mechanisms activated by imagery and memory: Eye movements to absent objects. *Psychological Research 65*, 235–241.

Spivey, M., & Marian, V. (1999). Cross talk between native and second languages: Partial activation of an irrelevant lexicon. *Psychological Science 10*, 281–284.

Spivey, M., Richardson, D., & Fitneva, S. (2004). Thinking outside the brain: Spatial indices to linguistic and visual information. In J. Henderson and F. Ferreira (Eds.), *The Interaction of Vision Language and Action.* San Diego, CA: Academic Press.

Spivey, M., & Tanenhaus, M. (1998). Syntactic ambiguity resolution in discourse: Modeling the effects of referential context and lexical frequency. *Journal of Experimental Psychology: Learning, Memory, and Cognition 24*, 1521–1543.

Spivey, M., Tanenhaus, M., Eberhard, K., & Sedivy, J. (2002). Eye movements and spoken language comprehension: Effects of visual context on syntactic ambiguity resolution. *Cognitive Psychology 45*, 447–481.

Spivey, M., Tyler, M., Eberhard, K., & Tanenhaus, M. (2001). Linguistically mediated visual search. *Psychological Science 12*, 282–286.

Spivey, M. J., Tyler, M. J., Richardson, D. C., & Young, E. E. (2000). Eye movements during comprehension of spoken scene descriptions. *Proceedings of the 22nd Annual Conference of the Cognitive Science Society* (pp. 487–492). Mahwah, NJ: Erlbaum.

Spivey-Knowlton, M. (1996). *Integration of visual and linguistic information: Human data and model simulations.* Ph.D. dissertation, University of Rochester.

Spivey-Knowlton, M., & Sedivy, J. (1995). Resolving attachment ambiguities with multiple constraints. *Cognition 55*, 227–267.

Spivey-Knowlton, M., Tanenhaus, M., Eberhard, K., & Sedivy, J. (1998). Integration of visuospatial and linguistic information in real-time and real-space. In P. Olivier & K. Gapp (Eds.), *Representation and Processing of Spatial Expressions* (pp. 201–214). Mahwah, NJ: Erlbaum.

Stanfield, R. A., & Zwaan, R. A. (2001). The effect of implied orientation derived from verbal context on picture recognition. *Psychological Science 12*, 153–156.

Swindale, N. (2001). Cortical cartography: What's in a map? *Current Biology 11*, R764–R767.

Talmy, L. (1983). How language structures space. In H. L. Pick & L. P. Acredolo (Eds.), *Spatial orientation: Theory, research and application.* New York: Plenum Press.

Tanenhaus, M., Spivey Knowlton, M., Eberhard, K., & Sedivy, J. (1995). Integration of visual and linguistic information during spoken language comprehension. *Science 268*, 1632–1634.

Tyler, M., & Spivey, M. (2001). Spoken language comprehension improves the efficiency of visual search. *Proceedings of the 23rd Annual Conference of the Cognitive Science Society* (pp. 1060–1065). Mahwah, NJ: Erlbaum.

Van Orden, G. C., Jansen op de Haar, M. A., & Bosman, A. M. T. (1997). Complex dynamic systems also predict dissociations, but they do not reduce to autonomous components. *Cognitive Neuropsychology 14*, 131–165.

Zwaan, R. A., Stanfield, R. A., & Yaxley, R. H. (2002). Do language comprehenders routinely represent the shapes of objects? *Psychological Science 13*, 168–171.

12

Connecting Concepts to Each Other and the World

Robert L. Goldstone, Ying Feng, and Brian J. Rogosky

Consider two individuals, John and Mary, who each possess a number of concepts. How can we determine that John and Mary both have a concept of, say, **Horse**? John and Mary may not have exactly the same knowledge of horses, but it is important to be able to place their horse concepts into correspondence with one another, if only so that we can say things like, "Mary's concept of **horse** is much more sophisticated than John's." Concepts should be public in the sense that they can be possessed by more than one person (Fodor, 1998; Fodor & Lepore, 1992), and for this to be the possible, we must be able to determine correspondences, or translations, between two individuals' concepts.

There have been two major approaches in cognitive science to conceptual meaning that could potentially provide a solution to finding translations between conceptual systems. According to an "external grounding" account, concepts' meanings depend on their connection to the external world (this account is more thoroughly defined in the next section). By this account, the concept **Horse** means what it does because our perceptual apparatus can identify features that characterize horses. According to what we will call a "Conceptual web" account, concepts' meanings depend on their connections to each other. By this account, **Horse**'s meaning depends on **Gallop**, **Domesticated**, and **Quadruped**, and in turn, these concepts depend on other concepts, including **Horse** (Quine & Ullian, 1970).

In this chapter, we will first present a brief tour of some of the main proponents of conceptual web and external grounding accounts of conceptual meaning. Then, we will describe a computer algorithm that translates between conceptual systems. The initial goal of this computational work is to show how translating across systems is possible using only within-system relations, as is predicted by a conceptual web account. However, the subsequent goal is to show how the synthesis of external and internal information can dramatically improve translation. This work suggests that the external grounding and conceptual web accounts should not be viewed as competitors, but rather, that these two sources of information strengthen one another. In the final section of the chapter, we will present applications of the developed ABSURDIST algorithm to object recognition, large corpora translation, analogical reasoning, and statistical scaling.

In this chapter, we will be primarily interested in translating between conceptual systems, but many of our examples of translation will involve words. Concepts are not always equivalent to word meanings. For one thing, we can have concepts of things for which we do not have words, such as the cylindrical plastic sheath at the tips of shoelaces. Although there may not be a word for every concept we possess, behind every word there is a conceptual structure. Accordingly, when we talk about a concept of **Horse**, we are referring to the conceptual structure that supports people's use of the word "Horse" as well as their ability to recognize horses, predict the behavior of horses, and interact appropriately with horses.

GROUNDED CONCEPTS

For a concept to be externally grounded means that, in one way or another, its meaning is based on its connection to the world. There are several ways for this to occur. First, aspects of the concept may come to us via a perceptual system. Our concept of **Red**, **Fast**, and **Loud** all have clear perceptual components, but most, if not all (Barsalou, 1999), other concepts do as well. Second, a concept may be tied to objects in the world by deixis – by linguistically or physically pointing in a context. When a parent teaches a child the concept **Horse** by pointing out examples, this provides contextualized grounding for the child's emerging concept. A final third way, which we will not be addressing in our work, is that meaning may be tied directly to the external world without being mediated through the senses. Putnam's (1973) famous "twin earth" thought experiment is designed to show how the same internal, mental content can be associated with two different external referents. Putnam has us imagine a world, twin earth, that is exactly like our earth except that the compound we call water (H_2O) has a different atomic structure (xyz), while still looking, feeling, and acting like water as we on real earth know it. Two molecule-for-molecule identical individuals, one on earth and one on twin earth, would presumably have the same internal mental state when thinking "water is wet," and yet, Putnam argues, they *mean* something different. One means stuff that is actually, whether they know it or not, made up of H_2O, while the other means stuff that is made up of xyz. Putnam concludes that what is meant by a term is not determined solely by mental states, but rather depends upon the external world as well.

The rest of the chapters in this book give excellent grounds for believing that our concepts are not amodal and abstract symbolic representations, but rather are grounded in the external world via our perceptual systems. Lawrence Barsalou has presented a particularly influential and well-developed version of this account in the form of Perceptual Symbols Theory (Barsalou, 1999). By this account, conceptual knowledge involves activating brain areas dedicated for perceptual processing. When a concept is brought to mind, sensory-motor areas are reactivated to implement perceptual symbols. Even abstract concepts, such as truth and negation, are grounded in complex perceptual simulations of combined physical and introspective events. Several lines of empirical evidence are consistent with a perceptually grounded conceptual system. Detailed perceptual information is represented in concepts and this information is used when reasoning about those concepts (Barsalou et al., 2003). Concepts that are similar to one another give rise to similar patterns of brain activity, and a considerable amount of this activity is found in regions associated with perceptual processing (Simmons & Barsalou, 2003). When words are heard or seen, they spontaneously give rise to eye movements and perceptual images that would normally be evoked by the physical event designated by the words (Richardson, Spivey, Barsalou, & McRae, 2003; Stanfield & Zwaan, 2001). Switching from one modality to another during perceptual processing incurs a processing cost. The same cost is exhibited during the verification of concept properties, consistent with the notion that perceptual simulation underlies even verbal conceptual processing (Pecher, Zeelenberg, & Barsalou, 2003).

Much of the recent work on perceptual and embodied accounts of concepts has involved verbal stimuli such as words, sentences, and stories. The success of grounded accounts of language is noteworthy and surprising because of its opposition to the standard conception of language as purely arbitrary and symbolic. An acknowledgment of the perceptual grounding of language has lead to empirically validated computational models of language (Regier, 1996; Regier & Carlson, 2001). It has also provided insightful accounts of metaphors for understanding abstract notions such as time (Boroditsky, 2000; Boroditsky & Ramscar, 2002) and mathematics (Lakoff & Nunez, 2000). There has been a recent torrent of empirical results that are inconsistent with the idea that language comprehension is based on concepts that are symbols connected only to each other. Instead, the data support an embodied theory of meaning that relates the meaning of sentences to human perception and action (Glenberg & Kaschak, 2002; Glenberg & Robertson, 2000; Zwaan, Stanfield, & Yaxley, 2002).

Consistent with Barsalou's Perceptual Symbols Theory, other research has tried to unify the typically disconnected literatures on low-level perceptual processing and high-level cognition. Goldstone and Barsalou (1998) argue for strong parallels between processes traditionally considered to be perceptual on the one hand and conceptual on the other, and that perceptual processes are co-opted by abstract conceptual thought. Other research indicates bidirectional influences between our concepts and perceptions

(Goldstone, 2003; Goldstone, Lippa, & Shiffrin, 2001; Schyns, Goldstone, & Thibaut, 1998). Like a good pair of Birkenstock sandals that provide support by flexibly conforming to the foot, perception supports our concepts by conforming to these concepts. Perceptual learning results in perceptual and conceptual systems that are highly related. Taken together, this work suggests that apparently high-level conceptual knowledge and low-level perception may be more closely related than traditionally thought/perceived.

The case for grounding conceptual understanding in perception has a long philosophical history. As part of the British empiricist movement, David Hume (1740/1973) argued that our conceptual ideas originate in recombinations of sensory impressions. John Locke (1690) believed that our concepts ("ideas") have their origin either by our sense organs or by an internal sense of reflection. He argued further that our original ideas are derived from sensations (e.g., yellow, white, heat, cold, soft, and hard), and that the remaining ideas are derived from or depend upon these original ideas. The philosophical empiricist movement has been reinvigorated by Jesse Prinz (2002), who argues for sensory information as the ultimate ground for our concepts and beliefs. Stevan Harnad has similarly argued that concepts must be somehow connected to the external world, and this external connection establishes at least part of the meaning of the concept. In his article "The symbol grounding problem," Stevan Harnad (1990) considers the following thought experiment: "Suppose you had to learn Chinese as a *first* language and the only source of information you had was a Chinese/Chinese dictionary. [...]. How can you ever get off the symbol/symbol merry-go-round? How is symbol meaning to be grounded in something other than just more meaningless symbols? This is the symbol grounding problem" (pp. 339–340).

CONCEPTUAL WEBS

In stark antithesis to Harnad's thought experiment, artificial intelligence researchers have argued that conceptual meaning *can* come from dense patterns of relations between symbols even if the symbols have no causal connections to the external world. Lenat and Feigenbaum (1991) claim that "The problem of 'genuine semantics' ... gets easier, not harder, as the K[nowledge] B[ase] grows. In the case of an enormous KB, such as CYC's, for example, we could rename all of the frames and predicates as G001, G002, ... , and – using our knowledge of the world – reconstruct what each of their names must be" (p. 236). This claim is in direct opposition to Harnad's image of the symbol-symbol merry-go-round, and may seem ungrounded in several senses of the term. Still, depending on the power of intrasystem relations has been a mainstay of artificial intelligence, linguistics, and psychology for decades.

In semantic networks, concepts are represented by nodes in a network, and gain their functionality by their links to other concept nodes (Collins & Loftus, 1975; Quillian, 1967). Often times, these links are labeled, in which case different links refer to different kinds of relations between nodes. **Dog** would be connected to **Animal** by an **Is-a** link, to **Bone** by an **Eats** link, and to **Paw** by a **Has-a** link. These networks assume a conceptual web account of meaning because the networks' nodes are typically only connected to each other, rather than to an external world or perceptual systems.

A computational approach to word meaning that has received considerable recent attention has been to base word meanings solely on the patterns of co-occurrence between a large number of words in an extremely large text corpus (Burgess, Livesay, & Lund, 1998; Burgess & Lund, 2000; Landauer & Dumais, 1997). Mathematical techniques are used to create vector encodings of words that efficiently capture their co-occurrences. If two words, such as "cocoon" and "butterfly" frequently co-occur in an encyclopedia or enter into similar patterns of co-occurrence with other words, then their vector representations will be highly similar. The meaning of a word, its vector in a high dimensional space, is completely based on the contextual similarity of words to other words.

The traditional notion of concepts in linguistic theories is based upon conceptual webs. Ferdinand de Saussure (1915/1959) argued that all concepts are completely "negatively defined," that is, defined solely in terms of other concepts. He contended that "language is a system of interdependent terms in which the value of each term results solely from the simultaneous presence of the others" (p. 114) and that "concepts are purely differential and defined not in terms of their positive content but negatively by their relations with other terms in the system" (p. 117). By this account, the meaning of **Mutton** is defined in terms of other neighboring concepts. **Mutton**'s use does not extend to cover sheep that are living because there is another lexicalized concept to cover living sheep (**Sheep**), and **Mutton** does not extend to cover cooked pig because of the presence of **Pork**. Under this notion of interrelated concepts, concepts compete for the right to control particular regions of a conceptual space (see also Goldstone, 1996; Goldstone, Steyvers, & Rogosky, 2003). If the word **Mutton** did not exist, then "all its content would go to its competitors" (Saussure, 1915/1959, p. 116).

According to the conceptual role semantics theory in philosophy, the meaning of a concept is given by its role within its containing system (Block, 1986, 1999; Field, 1977; Rapaport, 2002). A conceptual belief, for example, that dogs bark, is identified by its unique causal role in the mental economy of the organism in which it is contained. A system containing only a single concept is not possible (Stich, 1983). A common inference from this view is that concepts that belong to substantially different systems must have different meanings. This inference, called "translation holism" by Fodor and Lepore (1992), entails that a person cannot have the same concept as another person unless the rest of their conceptual systems are at least highly similar. This view has had perhaps the most impact in the philosophy of science, where Kuhn's incommensurability thesis states that there can be no translation between scientific concepts across scientists that are committed to fundamentally different ontologies (Kuhn, 1962). A chemist indoctrinated into Lavoisier's theory of oxygen cannot translate any of their concepts to earlier chemists' concept of phlogiston. A more recent chemist can only entertain the earlier phlogiston concept by absorbing the entire Pre-Lavoisier theory, not by trying to insert the single phlogiston concept into their more recent theory or by finding an equivalent concept in their theory. A concept can only be understood if an entire system of interrelated concepts is also acquired.

TRANSLATING BETWEEN CONCEPTUAL SYSTEMS

We will not directly tackle the general question of whether concepts gain their meaning from their connections to each other, or from their connection to the external world. In fact, our eventual claim will be that this is a false dichotomy, and that concepts gain their meaning from both sources. Our destination will be a synergistic integration of conceptual web and external grounding accounts of conceptual meaning. On the road to this destination, we will first argue for the sufficiency of the conceptual web account for conceptual translation. Then, we will show how the conceptual web account can be supplemented by external grounding to establish meanings more successfully than either method could by itself.

Our point of departure for exploring conceptual meaning will be a highly idealized and purposefully simplified version of a conceptual translation task. The existence of translation across different people's conceptual systems, for example between John and Mary's **Horse** concepts, has been taken as a challenge to conceptual web accounts of meaning. Fodor and Lepore (1992) have argued that if a concept's meaning depends on its role within its larger conceptual system, and if there are some differences between Mary's and John's systems, then the meanings of Mary's and John's concepts would necessarily be different. A natural way to try to salvage the conceptual web account is to argue that determining corresponding concepts across systems does not require the systems to be identical, but only similar. However, Fodor (1998) insists that the notion of similarity is not adequate to establish that Mary and John both possess a concept of **Horse**. Fodor argues that "saying what it is for concepts to have similar, but not identical contents presupposes a prior notion of beliefs with similar but not identical concepts" [p. 32]. In opposition to this, we will argue that conceptual translation can proceed using only the notion of similarity, not identity, between concepts. Furthermore, the similarities between Mary's and John's concepts can be determined using only relations between concepts *within* each person's head.

We will present a simple neural network called ABSURDIST (Aligning Between Systems Using Relations Derived Inside Systems Themselves) that finds conceptual correspondences across two systems (two people, two time slices of one person, two scientific theories, two cultures, two developmental age groups, two language communities, etc.) using only inter-conceptual similarities, not conceptual identities, as input. Laakso and Cottrell (1998, 2000) describe another neural network model that uses similarity relations within two systems to compare the similarity of the systems, and Larkey and Love (2003) describe a connectionist algorithm for aligning between graphs that is highly related. ABSURDIST belongs to the general class of computer algorithms that solve graph matching problems. It takes as input two systems of concepts in which every concept of a system is defined exclusively in terms of its dissimilarities to other concepts in the same system. ABSURDIST produces as output a set of correspondences indicating which concepts from System A correspond to which concepts from System B. These correspondences serve as the basis for understanding how the systems can communicate with each other without the assumption made by Fodor (1998) that the two systems have exactly the same concepts. Fodor argues that any account of concepts should explain their "publicity" – the notion that the same concept can be possessed by more than one person. Instead, we will advocate a notion of "correspondence." An account of concepts should explain how concepts possessed by different people can correspond to one another, even if the concepts do not have exactly the same content. The notion of corresponding concepts is less restrictive than the notion of identical concepts, but is still sufficient to explain how people can share a conversational ground, and how a single person's concepts can persist across time despite changes in the person's knowledge. While less restrictive than the notion of concept identity, the notion of correspondence is stronger than the notion of concept similarity. John's **Horse** concept may be similar to Mary's **Donkey** concept, but the two do not correspond because John's **Horse** concept is even more similar in terms of its role within the conceptual system. Two concepts correspond to each other if they play equivalent roles within their systems, and ABSURDIST provides a formal method for determining equivalence of roles.

A few disclaimers are in order before we describe the algorithm. First, ABSURDIST finds corresponding concepts across individuals, but does not connect these concepts to the external world. The algorithm can reveal that Mary's **Horse** concept corresponds to John's **Horse** concept, but the basic algorithm does not reveal what in the external world corresponds to these concepts. However, an interesting extension of ABSURDIST would be to find correspondences between concepts within an internal system and physically measurable elements of an external system. Still, as it stands

ABSURDIST falls significantly short of an account of conceptual meanings. The intention of the model is simply to show how one task related to conceptual meaning, finding corresponding concepts across two systems, can be solved using only within-system similarities between concepts. It is relevant to the general issue of conceptual meaning given the arguments in the literature (e.g. Fodor, 1998) that this kind of within-system similarity is insufficient to identify cross-system matching concepts.

Second, our initial intention is not to create a rich or realistic model of translation across systems. In fact, our intention is to explore the simplest, most impoverished representation of concepts and their interrelations that is possible. If such a representation suffices to determine cross-system translations, then richer representations would presumably fare even better. To this end, we will not represent concepts as structured lists of dimension values, features or attribute/value frames, and we will not consider different kinds of relations between concepts such as **Is-a**, **Has-a**, **Part-of**, **Used-for**, or **Causes**. Concepts are simply elements that are related to other concepts within their system by a single, generic similarity relation. The specific input that ABSURDIST takes will be two two-dimensional proximity matrices, one for each system. Each matrix indicates the similarity of every concept within a system to every other concept in the system. While an individual's concepts certainly relate to each other in many ways (Medin, Goldstone, and Gentner, 1993), our present point is that even if the only relation between concepts in a system were generic similarity, this would suffice to find translations of the concept in different systems. In the final section, we will describe an extension of ABSURDIST to more structured conceptual systems.

A third disclaimer is that ABSURDIST is not primarily being put forward as a model of how people actually communicate and understand one another. ABSURDIST finds correspondences between concepts across systems, and would not typically be housed in any one of the systems. Unless Mary knows all of the distances between John's concepts, then she could not apply ABSURDIST to find translations between John and Mary. If the primary interpretation of ABSUDIST is not as a computational model of a single human's cognition, then what is it? It is an algorithm that demonstrates the available information that could be used to find translations between systems. It is an example of a hitherto underrepresented class of algorithms in cognitive science – *computational ecological psychology*. The ecological movement in perception (Gibson, 1979) is concerned with identifying external properties of things in the world that are available to be picked up by people. Although it is an approach in psychology, it is just as concerned with examining physical properties as it is with minds. Similarly, ABSURDIST is concerned with the sufficiency of information that is available across systems for translating between the systems. Traditional ecological psychology proceeds by expressing mathematical relations between physical properties. However, in the present case, a computational algorithm is necessary to determine the information that is available in the observed systems. Thus, the argument will be that even systems with strictly internal relations among their parts possess the information necessary for an observer to translate between them. However, unlike a standard interpretation of claims for "direct perception," an observer using ABSURDIST would perform a time-extended computation in order to successfully recover these translations.

ABSURDIST

ABSURDIST is a constraint satisfaction neural network for translating between conceptual systems. Unlike many neural networks, it does not learn, but rather only passes activation between units. Each of the units in the network represents an hypothesis that two concepts from different systems correspond to one another. With processing, a single set of units will tend to become highly active and all other units will become completely deactivated. The set of units that eventually becomes active will typically represent a consistent translation from one system to the other.

Elements $A_{1..m}$ belong to System A, while elements $B_{1..n}$ belong to System B. $C_t(A_q, B_x)$ is the activation, at time t, of the unit that represents the correspondence between the qth element of A and the xth element of B. There will be $m \cdot n$ correspondence units, one for each possible pair of corresponding elements between A and B. In the current example, every element represents one concept in a system. The activation of a correspondence unit is bound between 0 and 1, with a value of 1 indicating a strong correspondence between the associated elements, and a value of 0 indicating strong evidence that the elements do not correspond. Correspondence units dynamically evolve over time by the equations:

$$C_{t+1}(A_q, B_x) = \begin{cases} C_t(A_q, B_x) + N_t(A_q, B_x)(1 - C_t(A_q, B_x)) \\ \qquad \text{if } N_t(A_q, B_x) > 0 \\ C_t(A_q, B_x) + N_t(A_q, B_x)C_t(A_q, B_x) \text{ otherwise} \end{cases} \quad (1)$$

If $N_t(A_q, B_x)$, the net input to a unit that links the qth element of A and the xth element of B, is positive, then the unit's activation will increase as a function of the net input, passed through a squashing function that limits activation to an upper bound of 1. If the net input is negative, then activations are limited by a lower bound of 0. The net input is defined as

$$N_t(A_q, B_x) = \alpha E_t(A_q, B_x) + \beta R_t(A_q, B_x) - (1 - \alpha - \beta)I_t(A_q, B_x), \quad (2)$$

where the E term is the external similarity between A_q and B_x, R is their internal similarity, and I is the inhibition to placing A_q and B_x into correspondence that is supplied by other developing correspondence units.

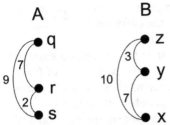

FIGURE 12.1. An example of the input to ABSURDIST. Two systems, A and B, are each represented solely in terms of the distances/dissimilarities between elements within a system. The correct output from ABSURDIST would be a cross-system translation in which element q was placed in correspondence with x, r with y, and s with z. Arcs are labeled with the distances between the elements connected by the arcs.

When $\alpha = 0$, then correspondences between A and B will be based solely on the similarities among the elements within a system, as proposed by a conceptual web account.

The amount of excitation to a unit based on within-domain relations is given by

$$R_t(A_q, B_x) = \frac{\sum_{\substack{r=1 \\ r \neq q}}^{m} \sum_{\substack{y=1 \\ y \neq x}}^{n} S(D(A_q, A_r)D(B_x, B_y))C_t(A_r, B_y)}{Min(m, n) - 1},$$

where $D(A_q, A_r)$ is the psychological distance between elements A_q and B_x in System A, and $S(F, G)$ is the similarity between distances F and G, and is defined as $S(F, G) = e^{-|F-G|}$. The amount of inhibition is given by

$$I_t(A_q, B_x) = \frac{\sum_{\substack{r=1 \\ r \neq q}}^{m} C_t(A_r, B_x) + \sum_{\substack{y=1 \\ y \neq x}}^{n} C_t(A_q, B_y)}{m + n - 2}.$$

These equations instantiate a fairly standard constraint satisfaction network, with one twist. According to the equation for R, Elements A_q and B_x will tend to be placed into correspondence to the extent that they enter into similar similarity relations with other elements. For example, in Figure 12.1, A_q has a distance of 7 to one element (A_r) and a distance of 9 to another element (A_s) within its System A. These are similar to the distances that B_x has to the other elements in System B, and accordingly there should be a tendency to place A_q in correspondence with B_x. Some similarity relations should count much more than others. The similarity between $D(A_q, A_r)$ and $D(B_x, B_y)$ should matter more than the similarity between $D(A_q, A_r)$ and $D(B_x, B_z)$ in terms of strengthening the correspondence between A_q and B_x, because A_r corresponds to B_y not to B_z. This is achieved by weighting the similarity between two distances by the strength of the units that align elements that are placed in correspondence by the distances. As the network begins to place A_r into correspondence with B_y, the similarity between $D(A_q, A_r)$ and $D(B_x, B_y)$ becomes emphasized as a basis for placing A_q into correspondence with B_x. As such, the equation for R represents the sum of the supporting evidence (the consistent correspondences), with each piece of support weighted by its relevance (given by the similarity term). This sum is normalized by dividing it by the minimum of $(m - 1)$ and $(n - 1)$. This minimum is the number of terms that will contribute to the R term if only 1-to-1 correspondences exist between systems.

The inhibitory Term I is based on a one-to-one mapping constraint (Falkenhainer et al., 1989; Holyoak & Thagard, 1989). The unit that places A_q into correspondence with B_x will tend to become deactivated if other strongly activated units place A_q into correspondence with other elements from B, or B_x into correspondence with other elements from A.

One problem with the original ABSURDIST algorithm described by Goldstone and Rogosky (2002) is that many iterations of activation passing between correspondence units is required before a single set of units converges. An analysis of the network dynamics often reveals that all correspondence units initially decrease their activation value, and then very gradually a set of consistent correspondence units becomes more activated. One strategy that has proven helpful in both speeding convergence in ABSURDIST and improving alignment accuracy has been to define a measure of the total amount of activation across all correspondences units,

$$T = \sum_{i=1}^{m} \sum_{j=1}^{n} C_{t+1}(A_i, B_j).$$

Next, if T is less than the intended sum if there were a complete set of one-to-one mappings, then each correspondence unit is adjusted so that it is more active. The adjustment is the difference between the ideal sum and the actual sum of activations, weighted by the ratio of the current activation to the total activation. Hence, the boost in activation for a correspondence unit should increase as the activation of the unit relative to the total activation of the network increases. These requirements are met by the following equation for dynamically adjusting correspondence units:

$$\text{if } T < \min(m, n) \text{ then } C'_{t+1}(A_q, B_x)$$
$$= C_{t+1}(A_q, B_x) + \frac{C_{t+1}(A_q, B_x)}{S}(\min(m, n) - T),$$

which would be applied after Equation (1).

Activations that would fall outside of the 0–1 range are assigned the closest value in this range. Correspondence unit activations are initialized to random values selected from a normal distribution with a mean of 0.5 and a standard deviation of 0.05. In our simulations, Equation (1) is iterated for a fixed number of cycles. It is assumed that ABSURDIST places two elements into correspondences if the activation of their correspondence unit is greater than 0.55 after a fixed number of iterations have been completed. Thus, the network gives as output a complete set of proposed correspondences/translations between Systems *A* and *B*.

ASSESSING ABSURDIST

Our general method for evaluating ABSURDIST will be to generate a number of elements in an *N*-dimensional space, with each element identified by its value on each of the *N* dimensions. These will be the elements of System *A*, and each is represented as a point in space. Then, System *B*'s elements are created by copying the points from System *A* and adding Gaussian noise with a mean of 0 to each of the dimension values of each of the points. The motivation for distorting *A*'s points to generate *B*'s points is to model the common phenomenon that people's concepts are not identical, and are not identically related to one another. The Euclidean distance between every pair of elements within a system is calculated. The correspondences computed by ABSURDIST after Equation (1) is iterated are then compared to the correct correspondences. Two elements correctly correspond to each other if the element in System *B* was originally copied from the element in System *A*.

Tolerance to Distortion

An initial set of simulations was conducted to determine how robust the ABSURDIST algorithm was to noise and how well the algorithm scaled to different sized systems. As such, we ran a 11 × 6 factorial combination of simulations, with 11 levels of added noise and 6 different numbers of elements per system. Noise was infused into the algorithm by varying the displacement between corresponding points across systems. The points in System A were set by randomly selecting dimension values from a uniform random distribution with a range from 0 to 1000. System *B* points were copied from System *A*, and Gaussian noise with standard deviations of 0–1% was added to the points of *B*. The number of points per system was 3, 4, 5, 6, 10, or 15. Correspondences were computed after 1,000 iterations of equation (1). α was set to 0 (no external information was used to determine correspondences), β was set to 0.4. For each combination of noise and number of items, 1,000 separate randomized starting configurations were tested. The results from this simulation are shown in Figure 12.2, which plots the percentage of simulations in which each of the proper correspondences between systems is recovered. For example, for 15-item systems, the figure plots the percentage of time that all 15 correspondences are recovered. The graph shows that performance gradually deteriorates with added noise, but that the algorithm is robust to modest amounts of noise. Relative to the ABSURDIST algorithm described by Goldstone and

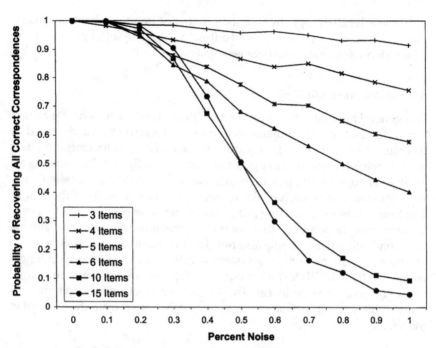

FIGURE 12.2. Probability of correctly translating every element in one system to every element in a second system, as a function of the number of items per system, and the amount of noise with which the elements of the second system are displaced relative to their positions in the first system.

Rogosky (2002) which lacked adaptive tuning of summed correspondence unit activation, the results in Figure 12.2 show about twice the noise tolerance and only one fifth of the iterations needed.

More surprisingly, Figure 12.2 also shows that for small levels of noise the algorithm's ability to recover true correspondences increases as a function of the number of elements in each system. Up to 0.2% noise, the highest probability of recovering all correct mappings is achieved for the largest, 15-item system. The reason for this is that as the number of elements in a system increases, the similarity relations between those elements provide increasingly strong constraints that serve to uniquely identify each element. The advantage of finding translations as the number of points in a system increases is all the more impressive when one considers chance performance. If one generated random translations that were constrained to allow only one-to-one correspondences, then the probability of generating a completely correct translation would be $1/n!$ when aligning systems that each have n items. Thus, with 0.7% noise, the 92% rate of recovering all 3 correspondences for a 3-item system is about 5.5 times above chance performance of 16.67%. However, with the same amount of noise, the 16% rate of recovering all of the correspondences for a 15-item system is remarkably higher than the chance rate of 7.6×10^{-13}. Thus, at least in our highly simplified domain, we have support for Lenat and Feigenbaum's (1991) argument that establishing meanings on the basis of within-system relations becomes more efficient, not harder, as the size of the system increases.

Integrating Internal and External Determinants of Conceptual Correspondences

The simulations indicate that within-system relations are sufficient for discovering between-system translations, but this should not be interpreted as suggesting that the meaning of an element is not also dependent on relations extrinsic to the system. In almost all realistic situations, translations between systems depends upon cues that are external to each system. For example, the alignment between John and Mary's **Horse** concepts is enormously facilitated by considerations other than within-system connections between concepts. Namely, strong evidence for conceptual alignment comes from the use of the same verbal label, pointing to the same objects when prompted, and being taught to use the concepts within similar cultures. Moreover, even though we have used within-system relations to represent conceptual webs, much of the basis for these within-system relations will come from external sources. It is possible that the only thing that somebody knows about flotsam is that it is similar to jetsam, but in most typical cases, the reason why two concepts are related to each other within a system is because of their perceptual-motor resemblances.

ABSURDIST offers a useful, idealized system for examining interactions between intrinsic (within-system) and extrinsic (external to the system) aspects of meaning. One way to incorporate extrinsic biases into the system is by initially seeding correspondence units with values. Thus far, all correspondence units have been seeded with initial activation values tightly clustered around 0.5. However, in many situations, there may be external reasons to think that two elements correspond to each other: they may receive the same label, they may have perceptual attributes in common, they may be associated with a common event, or a teacher may have provided a hint that the two elements correspond. In these cases, the initial seed-value may be significantly greater than 0.5.

Figure 12.3 shows the results of a simulation of ABSURDIST with different amounts of extrinsic support for a selected correspondence between two elements. Two systems are generated by randomly creating a set of points in two dimensions for System 1, and copying the points' coordinates to System 2 while introducing noise to their positions. When Seed = 0.5, then no correspondence is given an extrinsically supplied bias. When Seed = 0.75, then one of the true correspondences between the systems

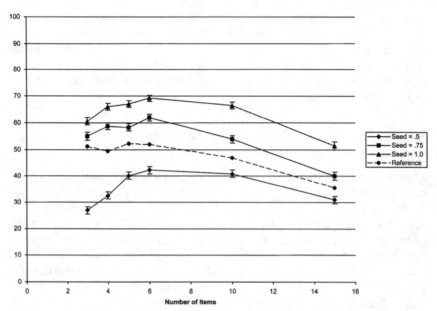

FIGURE 12.3. Percentage of correct alignments found by ABSURDIST, as a function of the number of items per system, and the amount of external bias that seeds a single correct alignment between two elements. As the strength of external bias increases, the percentage of correct correspondences increases, and this increase exceeds the increase predicted if seeding one alignment only affected the alignment itself (the "Reference" line). As such, the influence of extrinsic information is accentuated by within-system relations.

is given a larger initial activation than the other correspondences. When Seed = 1.0, this single correspondence is given an even larger initial activation. Somewhat unsurprisingly, when a true correspondence is given a relatively large initial activation, then ABSURDIST recovers a higher percentage of correct correspondences. The extent of this improvement is more surprising. For example, for a system made up of 15 elements, a mapping accuracy of 31% is obtained without any extrinsic assistance (Seed = 0.5). If seeding a single correct correspondence with a value of 1 rather than 0.5 allowed ABSURDIST to recover just that one correspondence with 100% probability, then accuracy would increase at most to 35.6% ($((0.31 * 14) + 1)/15$). The reference line in Figure 12.1 shows these predicted increases in accuracy. For all systems tested, the observed increment in accuracy far outstretches the increase in accuracy predicted if seeding a correspondence only helped that correspondence. Moreover, the amount by which translation accuracy improves beyond the amount predicted generally increases as a function of system size. Thus, externally seeding a correspondence does more than just fix that correspondence. In a system where correspondences all mutually depend upon each other, seeding one correspondence has a ripple-effect through which other correspondences are improved. Although external and role-based accounts of meaning have typically been pitted against each other, it turns out that the effectiveness of externally grounded correspondences is radically improved by the presence of role-based correspondences.

Equation 2 provides a second way of incorporating extrinsic influences on correspondences between systems. This equation defines the net input to a correspondence unit as an additive function of the extrinsic support for the correspondence, the intrinsic support, and the competition against it. Thus far, the extrinsic support has been set to 0. The extrinsic support term can be viewed as any perceptual, linguistic, or top-down information that suggests that two objects correspond. For example, two people using the same verbal label to describe a concept could constitute a strong extrinsic bias to place the concepts in correspondence. To study interactions between extrinsic and intrinsic support for correspondences, we conducted 1,000 simulations that started with 10 randomly placed points in a two-dimensional space for System A, and then copied these points over to System B with Gaussian-distributed noise. The intrinsic, role-based support is determined by the previously described equations. The extrinsic support term of Equation 2 is given by

$$E(A_q, B_x) = e^{-D(A_q, B_x)},$$

where D is the Euclidean distance function between point q of System A and point x of System B. This equation mirrors the exponential similarity function used to determine intrinsic similarities, but now compares absolute coordinate values. Thus, the correspondence unit connecting A_q and B_x will tend to be strengthened if A_q and B_x have similar coordinates. This is extrinsic support because the similarity of A_q and B_x's coordinates can be determined without any reference to other elements. If the two dimensions reflect size and brightness for example, then for A_q and B_x to have similar coordinates would mean that they have similar physical appearances along these perceptual dimensions.

In conducting the present simulation, we assigned three different sets of weights to the extrinsic and intrinsic support terms. For the "Extrinsic only" results of Figure 12.4, we set $\alpha = 0.4$ and $\beta = 0$. For this group, correspondences are only based on the extrinsic similarity between elements. For the "Intrinsic only" results, we set $\alpha = 0$, and $\beta = 0.4$. This group is comparable to the previous simulations in that it uses only a role-based measure of similarity to establish correspondences. Finally, for "Intrinsic and Extrinsic," we set $\alpha = 0.2$ and $\beta = 0.2$. For this group, correspondences are based on both absolute coordinate similarity, and on elements taking part in similar relations to other elements. Note, that both the intrinsic and

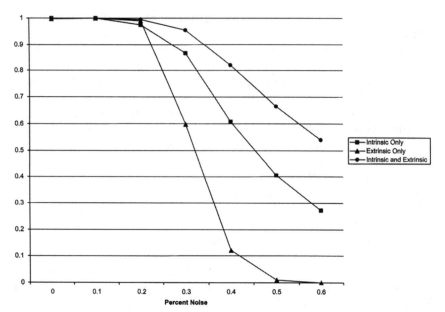

FIGURE 12.4. Probability of ABSURDIST achieving a perfect translation between two systems, as a function of noise, and the weighting of extrinsic and intrinsic information. Better performance is achieved when all weight is given to intrinsic information than when only extrinsic information is used. However, the best performance is achieved when both sources of information are weighted equally.

extrinsic terms are based on the same coordinate representations for elements. The difference between these terms centers on whether absolute or relative coordinate values are used.

Figure 12.4 shows that using only information intrinsic to a system results in better correspondences than using only extrinsic information. This is because corresponding elements that have considerably different positions in their systems can often still be properly connected with intrinsic information if other proper correspondences can be recovered. The intrinsic support term is more robust than the extrinsic term because it depends on the entire system of emerging correspondences. For this reason, it is surprising that the best translation performance is found when intrinsic and extrinsic information are both incorporated into Equation 2. The excellent performance of the network that uses both intrinsic and extrinsic information derives from its robustness in the face of noise. Some distortions to points of System *B* adversely affect the intrinsic system more than the extrinsic system, whereas other distortions have the opposite effect. A set of distortions may have a particularly disruptive influence on either absolute coordinates or relative positions. A system that incorporates both sources of information will tend to recover well from either disruption if the other source of information is reasonably intact.

DISCUSSION OF INITIAL SIMULATIONS

The first theoretical contribution of ABSURDIST is to show that translations *between* elements of two systems can be found using only information about the relations between elements *within* a system. ABSURDIST demonstrates how a conceptual web account of meaning is compatible with the goal of determining correspondences between concepts across individuals. Two people need not have exactly the same systems to create proper conceptual correspondences. Contra Fodor (1998; Fodor & Lepore, 1992), information in the form of interconceptual similarities suffices to find intersystem equivalences between concepts. Furthermore, it is sometimes easier to find translations for large systems than small systems. This is despite two large disadvantages for systems comprising many elements: there are relatively many opportunities to get the cross-system alignments wrong, and the elements tend to be close together and hence confusable. The compensating advantage of many-element systems is that the roles that an object plays within a system are more elaborated as the number of elements in the system increases.

The second theoretical contribution of ABSURDIST is to formalize some of the ways that intrinsic, within-system relations and extrinsic, perceptual information synergistically interact in determining conceptual alignments. Intrinsic relations suffice to determine cross-concept translations, but if extrinsic information is available, more robust, noise-resistant translations can be found. Moreover, extrinsic information, when available, can actually increase the power of intrinsic information.

The synergistic benefit of combining intrinsic and extrinsic information sheds new light on the debate on accounts of conceptual meaning. It is common to think of intrinsic and extrinsic accounts of meaning as being mutually exclusive, or at least being zero-sum. Seemingly, either a concept's meaning depends on information within its conceptual system or outside of its conceptual system, and to the extent that one dependency is strengthened, the other dependency is weakened.

In contrast to this conception of competition between intrinsic and extrinsic information, meaning in ABSURIDST is both intrinsically and extrinsically determined, and the external grounding makes intrinsic information more, not less, powerful. An advantage of this approach to conceptual meaning is that it avoids an infelicitous choice between reducing conceptual meanings to sense data and leaving conceptual systems completely ungrounded. Having concepts in a system all depend upon each other is perfectly compatible with these concepts having a perceptual basis.

OTHER COGNITIVE SCIENCE APPLICATIONS OF ABSURDIST

We have focused on the application of ABSURDIST to the problem of translating between different people's conceptual systems. However, the algorithm is applicable to a variety of situations in which elements from two system must be placed in correspondence in an efficient and reasonable (though not provably optimal) manner. A combination of properties makes ABSURDIST particularly useful for applications in cognitive science: (1) the algorithm can operate solely on relations within a system; (2) the within-system relations can be as simple as generic similarity relations; (3) the algorithm can combine within-system and between-systems information when each is available; (4) the algorithm has a strong bias to establish one-to-one correspondences; and (5) the algorithm does not require larger numbers of iterations for convergence as the number of elements per system increases.

Aligning Subsystems

In the simulations thus far considered, the systems to be aligned have had the same number of elements. This is not required for the algorithm. When different-sized systems are compared, the correspondences tend to be one-to-one, but many elements of the larger system are not placed into correspondence at all. One useful application of aligning systems of unequal size is finding subsystems that match a pattern. An example of this from conceptual translation might be the comparison of people with very different levels of knowledge about a domain. If Mary is a large animal vet, then she will have many more horse-related concepts than John. Some of Mary's concepts may not have correspondences in John, but it would still be useful to identify the equivalent of John's concepts in Mary's system. Figure 12.5A presents a simplified example of this scenario, in which a three-element pattern can be identified within a larger seven-element pattern by aligning the target three-element pattern with the larger pattern. In this fashion, ABSURDIST provides an algorithm for finding patterns concealed within larger contexts.

A second use of finding alignments between sub-systems is as a method of making consistent forced-choice similarity judgments. To decide whether Pattern A is more similar to Pattern Y or Z, ABSURDIST can be given Pattern A as System 1, and Patterns Y and Z as System 2. In Figure 12.5B, Patterns A, Y, and Z each consist of three elements. In this example, Y and Z correspond equally well to Pattern A. Even in this case, ABSURDIST creates a consistent alignment in which all of the elements of A are placed into correspondence with either elements from Y or Z, and each alignment occurs on roughly half of the simulations. The mutually supportive constraint satisfaction virtually assures that a consistent alignment will be found, similar to the consistent perception of ambiguous forms found

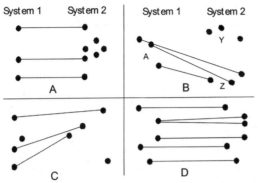

FIGURE 12.5. Four examples of ABSURDIST translations, with typical alignments shown by solid line connecting elements across the systems. In Panel A, the pattern represented by System 1 is aligned with the subsystem of System 2 that optimally matches this pattern. In Panel B, even though two subsystems of System 2 can correspond to the elements of System 1, one of the coherent subsystems will become strongly aligned with System 1 as the other loses its alignment to System 1 completely. In Panel C, the three pairs of elements that have mostly comparable similarity relations within their systems are placed into correspondence, but a fourth element of each system is not placed into any correspondence because it is too dissimilar to other elements in terms of its similarity relations. In Panel D, a two-to-one mapping is constructed because two elements from the System 2 have very similar relations to a single element from the System 1.

by Rumelhart, Smolensky, McClelland, and Hinton (1986). If Z aligns better with A than does Y, then it would be selected reliably more often.

A particularly challenging situation for ABSURDIST occurs if two systems have the same number of elements, but only a subset of them properly matches. For example, Mary and John both have concepts of **Horse**, **Stallion**, and **Pony**, but only Mary has a concept of **Palomino** and only John has a concept of **Pinto**. This situation is implemented in Figure 12.5C by having four elements per system, with three of the elements matching well across the systems, but one element from each system having no strong correspondence in the other system. This is challenging because ABSURDIST's one-to-one mapping constraint will tend to match two elements if neither participates in any other strong correspondences. Despite this tendency, given the situation shown in Figure 12.5C, ABSURDIST, will draw correspondences between the three pairs of elements that share the majority of their roles in common, but not between the fourth, mismatching elements. The unit that places the mismatching elements into correspondence does receive excitation from the three units that place properly matching elements into correspondence due to one-to-one mapping consistency. However, the lack of similarity between the mismatching elements' similarity relations to other elements overshadows this excitation.

Finally, unlike most computer science graph matching algorithms, ABSURDIST can violate a one-to-one mapping constraint under certain circumstances. Figure 12.5D presents one such configuration, in which two objects from a larger system enter into very similar similarity relations to a single object from the other system. This typically happens when the two objects from the larger system are themselves very similar. These particular circumstances allow ABSURDIST to aptly model conceptual change over development. For many domains, adults have more highly differentiated concepts than do children (Smith, Carey, & Wiser, 1985). To take examples from Carey (1999), the adult concepts of heat and temperature are not differentiated for children, nor are weight and density. In Figure 12.5D, System 2 might correspond to a part of an adults' conceptual system, with separate but close concepts for heat and temperature. Both of these concepts correspond to a single concept in the younger and less differentiated System 1. In this manner, ABSURDIST shows how it is possible to translate between conceptual systems even if the systems are differentially articulated. A second example of the situation shown in Figure 12.5D occurs when languages carve up the semantic universe in different manners (Gentner & Goldin-Meadow, 2003). Dutch, for example, uses the same word "Schaduw" to refer to things that, in English, would be called "Shadow" or "Shade." Conversely, English uses the word "Leg" to refer to things that, in Dutch, would be called "Been" (the legs of people and horses) or "Poot" (the legs of other animals and furniture) (R. Zwaan, personal communication, 2004). In these cases, ABSURDIST is able to align "Schaduw" from the Dutch system with two concepts from the English system.

Object Recognition and Shape Analysis

The ABSURDIST algorithm can be applied to the problem of object recognition that is invariant to rotation and reflection. For this application, a pictorial object is the system, and points on the object are elements of the system. Unlike many approaches to object recognition (Ullman, 1996), ABSURDIST's robustness under rotation is achieved automatically rather than being explicitly computed. Figure 12.5 shows the alignments obtained when one object is placed into correspondence with a rotated version of itself. These alignments are useful for object recognition. For example, if the form on the left side of Figure 12.6 were memorized, then the form on the right can be identified as an exact match to this memorized form without needing to rotate either form. Rotation is not required because ABSURDIST uses relative distances between points to determine correspondences. Distances between points are not affected by rotation or reflection.

A standard solution to recognizing rotated objects is to find critical landmark points that are identifiable on a stored object and a presented input

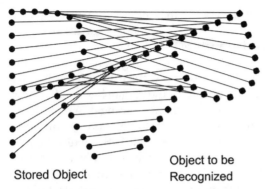

Stored Object

Object to be Recognized

FIGURE 12.6. ABSURDIST can be applied to orientation- and translation-invariant object recognition. An object to be recognized can be aligned to a stored version of the object without requiring either object to be rotated, and without requiring predetermined matching points to be available. Within-object relations suffice to unambiguously align any asymmetric object to a stored version of itself.

object. For example, a distinctive angle or colored point may be unambiguously identified on stored and probed objects. Ullman (1989) has shown that if three such landmarks can be identified, then two views of the same 3-D object can be perfectly aligned. ABSURDIST shows that even if zero extrinsically aligned landmarks can be identified, it is still possible to align the objects. ABSURDIST does so by taking advantage of the wealth of information in the form of within-object relations (see also Edelman, 1999). Object recognition algorithms have typically used extrinsic information without considering the useful constraints provided by solely intrinsic information.

ABSURDIST gets rotational and reflection invariance for "free" because inter-point distances are used and these are inherently relational. Size invariance is easily achieved by normalizing distances between points of an object so as to fall in a 0-to-1 range. In situations where rotation or size *does* make a difference ("b" is not the same object as "d"), extrinsic, absolute information can be added to Equation 2 to supplement the intrinsic information. Alternatively, a point can be added in a specific location, such as the upper left hand corner, to both the memorized and probed objects. If these anchor points are added to the system, then ABSURDIST correctly predicts that, up to 180 degrees, as the angular disparity between two objects increases, so does the time required to align them (Shepard & Cooper, 1986). In particular, if we measure ABSURDIST's response time by the number of cycles of activation passing required to reach a threshold level of summed unit activation, then rotating one object relative to the other slows response times. If the anchor points are not included, then ABSURDIST is completely unaffected by rotation, which improves the algorithm's object recognition speed, but at the cost of making it less psychologically plausible.

ABSURDIST can also be used to analyze the symmetries of an object for shape analysis. A symmetry is a distance-preserving transformation that copies an object exactly onto itself. For example, the capital letter "A" has a reflection symmetry because every point of the A matches another point on the A if they are reflected across a vertical line running down the center of the "A." A square has eight symmetries (four rotational symmetries multiplied by two reflectional symmetries). ABSURDIST determines the symmetries of an object by finding translations *between* the object and itself. For a random set of points, the only translation that ABSURDIST is likely to find is the one that aligns each point with itself. However, for four points arranged in a square, eight different sets of correspondences are equally probable, corresponding to the eight symmetries of a square. An equilateral triangle produces six different translations; points A, B, C (ABC) correspond with equal likelihood to ABC, ACB, BCA, BAC, CAB, or CBA. An isosceles triangle has only two different translations, corresponding to an identity and reflection transformation. If some randomness is added to Equation (1), then the distribution of alignments reveals not only the symmetries of a shape, but also the near-symmetries of a shape, with the probability of an alignment denoting how close the associated symmetry is to perfection.

Pre- and Postprocessing for Multidimensional Scaling

The ABSURDIST algorithm bears some similarities to multidimensional scaling (MDS), but its input and output are fundamentally different. MDS takes as input a matrix of proximities by which each object in a set is compared to every other object, and the matrix is ordered such that each matrix entry is identified with a particular pair (e.g., "Entry {2,3} is the similarity of **Bear** to **Dog**"). The output to MDS is a geometric representation of the objects, with each object represented as a point and the distances between points approximating their dissimilarity. MDS also provides methods, such as individual Differences MDS (Carroll & Chang, 1970) that can be used to compare two people's MDS solutions and derive a common geometric solution for both people, as long as the same objects are given to the two people, and they are ordered in an identical manner in the two persons' proximity matrices. ABSURDIST supplements MDS by applying in situations where the two people are comparing similar set of objects, but the people do not use the same labels for the objects (e.g., one person is comparing objects in Chinese, and the other in English), or the matrices are not in the same order. The output of ABSURDIST is a suggested way to reorder the matrices (a translation).

Using a pre-processor to MDS, ABSURDIST can reorder proximity matrices so that they are in the best alignment possible. For examples, a set of common concepts or objects can be evaluated by different cultures, language groups, scientific fields, or philosophical movements. A single, grand MDS can be derived for all of these groups once ABSURDIST has aligned the different groups' concepts as well as possible. The stress in ABSURDIST's alignments can be used to gauge how appropriate it is to generate a single geometric solution to represent several groups' assessments of similarity. Stress would be measured by finding the cumulative dissimilarity between the systems across of all the aligned distances.

ABSURDIST can also be applied as a post-processor once an MDS solution has been obtained. The distance measures between points in an MDS space are ideal inputs to ABSURDIST because they provide exactly the kind of relationally defined similarity matrix that ABSURDIST requires. We can use ABSURDIST to determine whether two different MDS solutions are in fact similar to each other, unaffected by reflections, translations, and rotations.

Interpretation of Neural Networks

ABSURDIST can be used to determine whether two neural networks have developed similar solutions to a problem. This application builds on a recent proposal by Laakso and Cottrell (1998, 2000) to compare neural networks by comparing the distances between their neural activities. By their approach, two neural networks offer a similar solution to a problem if input patterns produce similar, *relative* patterns of activation across the two networks. For example, if an input representing **Dog** produces similar hidden-unit activations to a **Cat** input in one network, and if they produce similar hidden-unit activations in another network, this would be some reason to believe that the networks are functionally similar despite any differences they might have in terms of their architecture. More formally, they compute all distances between activation patterns produced by a set of inputs, for each of two networks to be compared. They then compute the correlation between the distances for the two networks to determine their similarity.

Similar to ABSURDIST, Laakso and Cottrell's approach (2000) emphasizes the role-based, relative nature of similarity, and how it suffices to compare architecturally different systems. ABSURDIST significantly extends their approach by using even more relational, less absolute information to compare systems. Their technique requires that one know what stimulus is presented to the two networks (e.g., **Dog** in the example above). With ABSURDIST, two networks can be compared even if one cannot match up inputs to the networks in a predetermined way. All that is required is that the inputs to the two networks are sampled from essentially the same distribution of concepts/objects. This feature has a number of potential uses. It can be used when (1) the inputs to two networks are necessarily different because of differences in the architectures used for representing inputs, (2) the inputs to two networks are represented in different languages or representational formats and a direct translation is not available, and (3) there is a potentially infinite number of inputs, and one does not have control over the input that is presented to a network on a given trial. As an example of this third application, imagine that an infinite number of stimuli fall into 10 clusters with varying similarities to each other. Using some competitive specialization algorithm (Kohonen, 1995; Rumelhart & Zipser, 1985), a set of originally homogeneous hidden units can be trained so that each becomes specialized for one of the input clusters. By Laakso and Cottrell's approach, we can measure the similarity of two networks (that may differ in their number of hidden units) by feeding in known and matched input patterns to each network, and comparing the similarity of the networks' similarity assessments, measured by hidden unit activations, for all pairs of stimuli. Using ABSURDIST, we do not even need to feed the two networks exactly the same input patterns or match input patterns across the two networks. ABSURDIST can still measure whether the entire pattern of similarities among the hidden units is similar in the two networks. Along the way to determining this, it will align clusters of inputs across the networks according to relative, rather than absolute, input values.

Human Analogy and Comparison

As described earlier, ABSURDIST offers a complementary approach to analogical reasoning between domains. Most existing models of analogical comparison, including SME, SIAM, LISA, Drama, and ACME (Eliasmith & Thagard, 2001; Falkenhainer et al., 1989; Goldstone, 1994; Holyoak & Thagard, 1989; Hummel & Holyoak, 1997, 2003), represent the domains to be compared in terms of richly structured propositions. This is a useful strategy when the knowledge of a domain can be easily and unambiguously expressed in terms of symbolic predicates, attributes, functions, and higher-order relations. Determining the right symbolic encoding of a domain is a crucial, yet often finessed problem (Hofstadter, 1995). In many cases, such as single words or pictures, it is difficult to come up with propositional encodings that capture an item's meaning. In such cases, ABSURDIST's unstructured representation is a useful addition to existing models of analogical reasoning. From this perspective, ABSURDIST may apply when these other models cannot, in domains where explicit structural descriptions are not available, but simple similarity relations are available. For example, a German-English bilingual could probably provide subjective similarity ratings of words within the set {Cat, Dog, Lion, Shark, Tortoise} and separately consider the similarities of the words within the set {Katze, Hunde, Löwe, Hai, Schildkröte}. These similarities would provide the input needed by ABSURDIST to determine that "Cat" corresponds to "Katze." However, the same bilingual might not be able to provide the kind of analytic and structured representation of "Cat" that the other models require.

Psychologists have recently argued that similarity and difference are more similar than might appear at first (Gentner & Markman, 1994; Markman, 1996; Markman & Gentner, 2000; Medin, Goldstone, & Gentner, 1990). In particular, assessing the similarity *or* dissimilarity of two objects typically involves placing the objects into alignment as well as possible. One empirically confirmed prediction of this view is that it in many cases it is easier to find differences between similar than dissimilar objects (Gentner & Markman, 1994). Antonyms, while ostensibly opposites, are in fact quite similar in that all of their semantic attributes are perfectly aligned, with one attribute having opposite values. For example, **Black** and **White** are both terms for monochromatic, pure colors. ABSURDIST is consistent with this perspective. The alignment that it calculates would precede both similarity and dissimilarity judgments. Similarity judgments are based on the quality of alignment, and on the similarity of the corresponding elements. Dissimilarity judgments would be based on the dissimilarity of corresponding elements, and thus would also involve determining an optimal alignment between systems.

Large-Scale System Translation

The small-scale simulations conducted leave open the promise of applying ABSURDIST to much larger translation tasks. Although logistical and technical problems will certainly arise when scaling the algorithm up to large databases, the presented approach should theoretically be applicable to systems such as dictionaries, thesauri, encyclopedias, and social organizational structures. For example, ABSURDIST could provide automatic translations between dictionaries of two different languages using only co-occurrence relations between words within each dictionary. The input to the network would be the full matrix of co-occurrences between every word in English to every other word in English, and the same kind of matrix for a second language. The output would be a set of correspondences across the two language. If such a project were successful, it would provide a striking argument for the power of within-system relations. If unsuccessful, it could still be practically valuable if supplemented by a small number of external hints (e.g., that French "chat" and English "cat" might correspond to each other because of their phonological similarity).

We are not optimistic that a completely unseeded version of ABSURDIST would recover a very accurate translation between two dictionaries. We have collected a set of subjective similarities among a set of 134 animal words from two groups of subjects. The two groups were obtained by randomly assigning each of 120 Indiana University students to one of the groups. We used ABSURDIST to try correctly align the animal words across the two groups of subjects using only each groups' matrix of similarity assessments. ABSURDIST's performance rate of 34% correctly aligned animals was encouraging, but not nearly good enough to be practically useful. Furthermore, performance was higher than might generally be expected because of the high similarity between the groups, and the large number of subjects reducing extraneous noise. If we had tried to align a single pair of randomly selected subjects, ABSURDIST's performance would have been much worse. Although the unseeded ABSURDIST's performance was lackluster, we again found dramatic improvements when even a few animal terms were correctly seeded. An automatic dictionary translator could well be useful even if it needed to be seeded with 5% of the correct matches.

Translating Structured Representations

The simplicity of ABSURDIST's input representations is both a strength and a weakness. From a philosophical and rhetorical perspective, the ability of ABSURDIST to recover translations using only two similarity matrices to represent the compared systems is the strongest possible argument for the sufficiency of purely relational, within-system information for translation. However, in many cases, more structured information is readily available and could be used to improve translation performance. With this in mind, we have extended ABSURDIST so as to be able to handle generalized graph representations, including graphs with labeled relations, bidirectional or unidirectional relations, and sparse network topologies. These extensions allow ABSURDIST to be applied to many of the domains of focus for graph matching algorithms (e.g. Larkey & Love, 2003; Melnik, Garcia-Molina, & Rahm, 2002). One particularly timely application is the translation between XML documents on the web. XML is a meta-language for expressing databases using terminology created by database programmers. Unfortunately, different database programmers may use different terminology for describing essentially the same entities. For example, in Figure 12.7, two different designations, "worker" and "employee" have been used to describe essentially the same entity. The extended version of ABSURDIST, like other graph matching algorithms and analogical reasoning systems (Falkenhainer et al., 1989; Hummel & Holyoak, 2003), can be used to determine translations between the databases. Whether ABSURDIST offers tangible benefits over existing algorithms for structured graphs is not completely clear yet, but some potential advantages of ABSURDIST are: (1) it has a soft, rather than hard, 1-to-1 mapping constraint and so can find translations even when one database makes a distinction between two or more entities that are conceptually fused together in the other database; (2) it can integrate structured graph representations

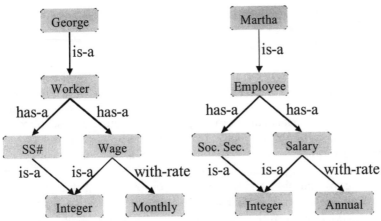

FIGURE 12.7. An example of the structured representations that the extended ABSURDIST algorithm can align.

with association-based similarity matrices; (3) it provides a natural mechanisms for incorporating external and internal determinants of meaning; and (4) the neural network architecture offers a framework for solving "correspondence problems" that has been shown to have neurophysiological plausibility in related perceptual domains (Marr & Poggio, 1979; Ullman, 1979).

Initial results with the graph-based version of ABSURDIST suggest a number of interesting trends (Feng, Goldstone, & Menkov, 2004). First, as expected, adding multiple types of relations such as **is-a** and **has-a** (see Figure 12.7) allows ABSURDIST to more accurately construct translations than it did with the single, generic similarity relation. Second, translations are more accurately found with asymmetric relations like **left-of** rather than symmetric relations like **next-to**. Third, the best translations are found when approximately half of the possible connections between concepts are present. The full connectivity that we have thus far been assuming does not give rise to the best translations. More sparsely connected systems actually have more unambiguous features that facilitate alignment. All three of these results are consistent with the idea that information that locally distinguishes concepts from each other leads to the best global translations.

CONCLUSION

Our simulations indicate that appropriate translation between conceptual systems can sometimes proceed on the basis of purely within-system conceptual relations. It is not viciously circular to claim that concepts gain their meaning by their relations to other concepts that, in turn, gain the meaning in the same fashion. Remarkably, a concept's connections to other concepts in the same system can suffice to give it a meaning that can transcend the system, at least in the sense of establishing proper connections to concepts outside of the system.

Despite the surprising power of within-system relations, our claim is not that translation typically *does* proceed with only this information. To the contrary, our simulations point to the power of combining intrinsic, within-system relations and external grounding. Conceptual-web accounts of meaning can offer an account of meaning, but they will be most effective when combined with an externally grounded component. In most real-world translation scenarios, external grounding is crucial. To return to our introductory example, translating between John and Mary's **Horse** concepts is immeasurably facilitated by virtue of the fact that they use the same words to refer to their **Horse** concepts, they originally learned their **Horse** concepts from the same kinds of inputs, and they gesture to the same things when asked to provide examples of horses. These are all external cues to translation, and play at least as large a role as within-system relations. However, our point is that we do not need to select either internal or external sources as the definitive provider of meaning. By choosing between or even separating these sources, their potential is weakened.

Like many of the other contributors to this book, we are impressed by the tight connection between our supposedly abstract, sophisticated concepts and our perceptual and motor capacities. The traditional split between research on low-level perceptual processes and high-level cognition is misleading and counterproductive. Elsewhere we have attempted to describe bridges between our perceptual and conceptual systems (Goldstone, 2003; Goldstone & Barsalou, 1998; Goldstone et al., 2000). In the present work, we have tried to strengthen this bridge by arguing that proponents of an approach to concepts grounded in perceptual-motor activity need not snub intraconceptual relations or claim that all thought reduces to sense data.

We believe that separating embodied cognition approaches from sensory reductionism makes embodied cognition substantially more palatable. One can maintain that all concepts have perceptual-motor components without claiming that concepts reduce to sensations and actions. A sensory reductionist easily falls into the trap of claiming that **Horse's** meaning is given by its parts – hoof, mane, tail, etc. These parts, in turn, are described in terms of their parts, and so on, until eventually the descriptions are grounded in elementary sensory elements. This account is dissatisfying because it overlooks much of people's rich knowledge associated with horses. Horses are associated with cavalries, Paul Revere, races, and cowboys. Several of the associated concepts that imbue **Horse** with its meaning, such as **Freedom**, **Domesticated**, and **Strength**, are less concrete than **Horse** itself. Sensory reduction can be avoided by positing interconceptual relations such as these, that coexist with perceptual groundings. We do not have to choose between meaning based on interconceptual relations or perceptual senses, and by not choosing we make it much more plausible that all of our concepts have perceptual-motor components. Moreover, it is not simply that these complementary aspects of meaning coexist. Internal and external bases of meaning are mutually reinforcing, not mutually exclusive.

ACKNOWLEDGMENTS

The authors wish to express thanks to Eric Dietrich, Shimon Edelman, Gary Cottrell, John Hummel, Michael Lynch, Arthur Markman, Robert Nosofsky, Diane Pecher, Richard Shiffrin, Mark Steyvers, and two anonymous reviewers. This research was funded by a grant from Lockheed Martin and NSF grant 0125287. Correspondence concerning this article should be addressed to rgoldsto@indiana.edu or Robert Goldstone, Psychology Department, Indiana University, Bloomington, Indiana 47405. Further information about the laboratory can be found at http://cognitrn. psych.indiana.edu/.

References

Barsalou, L. W. (1999). Perceptual symbol systems. *Behavioral and Brain Sciences 22*, 577–660.

Barsalou, L. W., Simmons, W. K., Barbey, A. K., & Wilson, C. D. (2003). Grounding conceptual knowledge in modality-specific systems. *Trends in Cognitive Sciences 7*, 84–91.

Block, N. (1986). Advertisement for a semantics for psychology. *Midwest Studies in Philosophy 10*, 615–78.

Block, N. (1999). Functional role semantics. In R. A. Wilson, & F. C. Keil (Eds.), *MIT Encyclopedia of the Cognitive Sciences* (pp. 331–332). Cambridge, MA: MIT Press.

Boroditsky, L. (2000). Metaphoric structuring: Understanding time through spatial metaphors. *Cognition 75*, 1–28.

Boroditsky, L., & Ramscar, M. (2002). The roles of body and mind in abstract thought. *Psychological Science 13*, 185–189.

Burgess, C., Livesay, K., & Lund, K. (1998). Explorations in context space: Words, sentences, and discourse. *Discourse Processes 25*, 211–257.

Burgess, C., & Lund, K. (2000). The dynamics of meaning in memory. In E. Diettrich & A. B. Markman (Eds.), *Cognitive Dynamics: Conceptual Change in Humans and Machines* (pp. 117–156). Mahwah, NJ: Lawrence Erlbaum Associates.

Carey, S. (1999). Knowledge acquisition: Enrichment or conceptual change. In E. Margolis & S. Laurence (Eds.), *Concepts: Core Readings* (pp. 459–487). Cambridge, MA: MIT Press.

Carroll, J. D., & Chang, J. J. (1970). Analysis of individual differences in multidimensional scaling via an *n*-way generalization of "Eckart-Young" decomposition. *Psychometrika 35*, 283–319.

Collins, A. M., & Loftus, E. F. (1975). A spreading-activation theory of semantic priming. *Psychological Review 82*, 407–428.

Edelman, S. (1999). *Representation and Recognition in Vision*. Cambridge, MA: MIT Press.

Eliasmith, C., & Thagard, P. (2001). Integrating structure and meaning: A distributed model of analogical mapping. *Cognitive Science 25*, 245–286.

Falkenhainer, B., Forbus, K. D., & Gentner, D. (1989). The structure-mapping engine: Algorithm and examples. *Artificial Intelligence 41*, 1–63.

Feng, Y., Goldstone, R. L., & Menkov, V. (2004). ABSURDIST II: A Graph Matching Algorithm and its Application to Conceptual System Translation. FLAIRS 2004.

Field, H. (1977). Logic, meaning, and conceptual role. *Journal of Philosophy 74*, 379–409.

Fodor, J. (1998). *Concepts: Where Cognitive Science Went Wrong*. Oxford: Clarendon Press.

Fodor, J., & Lepore, E. (1992). *Holism*. Oxford: Blackwell.

Gentner, D., & Markman, A. B. (1994). Structural alignment in comparison: No difference without similarity. *Psychological Science 5*, 148–152.

Gentner, D., & Goldin-Meadow, S. (2003). *Language in Mind: Advances in the Study of Language and Thought*. Cambridge, MA: MIT Press.

Gibson, J. J. (1979). *The Ecological Approach to Visual Perception*. Boston: Houghton Mifflin.

Glenberg, A. M., & Kaschak, M. P. (2002). Grounding language in action. *Psychonomic Bulletin & Review 9*, 558–565.

Glenberg, A. M., & Robertson, D. A. (2000). Symbol grounding and meaning: A comparison of high-dimensional and embodied theories of meaning. *Journal of Memory and Language 43*, 379–401.

Goldstone, R. L. (1994). Similarity, Interactive Activation, and Mapping. *Journal of Experimental Psychology: Learning, Memory, and Cognition 20*, 3–28.

Goldstone, R. L. (1996). Isolated and Interrelated Concepts. *Memory and Cognition 24*, 608–628.

Goldstone, R. L. (2003). Learning to perceive while perceiving to learn. In R. Kimchi, M. Behrmann & C. Olson (Eds.), *Perceptual Organization in Vision: Behavioral and Neural Perspectives* (pp. 233–278). Mahwah, NJ: Lawrence Erlbaum Associates.

Goldstone, R. L., & Barsalou, L. (1998). Reuniting perception and conception. *Cognition 65*, 231–262.

Goldstone, R. L., Lippa, Y., & Shiffrin, R. M. (2001). Altering object representations through category learning. *Cognition 78*, 27–43.

Goldstone, R. L., & Rogosky, B. J. (2002). Using relations within conceptual systems to translate across conceptual systems. *Cognition 84*, 295–320.

Goldstone, R. L., Steyvers, M., & Rogosky, B. J. (2003). Conceptual Interrelatedness and Caricatures. *Memory and Cognition 31*, 169–180.

Goldstone, R. L., Steyvers, M., Spencer-Smith, J., & Kersten, A. (2000). Interactions between perceptual and conceptual learning. In E. Diettrich & A. B. Markman (Eds.), *Cognitive Dynamics: Conceptual Change in Humans and Machines* (pp. 191–228). Mahwah, NJ: Lawrence Erlbaum Associates.

Harnad, S. (1990). The symbol grounding problem. *Physica D 42*, 335–346.

Hofstadter, D. (1995). *Fluid concepts and creative analogies*. New York: Basic Books.

Holyoak, K. J., & Thagard, P. (1989). Analogical mapping by constraint satisfaction. *Cognitive Science 13*, 295–355.

Hume, D. (1740/1973). *An Abstract of a Treatise on Human Nature*. Cambridge: Cambridge University Press.

Hummel, J. E., & Holyoak, K. J. (1997). Distributed representations of structure: A theory of analogical access and mapping. *Psychological Review 104*, 427–466.

Hummel, J. E., & Holyoak, K. J. (2003). A symbolic-connectionist theory of relational inference and generalization. *Psychological Review 110*, 220–264.

Kohonen, T. (1995). *Self-Organizing Maps*. Berlin: Springer-Verlag.

Kuhn. T. (1962). *The Structure of Scientific Revolutions*. Chicago: University of Chicago Press.

Laakso, A., & Cottrell, G. (1998). "How can I know what you think?": Assessing representational similarity in neural systems. In *Proceedings of the 20th Annual Cognitive Science Conference*. Madison, WI: Lawrence Erlbaum (pp. 591–596).

Laakso, A., & Cottrell, G. (2000). Content and cluster analysis: Assessing representational similarity in neural systems. *Philosophical Psychology 13*, 47–76.

Lakoff, G., & Nunez, R. E. (2000). *Where Mathematics Comes From: How the Embodied Mind Brings Mathematics into Being*. New York: Basic Books.

Landauer, T. K., & Dumais, S. T. (1997). A solution to Plato's problem: The Latent Semantic Analysis Theory of the acquisition, induction, and representation of knowledge. *Psychological Review 104*, 211–240.

Larkey, L. B., & Love, B. C. (2003). CAB: Connectionist analogy builder. *Cognitive Science 27*, 781–794.

Lenat, D. B., & Feigenbaum, E. A. (1991). On the thresholds of knowledge. *Artificial Intelligence 47*, 185–250.

Locke, J. (1690). *An Essay Concerning Human Understanding*. (http://www.ilt.columbia.edu/Projects/digitexts/locke/understanding/title.html).

Markman, A. B. (1996). Structural alignment in similarity and difference judgments. *Psychonomic Bulletin and Review 3*, 227–230.

Markman, A. B., Gentner, D. (2000). Structure mapping in the comparison process. *American Journal of Psychology 113*, 501–538.

Marr, D., & Poggio, T. (1979). A computational theory of human stereo vision. *Proceedings of the Royal Society of London 204*, 301–328.

Medin, D. L., Goldstone, R. L., & Gentner, D. (1990). Similarity involving attributes and relations: Judgments of similarity and difference are not inverses. *Psychological Science 1*, 64–69.

Medin, D. L., Goldstone, R. L., & Gentner, D. (1993). Respects for similarity. *Psychological Review 100*, 254–278.

Melnik, S., Molina-Garcia, H., & Rahm, E. (2002). Similarity flooding: A versatile graph matching algorithm and its application to schema matching. In *Proceedings of the International Conference on Data Engineering (ICDE)* (pp. 117–128).

Pecher, D., Zeelenberg, R., & Barsalou, L. W. (2003). Verifying properties from different modalities for concepts produces switching costs. *Psychological Science 14*, 119–124.

Prinz, J. (2002). *Furnishing the Mind: Concepts and Their Perceptual Basis*. Cambridge, MA: MIT Press.

Putnam, H. (1973). Meaning and reference. *The Journal of Philosophy 70*, 699–711.

Quillian, M. R. (1967). Word concepts: A theory and simulation of some basic semantic capabilities. *Behavioral Science 12*, 410–430.

Quine, W. V., & Ullian, J. S. (1970). *The Web of Belief*. New York: McGraw-Hill.

Rapaport, W. J. (2002). Holism, conceptual-role semantics, and syntactic semantics. *Minds and Machines 12*, 3–59.

Regier, T. (1996). *The Human Semantic Potential: Spatial Language and Constrained Connectionism*. Cambridge, MA: MIT Press.

Regier, T., & Carlson, L. A. (2001). Grounding spatial language in perception: An empirical and computational investigation. *Journal of Experimental Psychology: General 130*, 273–298.

Richardson, D. C., Spivey, M. J., Barsalou, L. W., & McRae, K. (2003). Spatial representations activated during real-time comprehension of verbs. *Cognitive Science 27*, 767–780.

Rumelhart, D. E., Smolensky, P., McClelland, J. L., & Hinton, G. E. (1986). Schemata and sequential thought processes in PDP models. In J. L. McClelland & D. E. Rumelhart (Eds.), *Parallel Distributed Processing: Volume 2* (pp. 7–57). Cambridge, MA: MIT Press.

Rumelhart, D. E., & Zipser, D. (1985). Feature discovery by competitive learning. *Cognitive Science 9*, 75–112.

Saussure, F. (1915/1959). *Course in general linguistics*. New York: McGraw-Hill.

Schyns, P. G., Goldstone, R. L., & Thibaut, J. (1998). Development of features in object concepts. *Behavioral and Brain Sciences 21*, 1–54.

Shepard, R. N., & Cooper, L. A. (1986). *Mental images and their transformations*. Cambridge, MA: MIT Press.

Simmons, K., & Barsalou, L. W. (2003). The similarity-in-topography principle: Reconciling theories of conceptual deficits. *Cognitive Neuropsychology 20*, 451–486.

Smith, C., Carey, S., & Wiser, M. (1985). On differentiation: A case study of the development of the concepts of size, weight, and density. *Cognition 21*, 177–237.

Stanfield, R. A., & Zwaan, R. A. (2001). The effect of implied orientation derived from verbal context on picture recognition. *Psychological Science 12*, 153–156.

Stich, S. P. (1983). *From Folk Psychology to Cognitive Science: The Case Against Belief*. Cambridge, MA: MIT Press.

Ullman, S. (1979). *The interpretation of visual motion*. Cambridge, MA: MIT Press.

Ullman, S. (1989). Aligning pictorial descriptions: An approach to object recognition. *Cognition 32*, 193–254.

Ullman, S. (1996). *High-Level Vision*. Cambridge, MA: MIT Press.

Zwaan, R. A., Stanfield, R. A., & Yaxley, R. H. (2002). Language comprehenders mentally represent the shape of objects. *Psychological Science 13*, 168–171.

Author Index

Subject Index

Abstract symbol, 1, 3, 283
ABSURDIST, 5, 283, 288, 289, 290, 292, 293,
  295, 296, 299, 300, 301, 302, 303, 304, 305,
  306, 307, 308, 309
Action, 1, 2, 3, 4, 8, 9, 10, 11, 12, 13, 14, 15, 16,
  17, 18, 19, 20, 21, 22, 23, 24, 25, 26, 27, 28,
  29, 30, 45, 47, 60, 61, 66, 67, 68, 71, 72, 73,
  74, 75, 86, 87, 88, 89, 90, 94, 95, 96, 97, 99,
  102, 104, 105, 106, 111, 115, 117, 118, 119,
  134, 140, 156, 200, 201, 202, 205, 206, 216,
  217, 218, 224, 227, 228, 229, 232, 240, 242,
  246, 247, 248, 251, 271, 274, 310
Affordances, 10, 11, 12, 13, 14, 15, 16, 17, 20,
  21, 22, 26, 28, 29, 30, 46, 60, 97, 200, 248
Amodal symbols, 8, 96, 97, 129, 273
Analogy, 151, 283, 306, 308
Aspect, 8, 13, 46, 66, 67, 72, 76, 77, 78, 79, 80,
  81, 82, 84, 85, 87, 89, 90, 94, 103, 130, 133,
  141, 144, 148, 151, 152, 190, 199, 202, 204,
  205, 213, 214, 218, 235, 239, 253, 254–257,
  258, 264, 265, 269, 270, 272, 283, 295, 311
Attention Vector Sum Model (AVS), 38, 39,
  40, 43, 44
Attentional frames, 45, 230, 232

Background entity, 45, 230, 231, 232
Binding theory, 211, 212, 213, 215, 218
Brain, and concepts, 1, 19, 27, 66, 67, 68, 90,
  97, 98, 132, 136, 199, 220, 224, 234, 242,
  272, 284
Brain, and emotions, 102, 103, 105, 121
British empiricists, 93, 95, 97, 103, 285

Categorization, 17, 18, 19, 26, 28, 95, 155
C-command, 211, 212
Chinese Room Argument, 115, 226

Clitic assimilation, 206, 217
Cognitive linguistics, 3, 5, 67, 68, 77, 79–83,
  88, 89, 194, 199, 246, 252, 254, 258, 264,
  265–266, 272, 274
Cognitive process, 1, 2, 9, 61, 120
Cognitive semantics, 164, 165, 166, 182, 187
Communication, 22, 29, 72, 73, 76, 122, 135,
  148, 152, 159, 198, 219, 220, 251
Compositionality, 225
Concept meaning, 1, 2, 71, 132, 133, 136, 225,
  238, 282, 283, 285, 286, 287, 289, 299, 309
Concepts, 2, 9, 25, 68, 93, 94, 95, 96, 97, 99,
  106, 111, 117, 118, 131, 133, 134, 152, 153,
  154, 155, 156, 157, 225, 253, 260, 282, 283,
  284, 285, 286, 287, 288, 289, 295, 299, 302,
  309, 310
Concepts, abstract, 29, 67, 68, 79, 83, 86, 87,
  130, 131, 132, 133, 134, 135, 136, 152, 153,
  154, 156, 157, 241, 250, 251, 253, 284
Concepts, concrete, 8, 9, 10, 20, 23, 26, 28, 29,
  93, 99, 129, 130, 131, 132, 134, 135, 136,
  152, 154, 156
Concepts, emotionally based, 4, 94, 99, 102,
  103, 106, 109, 110, 111, 115, 120, 125, 126,
  127
Concepts of good and bad, 4, 99, 106, 109,
  111
Concepts of ownership, 110, 111
Conceptual role semantics, 286
Conceptual webs, 287, 291, 295, 299
Construal, 37, 45, 61, 165, 169, 230, 231, 234,
  235, 236, 237, 238, 239, 240, 241, 242
Context, 3, 12, 19, 20, 25, 30, 37, 38, 43, 47,
  56, 57, 59, 60, 61
Co-occurrence, 227, 228, 229, 230, 239, 286,
  307